MSU BOOK
USED B

RENTAL RESOURCE SERVICE (RRS)
UNIVERSITY OF WISCONSIN-STOUT
Menomonie, Wisconsin 54751
Signing your resources is recommended
to prevent theft and if the resource
is lost and returned we can locate
it's owner.

(Signature)   6-13-88 (Date)

1 ~~Lynn A Buttonham~~
2 _____
3 _____
4 _____
5 _____
6 _____
7 _____
8 _____
9 _____
10 _____

245   06/88
POWERS (FOOD) (0026

— IMPORTANT —

1. Resources due last day of class.
2. $4.00 fine is assessed for the first resource plus $1.00 for each additional resource overdue.
3. User is responsible for the number of the resource checked out. Any damage to the resource will be charged at the discretion of the RRS staff.
4. Lost resources must be paid for.

FOOD SERVICE OPERATIONS: PLANNING AND CONTROL

WILEY SERVICE MANAGEMENT SERIES

THOMAS F. POWERS
Series Editor

INTRODUCTION TO MANAGEMENT
IN THE HOSPITALITY INDUSTRY
Thomas F. Powers

BASICS OF QUANTITY FOOD PRODUCTION
Jo Marie Powers

THE MANAGEMENT OF MAINTENANCE
AND ENGINEERING SYSTEMS
IN HOSPITALITY INDUSTRIES
Frank D. Borsenik

PURCHASING: SELECTION AND PROCUREMENT
FOR THE HOSPITALITY INDUSTRY
John M. Stefanelli

THE BAR AND BEVERAGE BOOK:
BASICS OF PROFITABLE MANAGEMENT
Costas Katsigris
Mary Porter

FOOD SERVICE OPERATIONS: PLANNING
AND CONTROL
Thomas F. Powers
Jo Marie Powers

FOOD SERVICE OPERATIONS: PLANNING AND CONTROL

Thomas F. Powers
and
Jo Marie Powers

University of Guelph
Guelph, Ontario

JOHN WILEY & SONS
New York / Chichester / Brisbane / Toronto / Singapore

*To our sons Tom, Mike, Peter, Joe and Pat
who made it all worthwhile and necessary.*

Copyright © 1984 by John Wiley & Sons, Inc.

All rights reserved. Published simultaneously in Canada.

Reproduction or translation of any part of
this work beyond that permitted by Sections
107 and 108 of the 1976 United States Copyright
Act without the permission of the copyright
owner is unlawful. Requests for permission
or further information should be addressed to
the Permissions Department, John Wiley & Sons.

Library of Congress Cataloging in Publication Data:

Powers, Thomas F.
   Food service operations.

   (Wiley service management series)
   Includes index.
   1. Food service management. I. Powers, Jo Marie,
1935–   . II. Title. III. Series.
TX911.3.M27P687 1984   642'.5   83-10364
ISBN 0-471-06107-7
Title and Series added entries

Printed in the United States of America

10 9 8 7 6 5 4

PREFACE

It is curious that the cost control systems most frequently studied by students are those least used in the real world of food service. Overelaborate control systems, expensive in their use of time and money, have largely been replaced by simpler, more cost-effective control systems. An important aim of this book is to help the student see how the control systems used by *profitable* food service operators are designed and used today. A second goal is to show how the general *control function* is shaped to fit the differing needs of the major elements of the industry: not only conventional restaurants and hotels but also fast-food services and institutions.

This text is designed principally for use in courses concerned with food, beverage, and payroll control. Materials have been included, too, to give it a good fit with a managerial accounting course elsewhere in the curriculum—or to permit the instructor to develop an introductory unit on managerial accounting as a part of the course.

Some instructors, however, will find the text useful in a food-service lab course to provide management theory as an accompaniment to the practical experience in the lab. The chapter on portion control, with its emphasis on the practical, will be particularly useful in a lab course. On the other hand, we firmly believe that detailed consideration of the "how to's" of portion control is also essential to a textbook on food, beverage, and payroll control.

How to Use This Book

The format of this book has been developed with students in mind but our procedure will be just as useful to operations people from industry. At the start of the chapter we state our general purpose and some key, specific learning activities that are the focus of the chapter. After reviewing them, you should turn to the key words and phrases and review questions at the end of the chapter and scan them. This overview will help you to know what to look for as you read the chapter. When you finish, the key words and questions at the end of the chapter permit a self-test that will ensure that you have mastered the material.

The first three chapters provide the context. Chapter 1 is concerned with the concept of control systems as it applies generally to the industry. Chapter 2 discusses the essentials of the most basic plan in food service: the menu. Chapter 3 shows how control systems work using computerized point-of-sale registers.

The functional chapters (4 to 13) show how the major control activities are carried out. We use forms to illustrate the use of control systems but have avoided detail in the "bookkeeping" aspects of how various forms are filled out or which copies go where. These details vary widely from system to system, but the functions of the activities remain the same. The last two chapters provide a basis for linking the food, beverage, and labor cost systems to managerial accounting and the financial side of operations.

Acknowledgments

The careful student may wish to take a close look at the acknowledgments because most of what we have written comes from our own practice of foodservice management. The people with whom we have worked and who have taught us what they know are a kind of pedigree for this text: When you know from whom we have learned, you are in a better position to judge what we have to say.

This text is a collaboration of authors each with a specialized background: one in foods and the other in management. Jo Marie Powers' early training was at Iowa State University, and she owes her earliest experience in the management of food commodities to the USDA Marketing Service, though her interest in foods is a lifelong one. Tom Powers began his management training at the Harvard Business School and moved on to the Stouffer Restaurant Corporation and then to Horwath and Horwath's food consulting staff. He thanks Jim Durkin who gave him his earliest understanding of payroll control. Much of this understanding is reflected in the text. Herb Beach of Horwath and Horwath drove home the importance of looking at the whole system in food service, beginning with receiving and moving right through to sampling the product.

Our collaboration in work as well as the rest of life began in our marriage, and we have been associated in operations, teaching, and consulting almost continuously since that time. We acknowledge the great personal influence and guidance in understanding the small operation that came from our early association with Ralph Lorenz of the Mayflower Hotel. We will always owe a great debt to Deanna Stoner and Edward Fowler with whom we worked at the Holiday Inn—Downtown in Atlanta. They helped us put to the test in a high-volume setting what we had learned up to that point. Deanna was later a helpful and stimulating colleague at Morris Brown.

Mattie Lou Waymer, chairperson of the Department of Home Economics at Morris Brown College, was the first to encourage us to develop formalized teaching materials and, though they have evolved a long way, the basics of many chapters first took instructional form at Morris Brown.

Our work on cost control became even more formalized when we developed "instructional modules"—a fancy term for parts of a textbook–for the associate degree program in Hotel and Food Service at Penn State University. This was done first for commercial food service under funding from the Research Coordinating Unit of the Pennsylvania Department of Education. We acknowledge the work of our coauthor in this effort, Suellen Wayda. These first modules were rewritten in a substantially more formal way under grants from the Public Health Service as correspondence courses for an associate degree program for dietetic technicians. Ellen Barbrow was our coauthor in that effort. We also thank Ken Burley, a senior colleague earlier at Horwath and Horwath, who served as a consultant in the development of the correspondence course on food and labor control. While most of the material has had to be approached somewhat differently in this text, we thank Dr. Edward V. Ellis, Associate Dean for Continuing Education of Penn State's College of Human Development, for securing for us permission to use any part of the correspondence course that we wished in our subsequent work.

The present work has benefited greatly from careful and thoughtful review by Frank H. Waskey of the Hilton School of Hotel Administration at the University of Houston, James A. Bardi of the Hotel and Food Service program at Penn State's Berks Campus; Jack E. Miller, Chairman of the Department of Hospitality Restaurant Management and Tourism of the St. Louis Comunity College; and Elizabeth Peters of the Hospitality Management Program at the Chicago City-Wide College.

We are also grateful for the contribution of colleagues with whom we have worked. The research of a colleague at Penn State, Theresa Huber, was most helpful in the chapter on menu planning and portion control. At Guelph, James Pickworth persuaded us to expand our coverage of beverage as well as food control and made many useful suggestions about how that should be accomplished. E. L. Fletcher reviewed the last two chapters and gave us numerous helpful suggestions. Finally, in Chapter 3 we have significantly relied on John Patterson's work on the computerization of cash registers and on his advice, throughout the text, where we deal with point of sales and electronic cash-register systems.

All of these people have been most helpful; however, we accept fully the responsibility for any errors that remain. Finally, we acknowledge the all-important contribution of our students who over the years have challenged and stimulated us and taught us a lot about how they learn.

Thomas F. Powers
Jo Marie Powers
Moon River, Ontario

CONTENTS

1 THE PROBLEM OF CONTROL IN FOOD SERVICE   1

2 MENU PLANNING: GOAL SETTING IN FOOD SERVICE   14

3 MONITORING OPERATIONS: POINT OF SALES SYSTEMS   38

4 PURCHASING POLICY AND PROCEDURE   76

5 DETERMINING PRODUCT QUALITY   106

6 RECEIVING AND STORAGE   132

7 FORECASTING: THE HEART OF PLANNING AND CONTROL   152

8 FOOD PRODUCTION CONTROL   184

9 PRECOSTING   212

10 PRODUCTIVITY ANALYSIS AND PAYROLL CONTROL   224

11 AN INTRODUCTION TO FOOD COST CONTROL   246

12 MONITORING PRODUCT COST PERFORMANCE   264

13 CONTROLLING BEVERAGE COST   200

14 BUDGETING FOR FOOD SERVICE OPERATIONS   308

15 EVALUATION AND DECISION MAKING IN FOOD SERVICE OPERATIONS   326

Appendix 1 Precosting   345
Appendix 2 Fortran Program   358
Glossary of Program Abbreviations   362
Index   366

THE PROBLEM OF CONTROL IN FOOD SERVICE

1

Why Control?

The Food Cost Control Cycle

The Food Service Industry

THE PURPOSE OF THIS CHAPTER

Many people are attracted to food service because of its glamour. The genial, well-dressed hotel manager or the tuxedoed maitre d' may come to mind, especially the ability to make a frowning guest smile. Other people will think of chatting pleasantly with patients in a hospital about their diet or perhaps watching youngsters at school "load up" with a nourishing meal. The glamour is in the guest; there's no doubt of that. But behind each of these scenes lies a great deal of planning and hard work. If the food operation were just smiling general managers, tuxedos, and diet interviews, it would soon be in trouble.

We do not mean to be spoilsports and rob food service of its glamour. Nevertheless this book is devoted to dealing with the less glamorous but vital work that makes guest satisfaction possible. This chapter introduces you to the general management tools of the "back of the house."

THIS CHAPTER SHOULD HELP YOU

1. Discuss the importance of cost control in profit and nonprofit organizations.

2. Define cost and describe the principal kinds of costs.

3. Describe the principal elements of the food cost control cycle.

4. Explain why a generalized approach that identifies the major control tools is necessary for the study of control in such a diverse industry.

WHY CONTROL?

Even though the answer to this question is obvious, this is such an important question that it should be asked. Very simply, we control to stay afloat and reach our profit goals. In one operation, for instance, mishandling of only four products resulted in a loss of nearly 10 cents on every dollar of sales! In another, just the mishandling of breakfast meats (e.g., bacon and sausage) consumed 1% of sales. And, in yet another case, overuse of soup bases accounted for nearly 1% of sales! In a business where profit margins in successful operations are commonly between 3 and 5% of sales, the proportionate significance of a single product or small group of products eating up 1 or 2% of sales is obvious—half the profit is lost!

WHAT ABOUT NONPROFIT?

Some students whose career interests lie, for instance, in health care food service or school food service may be getting a bit restless at this point because earning a profit is not the principal goal of their food service. A moment's reflection, however, should put those concerns to rest.

Health care food service is generally run on a nonprofit basis, and school food service is actually subsidized. However, it is easy to see that although nonprofit means zero profit or limited loss, it definitely does not refer to a dietary department that does not attend to costs.

Similarly school lunches, although subsidized in the United States and many Western European countries, do not earn a profit in the conventional sense. However, we could think of the dollar performance goal here as a minus or negative "profit" (that is, the operation plans to lose a certain amount of money, but no less). Conformity to a negative profit goal is absolutely essential—there just isn't any "extra money" around to defray costs that are overbudgeted in school or health care food service.

For this reason, whether your future lies in the commercial hotel and restaurant industry or in the nonprofit or subsidized segments of food service, you need the tools to manage your operation in line with budget targets. The well-dressed general manager (G.M.) who cannot control his or her operation's costs will soon be looking for another position, which is also true of the "caring" school or health care food service director whose operation is consistently over budget.

Throughout the book, we will present examples from all segments of the hospitality industry. We do this because, in terms of labor mobility (i.e., people moving from jobs in one segment to another) this is actually *one* industry. Although school and health care food service is now largely a specialized field operated by school systems and hospitals, commercial food service operators are taking a larger share of these markets. People entering the industry now really do not know where they will be working 5 or 10 years from now. We therefore hope you will regard all examples as relevant, not just those drawn from the segment of the industry that currently interests you.

DEFINITION OF COST

Cost, according to one authority, "means any monetary sacrifice—during a given accounting period."[1] In food service operations, several principal costs are of interest to us: first, the cost of food and beverage consumed in serving the guest; second, payroll and related costs such as employee benefits; and, third, "other direct operating expenses" (e.g., the cost of dishwashing detergent, guest supplies, and china). *The Uniform System of Accounts for Restaurants* refers to these costs as "controllable costs."

Discussion of another group of costs, capital costs (e.g., rent, depreciation, and interest) while significant, is beyond the scope of this book. For the most part these costs relate to the original investment to build and equip the operation and therefore are not within the province of the operation's manager. The focus of our concern is not on investment decisions but on the means of achieving a desired profit (or nonprofit goal) through well-controlled current operations.

---

[1] Robert N. Anthony, *Management Accounting: Text and Cases* (Homewood, Ill.: Richard D. Irwin, 1964), p. 65.

Costs may also be categorized as variable costs, fixed costs, and mixed costs, a subject dealt with at more length in Chapter 14.

Variable costs vary directly *with sales:* food cost, for example.

Fixed costs do not vary: real estate taxes remain the same regardless of sales volume, for example.

Mixed costs begin at some minimum level and vary to some degree with sales volume. Payroll begins at some minimum level "just to open the doors"; sufficient crew is hired to handle a moderate amount of business. On busier days, more employees must be added. Finally, for extra rushed periods—the Christmas holidays, Mother's Day, or Easter—a still larger crew size is needed. Since employees cannot be considered in "meal units" like a scoop of ice cream, the level of cost rise may not be directly proportionate to sales.

THE FOOD COST CONTROL CYCLE

As Figure 1.1 indicates, management approaches the operation from three different perspectives: the planning mode, the operating mode, and the monitoring mode. Each of these modes requires control activities.

To control costs, it is necessary to set performance targets, determine how to reach them, operate in a controlled fashion, and monitor results against plan. In short, control of costs requires planning.

Before we detail the activities of management and supervision, it is useful to develop an overview of a food service operation from the point of view of control. This is the subject of much of the first part of this text (Figure 1.1). The overview is intended to show the interrelationship between the various aspects of the cost control cycle.

THE PLANNING MODE

Menu Development
Planning in food service begins with the menu and menu planning. Clearly, planning must begin with the guest's needs and wishes. No menu can be successful that does not take the guest into account.

The menu will also be affected by the style of service, location of the operation, and competition in the market. A cafeteria may offer wide variety of foods whereas the attraction of a beef restaurant will be it's simple specialized menu. If the restaurant is located to serve people in a hurry, the menu will be designed to ensure fast service; in contrast an operation that features luxury dining will allow for more leisurely service.

4 THE PROBLEM OF CONTROL IN FOOD SERVICE

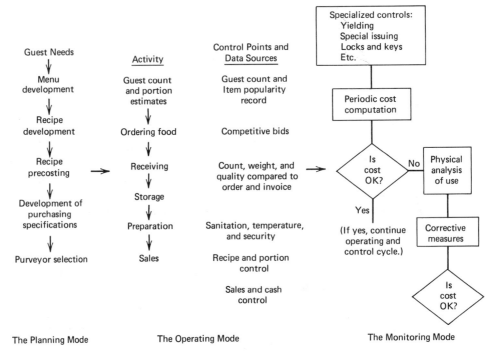

FIGURE 1.1 The food cost control cycle.

Related to location in institutional food service is function. If the operation is intended to service office workers who have limits on both the price they are willing to pay and the time they have available to eat, the menu will take price and speed of service into account. On the other hand, cost and speed of service are less important in a senior staff dining room designed to serve the medical and senior administrative staff in a hospital.

Also, knowing the competition and meeting its challenge are part of almost all food service. Although this is obvious for commercial food services, high schools have also found that neighborhood fast food outlets can be significant competition.

Similar circumstances arise in health care food service. In one city where there were a large number of corporate headquarters, the annual physical checkups of senior corporate staff brought considerable revenues to the hospital chosen for the four- or five-day physicals. One hospital developed a roof top restaurant at which the executive could entertain his or her family while going through the physical. This extra service, and the menu to accompany it, gave the hospital a real advantage in attracting corporate patronage. This creative marketing helped it to support its necessary and costly public service activities.

Our point is that designing operations according to customer needs and revenues available is an integral part of food service operations. (Chapter 2 is devoted to a discussion of guest centered menu planning.)

Production Strategy

Once the menu is written, the means to produce it must be decided on. We advocate the use of written standard recipes or written procedure cards because these help ensure a product that is standard in both quality and cost. A recipe is really a standard operating procedure, a simplified form of a plan (see Chapter 8). Once recipes have been prepared, the cost of a serving of each item on the menu (precosting) must be determined in advance, based on reasonable estimates of costs. Precosting (see Chapter 9) provides the basic information necessary for pricing (the competition's prices are significant here, too). In institutions, this information is used to determine the food cost per patient day or the food cost per student meal. This is an important part of the budget of a nonprofit or subsidized operation's budget and, in college food services is used to set the price for various board plans. The cost per day or board plan rate are absolutely essential elements in overall operations planning.

Purchasing Strategy

To develop final costs, it is necessary to specify the kind of product to be used and to select the suppliers. In short, purchasing must be carefully planned and, wherever possible, reduced to routine (see Chapters 4 and 5).

THE OPERATING MODE

One of the most important steps in day-to-day control is to estimate the amount of sales for any given day to avoid both excessive buying and preparation, which are major sources of waste. This sales estimate is based on the expected total number of guests, which items they will choose from the day's menu, and the timing of their arrival and ordering.

Next, food must be ordered so that the correct amount is delivered at the lowest price consistent with quality. Food must be checked in; this will ensure that the operation knows it is getting what it ordered and paid for. Similarly, it must be stored to prevent both spoilage or pilferage (Chapter 6).

Food standards based on quality and quantity to be served are best maintained by written recipes, as we have noted. It is important also to have available the necessary tools of portion control—numbered scoops, portion scales, different sized ladles—to be sure that plans are carried out precisely. A "heavy hand" in portioning can be costly. (Production control is covered in greater detail in Chapter 8.)

Finally, we must be sure that the guests pay for the food they receive. Cash controls focus on reducing the temptation to employees to give away food without charging for it or pocketing the money a guest pays for a meal instead of turning it over to a cashier. Chapter 3 considers current electronic cash register and point of sales systems used to control cash in modern food service.

In summary, key control steps must be built into the operating plan, and the means to collect information on performance must be an integral part of an operation if performance against budgeted target is to be maintained.

THE MONITORING MODE

Specialized food cost controls are an important part of monitoring (Chapter 12). Issuing high-cost items such as steaks and accounting for their use on a daily basis is a good example of one such procedure. The practice of restricting access to some store rooms by locking them is another simple example.

The most basic monitoring activity is the periodic computation of the cost of food consumed. This "food cost" is stated as a percent of sales, and the food cost percentage is compared to budget, previous performance, and industry averages for similar operations. The formula for computing food cost is: Beginning Inventory *(BI)* plus Purchases *(P)* minus ending inventory *(EI)* equals food cost *(FC)*; the food cost percent is found by dividing dollar food cost by dollar sales. These formulas may be stated more simply:

$$BI + P - EI = FC$$
$$FC\% = \frac{FC}{S} \times 100$$

If the cost is acceptable, then food service managers concern themselves with guest satisfaction, sanitation, service, and other aspects of the operation.

In the past 10 years, a revolution in food service information technology has resulted in an explosion of control information. The development of computer-driven point of sales (POS) register systems and electronic cash registers is now reshaping food service operations. Chapter 3 is devoted to describing POS systems and showing how they work. This topic is also discussed, where appropriate, throughout the rest of the book.

It is important to note here accumulating numbers—in a computer or in a file drawer—without analyzing their significance and taking corrective action is a waste of time. It gives the illusion of control—"See how many reports I have!"—but does not actually lead to any real changes.

CORRECTIVE MEASURES

If food costs are too high, corrective measures have to be taken. A first step is to find out which specific food products are causing the problem by comparing, for instance, the amount of beef products used up (e.g., pounds of rib roast) with the sales record. Once the problem items have been identified (these items are problems because product use is not accounted for by product sale), management will take corrective measures based on a study of how those products are being controlled.

For example, when an analysis of use revealed that ham and turkey roll were being used out of proportion to sales, a review of purchasing specifications revealed that poor quality products were being purchased; these contained excessive gelatin and fat and fell apart when cut, resulting in excessive waste. Spot checks of these products as they were prepared to be served revealed that both of them were consistently overportioned. An additional portion scale was used, a higher quality product was purchased, and costs quickly came back into line.

LABOR COST: AN OVERVIEW

We have just glanced at the highly interrelated activities that go into planning, operating, and monitoring a food service operation. Had we selected labor as a subject we would have seen a similar cycle in which a staffing strategy is planned based on tasks identified as necessary to the operation. Once the tasks have been identified, skill levels are determined; tasks are then put together in jobs for which individuals are to be hired. The process of relating similar tasks includes keeping the levels of skill required to do one job related to the skill level required to do another similar job so that highly paid skilled workers are not using expensive time to do unskilled jobs.

In the operating mode, schedules must be prepared that reflect variation in the need for workers during particular hours of the day and days of the week. Monitoring begins with evaluating payroll cost against budget target. If performance is off target, more strenuous analysis and corrective action are undertaken.

As with the food cost control cycle, the topics in this overview will be discussed in greater detail in Chapter 10. Right now, we need only have an understanding of the idea of the control cycle to appreciate the ideas that follow.

THE FOOD SERVICE INDUSTRY

Table 1.1 shows the National Restaurant Association's Estimated Food and Drink Sales for 1980. Although these industry statistics may seem to have little to do with the problem of food service control, they can influence our concept of food service in important ways. In fact, a few key statistics have helped to establish this book's frame of reference.

In food service, fast food is becoming more and more important. Limited menu restaurants—the U.S. Census Bureau's name for fast food—account for nearly one quarter (23.9%) of *all* food sold outside the home in the United States. If you consider fast food as a percent of restaurant sales (in the Census figures, "eating places"), fast food stands out even more significantly at 40% of the market and 42% of all restaurant units. Moreover, fast food had the highest growth rate in 1980, 10% of any of the major components of food service. Fast food operations clearly are an important part of food service, and fast food has special characteristics in regard to the problems and procedures of control that are especially well-addressed by POS systems.

Let us turn to another significant component of food service. If we combine food contractors (in Commercial Feeding)—private companies such as ARA and Saga who operate the food service for many institutions—with sales of institutions that operate their own food service (all of Group II) we see that institutional food service accounts for nearly 21% of food sales away from home. Because the relationship of cost to sales price tends to deflate sales in this area (for instance, notice that sales are *less* than food cost in school food service) a better measure of the relative importance of institutional food service may be the ratio of their food and drink *purchases* to total purchases. By this measure, just over a quarter

TABLE 1.1 NATIONAL RESTAURANT ASSOCIATION'S ESTIMATED FOOD AND DRINK SALES FOR 1980

Number of Units	Type of Establishment	Estimated Food and Drink Sales (000) 1980	Estimated Food and Drink Purchases (000) 1980
	Group I: Commercial Feeding Group		
	Eating places		
121,461	Restaurants, lunchrooms	$ 36,037,601	$ 13,531,128
101,587	Limited menu restaurants	27,434,837	9,842,465
6,856	Commercial cafeterias	2,163,965	820,827
3,380	Social caterers	775,944	302,514
8,749	Ice cream, frozen custard stands	1,289,479	406,186
242,033	Total—Eating Places	$ 67,701,826	$ 24,903,120
38,879	Bar & Taverns	7,779,573	491,593
280,912	Total—Eating and drinking places	$ 75,481,399	$ 25,394,713
7,836	*Food contractors*		
	Manufacturing & industrial plants	2,121,483	988,590
	Commercial and office buildings	603,906	281,414
	Hospitals and nursing homes	832,480	332,992
	Colleges and universities	1,139,972	396,713
	Primary and secondary schools	628,966	305,237
	In-transit feeding (airlines)	512,914	246,188
	Recreation and sports centers	977,788	355,915
	Total—Food contractors	$ 6,817,509	$ 2,907,049
	Lodging places		
13,768	Hotel restaurants	4,439,576	1,521,065
2,423	Motor hotel restaurants	791,227	271,413
13,651	Motel restaurants	1,368,009	481,225
29,842	Total—Lodging places	$ 6,598,812	$ 2,273,703
	Retail hosts		
8,619	Drug and proprietary store restaurants	357,572	135,877
1,644	General merchandise store restaurants	52,643	19,478
5,202	Department store restaurants	1,039,838	405,537
5,111	Variety store restaurants	453,231	172,228
3,967	Food stores except grocery	171,580	58,337
23,001	Grocery stores restaurants	705,431	253,955
8,232	Gasoline service stations	383,073	137,906
3,608	Miscellaneous retailers (liquor, cigar, etc.)	139,505	49,524
59,384	Total—Retail hosts	$ 3,302,873	$ 1,232,842
	Recreation and sports		
2,882	Drive-in movies	167,213	55,180
3,933	Bowling lanes	500,922	187,846
N/A	Recreation and sports centers	701,768	255,443
6,815	Total—Recreation and sports	$ 1,369,903	$ 498,469

Number of Units	Type of Establishment	Estimated Food and Drink Sales (000) 1980	Estimated Food and Drink Purchases (000) 1980
	All other		
3,267	Vending and nonstore retailers	2,528,229	844,428
N/A	Mobile caterers	466,720	160,085
3,267	Total—All other	$ 2,994,949	$ 1,004,513
388,056	TOTAL—GROUP I	$ 96,565,445	$ 33,311,289
	Group II: Institutional Feeding Group—Educational, government or institutional organizations that operate their own food service		
	Employee feeding		
4,000	Industrial and commercial organizations	$ 1,376,668	$ 673,232
551	Sea-going ships (1,000+ tons)	55,919	33,551
4,248	Inland waterway vessels	202,649	121,589
8,799	Total—Employee feeding	$ 1,635,236	$ 828,372
	Educational feeding		
95,471	Public & parochial elementary and secondary school (94,535 national school lunch program)	2,312,195	3,117,110
1,017	Public colleges and universities	1,625,118	782,388
1,533	Private colleges and universities	672,954	377,910
98,021	Total—Educational feeding	$ 4,610,267	$ 4,277,408
	Transportation feeding		
68	Passenger/cargo liners	115,664	63,615
63	Airlines	475,494	236,848
2	Railroads	32,775	25,654
133	Total—Transportation feeding	$ 623,933	$ 326,117
	Hospital feeding		
4,052	Voluntary and proprietary hospitals	4,771,098	1,908,439
1,852	State and local short-term hospitals	723,645	505,254
702	Long-term, general, TB, nervous and mental hospitals	854,510	341,804
359	Federal hospitals	318,995	261,539
6,965	Total—Hospital feeding	$ 6,668,248	$ 3,017,036
25,130	Nursing homes, homes for the aged, blind, orphans, mentally and physically handicapped	2,416,239	1,527,667
	Miscellaneous		
10,310	Clubs	1,055,919	498,394
2,249	Sporting and recreational camps	114,244	68,558
16,010	Community centers	351,233	414,448
N/A	Convents and seminaries	***	118,090
28,569	Total—Miscellaneous	$ 1,521,396	$ 1,099,490

Number of Units	Type of Establishment	Estimated Food and Drink Sales (000) 1980	Estimated Food and Drink Purchases (000) 1980
620	*Penal institutions* Federal and state prisons	***	$ 258,340
3,493	Jails	***	205,703
4,113	Total—Penal institutions		$ 464,043
171,730	TOTAL—GROUP II	$ 17,475,319	$ 11,540,133
559,786	TOTAL—GROUPS I & II	$114,040,764	$ 44,851,422
	Food furnished food service employees in groups I and II		3,329,160
	TOTAL—GROUPS I, II and FSE	$114,040,764	$ 48,180,582
	Group III: Military Feeding Group		
	Defense personnel	***	$ 1,664,390
700	Officers & NCO clubs ("open mess")	$ 392,531	145,854
556	Food service-military exchange	219,800	95,343
1,256	TOTAL-GROUP III	$ 612,331	$ 1,905,587
561,042		$114,653,095	$ 50,086,169

Source: National Restaurant Association.

(28.8%) of all food and drinks purchased for resale to guests away from home is for institutional food service.

Some students of cost control employ a system used in large hotels and clubs as their model for food cost control. Significantly, if all hotels and clubs used that system, it would account for less than 6½% of food sales. In practice, because only a minority of establishments use this system, we can no longer safely prepare students for management with an understanding of just that one system. The well-prepared student needs to be aware of how controls are put into effect in the several major components of the industry.

For instance, fast food operations because of their very simple menu can control food use so closely that the number of wasted pieces of chicken or hamburger patties can be (and are!) determined daily. On the other hand, such precision is still generally too expensive for operations with more complex menus. However, computerized systems make such control possible.

Institutional food service has more predictable sales than do restaurants. Because both guest count and item choice can be forecast with a good deal of accuracy, the operating and control picture is changed in some important ways.

Even more significant, a great deal of institutional food service is managed by large companies or large institutions such as a city school system or a large university. Generally the unit belongs to a larger, more complex system of multi-unit operations that have much in common with fast food services, most of whose units are part of a chain.

Food service *systems* have specific solutions to the problems of food and labor cost control. For instance, quality checks in conventional receiving in single unit operations are handled in large companies by special inspection staffs and area supervisors, though a rudimentary receiving function remains at the restaurant[2].

Most students should have some knowledge of the variety of food service types because, as we noted earlier, they can expect to work in more than one segment of the hospitality industry in the course of their professional career.[3] For this reason this book emphasizes the major control *functions,* rather than the "paperwork" that goes with any single control system. Particularly where most segments of the industry have a common approach to a problem, we will present considerable detail and offer problems for students to work through. However, instead of emphasizing one particular kind of accounting form as "the best," we will offer one or more examples to show how a particular control function is carried out in various circumstances.

In fact, we describe controls as they would operate in an independent, free-standing restaurant with a reasonably complex menu and a modern control system. This means we will illustrate the various functions of control (such as those described in the discussion of the food cost control and payroll control cycles). As necessary, we will also note how control problems are commonly handled by institutional food service and fast food operations. In our discussion of food cost control, a chapter will be set aside for an analytical discussion of the traditional system; it will be followed by a chapter describing the way food cost control is practiced in modern food services. In Chapter 3 we illustrate how POS systems are used in food service; we will also describe control activities as they are carried on without the computerized systems because much of the industry students will encounter in their working experience is still in the process of adopting the new technology.

Throughout the book, our approach will be to identify the problems and functions of control and then to give examples of how different systems deal with these problems. Ultimately, each company has its own control system; thus well-prepared graduates will be able to understand the challenge of control and quickly master whatever system they are confronted with in their early career. Later, as your responsibility grows with your career, our approach to studying control will equip you to participate in control system *design* as the problems of control in an evolving food service continue to change, requiring new approaches and solutions.

---

[2]For a fuller discussion of the contrast between management of traditional food service with complex food service systems, see Thomas F. Powers, "Complex Food Service Systems" *Cornell Hotel and Restaurant Quarterly,* November, 1979, pp. 49–58.

[3]For a fuller discussion of this subject, see Thomas F. Powers, *Introduction to Management in the Hospitality Industry* (New York: Wiley, 1979), especially Chapters 1 and 16.

KEY WORDS AND CONCEPTS

Back-of-the-house
Control
Profit goals
Nonprofit goals
Zero profit
Negative "profit"
Positive profit
Cost—definition
Principal costs
Food and beverage
Payroll and related costs
Direct operating expenses
Capital costs
Variable costs
Fixed costs
Mixed costs
Food cost control cycle
Planning mode
Operating mode

Monitoring mode
Performance targets
Menu development
Production strategy
Purchasing strategy
Sales estimate
Food ordering, receiving and storage
Portion control
Cash control
Food cost as percent of sales
$BI + P - EI = FC$
Food cost percent formula
An "illusion of control"
Corrective measures
Labor cost
Staffing strategy
Evaluating cost against budget
Control system design

DISCUSSION QUESTIONS

1. If a food service operation has sales in the neighborhood of $2 million per year, what is the cost of a 1 percent loss due to the lack of control?

2. A food service director for a group of nursing homes states that he must watch costs more closely than when he was in the restaurant business. "Every penny counts on my bottom line." Why would costs be significant in a so-called "nonprofit" operation? Discuss.

3. Give examples of variable costs, fixed costs, and mixed costs.

4. Do you know the food cost percentages of food service operations where you have worked? Is there variation or common ground between types of operations—say fast food, hotels, family restaurants, or hospitals? How about labor costs? Discuss reasons for the differences, if any.

5. Discuss a food service operation in your locality that has done something special—successfully—or used creative marketing. How did they fill their customers needs?

6. Discuss how you think control systems could vary between different segments of the food service industry such as fast food and a large metropolitan hotel with 5 or 6 dining rooms.

MENU PLANNING: GOAL SETTING IN FOOD SERVICE

2

The Customer and Market Planning

Basic Menu Planning Concepts

Types of Menu Plans

Modification of Set and Cycle Menus

Trend to Limit Menus

Menu Balance

Menu Planning in Specialized Operations

Conclusion

THE PURPOSE OF THIS CHAPTER

The menu is *the* basic document in food service. When an operation's menu has been written, the customer has been selected and the food and payroll costs determined. Indeed, the final profit (or nonprofit) goal is written into the menu. Any menu writer who does not know the truth of this statement designs an operation by chance—hardly the best way to proceed. Since writing a menu begins with the customer, let us start this chapter with the customer in mind.

THIS CHAPTER SHOULD HELP YOU

1. Determine the necessary relationship between customer needs and menu planning.

2. Identify basic menu planning concepts.

3. Relate variations in sales volume and food production needs to menu planning.

4. Become familiar with problems in menu planning for specialized operations.

THE CUSTOMER AND MARKET PLANNING

We must first turn our attention to gaining a market since there are no costs to control without sales. Although a specific clientele is generally selected for a new restaurant, let us begin our study of market planning by looking at the market for an existing operation, perhaps the one in which you work.

Peter Drucker, the management consultant, begins this analysis by asking "Who are my customers and what are they doing?" Applying the first part of Drucker's question, we observe characteristics such as age, sex, estimated income, and occupation. If your operation serves upper middle income people with an average age in the mid-thirties, your menu can be richer both in calories and prices charged than if your guests are principally price-sensitive retirees.

The second part of Drucker's question is equally important. What is your customer doing. Is yours an "occasion" type restaurant, or is it a coffee shop in a shopping mall. Obviously each kind of restaurant would require a different menu.

LOCATION ANALYSIS

Location is an important clue, of course, to what a customer needs and wants from an existing operation. For instance the number of fast food shops next to large apartment complexes suggests that working mothers want an inexpensive, quick place to eat out or from which to take home a meal. Location in a wealthy suburb requires one kind of menu while the operator of the employees' cafeteria in a hospital faces quite a different challenge. Some operations choose locations next to high vehicular or pedestrian traffic. Certainly the location chosen largely determines the likely customers.

Remember too, that in institutional food service *function* is analogous to location. An executive dining room in a bank requires one kind of menu; an employees' cafeteria in an office building where the guests are principally young, diet-conscious women calls for a different menu; and, an industrial plant food service catering to men involved in substantial physical exertion suggests a third menu.

ANALYSIS OF COMPETITION: MENU COMPARISONS

The kind of guest an operator wants to serve determines the price and quality of the food offered on the menu. Competition also affects menu planning. While your operation may not offer every item your competitor does, it must take into account the choices that similar operations in the market are offering. A good way to analyze restaurant competition is to prepare a comparative summary of their menus. Table 2.1 shows a comparative summary of the entrees and sandwiches offered by the four competing coffee shop restaurants serving a medium-sized community. All the entrees and sandwiches offered in all five restaurants are listed on the left. Although similar products may have different names, we have used the most common name for convenience. The next five columns indicate the prices charged; an X indicates that no such item is listed.

TABLE 2.1 A COFFEE SHOP OPERATOR'S COMPARISON OF HIS MENU PRICES WITH THOSE OF COMPETITORS IN THE AREA.

	Comparative Menu Analysis				
Menu Items	Our Restaurant	Competitor 1	Competitior 2	Competitor 3	Competitor 4
Entrees					
Fried chicken	$3.60	$3.55	$3.15	$3.95	$3.25
Roast beef	3.25	X	X	3.50	X
Sirloin steak	4.95	4.70	3.95	X	X
Ham steak	3.60	3.65	3.05	X	X
Fried shrimp	4.60	X	3.95	X	4.25
Chili	2.10	X	1.95	1.95	X
Sandwiches					
Ham	1.95	1.40	1.40	1.50	X
Bacon, lettuce, and tomato	1.70	1.40	X	1.40	1.50
Tuna Salad	1.95	1.50	1.25	1.50	X
Hamburger	1.70	2.60	1.75	1.85	1.75
Roast beef	2.15	X	2.30	2.30	X

VALUE OF A CUSTOMER AND COMPETITION SURVEY

In an existing operation, an analysis of the kind outlined above should be conducted at least once a year. It will tell the operator whether the competition is changing and may shed light on why guest counts and item popularity (two subjects discussed in detail in Chapter 7) are changing. In addition, price comparisons may need to be made more frequently when price levels are changing.

The form of this analysis is used in the course of planning a new operation. At this time, of course, one does not know the flow of guests but must instead look at the location and market in the area. Management's object is to determine which guests are to be attracted and what kind of service to offer them.

NONCOMMERCIAL OPERATIONS

College food service operators make considerable use of menu popularity surveys, as do other noncommerical operators. In one study of institutional operators, nutrition ranked first as an influence in menu writing in hospitals and in school food service, while consumer preference ranked a close second. In colleges and universities, however, consumer satisfaction ranked ahead of nutrition. In all three categories (hospitals, schools, and colleges) cost ranked third.[1] Clearly then, determining the consumer's point of view is important in noncommerical operations, too.

BASIC MENU PLANNING CONCEPTS

PREPARED AND PREPARED-TO-ORDER FOODS

The following experience may help you understand why menu planners for food services tend to choose either prepared or prepared-to-order foods for their menus.

> In my first job as manager, I ran a small club. One evening we had a special wine tasting party. It was an obvious success because every table in the house was quickly reserved. The chef and I put our heads together to make up a menu of favorites. When the great night came, however, we had a rough time because we hadn't noticed that every item offered on the menu had to be cooked-to-order. Everybody arrived at about the same time, all the orders hit the kitchen at once, and there was the poor chef trying to cook 120 different meals at once! Not only was the staff over-loaded but equipment was overloaded too.

---

[1]Theresa C. Huber, Menu Planning Priorities for Non-Purchasing Consumers. Unpublished Master's Paper, The Pennsylvania State University, 1976. p. 61.

Most menu items can be classified as "prepared" foods or "prepared-to-order" foods. "Prepared foods" are foods that are completely cooked and ready to serve when the meal begins. They need only be dished onto the plate. (Serving this type of food would have prevented the disaster just described.) "Prepared-to-order" (PTO) (or "cooked-to-order") foods are steaks, fried shrimp, or hamburgers. If cooked and held they typically lose flavor. Prepared-to-order foods often require a good deal of preparation before the meal—for example, portioning, breading, cutting, and shredding—but the final cookery is accomplished just before serving. Prepared foods generally create leftover problems while PTO foods can be held. PTO foods, however, as you learned above, create production problems when the demand for many prepared-to-order foods comes at one time.

Either prepared or PTO foods tend to dominate in specific food service operations. Commerical restaurants tend to prefer PTO foods and with good reason. Commerical restaurants cannot dictate when their customers will arrive and, although modern forecasting techniques can keep overproduction to a minimum, many cooked foods are lost the next day or require additional labor to work them into other dishes. For example, a baked chicken half is tender and juicy when taken from the oven but when reheated the next day would not satisfy the least discerning guest. However, a raw chicken half keeps well uncooked, which explains why fried chicken is offered in restaurants more frequently than baked chicken. Restaurants, then, tend to study each item added to the menu and analyze how it will hold if it must be completely prepared. Foods such as soups, stews, and certain sauces may improve in taste the following day, and these are the type of prepared foods that you will most often see on commercial restaurant menus. In fact, restaurants may cleverly turn a prepared food into a PTO item if they wish to have the food on their menu. For example, a restaurant may partially cook several pans of manicotti at a time, then chill them; the short order cook removes an order as needed and finishes cooking the manicotti in a microwave.

Another way to offer a variety of foods, including foods that seem to be "prepared", is to use frozen prepared foods as a part of a menu. Although the variety and sometimes the quality available present some difficulties, the major problem is cost. Since the manufacturer's labor and overhead costs are added to the product's cost, such foods are unusually expensive. Where preparation staff is available, operators often choose to limit the use of frozen prepared entrees.

Institutions or services offering foods that must be held, choose prepared foods. Foods such as fried shrimp or breaded veal are avoided because they just do not taste as good after being held a few hours as they did when they were freshly cooked. Airlines, for example, serve predominately prepared rather than PTO foods.

Usually before beginning to plan a menu it is important to determine which type of foods—prepared or PTO—will dominate your menu. This will affect the quality of serivce and can reduce production problems.

TYPES OF MENU PLANS

Traditionally, restaurant operators planned their menu for the week, made sales forecasts, purchased the food supplies, and went into operation. Their planning was dictated by their experience, perhaps based upon availability of good buys in the market, a request by the customer, or just what the restaurant operator wanted to put on the menu.

Today this menu planning strategy is less and less common because it does not usually reflect good management practice. Changing the menu means changes in production, additional training, and invariably, more waste product. Accurate forecasting also is difficult, often leading to over-or underproduction.

There are two types of menu plans used in the industry that have an overall effect of reducing labor and food cost. One is a "set" menu and the other is a "cycle" menu. A set menu is a menu plan that does not change from day to day. In essence, customers are offered the same menu whenever they go into that restaurant (Figure 2.1). A cycle menu is planned for a particular period of time and then repeated (Figure 2.2).

SET MENU

A set menu is appropriate when you expect customers to dine in your establishment only occasionally (expensive dinner house), when your menu has sufficient variety to satisfy customers that may dine with you frequently (family restaurants), when your guests are transient (an expressway restaurant), or when your image requires an unchanging menu (restaurant chains).

With high food costs and labor costs, most menu planners choose a set menu if possible. The set menu reduces skill training since menu items are repeated over and over; by contrast a changing menu presents new recipes each day. Waste is reduced with set menus since carryover of most food products is accomplished by proper rotation techniques.

CYCLE MENU

Although food service may prefer set menus, often their clientele will not allow it. When the customer has no choice but to dine in your establishment every meal and every day, the menu must change and a cycle menu (or menu rotation) is a strategy commonly used. The operator determines the average guest stay (such as in a hospital or college) and decides how often a set of menus can practically be repeated. For example, in a factory cafeteria, it may be management's decision to change the entrees daily for a period of three weeks and then repeat. Cycle menus reduce production planning because recipes can be reused, cooks trained, and raw food costs predicted. (Production planning is done once.) Most important, cycle menus provide a forecasting tool; every time a menu is changed, so does the sales mix.

A cycle menu concentrates the planning of the menu in an initial intensive effort. Subsequent revisions are less time-consuming. A cycle menu assures variety adequate to the clientele served. For instance, a vacation resort with a package that included meals might select a one week cycle if that were the length of a guest stay. On the other hand, a large university might operate on a 28-day or longer cycle with provisions to avoid exact duplication of any day's offering during a quarter or semester.

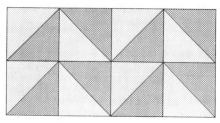 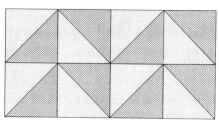

Soups

All soups are served with fresh bread or biscuits

Cream of Watercress with Shrimp
French Onion Gratinée
Just Plain Homemade Oxtail with Chunky Vegetables
Modest Bowl 1.00   Immodest Crock 1.50

Check the Blackboard for our daily selection as well as our regular offerings:

Salads

Salad of Greens
 including Romaine and Boston Bib lettuces, served with Arnold's dressing .85
Basque Salad
 fresh vegetables blanched, refreshed and marinated in a herbed vinaigrette 1.45
Fresh Pickings
 assortment of fresh, raw vegetable tidbits with a country-style dill dip 2.00

Beverages

Teas
Apricot - Scented .45
Orange Pekoe .35
Earl Grey .35
Peppermint .35
Sleepy Time .45

Coffees
Club .40
Espresso .65
Cappuccino .75
Sanka .50

Our coffees and teas are brewed with charcoal-filtered water.

Large Milk .45   Small Milk .30
Apollinaris Mineral Water .75

Main Courses

Your choice of our homestyle stews and casseroles 3.25
Irish Lamb Stew with Dumplings
Beef Bourguignon
Ratatouille with Emmenthal and Cheddar
 fresh vegetable stew with a broiled cheese topping
Escalloped Chicken and Veal Gratinée
 served on buttered egg noodles
Russian Pie
 mushrooms, sliced egg, onion and cabbage in herbed cream sauce
Every crock and casserole is served with fresh bread and sweet butter curls

Classic Luncheons

Bowl of Soup
Fresh Bread with Sweet Butter
Salad of Greens or Choice of Dessert
Glass of Selected Wine
3.00
Omelette of the Day
 selected fillings and served with French fries;
 check our blackboards
2.50

Desserts

Unpretentious ... but Great
Gooey Chocolate Brownie
 with Vanilla Ice Cream .75
The Best Rice Pudding
 with cinnamon, lots of raisins and fresh cream .75
Citrus Sherbet or Vanilla Ice Cream .60
Frozen Yoghurt with Crispins Fruit Topping 1.00
Or check our Blackboard for the selection of fine flans or cakes.

FIGURE 2.1 Example of a set menu. In this restaurant daily specials are listed on a blackboard (in lieu of a "clip-on"). (Courtesy Morris Graphics Limited, Hospitality Division.)

THE CUSTOMER AND MARKET PLANNING 21

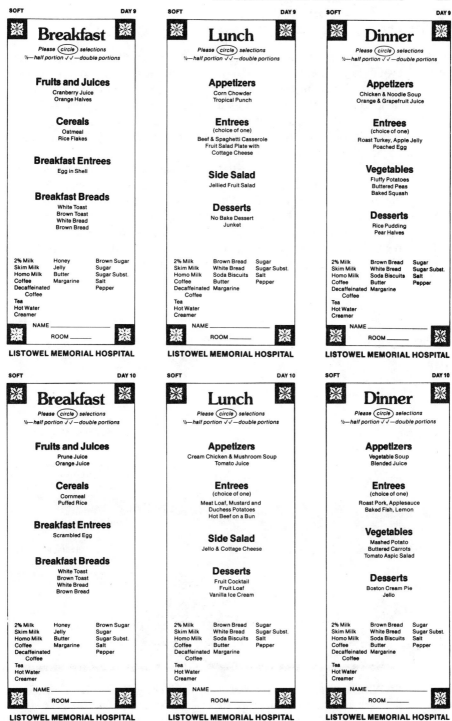

FIGURE 2.2 Two days of a hospital cycle menu that rotates every 14 days. (Courtesy Morris Graphics Limited, Hospitality Division.)

MODIFICATION OF SET AND CYCLE MENUS

Even food service operators that have a "captured" clientele have been able to switch to set menus. For example, student centers in universities traditionally served cafeteria lunches with a different variety of food each day. Now there is a trend to have a cluster of fast food outlets in the student centers—for example, a sandwich fast food, a health-food fast food, and a snack bar outlet (also called the scramble system). Thus, the customer has a choice, but the operator has the advantage of the set menu.

Another commonly used strategy of restaurant operators wishing to lure customers back each day is to use a base "set" menu combined with a clip-on. The clip-on is just that: a variable menu that may change each meal, and that is fastened to or slipped into the set menu (Figure 2.3). The variable menu may be a cycle menu, or it may be the place in which the operator wishes to introduce new menu items, take advantage of good buys, or respond to customer requests. The clip-on offers a convenient way to iron out menu problems. The set menu when

FIGURE 2.3 Here a variable restaurant menu, changed daily, is designed as a table tent to accompany the set menu. This particular restaurant is Canadian and restaurant menu offerings are listed in both English and French. (Courtesy Morris Graphics Limited, Hospitality Division.)

first established may need adjustment. When the menu is printed you may not be able to change it for a few months. Allowing space for an insert or clip-on allows the operator flexibility if the customer's tastes have been miscalculated.

TREND TO LIMIT MENUS

Students are often surprised to learn that much of restaurant food is prepared in small quantity rather than for vast numbers. Consider a restaurant with 100 chairs and 1 ½ turns at dinner, or a total of 150 guests. If there are 15 entree choices on the menu, then an average of only 10 orders will be needed of each menu item. This is not, however, the way the ordering usually breaks down—there could be 40 orders of one menu item and only 1 or 2 orders of another menu item.

Each menu item entails inventory, production planning, preparation, and carryover problems. With cooked foods, there is the ever present problem of reheated leftover food with a distinct loss of quality. For good reason then, food service operators attempt to trim their menu to the least number of items while still providing menu variety. This trend is seen in the proliferation of specialized dinner houses and new varieties of fast food outlets. For example, there are restaurants serving a variety of crepes that are actually fast food restaurants with a service component. Then there are bright young chefs appearing on the haute cuisine scene with limited offerings of *cuisine courante* and a view to do a few things well rather than many things poorly.

MENU BALANCE

A menu must be balanced according to guest preference and in the demands it makes on the kitchen. Moreover, it must offer a range of prices appropriate to its market. Finally, some specialized operations have special menu planning requirements. We shall deal with each of these topics in this section.

PRESENTATION AND FLAVOR

"We eat with our eyes" is a very trite saying, yet it is still true. A plate that is set before a guest should have an attractive appearance. Colors and shapes should be varied. You would not, for instance, serve a breast of chicken, boiled peeled potatoes, and cauliflower on the plate because each item would have a color and similar shape. Substituting green beans and new potatoes with "their jackets on" (i.e., unpeeled) would vary both color and flavors. Menu planning also includes planning colorful and contrasting garnishes for plates particularly when the guest chooses a lifeless plate combination.

The texture of foods also should offer variety. A plate presenting creamed chicken, whipped potatoes, and mashed squash might make the customer think you feared they had no teeth. (Of course, in health care food service the combination of soft foods in a "soft diet" is often clinically appropriate.) One way to compliment the creamed chicken, however, would be to serve it with spears of broccoli and crispy carrot curls. Considerations of balance of color, texture, and shape are especially important in situations where the guest has no choice, such as school lunch, the regular diet in hospitals without selective menus, and banquets.

A menu should offer balance in the temperature of foods. Particularly at lunch in the summer, the guest should be able to choose a cool salad or fruit plate as well as a cold sandwich or hot entree.

Obviously, every operator wants to offer good tasting food, but the conventional, full service menu should offer enough variety so that all guests can find a choice that pleases them. For this reason, many steak houses offer some fish and chicken items, just as fish specialty restaurants often have steaks available.

NUTRITION BALANCE

Today, customers are concerned about their diet and its effect upon their health. Twenty years ago when families dined out perhaps once a month, nutrition was furthest from their minds; They were not concerned with an occasional unbalanced meal. Today, however, families dine out more frequently, particularly when the mother works, and proper nutrition for the family may influence the family choice of restaurant. Fortunately, nutritionists have devised a simple chart to check our menus to see if they include everything that is necessary for a balanced diet. The chart is composed of the "Basic Four" food groups (Table 2.2). If your menu includes choices from each group, you can be assured that your customer can choose a nutritious diet.

A common criticism of fast food is that the foods are not nutritious. Although the opposite has been shown to be true, the correct choice is up to the customer. In most commercial restaurants we cannot tell customers to choose a well-balanced nutritious meal, but we can provide them with a nutritious choice if they care to make it.

PRODUCTION BALANCE

While planning the menu it is a good idea to keep in mind the labor involved in preparing each menu item and attempt to allocate kitchen production among the tasks to be performed. Work allocation is highly dependent upon the type of operation, of course. Some restaurants cannot afford any "labor intensive" menu items (labor intensive items require much hand labor). Even if you have had little experience in cooking, it is not difficult to decipher a recipe and rate it for labor intensity. The number of preparation steps can be a guide. For example, a broiled T-Bone steak is certainly less labor intensive than Swiss steak. The Swiss steak involves chopping vegetables, preparing a sauce, and breading the steaks, while a pre-portioned T-Bone steak involves one-step broiling.

A dilemma for food services is that they must keep food costs low. Many less expensive foods require additional preparation steps. Meatless dishes are noto-

TABLE 2.2 THE "BASIC FOUR" FOOD GROUPS USED IN MENU PLANNING

Serving Recommended	What Counts as a Serving
Meat group 2 or more servings	2–3 ounces of lean meat, poultry, or fish. One egg; 1/2 cup cooked dry beans, dry peas or lentils; 2 tablespoons of peanut butter replace 1/2 serving of meat.
Fruit-vegetable group 4 or more servings including: A good source of Vitamin C	Count as a serving 1/2 cup fruit or vegetable; or the portion ordinarily served. For example, 1 medium apple, orange, or potato, half a medium grapefruit. Grapefruit or grapefruit juice; orange or orange juice; cantaloupe, raw strawberries; watermelon; broccoli, brussel sprouts; tomatoes or tomato juice; and green pepper.
A good source of Vitamin A	Dark green and deep yellow vegetables and fruits: apricots, broccoli, cantaloupe, carrots, chard, collards, kale, pumpkin, spinach, sweet potatoes, turnip greens and other dark green leaves, and winter squash. Count as a serving 1/2 cup or the portion ordinarily served. For example, 1 medium orange *or* banana.
Bread and cereal group 4 or more servings	Count as 1 serving: 1 slice of bread; 3/4 cup ready-to-eat cereal; 1/2 to 3/4 cup cooked cereal, cornmeal, grits, macaroni, noodles, rice, or spaghetti. Whole grain or enriched breads and cereals including ready-to-eat cereals, cooked cereals, macaroni, noodles, spaghetti, rice, crackers, quick breads, and other baked goods made from whole grain or enriched flour.

Milk group
 Child under 9
   2–3 servings
 Child, 9 to 12
   2 or more servings
 Teenage
   4 or more servings
 Adults
   2 or more servings
	Count as a serving: 8 ounce cup of whole, skim, buttermilk, or evaporated or reconstituted dry milk.

rious for their labor intensity. Lasagna, for example, involves cooking a sauce, cooking lasagna noodles, and layering cheeses, sauces, and noodles. To avoid overloading the kitchen on some days and having light days at other times, we balance the labor intensive foods with those that require little preparation. Another way we balance production is to plan for equipment usage. If all items on the menu must go into the oven, there may not be sufficient equipment capacity.

In thinking about balancing a menu for production, we must also estimate the sales volume for a particular meal. In an operation where, for instance, Monday and Tuesday evenings are very slow it is probably best to list only prepared-to-order items on those evenings because any food that is ready to serve (such as roast beef) may be left over. Even if it can be used the next day, leftovers are often of lower quality and frequently are used in lower cost dishes. What this means is that, because of the ingredients in lower cost dishes, we cannot get the return required from the high purchase cost of the ingredient. Thus, when we use that as a leftover we cannot make our food cost target.

In our example restaurant, let us assume that business on Wednesday and Thursday is brisk but that the premises are not overcrowded. On these nights the menu can readily afford to have one or two prepared items, particularly if these items *can* be reused without quality loss, such as baked ham. These foods are sometimes called *extendible*.

If we suppose further that Friday and Saturday night are really busy, with waiting lines at the door shortly after we open for dinner, the menu would need to balance prepared-to-order items with ready-to-serve foods and could even list ready-to-serve foods that are not fully reusable (those that do not have acceptable quality as leftovers). These are sometimes called "runouts" because management may plan to run out of roast prime rib of beef an hour or so before the restaurant closes for the evening to avoid having any of this expensive product left over.

A strategy used for "planned" runouts is to use small cards (sometimes called a "tip-on") that can be removed when the item is sold; this will prevent a guest from being disappointed. Figure 2.4 shows the production strategy appropriate to our example.

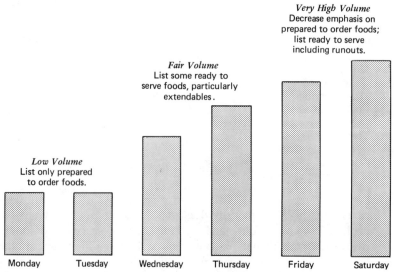

FIGURE 2.4 Production strategy varies with sales volume.

THE CUSTOMER AND MARKET PLANNING 27

PRICING BALANCE

Although pricing strategy is a subject that deserves fuller discussion, probably in a marketing course, we need to note some major considerations in this area as they relate to menu balance.

In the nonprofit and subsidized operation, pricing is generally strictly a function of cost. If the cost of food for an entree is $0.75 and the target food cost per cent 50%, then the food item will be sold for $1.50.

In the commerical sector, pricing is both a function of cost *and* the price a customer is willing to pay. A primary influence on what people will pay is the cost of similar products in competitive restaurants. This is one of the reasons why periodic menu surveys, discussed earlier, are so important.

A practice of mechanically "marking up" every item so that each yields some standard food cost percentage may result in some products, for instance steaks, being overpriced relative to the competition while others are underpriced relative to the market. An alternate strategy would be to list steaks with a price that yields a higher food cost and seek out lower cost items, such as fish and chicken, that can be priced to have a lower food cost so as to have a menu balanced to yield the target food cost on an overall basis—and still be a menu that will attract guests to your operation.

Many operators think it foolish to base menu price exclusively on food cost. They may explain that it is the total profit that is significant and that lower prices may bring increased sales volume, which yields lower labor costs and higher profits. Put simply, would your rather, assuming labor and other costs stay the same, sell a steak for $10 with a 50% food cost or fried chicken for $3 with a "better" food cost of 33%? In the first case, the contribution to fixed costs and profit is $5; in the second case, it is $2.

Different kinds of operations arouse different expectations about prices. A family restaurant, for instance, may list dinners from $2.90 to $5.95. It chooses this range because it has found, through experience that these are the prices its customers expect. If the cost on a popular item rises dramatically, the restaurant has three options. The first option is to absorb the increased price and raise other prices on the menu to offset the poorer cost performance of the high cost but popular item. However, this is an option that can hurt overall profit if the prices of the other items are raised too high.

A second option is to substitute lower grade ingredients or reduce portion size. This option, too, has its hazards. Cheapening the quality can—and often does—have an adverse effect on the restaurant's image. If shrimp rises dramatically in price, switching from a 20–26 count to 26–30 count is something the customer will notice and that customer may decide that everything else has been cheapened too, and go elsewhere.

The third option is to remove the overpriced item and substitute a similar item. If the price of clams has remained in line while shrimp have become too expensive to fit the price range, then a fried clam basket may be featured and french fried shrimp dropped from the menu entirely.

Our major point here is that the menu must be balanced in its overall price range so as to present a consistent image of the operator to the guest, listing no item whose price is so low or so high as to clash with that image. Finally, the cost of this mix of food products must yield the desired overall cost of the operation.

BOARD PLAN PRICING

Board plan pricing is a special case of the need to balance menu prices. In these cases, there is a single "price" that customers pay for meals over a certain period of time and the menu must be balanced over that period to that price. A 12-week contract may include meals featuring sirloin steak and macaroni and cheese. It is necessary that the cost of items balance over the period of the board plan to fit the board plan price. In many institutional operations, especially colleges, the guest buys meals for an entire semester or quarter. More commonly a variety of board plans are offered; for instance, a seven day, three meal plan; weekday meals only; weekday lunch and dinner. Often several different board plans are offered at the same institution.

However varied, the board plan is a contract over a fairly long period of time. The price is set by negotiation between the contract company (or the institution's own food service department) and the client—that is, the institution's administration—to suit institutional goals such as student satisfaction, breakeven or profitable operation or, perhaps, prestige.

The guest (here we mean the individual student) who has bought the contract finds that the operator has included several variables in the price negotiated with the client. One important consideration is absenteeism. The more meals included in the program, the higher the proportion of meals that will be missed by the average student. Some students sleep late and miss breakfast, others occasionally go away for the weekend. Absenteeism has two effects. First, it lowers the price of the total semester or quarter meal plan because the price takes missed meals into account. Second, it provides some flexibility in menu planning: the money saved from absentee diners may be used to break the monotony of a menu by occasionally offering a steak dinner or Hawaiian Luau. On the other hand many of the meal options other than a 21-meal week are designed and priced to let the guest decide to be absent for a given number of meals whenever he or she wants.

THE PRINTED MENU

Most table service restaurants have a permanent menu printed on a heavy paper stock (the set menu). This is sometimes called the "hard back menu." Inside the menu a daily variable menu may be affixed, sometimes called a "hot sheet," indicating the cooked items offered on that day at lunch or at dinner. "Clip ons" may be attached to the hard back to advertise a house special.

Operations such as family restaurants use only a permanent hard back menu. Sometimes the permanent menu is printed on a place mat. Some restaurants use a hardback menu with tip-on (small cards usually featuring one or two items) but no hot sheet or daily variable menu. Hotel restaurants and many higher priced table service restaurants have a hard back menu that lists the items available from opening to closing, inserting a hot sheet or daily variable menu. Other large operations that vary their menu actually print their daily menu on hard stock, a very expensive practice, while still others have a set of printed menus that are used in a cycle. It is most important that the student see what the principal elements of the menu are: the hard back, the daily variable menu, and tip ons.

Of course, not all menus are printed. Cafeterias usually list the items available and their prices where guests moving through the line can see them. Fast food operations have a menu board permanently fixed behind the counter from which the guest can order.

MENUS FOR DIFFERENT MEALS

The typical operation that is open for three meals usually has two or three menus, one for breakfast and a second for lunch and dinner or, commonly, a second menu for lunch and a third menu for dinner.

The breakfast menu must cater to several tastes. Some guests are light eaters. Others are in a hurry. Still others like a heavy breakfast. For this reason, a breakfast menu always invariably includes a large number of a la carte listings (single items that may be ordered alone); one or more "quickie" featured breakfasts; and club breakfasts that include juice, main item (such as eggs and bacon), toast, and beverage. Usually the cost of a club breakfast is less than the cost of all items if ordered a la carte. Breakfast menus do tend to be set menus for restaurants and cycle menus.

The lunch menu must offer a sufficient variety to cater to the heavy eater, the moderate eater, and the weight watcher. For this reason the "hot sheet" may offer some items similar to those offered for dinner such as roast beef but with a smaller portion and, hence, at a lower price. Sandwiches and salads are invariably part of the lunch menu, too. Appetizers are important because they are usually part of a complete luncheon, which also includes main course, surrounding courses (such as salad, vegetables, rolls), and dessert. Like the club breakfast, the complete luncheon is usually offered at a slight discount from the total a la carte (or individual item listing) if added up for all items. One use of the appetizer course is the very combination of a soup and sandwich special. Dessert listings are always a part of the luncheon menu and offer an important means of increasing the average sale per guest.

The dinner menu features fuller meals and larger portions and may offer salad only as an accompaniment to the meals. Many operations offer "Complete Dinners" which, like the complete luncheon and club breakfast, offer a choice of every course together with the entree. (In fact, this is probably the source of the phrase "from soup to nuts.")

Other menus offered in various operations such as a late supper menu or an afternoon menu typically feature desserts and lighter food. To promote desserts, some operations have a special dessert menu that waitresses or waiters present as soon as the main course is cleared.

MENU PLANNING IN SPECIALIZED OPERATIONS

The menus we have considered are, for the most part, typical of the freestanding full service restaurant and of restaurants found in small and medium sized hotels. Several specialized menus need to be considered briefly to complete our view of the food service field.

SCHOOL FOOD SERVICE

The National School Lunch Program in the United States requires that school lunches conform to a basic pattern and provide one third to one half a students's minimum daily nutritional requirements. Four elements must be present in the prescribed quantities:

1. Body building foods like meat, fish, eggs, and cheese that provide protein and iron. (Bread and butter are served with these foods to supply carbohydrates and fat.)
2. Vegetables or fruits high in vitamin A.
3. Vegetables or fruits high in vitamin C.
4. Milk to provide calcium as well as protein.

The reimburseable meal pattern, as school lunches fulfilling these requirements are called, provide not only a nutritionally sound meal but are part of an *educational program* to teach students what foods are necessary for health and growth. Cycle menus are commonly used as a base plan in school lunch feeding, but the cycle is generally flexible to allow use of surplus commodities.

HEALTH CARE FOOD SERVICE

Because of the careful calculations that go into special diets, health care facilities make use of cycle menus. The length of the cycle is usually based on the average patient stay.

Three kinds of problems present themselves in health care. The first is special diet. Although most patients are usually on a regular diet, some patients require modified diets. Common modified diets are calorie restricted diets, diabetic diets, low cholesterol diets, fat controlled diets, sodium restricted diets, soft diets, and bland diets. In planning menus for health care operations, we try to use base foods for the regular diet, which can be modified for most of the other diets. Roast or baked chicken, for example, can be used on calorie controlled, low cholesterol, fat controlled, bland, and diabetic diets, but fried chicken is not as versatile.

The second problem is coordinating patient food service with the food service provided for professional staff, other employees, and visitors (which may constitute a larger volume of business than patient feeding). Generally all three nonpatient groups are served in a single food service unit, usually a cafeteria. The need for a change in menu for this clientele, most of whom eat at least one meal per working day in the cafeteria, month in and month out, may require a different menu plan than that used for patients. To ease production requirements, foods for patients are included on the staff menu, which is often then extended. A prepared-to-order sandwich menu, for example, may be offered along with the patient meals, a snack-food menu, or a longer-cycle menu.

A third problem in health care menu planning is patient diet education. Operators must be concerned with the cultural background of their patients (their likes and dislikes) and not include foods that can or will not be prepared by the patients when they return home (or left untouched during their hospital stay). The hospital is a learning place for many patients who should be introduced to a variety of foods that they may have (and like) when they return to normal life.

HOTEL FOOD SERVICE

In the hotel business, the rental of rooms is generally much more profitable than food service. For this reason, hotel dining rooms open earlier for breakfast and close later in the evening than would a typical freestanding restaurant—and some food service facility in most well-run hotels is open all day. This is done as an accommodation to keep profitable room guests coming back.

Similarly, hotel menus often include special features designed to please the hotel guest rather than strictly to earn a profit. For instance, many hotels serve freshly squeezed orange juice, which is much more expensive than a good frozen juice, yet do not charge more for it because they found it is a frill that earns repeated patronage from some room guests.

Many hotels offer not only luxury dinner items but also one or two inexpensive entrees. The lower priced items reduce the average sale per guest but may allow guests to have a drink or two before the inexpensive meal and remain within the limits of their expense accounts (see Figure 2.5). Once again, the hotel's concern is with the $30 or $50 (or more) room sale (with the *variable cost* of that sale $2 to $4), more than it is with the food sale. Banquet sales, high profit for hotel food service, require separate menus from the hotel dining room menus. Since banquet meals are served at one time, the food must be prepared and quickly dished. Prepared foods lend themselves to banquet menus. Steaks, for example, an ever-popular menu item, can cause production problems in a banquet of more than 25 persons. (In addition to having banquet menu plans, persons selling banquets need to be apprised of production problems with certain menu items and not sell a steak dinner to 1000 persons unless the production capacity is available.)

FIGURE 2.5 A hotel menu with entree prices ranging from $4.75 to $12.55. (Courtesy Morris Graphics Limited, Hospitality Division.)

INSTITUTIONAL MENU PLANNING

In institutional food service, where the total number of meals and the relative popularity of individual items are known, having a cycle menu permits those in charge of purchasing to forecast demand for various items of food over a period of months or a year's time. They can then undertake bulk purchases at substantial savings.

Most institutional menus are prepared by hand. Kotschevar suggests "beginning with a sheet large enough to hold the menu for an entire period"[1] if the period is not so long as to make that impossible. Kotschevar describes the process of drawing up an institutional cycle menu in these words:

> Most planners start with the main dishes for a meal, beginning first with dinners, then with lunches and then breakfasts. Balance and variety must be sought between days and also between the meals of a day.

---

[1]Lendal Kotschevar, *Management By Menu* (Chicago: National Institute for the Food Service Industry, 1975), p. 73.

The frequency of the types of meats to use should be established and a table can be set up for this. For instance, in a week beef may be served twice, pork or cured pork once, poultry once, fish or shellfish once, a casserole dish once along with an occasional selection of variety meat, veal, lamb, sausage, eggs, cheese or other non-meat dish. Similarly, a table may be set up to indicate the frequency desired for various vegetables and other foods. A desired frequency table can be set up for breakfast and lunch items also.

After the main dishes are selected, the vegetables and potato, or other starch items, are added, followed by salads, and dressings. Again, these must be balanced against the various foods used in a day and from day to day. After adding these major items, the planner may select the breakfast fruits and cereals. Breads for each meal, desserts and beverages can follow in that order.

After this, the menu is checked to see that balance has been maintained, nutritional needs met, cost restraints not exceeded and other factors such as equipment balance, skill of labor, etc., considered. Modified diets based on this general menu, should be planned by an individual trained in nutrition.[2]

Some large institutional operations use computerized routines in the planning process just described.

FAST FOOD

Most fast food menus are extremely rigid compared to other menus both because of "image" and limited production plant. The latter is fairly obvious. Where a fast food operation uses principally grills to prepare their food, addition of fried chicken may be difficult or impossible because of limited fryer capacity or limited kitchen space for adding fryer capacity. The fast food production area is designed with a specific menu in mind. Only the equipment and space needed for that menu are provided. Consequently, except where a new product can use existing equipment (fried eggs can be prepared on the same grill used for hamburgers) changes in menu are very difficult.

Equally important to most fast food operations is retaining a consistent and clear identity in the marketplace. Although fast food menus are expanding, such menu expansion takes place only after careful test marketing to determine consumer acceptance of the new item *and* and impact of the new item on the consumer's concept of the total operation.

Finally, many fast food chains do not add an item that will just "steal sales" from another item. The new item must either move the operation into a new market (as with the Egg McMuffin and other breakfast products at McDonald's), increase the average sale, round out a menu (by building additional dessert business as with pies, then cookies, and most recently sundaes at McDonald's), or meet competition.

Several examples of meeting competition were offered when roast beef sandwich restaurants added fried chicken to their menus to meet the competition brought on by addition of roast beef to the menu in chicken fast food chains.

[2]Kotschevar, p. 73

THE FAMILY RESTAURANT

Some operations, as noted earlier, have a simplified menu that is the same for all meals. Sometimes called the "California menu" after the place where this kind of operation originated, these menus offer breakfast at any time of the day—and in effect, lunch and dinner any time, too. Such operations cater not only to people eating the customary meal at the customary hour but to people working afternoon or evening shifts, travelers from a different time zone, as well as people who just feel like having bacon and eggs or a waffle for lunch, dinner, or a late night snack.

MENUS FOR CAFETERIAS

Profit in cafeterias is a function of the number of customers moving through the line per minute. A slowdown anywhere in the line can have an adverse effect upon volume. Thus, in planning the menu for cafeteria service, we include foods that can be predished or dished and served rapidly. Naturally, prepared foods are used in cafeteria menus, but we must go even further and look at the steps in dishing out cafeteria foods. For example, a crepe could be stuffed and rolled before it is placed on the cafeteria line. Adding a sauce and a pickled peach garnish would mean two additional serving steps for this menu item. Another example is French onion soup, which has several steps: dishing of the soup (step 1), adding toast (step 2), sprinkling on cheese (step 3), and, adding crackers (step 4). Servicing the soup might be changed to make it a one step process or the planner might be forced to remove the four-step item from the menu. Occasionally one encounters a prepared-to-order counter in the cafeteria line where the server makes sandwiches to order. This immediately slows the entire line to a halt. To meet customer demands for some PTO foods, cafeterias have used the "scramble" system in which mini-units containing foods requiring different times to prepare or serve are placed around a room. The guest, for example, may go to one place for a hot sandwich, another for a salad, and still another for dessert and take their tray to a centralized cashier.

MENU PLANNING FOR NEW FOOD SERVICE SYSTEMS

These systems encompass ready food systems (chilled and frozen), total convenience systems, and commissaries.

We cannot anticipate all problems in new food service systems because we have not had enough experience with them. The critical part of menu planning for these systems is to be sure to follow each menu item through the entire system to determine if it is suited for the system. A recent graduate of a food service program explained this problem well:

> Someone added a parfait to the menu, sending us the glasses and recipe, but had not considered the height of the parfait. The glasses were too high to fit into the carts transporting the food. They needed to be carried on separate trays and the jiggling during transport knocked many of them over. As it turned out, the food service purchased parfait glasses unnecessarily as the item had to be dropped from the menu.

THE CUSTOMER AND MARKET PLANNING

FIGURE 2.6 This menu features frozen prepared entrees, allowing the hospital to offer patients a selection of foods each day. (Courtesy Morris Graphics Limited, Hospitality Division.)

Noon & Evening Meals
The following items are available for both noon and evening meals

Appetizers
Orange Juice
(1 Fruits & Vegetables choice)
Diet Lemonade
(Extra)
Tomato Juice
(Extra)
Cream of Mushroom Soup
(½ Starch & 2 Fat)
Chicken Noodle Soup
(½ Starch & ½ Fat)
Soup of the Day
(Varies)

Side Salads
Your choice of one of the following...
Tossed Side Salad
with diet dressing
(Extra)
Diet Cabbage Side Salad
(Extra)
Side Salad of the Day
(Extra)

Garden Vegetables
Sweet Green Peas
(1 Fruits & Vegetables choice)
Carrot Coins
(1 Fruits & Vegetables choice)
Spinach
(Extra)
Wax Beans
(Extra)
Vegetable Medley
(1 Fruits & Vegetables choice)

All vegetables are prepared in a manner which provides maximum nutritional value, and may be somewhat firmer than those prepared by conventional methods.

Beverages
2% Milk
Skim Milk
Whole Milk
Coffee
Tea
Decaffeinated Coffee

Salad & Sandwich Entrees
Your choice of one of the following or a hot entree . . . . .

Assorted Cold Meat Plate
Thinly sliced assorted cold meats served with potato salad and a vegetable garnish.
(2 Protein choices + 1 Starch choice + 1 Fat choice)

Cottage Cheese Fruit Salad Plate
Seasonal fresh and preserved fruit with refreshing cottage cheese arranged on a lettuce bed.
(2 Protein choices & 2 Fruits & Vegetables choice)

Zesty Sandwich Platter
Attractively garnished, and different every day.
(2 Starch choices & 1 Fat choice & 2 Protein choices)

Submarine Sandwich
A variety of meat and cheese served with lettuce and tomato on a long bun.
(2 Starch choices & 1 Fat choice & 2 Protein choices)

Potatoes & Rice
(Each serving equals 1 Starch choice)
Fluffy Whipped Potato
Parsley Boiled Potato
Baked Potato
Steamed Rice

Breads
(Each serving equals 1 Starch choice)
100% Whole Wheat Bread
Enriched White Bread
Crackers

Desserts
Seasonal Fresh Fruit
(1 Fruits & Vegetables choice)
Water-Packed Canned Fruit
(1 Fruits & Vegetables choice)
Diet Milk Pudding
(1 Milk choice)
Plain Yogurt
(1 Milk choice)
Vanilla Ice Cream
(1 Fruits & Vegetables choice & 1 Fat choice)
Fresh Baked Muffin
(1 Starch choice & 1 Fat choice)
Crackers & Cheese
A nutritious way to end your meal - zesty cheese served with crackers.
(1 Protein choice & ½ Starch choice)

Noon Meal Entrees
These items are available for the **Noon Meal** only.
Your choice of one of the following or a cold entree . . . .

Baked Chicken
Succulent pieces of skinless chicken baked with a lightly seasoned coating.
_____ Protein Choices

Shepherd's Pie
Layers of ground beef, vegetables and potato topping combined to make a hearty meal.
(2 Protein choices & 1 Starch choice & 1 Fat choice)

Baked Fish Fillet
Fresh fish fillet served with a lemon wedge.
_____ Protein Choices

Chunky Turkey Stew
Chunks of turkey and vegetables, simmered in a flavourful gravy.
(2 Protein choices & 1 Fruits & Vegetables choice & 1 Fat choice)

Roast Pork
Slices of lean pork served with unsweetened applesauce.
_____ Protein Choices

Omelet
Fresh and fluffy egg dish
_____ Protein Choices
Available with Whole Wheat toast and corn oil margarine
_____ Starch choices & _____ Fat choices

Shrimp Bayou
Tender Shrimp in a creole sauce
(2 Protein choices & 1 Fruits & Vegetables choice)

Charbroiled Burger
Juicy all-beef burger charbroiled to perfection and served with appropriate condiments.
(2 Protein choices & 2 Starch choices)

Evening Meal Entrees
These items are available for the **Evening Meal** only.
Your choice of one of the following or a cold entree . . . .

Chicken a la King
Tender chicken with vegetables in a smooth white sauce.
(2 Protein choices & 1 Fruits & Vegetables choice & 1 Milk choice)

Roast Beef
Tender slices of beef served with gravy if desired.
_____ Protein choices & _____ Fat choices

Macaroni & Cheese
Elbow macaroni baked in a mild cheese sauce.
(2 Protein choices & 1 Starch choice & 1 Milk choice)

Roast Turkey
Succulent turkey served with unsweetened cranberry sauce, and gravy if desired.
_____ Protein choices & _____ Fat choices

Baked Liver
Baby beef liver baked in a tomato sauce.
(2 Protein choices)

Golden Souffle
A light and airy blend of eggs
(2 Protein choices & 1 Starch choice)
Available with Whole Wheat toast with corn oil margarine
_____ Starch choice & _____ Fat choice

Poached Sole ☺
Delicately flavoured portions of sole poached in an herbed broth.
_____ Protein choices

CALORIE RESTRICTED

Please select your choice of condiments on the daily order sheets.

You will certainly wish to determine in advance whether prepared or prepared-to-order foods are appropriate. Here, PTO foods can be partially prepared up to the point of cookery and are not necessarily eliminated from new systems depending upon the final cookery system available.

With total convenience systems a primary consideration in menu planning is availability of product (see Figure 2.6). If not successful in the market a new convenience food may cease to be manufactured. If your menu relies on this convenience food you may have to reprint menus or worse, scratch it from your printed menu. Before adding a prepared food, check its availability, especially from the supplier who must be able to supply it as often as you need it. If possible, use a flexible menu plan, a printed menu that can be inexpensively altered.

CONCLUSION

Regardless of the kind of menu a manager writes, we do well to remember that either by design or by accident, the menu is a marketing strategy aimed at a specific market, as well as a production strategy that dictates kitchen lay out, labor requirements, and food cost. The menu is *the* plan in food service. As such, it deserves more attention than any other planning activity.

KEY WORDS AND PHRASES

Who is your customer
Income
Occupation
What is your customer doing?
Location analysis
Competition analysis
Menu comparison
Price comparisons
Menu popularity surveys
Basic menu planning concepts
Prepared foods
Prepared-to-order foods
Menu plans
Set menu
Cycle menu
Menu rotation
Average guest stay
Clip-on menu
Limiting menu items
Chair turns
Menu balance
Guest preference

Guest preference
Kitchen demands
Price appropriate to market
Presentation and flavor balance
Color, shape, texture, temperature, variety
Nutrition balance
Production balance
Extendible menu items
Planned run-outs
Pricing balance
Strategies for yielding
Target food cost
Contribution to profit
Price range
Board plan pricing
Printed menu
Hard back menu
Variable menu
Tip-ons
Meal menus
Specialized menus

DISCUSSION QUESTIONS

1. What restaurant or food service operation do you frequent most often? Discuss who is this restaurant's customer (age, sex, income, and occupation) and what the customer is doing. Is the menu appropriate for the market? Could the menu be improved? Does this restaurant use a cycle or a set menu?

2. Make a list of 10 favorite prepared foods and a list of 10 favorite prepared-to-order foods.

3. Discuss why breakfast foods like eggs, bacon, and pancakes are generally good in table-service restaurants and a problem in institutional food service.

4. Why do food service operators tend to limit menus whenever possible?

5. You have just been hired as head cook for an ocean freighter and your first job is to write a menu for its crew of 30 men. The ship comes into port every two weeks. When at sea, the seaman's only diversion is mealtime and your company does not scrimp on food cost. The seamen put in 8-hour shifts and the work is generally strenuous manual labor. To plan the menu you need to decide whether to use a cycle or set menu, the meal periods (there are three 8-hour shifts a day) and the type of foods (prepared or PTO). Design a menu for your freighter using basic menu planning concepts.

6. Identify a favorite fast food restaurant. Can you choose a nutritionally balanced meal from their menu? (Include a selection from each food group.)

7. Identify the labor intensive foods from this list: roast beef, steak, breaded stuffed pork chops, meat loaf, chicken pot pie, cole slaw, tossed salad, apple pie, ice cream, cheese cake.

MONITORING OPERATIONS: POINT OF SALES SYSTEMS

3

Control in the Hospitality Industry

Point of Sales in Food Service

POS Control Functions

THE PURPOSE OF THIS CHAPTER

A technological revolution has been sweeping the business world since the end of World War II because of the development of the computer. In the past, information had been relatively expensive to collect and process, and its accuracy often open to question because of human error. Because of the limitations of cost and the speed at which humans can work, reports were often out of date by the time they were prepared for study by management. This chapter introduces you to the information revolution in the hospitality industry that has resulted from the introduction of point of sales systems. In order to understand the significance of the point of sales system, we need to develop some basic concepts more fully. The chapter begins, therefore, with a discussion of management control and management information systems.

THIS CHAPTER SHOULD HELP YOU

1. Place control of food service operations in the overall perspective of management control.

2. Become familiar with the major point of sales systems used in food service.

3. Identify the principal hardware available for POS systems and their functions.

4. Identify and explain the principal categories of POS reports.

5. Work through one example of the kinds of reports a POS system offers food service operators.

CONTROL IN THE HOSPITALITY INDUSTRY

At least three kinds of control can be distinguished:[1]

1. *Management control* is the means by which management assures itself that the organization will carry out its (plans) effectively and efficiently.

2. *Operational control* is the management process of assuring that specific tasks are carried out effectively and efficiently.

3. *Strategic planning* is the process of deciding on the goals of the organization and on the broad strategies to be used in attaining these goals.[2]

---

[1] We draw heavily in this section of the work of Robert N. Anthony and John Dearden, *Management Control Systems*, 4th ed. (Homewood II.: Richard D. Irwin; 1980). The interested student may wish to consult their text, in particular, Chapter 1, "The Nature of Management Control," p. 3–20.

[2] Anthony and Dearden, *Management Control Systems*, p. 7.

Although we concerned ourselves with some elements of strategic planning in the last chapter, this book is principally concerned with the way the first two of these processes are carried out in the food service industry (Table 3.1). Here is an example of each process.

> The management team sits down to review an operator's performance against budgeted goals at the end of the month. The team members are engaged in mangement control.

> A cashier fills out a shift report turning over the cash and change as received from customers and showing the amount of cash over or short at the end of the shift along with other information required in that report. That report is consolidated with others and a bank deposit is made, a copy of which is supplied to accounting. Here, we are dealing with operational control.

In management control, results are interpreted and a judgment is made about what (if any) corrective measures are needed. The meeting described above might lead, for instance, to a concensus that "food cost is above target by one point but that is because of a temporary jump in the price of fish last month. Since the price has come back down, no action is called for."

On the other hand, operational control sets limits within which significant routine *activities* are carried out. A quick review of the days cashier's reports might reveal that overages and shortages were within acceptable limits or might lead to a statement by the manager that "Mary is short more than $10 for the third day in a row. We'd better decide what to do."

It is useful to draw out the distinctions between management and operational control. Operational control relates input (resources used, such as raw food) to outputs (product or service rendered, such as a finished meal) in a way that can best be described as *engineered*. For example, a yield per pound target is established for a roast and a cook is asked to weigh every portion. At the end of

TABLE 3.1 A COMPARISON OF MANAGEMENT CONTROL AND OPERATIONAL CONTROL

Characteristic	Management Control	Operational Control
Focus of activity	Whole operation	Single task; related transactions
Judgment	Relatively much; subjective judgments	Relatively little; reliance on rules
Nature of information	Integrated; approximations accepted; future and historical	Tailor-made to the operation; precise; often real time
Persons primarily involved	Management	Supervisors and lead employees
Mental activity	Administrative, persuasive	Follow directions
Source discipline	Social psychology	Economics; physical sciences
Time horizon	Weeks, months, years	Shift to shift; day to day
Types of costs	Judgmental	Engineered

Source. Adapted from Anthony and Dearden, *Management Control Systems*, p. 17.

the shift, the cook submits a yield report showing raw weight, cooked weight, portions served, waste and scrap. The acceptable amount of variance from target in this case will be very small.

On the other hand, if a manager has a 27.5% payroll cost target for the month, the large number of variables to be handled prevent us from treating the results as mechanically as we might with a yield report. The yielding process makes portioning a roast a *programmed activity,* but payroll control involves too much judgment to be reduced to a set of simple procedures.

Management control focuses on the entire organization while operational control deals with a single task or series of related tasks or transactions. Management control is more difficult because it requires judgment rather than the enforcement of a rule or set of rules, as with operational control.

Operational control, because it deals with a specific task or process uses exact information; for example, how much the cashier was short, or how many portions per pound the roast yielded. Management control can often be satisfied with approximations. A payroll report might summarize employee hours by department rounded to the nearest hour or tens of hours or indicate that banquet department productivity has ranged from 27 to 35 covers per man-day over a recent period.

Data relevant to operational control are determined by the *process*. The cashier's report is related to cash and charges. (The number of each product sold doesn't enter into the process of assessing the cashier's deposit.) The same set of transactions, however, can be used to show how management control integrates a variety of data. Unit sales, for instance, can be used to gauge marketing in one report and to assess food cost performance in another. Thus, data in a management control system can be used in an integrative way to develop a large number of reports that are varied in purpose and content.

Finally, in management control, the system itself is only a part of the management process. The control system is helpful but can not replace the manager's judgment and knowledge nor their interpersonal skill. In operational control, on the other hand, the system (e.g., use of the cash register, preparation of the cashier's report, submission of deposit) is relatively much more important. The *system* tells the cashier what to do and the cashier's success or failure in the job is measured by the ability to follow the system.

This distinction between management control and operational control is especially crucial as point of sales (POS) register systems become more widely used. POS give management much more information, more accurately and more quickly, and makes it possible for whole areas of unit management to be shifted from time-consuming management control to the much more routinized operational control.

This simplification of much of unit management's work should not deceive you: it does not mean management has been made easier. Rather, it means that managers now have more time available to concentrate on other important tasks that can never be automated, such as employee and guest satisfaction.

MANAGEMENT INFORMATION SYSTEMS

Although management information systems (MIS) have been around for a long time, it is only recently that the concept has been formalized and that information systems have been used so extensively. Let us look at an MIS in its most simple form.

> Joe had a hot dog stand at the entrance to the fairground. He sold hot dogs and soft drinks during the fair. He put the money he received in a cigar box and made change from the cigar box. At the end of the day, he counted up his money.

The elements of a food service MIS are contained in this example. Here are a set of transactions that need to be summarized to provide management with information about how to interpret them. (Information is here defined as data that increases what we know.) In this very simple operation, Joe can tell at the end of the day *whether* or not he has had a good day just from knowing how busy he has been; but counting up cash in the cigar box tells him just *how* good (or bad) the day has been. His intuition—"it's been a good day"—is less precise than his total dollar sales: "Sales went over $500. That's the best day I've had." MIS, though, are tailored to the operation's needs, and Joe has generated only the information he needs.

Since Joe runs the stand by himself and knows how careful he is, he probably doesn't feel the need to compare sales to inventory reduction. Let's suppose, though, that next year the fairground opens a second gate and Joe manages to secure a second stand at that gate. Now, he has an employee running one stand and, at the very least, wants to know how much money is in the cigar box (sales) as well as how much product is left unsold at the end of the day; we thus have the makings of the most basic information summary in an industry, the daily report (Table 3.2).

TABLE 3.2 JOE'S DAILY REPORT

	Closing Cash	$ 295
	Opening Cash	5
		$ 290

	Hot Dogs	Soft Drinks
Opening inventory	100	80
Received	400	120
	500	200
Closing inventory	100	20
	400	180
Sales value/unit	0.50	0.50
Total sales value	$200	$ 90

Table 3.2 suggests that Joe made a good choice in staffing his second stand because both sales and inventory reduction coincided.[3]

If we assume continuing success for Joe, in a few years he may have a chain of "Hot Dog Heaven" restaurants spread across a wide territory.

As his operation grows in size and geographic spread, his information needs expand. At some very early point, a cigar box, a piece of paper, and a pencil will no longer do. Dishonesty and human error would quickly put him out of business. In today's restaurant industry, Joe would most certainly purchase point of sale registers for his operations and develop a more formal and accurate management information system.

One authority defines a management information system in this way:

> A management information system, as the term is generally understood, is an integrated man/machine system for providing information to support the operations, management, and decision making function in an organization. The system utilizes computer hardware and software, manual procedures, management and decision models, and a data base.[4]

What an MIS "looks like" depends on your vantage point. A cashier sees the MIS as the hardware used to look up prices and record sales. A supervisor may emphasize the reports in the system he or she is responsible for: a shift sales report and a labor hours summary; and the store manager sees it as a series of summary reports on the unit on a daily, weekly, and monthly basis. On the other hand, staff people in the home office see an MIS as summarizing information about each store with regard to their special functional interest: personnel, building operations, sales, control, etc. Finally, the multi-unit line reports for their area, for each unit in their area, and provides comparative data between units.

In today's food service industry, POS systems lie at the heart of management information systems (MIS) (though, of course, there have been and still are MIS that do not use POS systems). We use the term POS to encompass the mangement information systems (MIS) they implement. Certainly, without a well-developed control system, the benefits of POS systems are likely to be very limited. Here is a summary of the elements of a POS system.[5]

---

[3]Fortunately for Joe, the unit value of his product is low and so is the mark up—the amount of money he adds to the cost to make a profitable selling price. There is probably not enough incentive to engage in the more elaborate kinds of fraud our industry experiences. If he were selling beer for $2.00 a bottle, each of which cost him $0.50 to buy, he might discover a bartender bringing in his own cases of beer, substituting them for the house's, and pocketing the profit for himself. If this happened, at the end of the day, dollar sales and the amount of the house's beer that had disappeared would perfectly match,—but the bartender would have defrauded the house. Our example, then, is deliberately simplified to make a point; it *does not* deal with all the problems of control.

[4]Gordon B. Davis, *Management Information Systems: Conceptual Foundations, Structure, and Development* (New York: McGraw Hill, 1974) p. 5.

[5]Adapted from Davis, *Management Information System*, p. 15–16

1. Computer hardware. This includes POS *registers* and other *terminals* as well as *peripheral equipment* such as guest check printers, remote (kitchen) printers, or disk storage units.
2. Software. This is the program. In simple systems this may be very simple, completely programmed at the time of purchase and unlikely to be changed. In more elaborate systems, the program can be complex, subject to reprogramming by unit management, and designed for continued updating.
3. Data base. This refers to all the information put into the system other than the software or computer program. Typical elements in the data base are a sales transaction, and employee time in and time out. Some systems may be designed to record paid outs, receipt of product, discount, and other information as part of the data base.
4. Procedures. These include management rules regarding how sales are to be recorded, when summary reports are to be taken, who shall have the authority to take readings and to clear the machine, etc.
5. Operating personnel. All the employees who interact with the system are included in this category.

While our attention will focus on the POS system in terms of the first three items above, it is important to remember that people and the way they use the system is an integral and important element in the system.

POINT OF SALES IN FOOD SERVICE

In this section we will consider the major kinds of POS systems in use, the POS hardware, and the reports summarizing transactions made possible by POS software. After we look at these elements, we will review an example of a system in operation.

MAJOR POS SYSTEM TYPES

There are three major POS systems in use today. First, we have the stand-alone electronic cash register or registers, each of which functions as a self-contained system. The second system is the back office computer system; here a group of keyboards is connected to a computer with a substantial computing and memory capacity. The third system is the master–slave system in which one of the terminals includes a minicomputer (the master) that controls the operations of the other terminals (the slaves), particularly with regard to summary reporting. Each has advantages and disadvantages that vary in importance with the kind of operation the POS system is designed to serve; it is therefore reasonable to say that no one system is "the best." Moreover, since the technology available is still in a state of rapid growth, it is diffcult to assess what kinds of systems may emerge and what kind of advantages may be available when the next generation of POS devices is developed.

Stand Alone
Until the early 1970's, the standard cash register was an electromechanical unit (Figure 3.1). Many of these registers are still in use today, although they are no longer manufactured in North America. They have been replaced by the Electronic Cash Register (ECR) (Figure 3.2). THe ECR offers significant advantages in the kinds of management reports it can generate, as compared with the electromechanical cash register. Another major advantage is the availability of "presets. Some ECRs can be programmed so that each menu item has a key of its own. Thus a key named "Salisbury Steak" is depressed when that item is sold. In this transaction the ECR automatically records the preprogrammed price of a Salisbury steak, enters that price on a guest check and, for report purposes, increases the totals of both dollar sales and unit sales. The ECR also offers multiplication (versus repeat addition on the old register) and can be programmed to include a tax table function that automatically and accurately computes taxes on each sale. ECRs can also provide automatic change calculation. In addition to

FIGURE 3.1 An early mechanical cash register. (Courtesy Data Terminal Systems.)

FIGURE 3.2 Electronic cash register (ECR). (Courtesy Data Terminal Systems.)

the expanded report production capability, the ECR offers speed in registering transactions, simplification of report preparation, and accuracy.

In high volume operations, faster registers translate into more sales, fewer guest delays, and less cashier payroll. Speed and simplification are even more important because they affect managers' duties.

> At one time, Burger King managers had to fill out 26 different forms each day as inventory, sales, variance reports, labour scheduling, etc. With the use of systems, these were reduced to one sheet of figures—manager time spent doing paper work was reduced from three hours to less than one hour. Managers now had the opportunity and information necessary to make decisions based on timely accurate information, not intuition.[6]

Finally, accuracy in computation is a significant factor, with one fast food chain estimating their savings *per register per day* at $5 to $6 solely from eliminating arithmetic errors.[7]

While the ECR is the least expensive equipment for the smaller operation, the disadvantages of the ECR mount when more than three registers are needed. Since each ECR is completely independent, all consolidation of reports must be

---

[6] Jack. B. Levine and Alfons Van Wijk. *Counting on Computers* (New York: Lebhar Friedman, 1980), p. 80.
[7] Levine and Van Wijk, *Counting on Computers,* p. 78.

done by hand. The ECR is based, moreover, largely on memory built into the machine called Read Only Memory (ROM). ECRs typically have a minimum of Random Access Memory (RAM), which is considerably more flexible. ROM requires actual physical changes to the equipment to change its function, while RAM permits program change through reprogramming entries input on the unit keyboard. (That is, RAM is memory that can be accessed and changed as part of the operation of the computer in which the RAM is housed.) The inflexibility of the ECR, because of its limited RAM capacity, is one of its major drawbacks. Many of the ECRs being sold now have very simple key boards that limit severely the number of presets available. Most complex operations that require extensive presets have moved up to a POS system with its greater flexibility and depth in management reporting capacity.

Remote Computer

At the other extreme from the ECR is a system in which a series of point of sales (POS) registers are connected to a computer. The registers have no computational capacity of their own and act solely as terminals of the computer. In this system, the register is little more than a keyboard. The remote computer configuration provides the greatest amount of computing capacity because of the computer's large memory (Figure 3.3)

FIGURE 3.3 Remote computer. A back office or remote computer can monitor system and interact to change the register data base. (Courtesy Data Terminal Systems.)

The remote computer offers several advantages. It can be reprogrammed in different ways, and can accommodate additional terminals. In this system, terminals can include not only registers but remote printers in the kitchen, at a service bar as well as input terminals in the receiving area. Other features, which increase the flexibility of the remote computer, are available and will be discussed in the next section.

Not surprisingly, the remote computer is the most expensive configuration and is normally installed only when there are more than five terminals. A system where all the intelligence is in a central computer is said to have "integrated intelligence," or what might be called centralized or concentrated intelligence. One difficulty with a remote computer occurs when the central unit fails. Since the terminals in this kind of system cannot operate independently, the whole system goes down. Although there are means to maintain the information that was in the system, the inconvenience of losing the whole cash and operating control system for a portion of an operating day or more is more than just an inconvenience.

Master–Slave[8]

It is quite possible to think of the third configuration as a variation of the second. In it, one of the registers is upgraded by having a microprocessor included in it (Figure 3.4). This register, with its microprocessor, provides most of the operations-wide reports. In effect, the microprocessor is substituted for the remote computer. In this system, however, there is a good deal of intelligence in each register. In fact, these registers are sometimes referred to as "smart" registers and the system is said to have "distributed intelligence."

One of the major advantages of this system, in fact, is that each register can perform independently in the operating mode and can generate some reports on its own. This is an advantage because if the "master" register fails, the rest of the system can continue to operate. In a remote computer system, if the computer goes down, the whole system is down.

This system is also less costly than a centralized computer. It can also support much of the peripheral equipment that the remote computer utilizes. While the master unit does not have the memory capacity of a larger computer, it can produce a wide variety of reports and is *pollable*—that is, it can interact with a

---

[8]The variety of terminology in use from one company to another is dizzying to the layperson. For instance, the relationships we describe here as master–slave is referred to in the industry as an "advance stand alone POS concept." In this view, what we are describing is made up of a master processor in one unit and a backup (master) processor in a second unit with the balance of the units having "united intelligence," that is, the ability to exchange information from one unit to another while, at the same time, being able to perform transaction recording even if operating alone. This is an equally useful way of describing the process but less direct than our description. The important point to remember, however, is that the terminology often varies.

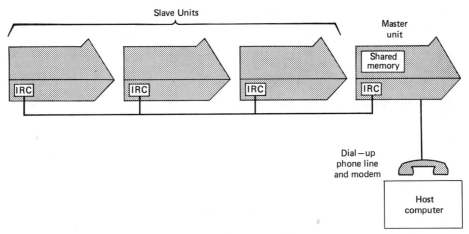

FIGURE 3.4 Inter-register communication (IRC). The master unit in this system operates as a register; it also stores transaction records of other registers and contains programming to generate management control reports for other registers. The master is connected via modem and phone lines to a host computer. (Adapted from Data Terminal Systems.)

home office computer.[9] The interaction referred to as polling (see Figure 3.5) commonly involves the central office computer "calling up" the unit minicomputer at the end of the business day (in the middle of the night, in fact, when phone rates are lowest) by a long distance call and in seconds receiving a summary of the business of the day. These data can then be further analyzed by the home office computer, results can be compared with those of similar units, and information can be consolidated according to area, region, or throughout the company. In some systems, the individual store data are analyzed at the central office (Figure 3.6) and a report summarizing some or all of that analysis is sent back to the store electonically by a process called *downloading*. Downloading is the ability of the central computer to send information to stores as well as to receive it (i.e., to poll it).

In a chain, the auxiliary computing capacity for financial report computation, accounts receivable, and accounts payable, for example, can be handled centrally while operational reports of interest to unit management are computed automatically on site by the master terminal. In some cases, the central computer can be used to download new programs for store minicomputers or to provide store minicomputers with information such as new price lists or updated recipe file costs.

---

[9]The polling function is not, however, universal and depends on the ability of the equipment in the unit to interface with the home office computer. In general, a computer manufacturer's own terminals can "talk to" their own computers but may or may not be able to interact with other manufacturers' equipment. Some manufacturers also have standard "protocols" that make their POS system able to communicate with different kinds of host computers.

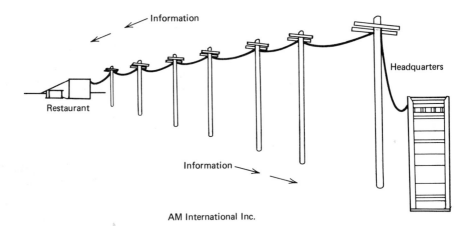

FIGURE 3.5 Polling. Two-way flow of transaction information and reports from unit, management instructions and reprogramming are possible via telephone system. (Courtesy Data Terminal Systems.)

FIGURE 3.6 Home office management reports. By using phone communication data links, the host computer makes management reports available on a store or regional basis to home office, thus facilitating rapid followup where problems emerge. (Courtesy Data Terminal Systems.)

POS vs. ECR

Let us compare the POS system with the ECR. Where only one or two registers are needed and limited analytical reports are required, the lower cost of the ECR is a major advantage. In a small and relatively simple operation, then, the ECR may be chosen.

The POS has all of the advantages of the ECR in operation. POS terminals, whether operating with integrated or distributed intelligence, have preset keys and therefore offer the same speed and accuracy. Like the ECR, the POS can be programmed for tax and other automatic computation. The POS, however, has a much greater array of management reports available that will cover not just one register but the total operation. Table 3.3 compares and contrasts the ECR with

TABLE 3.3 ECR/POS INTEGRATED SYSTEM COMPARISON

Function	POS System	ECRs
Input	Keyboard typically with over 100 preset keys. Scanning systems have also been built.	Keyboard
Output	CRT (large information content displays).	Limited displays, up to 20 alpha/numeric characters.
Telecommunications	Flexible interrogation; Unrestricted; can download changes and programs	Inflexible Limited
Management reporting	Extensive: 35 or more reports	Limited but expanding
Interface to peripherals	Industry standard	Unique, very limited
Programming	Totally programmable general purpose system; programming can be done by knowledgeable customer; readily modified to accommodate changes in business operations.	Generally fixed ROM program traditionally but more manufacturers now leaning toward increased RAM
Failsafe	If master fails, the system goes down. With optional disk backup, users have total protection.	Full backup; if one ECR fails, others in restaurant still function.
Peripherals	Large number, almost unlimited potential	Limited
Price	Price/benefit effectiveness increases in proportion to number of terminals in system, size of memory, and input/output devices.	Low for single, dual register operation; price factor increases with additional register

Source. AM International Documentor Division.

the POS integrated systems while Table 3.4 summarizes some of the principle characteristics of POS systems.

In the next sections we describe some of the POS equipment options and the kinds of functions and reports a POS system offers. A POS system encompasses either the integrated remote computer or the distributed intelligence in which a microprocessor is built into one of the registers. What really sets the POS system off from the ECR is its intelligence—its capacity for on-site managerial report preparation.

POS SYSTEM HARDWARE OPTIONS

To indicate what a POS system can do, we will describe some of its principal hardware features, usually referred to as peripherals along with their functions (Figure 3.7).

Remote printers are said to be on line to the system, that is, they are plugged into the system, which is literally true since they are connected by a wire similar to a telephone cord. When a server enters an order at a register in the dining room, that order is printed out in the kitchen and/or at the service bar (Figure 3.8). Servers can time their trip to the pantry or bar when they think the order is ready for pickup. (In some operations runners deliver orders to the server, who never leave the dining room.)

Other remote terminals are available. For instance, a terminal equipped with a wand reader (Figure 3.9) at the receiving deck can automatically read the uniform product code (Figure 3.10) on goods received and enter these receipts into the system. Goods that arrive without a machine readable code can be entered manually. In some operations the "smart-box"—the terminal with the microprocessor—is located in the manager's office. This serves to keep the data private as well as being convenient for the manager.

TABLE 3.4 CHARACTERISTICS OF POS SYSTEMS

Integrated operation
High utilization of RAM and therefore highly programmable
System design similar to standard computer systems
    Central Processor—may be packaged within one of the terminals
    Terminals act as input/output devices
    In most cases remote terminals are nonintelligent
Ability to communicate with peripheral devices
    Unlimited peripherals flexibility
    Original equipment manufacturer peripherals
Printers as systems peripherals
Very sophisticated telecommunications capability
    Total downloading capacity
Capability for customized application programs

Source. John Patterson, *New Technology in Food Services—ECR-POS Systems Workshop Notebook.*

FIGURE 3.7 Variable presets. Presets may be varied from one meal to another by (*a*) inserting the printed key identification appropriate to the meal as shown and (*b*) keying in the information to "tell" the register which meal pattern it is to use. (Photo Courtesy AM International.)

FIGURE 3.8 Remote printing. Data input at waitress station can be transmitted to a remote printer such as kitchen printer shown here. (Courtesy Data Terminal Systems.)

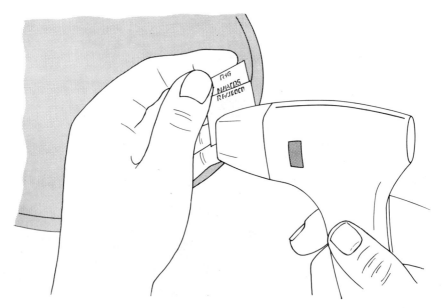

FIGURE 3.9 Wand reader can be used by receiver to record items marked with the uniform product code. (Courtesy Data Terminal Systems.)

A *modem,* an abbreviation for modulator-demodulator, permits the telephone transmission of information from the computer to the home office main frame computer.

Disk storage provides large storage capacity for information that is not presently active on the system (Figure 3.11). Thus, the disk can be used to store data if a new program is to be used or can be set up to reprogram the computer in case the program is lost through a power failure. Since disk storage is nonvolatile (that is, does not require electrical power to be maintained), it is not lost in a power failure. Most POS have back up battery power that will maintain the computer's volatile memory during a limited power outage.

FIGURE 3.10 Uniform product code (UPC). UPC presents a unique configuration for each product coded and within products for each container size.

FIGURE 3.11   Disk storage is used to store data. (Courtesy Data Terminal Systems.)

CRT Display

A cathode ray tube (CRT) (Figure 3.12) is a useful way of providing information visually to workers. Thus, a kitchen station may use a CRT to display orders to cooks, who prepare and assemble them. They are also used to show a cashier or other person entering data on a terminal what has previously been entered; this enables the cashier to verify the data prior to printing "hard copy" such as a written guest check. The greatest use of this equipment, however, is in fast food prep areas and for assembling drive-through orders.

Check (Tab) Printer

This document printer, usually located near the terminal used by the server, records the particulars of an order and interacts with the computer or microprocessor to determine the guest charges (Figure 3.13). The hard copy that is produced is clear, legible, and accurate.

Magnetic Stripe Reader

The magnetic stripe reader senses magnetically coded strips on plastic cards. Such cards may be used by employees as identification cards to log in and out of work. The reader can also read account numbers from credit cards that provide the appropriate magnetic stripe; this means it can also record credit card transactions.

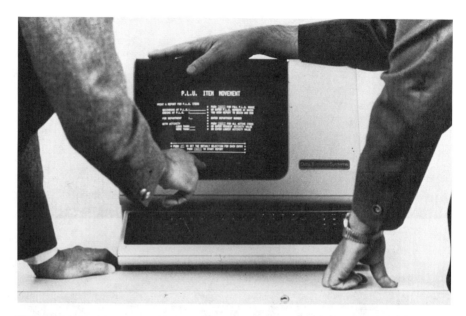

FIGURE 3.12 Cathode ray tube display (CRT). A CRT reproduces data and reports on a "TV screen." It is used as an intermediate communication device; when connected to a printer it can provide "hard copy" where a permanent record is required. (Courtesy Data Terminal Systems.)

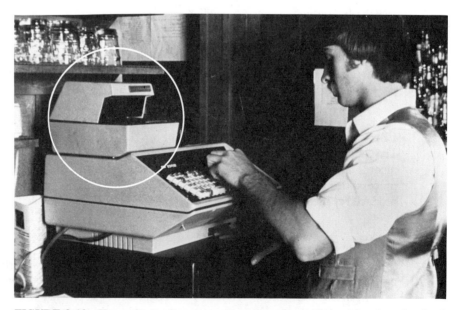

FIGURE 3.13 Here a bartender enters a transaction that will be printed on the check printer seen on top of the register. (Courtesy Data Terminal Systems.)

CONTROL IN THE HOSPITALITY INDUSTRY 57

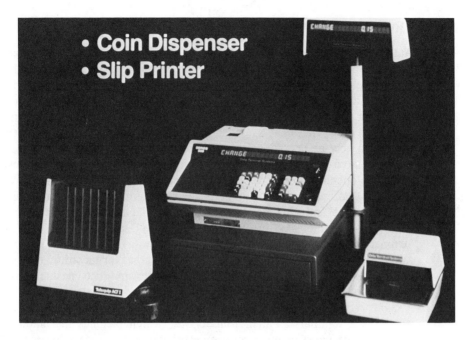

FIGURE 3.14 Coin dispenser and slip printer. The slip printer may be used as a receipt in lieu of guest check. The coin dispenser speeds the cashier process and ensures accuracy in change making. (Courtesy Data Terminal Systems.)

A cassette unit reads information from a tape cassette. It is sometimes used to load the program into a new system or to provide back up if the program is lost through power failure. Cassettes can also record transactions and this, too, can provide a back up on the day's business in case of power failure. Some companies mail a cassette recording of the day's transactions to the home office instead of using telephone lines to transmit them.

Scales
In operations where items such as salads are sold by weight, on-line scales transfer weight information for price computing and recording.

Coin Dispenser
The dispenser speeds service by issuing the correct change automatically (Figure 3.14).

As this discussion makes clear, the interactive POS system provides valuable functions to guest, employee, and management. In the next section we will focus on the functions that the system provides.[10]

---

[10]This section and the one that follows draws heavily on the work of John W. Patterson, School of Hotel and Food Administration, University of Guelph, Guelph, Ontario.

POS CONTROL FUNCTIONS

At the start of the chapter, we distinguished between operational and managerial control. Operational control is programming an activity, such as cash handling or a meat yield report. Managerial control, on the other hand, involves judgment based on current, accurate information delivered by the POS system. As discussed earlier, one of the major benefits of the POS systems was that it permitted many activities classified as managerial control (involving judgment) to be developed now as operational control (following rules). Although managerial control is more demanding than operational control, both are essential to ensuring profitable operations, and we will give examples of both kinds of control.

Before detailing the kinds of reports a POS system provides and relating them to major control and other management activities, let us give a general description of what is accomplished by the system. Figure 3.15 provides a brief visual summary of system operations. At the start of any day, the system's computer or microprocessor is ready for business with a program for recording transactions and sorting the data of those transactions so that they produce guest records, shift reports, and managerial reports.

Guest records may be "hard copy" printed guest checks that are presented to guests as a summary of their transactions, which includes the amount due. However, the guest record may not be printed at all. Especially in fast food operations, the record may be held while the order is being prepared and assembled. When the order is ready, the order is totaled, money is collected from the guest, and the register cleared (Figure 3.16).

Shift reports summarize activities for which supervisors (e.g., shift supervisor, assistant manager) and key employees (cashiers) are responsible. Shift reports generally lie in the area we have described as operational control. Shift reports supply feedback on how well rules and procedures have been followed.

Management reports can range from daily or even shift summaries of a single store to the period-to-date (week, month, or year) summaries at the store level. At

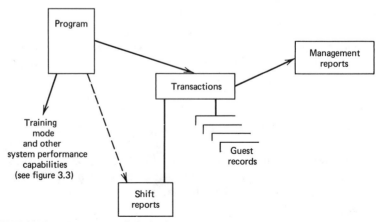

FIGURE 3.15 POS system functioning.

```
         CUSTOMER GUEST CHECK
   SERVER  41  TABLE  20/ 1  TIME 13:18

         1 ALMADEN RD GL    2.95
         1 STEAK SANDW.     5.95
         2 ALMADEN RD GL    5.90
         1 COFFEE           0.70
                          --------
               TOTAL       15.50
               TAX          1.36
                          --------
            GRAND TOTAL    16.86
   GRATUITY..........

   CARA INN THANK YOU-MERCI 678-1400

   ROOM NO:.......SIGNATURE.............

       82-08-09   1 GUEST   NUMBER 0203
```

FIGURE 3.16 Guest check.

the region, district, or home office level more comprehensive reports may make a number of interstore comparisons. Figure 3.17 summarizes typical system performance capability.

PRINCIPAL CONTROL FUNCTIONS

A training mode offered on most systems enables a register to be operated while training new employees in the use of the system without affecting any operating control totals. To show the degree to which the training mode has been used—that

FIGURE 3.17 SYSTEM PERFORMANCE CAPABILITIES

Telecommunications _____	Check digit verification _____
Pre-sets _____	Automatic change computation _____
P.L.U. _____	Cashiers _____
Departments (open) _____	Credit authorization _____
Server totals _____	
Previous balance recall _____	Keys _____
Employee time recording _____	Training mode _____
Automatic tax calculation _____	Menu explosion-inventory control _____
Price extension _____	Check tracking _____
Numeric data key _____	Automatic line finder _____
Modifier keys _____	Automatic slip feed _____
Inventory tracking _____	Buffered keyboard _____
Menu explosion _____	

Source. John Patterson, *New Technology in Food Services—ECR-POS Systems Workshop Notebook.*

is, to prevent dishonest use of the training mode during operations—most systems accumulate a training mode total as a part of the running total locked in the machine.

There is a wide variety of reports in the field because many restaurants or restaurant chains use customized reporting systems. The variety of practice is also increased because a shift report in one company may be taken only daily in another company and only weekly or monthly elsewhere. Therefore, in this section we intend not to reproduce "the best of" or "all of" the reports, but simply to illustrate, using actual reports, the kinds of control and other management functions POS systems can deliver. As we have noted, we do not distinguish between shift and daily reports because of the great variety of practice in the field.

For purposes of analysis we will divide POS reports into these categories:

Daily summaries
Cash and other media
Food cost control
Inventory
Security
Productivity and payroll control
Marketing

DAILY SUMMARY

POS systems produce automatically a daily report such as the one shown in Figure 3.18.

FIGURE 3.18 Daily report.

CASH AND OTHER MEDIA REPORTS

A cashier's deposit can be summarized in terms of cash, checks, and charges and, as in Figure 3.19, show paid-out transfers from cashier to main office (identified as loans) and other details. An important control relates to "locked totals" (Figure 3.20). This report gives a sales summary tied to a nonresettable total. Today's nonresettable total is compared with today's business plus yesterday's nonresettable total to be sure that no employee has operated the register for any period without depositing the cash received along with the rest of the day's business.

Figure 3.21 gives information on a single cashier, reconciling total sales after pickups, transfers to other cash banks (loans) and paid outs, to determine this cashier's "accountability" or deposit. The deposit is made up of several kinds of payment media, conveniently summarized by the report: cash, checks, charge, and vendor discount vouchers (coupons). Total media, in turn, are explained by the categories following that entry: discounts, reverse entries (i.e., voids), returns, and refunds. Note that the number in the left-hand column show the

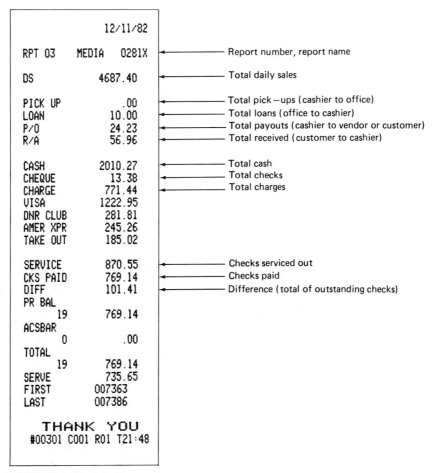

FIGURE 3.19 Media report.

62 MONITORING OPERATIONS: POINT OF SALES SYSTEMS

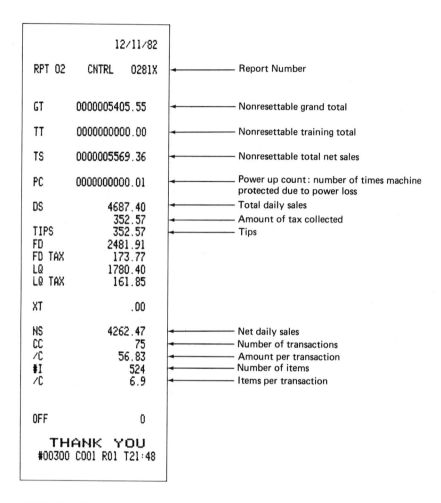

FIGURE 3.20 Control report.

physical count (number of charge guests, for instance) while the right-hand column reports the dollar amount.

Food cost reports permit management to determine food cost for any item at current prices, food cost for the day or period to date, finished and raw waste, and to compare the actual cost of food consumed with the amount called for if food were prepared and served exactly according to approved recipes and procedures, that is, to compare actual cost against a standard cost.

Figure 3.22 shows an inventory variance report that indicates usage for the period for breaded shrimp, summarizes raw and finished waste both in dollars and as a percentage of sales of this item, and compares actual usage with computed or standard usage. The "total" line under "actual and computed" is stated in units and indicates that although 416 shrimp are accounted for by sales, 421 shrimp

```
              CASHIER REPORT, CASHIER TOTALS ONLY REPORT
                         #6, #7   X, Z Mode

              (Note:  Cashier must be logged off)



                        07/20/81         Date
         RPT  07   CASTT   0011Z         Report Number, Report Name, Z Report
                                           Counter, Mode
                             2#          Cashier Number
         NO                   0          No Sale Count
         #C                  80          Customer Count
         #TS              685.61         Total Sales for this Cashier

         PICK UPS                        Pick ups:
              2             180.00              Count, Total
         LOANS                           Loans:
              1             100.00              Count, Total
         PAYOUTS                         Payouts:
              1               5.00              Count, Total
         RECD ACC                        Received on Account:
              0                .00              Count, Total₁
         ACTBY              600.61       Cashier Accountability

         CASH                            Total Cash:
             11             223.52              Count, Total
         CHECK                           Total Check:
              1              48.58              Count, Total
         AMEX                            Total Charges:
              5             227.85              Count, Total
         VISA
              2             100.66              Count, Total
         TLMED              600.61       Total Media²
         OVER                 .00        *Total Amount Cashier's Drawer is Over
         SHORT              600.61       Total Amount Cashier's Drawer is Short
         OV/SH              600.61       Net of the Overage and Shortage Totals

         DISCOUNT                        Total Discounts:
              2              15.82              Count, Total
         CR SALES                        Total Credit Sales
              0                .00              Count, Total

         ¹Accountability = Total Sales + Loans + Received on Account - Pickups - Payouts
         ²Total Media = Sum of All Media = Accountability
          *A cashier is either over or short if the amount of media taken from the till
           in pick-ups does not equal the sum of the Total Sales, Loans from the office,
           and transactions with outside vendors
```

FIGURE 3.21 Cashier report, cashier totals only report.

were actually used. The next line (V) summarizes the variance, which was five shrimp or 1.18% of sales. The variance had a value of $2.22. At the bottom of the report a sales and waste summary for all items is presented to provide a standard for comparison.

```
           CASHIER REPORT, CASHIER TOTALS ONLY REPORT cont. -




VOID                                Total Voids:
    1                    7.95              Count, Total
RETURN                              Total Returns:
    0                     .00              Count, Total
REFUND                              Total Refunds:
    1                   24.95              Count, Total


APPTZR                              Department Groups:
   29                   36.25              Count, Total
ENTREES
   78                  503.70       (Department Groups take the
DESSERTS                             descriptor of the first
   31                   49.20        department in the Group.)

IC                       1.73       *Items Per Customer
#1                        138       *Item Count
OPEN                     7.95       *Logged on Time
UNLCK       100.00%      7.94       *Hours Active: Percentage, Total
CS/HR                   10.06       *Customers Per Hour
SL/HR                   86.24       *Dollar Sales Per Hour

#00387   C002   R05   T11:19        Transaction Counter, Manager Number,
                                    Register Number, Time

*The Cashier Totals Only Report does not include productivity data




        OPEN TIME:    Log-On to Permanent Log-Off

        UNLOCKED TIME:   Time A - Key On

        CUSTOMERS PER HOUR:   Customers ÷ Open Time

        SALES PER HOUR:   Sales ÷ Open Time
```

FIGURE 3.21   *(continued)*

Figure 3.23 shows a recipe explosion. The recipes are stored in what is called a Price Look Up (PLU) table and the recipe's number—in the system illustrated here as well as in many other systems—is called PLU number. The first recipe, fried shrimp (recipe number 1060), sells for $5.95; the recipe calls for six units of breaded shrimp for a total recipe cost of $2.664 and represents 44.7% of the selling price. As costs change and the changed costs are entered into the system, these costs will be adjusted automatically so that precosting is always current with the prices in the system.

In Figure 3.24, a finished waste report shows the amount of finished product

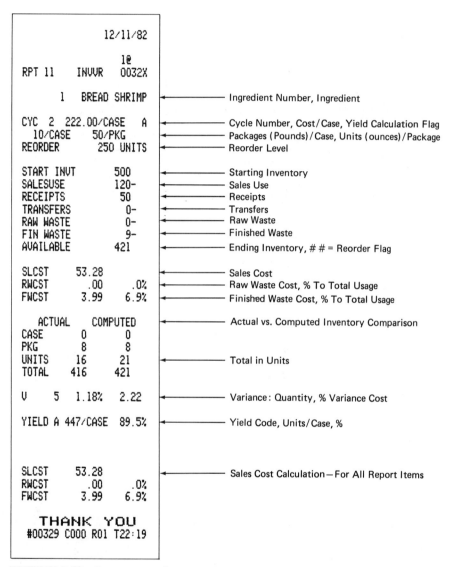

FIGURE 3.22 Inventory variance report.

discarded. This system can reflect two selling prices for the same product (for instance, a la carte and complete dinner). Notice that waste is shown in physical units (rather than dollars).

Sales control reports pertaining to security of sales permit management to determine which checks are outstanding—and, at the end of the shift, which checks are missing—and to follow specific menu items to see if they are being rung up and by which servers.

A waiter tracking report, shown in Figure 3.25 shows the outstanding total for any server for both kitchen and bar, paid totals and total sales at the point the

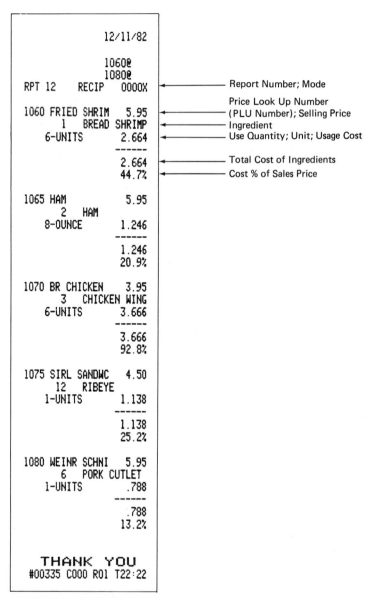

FIGURE 3.23 Recipe report.

report is requested. At the end of the shift this report indicates the value of sales, by department (food and bar), on a check not yet paid. Such a report, taken before a server leaves work, serves as a basis for requesting an accounting from a server for any missing checks. (Note that the report, by showing sales totals, is a good reflection of a server's productivity.)

Figure 3.26 gives the name of the server using that check, the check number, a

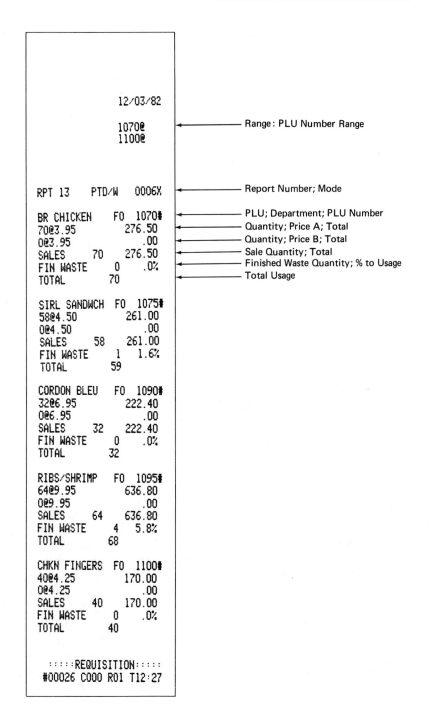

FIGURE 3.24 Period-to-date and finished waste report.

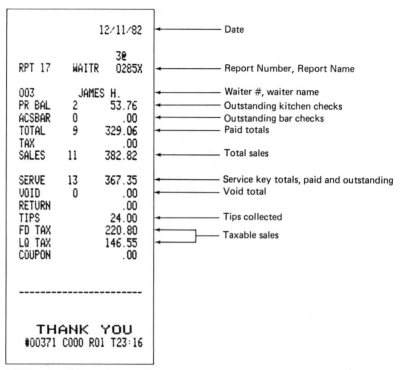

FIGURE 3.25 Waiter tracking report.

number assigned by the POS to that check to keep track of it while it is in use, and the dollar total of the missing check. At the end of the meal, any missing checks can be readily reconstructed. Such a report is available for every server logged into the system.

Figure 3.27 shows a selective sales itemizer report. A limited number of menu items of a summary group of items such as desserts may be selected for study in any single period. The system will indicate the number sold, by server, of each item at the end of a shift or other period. Thus, if a dessert promotion is underway, management can determine how many desserts are sold by each server.

The itemizer can also be set to track a single item to determine error or dishonesty. For instance, an operator was concerned that his servers were not bothering to ring up coffee and just giving it to the guest. His guest count was 1500 persons on an average day and each coffee sold for $0.50. The operator thought most customers had at least one cup of coffee. Thus, his loss exposure was on the order of $750 per day. By tracking coffee, he was able to determine how much coffee was recorded as sold by each server and compare it to the total sales for that server. This gave him a basis on which to discuss coffee sales with individual servers.

Productivity and labor costs are high on any manager's list of crucial control

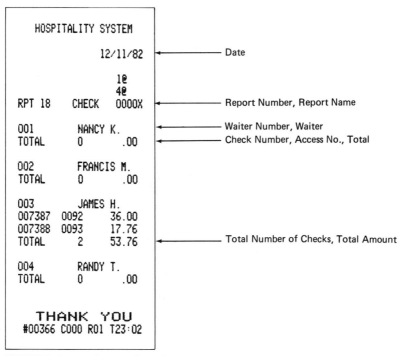

FIGURE 3.26 Outstanding check report.

points. A number of reports are available to managers from POS systems to help control labor costs. Figure 3.28 shows an employee time clock report. An employee is identified by an employee number, requiring the same number of digits as a social security number, and name. The entry shows the job code designating category of worker (e.g., cook, waitress, and dishwasher), the day of the month, the time in and time out. Figure 3.29, a labor cost summary report, converts time clock data to actual cost and summarizes both hours and costs.

A more analytical labor report is shown in Figure 3.30, a periodic productivity report. In the first part of the report data are collected for time periods—in the example shown, one-hour segments. Collecting data in this fashion permits us to assess scheduled hours against customer demand with a view to revising schedules for maximum productivity. In the latter part of the report, the total figures for the period under review—a shift, a day, or some longer period—are summarized showing labor hours and cost in relation to sales both in dollars and in numbers of guests. The last two figures, dollar sales and guests per man-hour, provide important measures of productivity. We should just note again that the waiter tracking report (Figure 3.25) provides comparative data on server productivity and the selective sales itemizer, (Figure 3.27) can also be used for that purpose.

In the balance of the text we will consider various kinds of control problems

```
                    WAITER PRODUCTIVITY REPORT

                       #21 MACRO  X, Z MODE*


                 07/20/81              Date

        RPT 21              2@         Single Range Waiter Report

        TROMBLEY            2          Waiter Name, Waiter Number

            CKS  CVRS SALES            Checks, Covers, Sales For:
        IN  32   68   590.15           Check Trak^tm Sales
        TO   2    2    10.23           Cash Sales
        TL  34   70   600.38           Total Sales

        AV CR IN          8.67         Average Check Trak^tm Sale per Cover
        AV CR TO          5.11         Average Cash Sale per Cover
        TL AV CR          8.57         Average Total Sale per Cover

        AV CK IN         18.44         Average Check Trak^tm Sale
        AV CK TO          5.11         Average Cash Sale
        TL AC CK         17.65         Average Sale

                                       Waiter Itemizer Totals:

        ITEM 1           10.45         Itemizer 1
        ITEM 2             .00         Itemizer 2
        ITEM 3           24.25         Itemizer 3
        ITEM 4            7.50         Itemizer 4

        STORE TL                       Store Itemizer Totals:

        ITEM 1           75.15         Itemizer 1
        ITEM 2           12.40         Itemizer 2
        ITEM 3          198.75         Itemizer 3
        ITEM 4           42.50         Itemizer 4

        #00406 C001 R05 T14:18         Transaction Counter  Manager Number,
                                          Register Number, Time


        *A 21 Z Report will Z the 20 Report.
```

FIGURE 3.27 Selective sales itemizer.

and the procedures that have been developed to deal with them. We will discuss control activities that are independent of POS systems and, where appropriate, activities that use POS. A basic point to keep in mind, however, is that the principal controls are easier to implement with a computer-based POS system but the control activity *can* be carried on without POS. We will show how POS facilitates control, but we will not see control as dependent on POS.

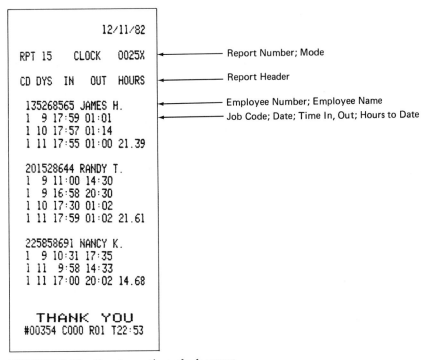

FIGURE 3.28 Employee time clock report.

KEY WORDS AND PHRASES

Three kinds of control
Management control
Interpretation of results
Judgments
Whole organization
Integrative
Operational control
Relate input to output
Programmed activity
Single or series of related tasks
Process oriented
POS
MIS
Daily report
Kinds of information
Elements of POS systems
Computer hardware
Software

Master-slave
Microprocessor
Pollable
Downloading
POS vs. ECR
POS hardware
Remote printers
Modem
Disk storage
CRT display
Check (Tab) printer
Magnetic stripe reader
Cassette unit
Scales
Coin dispenser
POS control functions
Guest records
Shift reports

72 MONITORING OPERATIONS: POINT OF SALES SYSTEMS

X, Z Mode

(Note: taken after a 15Z)

```
                    07/20/81     Date
RPT  16   LABOR     0002X        Report Number, Report Name Z Report
                                   Counter, Mode

CD   RATE   HOURS    COST        Code, Rate per Hour, Hours Worked, Cost

018416312   WAKEFIELD            Employee Number;  Employee Name
6    2.20    4.55    10.01       Job Code: Rate Per Hour;  Hours;  Total
TOTAL        4.55    10.01       For All Job Codes:  Total Hours; Total Cost

212783567   POIRIER
3    3.50    4.00    14.00
Total        4.00    14.00

012543121   TROMBLEY
6    2.20    4.08     8.98
             4.08     8.98
---------------------------

---------------------------
101274651   HOPKINS
4    4.00    2.00     8.00
5    4.75    5.75    27.31
TOTAL        7.75    35.31
                                 Job Code Summary:
CD         HOURS      COST
                                 * Job Code;  Total Hours Per Code; Total Cost
2           5.51     17.52         Per Code
3          42.60    144.84
4          16.76     67.04
5           5.75     27.31
6          30.73     67.61
7           8.07     46.40

TOTAL HOURS         109.42       Total Hours For All Codes

TOTAL COST          370.72       Total Cost For All Codes

AVG COST              3.39       Average Cost Per Labor Hour


#00394  C002  R05  T11:27        Transaction Counter, Manager Number,
                                   Register Number, Time
```

*Only job codes worked will be summarized

FIGURE 3.29 Labor cost summary report.

CONTROL IN THE HOSPITALITY INDUSTRY   73

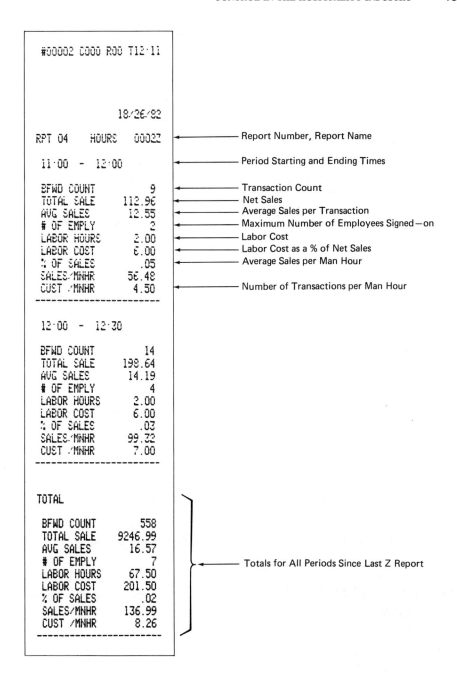

FIGURE 3.30 Periodic productivity report.

KEY WORDS AND PHRASES

Three kinds of control
Management control
Interpretation of results
Judgments
Whole organization
Integrative
Operational control
Relate input to output
Programmed activity
Single or series of related tasks
Process oriented
POS
MIS
Daily report
Kinds of information
Elements of POS systems
Computer hardware
Software
Master-slave
Microprocessor
Pollable
Downloading
POS vs. ECR
POS hardware
Remote printers
Modem
Disk storage
CRT display
Check (Tab) printer
Magnetic stripe reader
Cassette unit
Scales
Coin dispenser

POS control functions
Guest records
Shift reports
Data base
Procedures
Personnel
Types of POS systems
Stand alone
ECR
Presets
Speed and simplification
Accuracy
ROM
RAM
Remote computer
Series of POS registers
Integrated intelligence
System failure
Management reports
Principal control functions
Training mode
Daily summary
Cash and media reports
Control report
Cashier reports
Food cost reports
Inventory variance report
Price look up (PLU)
Recipe report
Finished waste report
Outstanding check report
Sales control reports
Labor cost reports

DISCUSSION QUESTIONS

1. Explain the differences between management control and operational control. Give an example of each type of control.

2. Define the elements of POS systems: hardware, software, data base, procedures, and operational personnel.

3. In a fast food restaurant there are six POS registers—one for each serving station. In the manager's office there is a computer terminal (which looks just like the POS registers). The terminal gathers information from the six stations—and summarizes the restaurant unit's performance each day. In addi-

tion, as each employee comes to work, they "lock-in" by wanding their ID card on the terminal. What type of POS system is this?

4. A recreation theme park contains eight restaurants. Each restaurant has a POS register with a microprocessor capable of providing each unit with daily cash and labor reports. In addition, the central computer polls each POS register for information so that the park has a daily summary of the performance of each unit (e.g., sales, food cost, and productivity) What type of POS system is this? Why do you suppose they chose this system rather than the system in question 3?

5. What are the differences between ECR and POS registers?

6. Identify the usefulness of each piece of POS hardware described in the text for a hotel containing the following food and beverage outlets: main dining room (serving beverages), coffee shop (no beverage service), steak house (serving beverages), two cocktail lounges, and three banquet rooms.

7. List the principal control functions provided by POS systems. Then describe the information that would be useful for each function. You may wish to use the examples provided in the text (Figures 3.5 to 3.15).

PURCHASING POLICY AND PROCEDURE

4

A Definition of Purchasing

Criteria for Choosing Suppliers

Defining Quality in a Food Product

Approaches to Purchasing

Group Purchasing

"Keeping Them Honest"

Determinants of Purchasing Policies and Procedures: A Summary

Being a Good Customer

Ordering: Analyzing the Menu

Logistics: Purchasing in Complex Food Service Systems

Summary

THE PURPOSE OF THIS CHAPTER

In this chapter, we will view the purchasing function from the perspective of, first, a medium-sized independent restaurant, and then, a large multi-unit operation. Throughout the chapter, we will focus on purchasing as a management activity guided by policies and, generally, carried out by management routines.

THIS CHAPTER SHOULD HELP YOU

1. Describe the difference between ordering and buying.

2. Explain the criteria generally used to select suppliers.

2. Discuss the importance of specifications and describe their common elements.

4. Understand open market buying and forward buying and know the differences between the various buying methods.

5. Define a "good customer."

6. Discuss ways of keeping suppliers honest.

7. Describe a general approach to preparing a purchase order.

8. Differentiate between operational-level and system-level considerations in complex food service systems.

A DEFINITION OF PURCHASING

Purchasing includes the determination of your needs and the placement of orders with those suppliers who offer the lowest price for items of stated qualities. Note that the entire purchasing process, includes two different kinds of activities, ordering and buying.

Ordering may be defined as the accurate determination of the quality and quantity of food necessary to fulfill menu requirements with minimum waste. Ordering is essentially a supervisory *routine*, and in many operations it is handled by the chef or some other food service supervisor. Ordering can also be accomplished by a skilled employee such as a cook, as is frequently the case in the smaller operations. Once an order has been determined, a clerk or secretary can be assigned the task of calling in the actual orders to the approved suppliers.

Depending on the size of your operation, then, *ordering* may be carried out by the chef, by a food service supervisor, or even, in part, by the manager's secretary.

By suggesting that ordering can be done by a skilled employee rather than an administrative person, we certainly do not mean to imply that it is a casual function. On the contrary, when the food service runs out of milk during breakfast or bread during lunch because someone has failed to order enough, the critical importance of ordering becomes painfully obvious. Similarly, if you have to throw away perfectly good food because too much has been ordered, your operational costs will soar—another illustration of the importance of accurate ordering.

Although the actual process of ordering does not require top management participation, the ordering agent usually maintains records showing that approved suppliers are being used and that competitive prices are being obtained.

Buying involves deciding where to place orders on the basis of quality, price, and service. In most cases, buying is a management function; therefore, a senior member of management decides what suppliers an operation will deal with.

Buyer and *Customer* are used interchangeably to refer to the food service operation (or one of its members) acting in a purchasing capacity.

Supplier and *Vendor* refer to the companies or people who sell food products.

Because all of the different levels of activity grouped under the title "Purchasing Policies and Procedures" often are referred to simply as "purchasing," some students have trouble understanding exactly what purchasing involves. Consequently, we will use a step-by-step approach to explain the activities involved in purchasing.

CRITERIA FOR CHOOSING SUPPLIERS

When selecting suppliers, you should take into account four factors.

QUALITY OF THE SUPPLIER'S PRODUCT

Quality is always of paramount importance. From the buyer's standpoint, however, quality does not necessarily mean "the best": in terms of purchasing, quality means getting the best quality commensurate with the intended use of the product. For example, an expensive gourmet restaurant that served a dessert with a cooked peach filling probably would purchase sliced canned or frozen peaches, rather than higher-quality fresh whole peaches, which might be chosen for a dessert such as peach melba. Similarly, meat that is to be served as a tender broiled steak must be obtained from a limited number of cuts, whereas meat for Swiss steak can be obtained from a variety of inexpensive cuts. So the ability of a supplier to deliver the *appropriate* quality is a crucial criterion.

In addition to purchasing for intended use, buyers must consider the product in terms of its own characteristics—how good or bad it is—rather than in terms of the supplier's brand name. Some suppliers spend a great deal of money on brand name promotions, buyers, however, should never let the brand name alone influence their purchasing decisions, unless they, in turn, intend to advertise a product to their customers by its brand name—a practice followed in only a few cases, such as table top condiments (catsup, mustard, etc.). Essentially, then, you must become a "rational buyer": one who studies the products carefully to determine which of them provides the best quality for the money. In any market, it takes time to learn which suppliers and labels yield the best results, but it is time well spent in the long run.

SANITATION AND CLEANLINESS OF THE WHOLESALER'S PRODUCTION OPERATION

To assure themselves that the products purchased are carefully packed or packaged, buyers should drop in at suppliers' production facilities from time to time to see how operations are conducted. Buyers need not insist on formal inspections; awareness that their plants will be visited should suffice to encourage suppliers to maintain high standards of cleanliness. It is important that buyers take this inspection responsibility seriously, since the food service itself ultimately will have to assume responsibility for any low-quality or contaminated food served to its customers.

PRICE

Although most buyers are aware of the importance of considering the price of the product they buy, they sometimes fail to put price into a proper perspective with other factors that affect the suitability of particular products. Consequently, they sometimes put too much emphasis on buying the cheapest product and, as a result, actually end up paying more in terms of cost per portion and preparation time.

In one particular market area, for example, there were three suppliers of roast round of beef. Two of them consistently offered an inside round at a lower price than the third, but careful yield-testing of the product—that is, determination of how many portions were obtained for the total dollar cost—indicated that the company with the highest price really was offering the best buy. The higher-priced roasts had less excess fat and so provided a more usable product for the total cost.

Canned products also should be evaluated according to this price-yield ratio. Canned products priced considerably below competing products may contain a substantially smaller amount of fruit or vegetables, with more juice or water making up the weight; or the quality itself may be inferior. We are not saying, of course, that lower-priced commodities are always inferior, but simply that buyers should conduct tests to determine for themselves the quality and yield of specific products.

The only way to judge canned products effectively is to open a can and inspect the contents. If inspection reveals, for example, that a can of peaches contains fruit with several bruises, the buyer will know that those peaches are not suitable for use in a salad, where appearance is an important factor, and consequently will reject that particular product as unsatisfactory for its intended use. To measure the yield of a canned product, the buyer should determine the product's net drained weight, which is the weight of the fruit or vegetable after the liquid has been drained off. The net drained weight in ounces divided into the cost per can gives the cost per usable ounce. In considering the price of a product, therefore, buyers must relate the cost to the amount of the product rather than just to how much is paid per can.

SERVICE

Many salesmen emphasize that they will "give more service," by which they often mean that they will be friendly and will perform small favors such as taking buyers out to dinner or sending them Christmas presents. Wise buyers never misconstrue this type of "service" as a sound business practice. To the contrary, the acceptance of personal gifts and favors from suppliers not only is unethical but could also compromise the buyer, who may feel obligated to do business with that supplier even when it is not in the best interest of the food service. And some suppliers will not hesitate to apply subtle pressure to people "in their debt." Only a naive buyer thinks that gifts and favors received are free. They are eventually paid for by the small amounts added to the cost of the orders placed with that particular company.

The concept of "good service" should refer, instead, to a positive attitude on the part of the supplier and the ways in which this attitude benefits the entire food service operation rather than the individual employee. The supplier who gives good service

- Will deliver when the food service operation needs a shipment and is ready for it.

- Consistently provides the quantity and quality that the buyer has asked for.

- Keeps prices in line with the market.

- Is concerned about the reputation of his or her firm and strives to maintain high standards of quality and service.

- Acts as a constant source of information about new products, market trends, and other important developments.

Service, then, encompasses the consideration a buyer can expect from a firm that straightforwardly conducts a business, values its clients, and works hard to keep them satisfied. Friendship is a wonderful thing, but service is what you pay for.

DEFINING QUALITY IN A FOOD PRODUCT

No experienced food service operator will buy the "best of everything." In practice, they will buy the best quality for the intended use of the product.

Consider a hospital that caters to a wealthy clientele (or a resort or restaurant with the same kind of customers). In buying tomatoes for use in a salad in which the tomato would be highly visible, such an operation undoubtedly would specify the highest-quality fresh tomatoes—firm skin, glossy and bright, free from bruises. On the other hand, the same operation probably would order a much less expensive tomato if the product was intended to be cut up and used in a soup.

A fine hotel probably would order USDA-grade top Choice T-bone steak, or perhaps even Prime aged T-bone steak, for its prestige steak house—but another division of the same company might buy unaged, Commercial-grade T-bone steaks for a low-cost steak house on a busy street front. Clearly, then, the intended use of the product, and not some absolute standard, should determine what "quality" means.

In normal use the word *quality* denotes a degree of excellence. As we have just seen, however, the *use* of the product is the principal determinant of quality; this gives us a clue that characteristics *other than product excellence* must be included in a working definition of quality. These quality considerations are surprisingly commonplace: size, weight, and market form.

Size. An undersized apple (such as a #125 apple) would not look very good on a dessert tray of fresh fruits and cheeses. On the other hand, if fresh fruit pies were the intended product use, size would not be very important.

Weight. If your menu price is based on a 14 oz steak, a supplier who ships 16 oz steaks (charging you by the pound, of course) could not give you the quality you needed, no matter how fine the steaks shipped.

Market Form. This term refers to the state in which the product is to be shipped. Some examples of market form are fresh (for fairly rapid use), portion cut (to fit a staffing plan that does not include a butcher), frozen, and canned or dried (for longer storage).

Quality, then, is a relative value determined by the needs of your operation and the use to which the food is to be put.

SPECIFICATIONS

The customary way in which food quality is described for purposes of purchasing (as well as for receiving and food production planning) is through specifications, or "specs," prepared for that product. Specifications describe the principal characteristics of a particular product in sufficient detail to ensure that

- The supplier knows what you want.
- You have a standard against which to measure product when it is received.

In many operations, specifications *appear* to be lacking, but inquiry may reveal that specifications were written down and discussed with suppliers when the operation started up. Because both supplier and operator now know what is wanted, the written specifications no longer seem to be used. In fact, however, they form the basis of understanding between buyer and seller. This pattern is especially common in owner-operated establishments and other situations in which management turnover is low. In other cases, buyer and seller have dispensed with written specs in favor of a quite specific informal or oral understanding. Although either of these situations in which specs do not seem to be used *may* yield generally satisfactory results, they also leave room for much variability in products ordered and accepted.

The best professional opinion, then, is that written specifications should be developed for products—and especially for those that are costly or purchased in large volume—and that the specs should be readily available whenever operational management wants to check a detail before ordering or accepting a product.

Where formal fixed-price purchasing is the practice, highly detailed specifications to ensure conformance of product to planned use are the rule. In very large multi-unit companies and government food service operations, specifications may be drawn up by food scientists or other highly skilled staff personnel. Consider the case of the specifications developed for the hamburger bun used by a fast food chain, noting how closely the specs are tied to the use of the product.

> The hamburger buns' sugar content is the occasion of some complaint by consumerists but it is essential to the product design. Under pressure and high heat, when the bun is finished for service, the sugar rises to the surface to create a hard, carmelized surface. Without this, other ingredients—catsup, mustard pickles—would disappear into the bun and a soggy product and one on which the guest couldn't see the "fixins" would result. The specifications prescribe contents, dimensions and standards but the formula varies with altitude and humidity.
>
> This same bun, by the way, is steamed when it is served with fish to give a moister flavor to balance the somewhat drier fish product. Since it's not toasted, the sweet flavor doesn't come out.[1]

Examples of product specifications for fruits, vegetables, and meat can be found in Tables 4.1, 4.2, and 4.3. As you can see, specifications generally include the following information.

- The name of the item.
- Your specific quality requirements.

---

[1] This quotation is taken from the original manuscript submitted to Cornell Hotel and Restaurant Quarterly by Thomas F. Powers.

TABLE 4.1 SAMPLE GENERAL PURCHASING SPECIFICATIONS FOR FRESH FRUIT

Item	Purchase Unit	Quality	Desired Weight or Count
Apples	Box	U.S. #1 Red, Delicious, firm, well-formed, good color, no blemishes, clean	113 size
Bananas	Hand	Firm, golden yellow	4–5# to hand
Grapes	Lug	Thompson Seedless, firm, tight stemmed	25–28#/lug

- The weight, size, amount, or number of items you require.
- The item's market form (fresh, canned, frozen, etc.).
- How often you require this amount. (You may also include statements about delivery days, dates, or hours, or any other specific information helpful to the supplier.)

Essentially, the writing of purchasing specifications requires a buyer to determine the intended use of the items ordered and the best form in which to buy them.

STANDARD OF IDENTITY

For many products, government regulations specify that a product name may not be used unless certain characteristics are satisfied. For example, corned beef hash must contain at least 35% corned beef on a cooked basis, plus potatoes. Onion, garlic, seasonings, curing agents, beef broth, and beef fat are optional, and moisture content must not exceed 72%. Anyone who purchases canned corned beef hash thus can be sure of it's corned beef and moisture content. Variation

TABLE 4.2 SAMPLE GENERAL PURCHASING SPECIFICATIONS FOR VEGETABLES

Item	Grade	Purchase Unit	Weight or Count	Quality
Asparagus	Fancy	Crate-California 30# avg.	12/bunches crate 14–16 spears per #	Fresh, straight, crisp, green
Cabbage, spring (new)	Fancy	Sack or crate	50# Heavy head	Heads solid, firm; other leaves close to base
Celery	Fancy	Crate—60 to 70# 4 doz/crate	12 to 15 lb per dozen	Brittle, clean, solid

TABLE 4.3 SAMPLE PURCHASING SPECIFICATIONS FOR MEAT

Imps[a] No.	Item	Grade	Purchasing Unit	Description
#168	Top (inside) round	USDA Choice	18–20 lb	Each roast to be tied, weight each roast not to be above or below specified range; maximum average fat thickness ¾ in., not to exceed 1 in. at any point; send chilled
#1180	Strip Loin steaks, boneless, short cut	USDA Choice	8 oz each packed 24 per box	Aged 10 days, cryovac package; ½ oz weight tolerance; fat must not exceed ½ in. in thickness at any one point; send chilled.
#539	Bacon, sliced (cured and smoked), sknls.	USDA #1	22–26 slices/lb packed in 12 lb box	Preset; send chilled

[a]*Note*: Clear and specific specifications for virtually all meat products are available from the USDA in Institutional Meat Purchasing Specifications (IMPS).

between brands typically stems from seasoning, where more flexibility is allowed. Standards of identity protect us from buying corned beef hash that is all potatoes and no corned beef! When buying prepared foods (meat pies and stews are a good example), you should realize that the standard of identity for quantity of meat may be lower than you wish, and that you may need to specify a higher quantity of meat or other ingredient.

APPROACHES TO PURCHASING

Generally, there are two approaches to purchasing: 1. open market buying and 2. forward buying. Open-market buying (also called "hand-to-mouth" buying) means buying at current market prices, whereas forward buying involves buying ahead or establishing a price for a commodity that will not change for a specified period. In the marketplace, large and small operators alike can use both approaches to advantage.

OPEN MARKET BUYING

Products that display frequent price swings or that cannot be stored are purchased on the open market. Produce, fresh meats, and seafoods commonly are purchased at open market prices. For example, restaurants usually buy lettuce on the open market paying the going price per case—one week the price might be $7.00 a case, the next week $10.00, depending upon supply and demand.

Food service operations have different methods of buying on the open market. These methods include competitive bid buying, buying through selected suppliers, one-stop shopping, and a combination of these methods.

Competitive Bid Buying

The recommended method for open market buying is competitive bidding, in which the buyer secures periodic quotations from suppliers for major commodities and then awards the day's (or period's) purchases according to the lowest net cost per order. Usually buyers solicit bids from three suppliers, although some buyers request bids from as many as five. Theoretically, expanded competition among suppliers should allow the buyer to gather a great deal of comparative data and would seem to guarantee the lowest net cost. In practice, however, this method is expensive, because it requires the purchasing staff to spend a great deal of time taking bids, usually by phone. Moreover, this system hinders the development of the close relationship with suppliers that is especially helpful in times of product scarcity or in periods of limited availability of high-quality products. Many food services, therefore, designate only certain food groups for competitive bid buying. Foods whose prices fluctuate over short periods of time lend themselves to competitive bid buying—produce, fresh meat, poultry, and seafoods, for example.

Figure 4.1 shows a sample form used to accumulate bids or price quotations as they are received over the telephone. The compilation of all bids on one sheet facilitates the comparison of prices and the selection of a supplier for particular items.

Selected Suppliers

Many operations recognize the benefits of competitive bid buying but select one or more suppliers for all their needs, most commonly because of the management time and expense involved in competitive bid buying. Independent operators in particular tend to buy from "selected" suppliers. The key word here is *selected:* The operator must analyze carefully the quality and prices of competing suppliers in the area, as well as their capabilities for supplying the quantity at the time the product is needed.

Another reason for using selected suppliers is relative stability of prices. As a purchaser for a medium-sized hotel noted, "At first, I spent a great deal of time getting quotes from a number of suppliers, just to find that there was not more than a penny variation between prices, and I found that it was just too time consuming." Processed foods are relatively stable in price and commonly are purchased from one supplier.

Large as well as small operations use this buying strategy for some items. In fact, many large operations carry the selection process to the extreme in what is termed one-stop shopping.

FOOD PURCHASING QUOTATION SHEET
Operation _____
Ordered _____ Delivery Date _____

Item	Quantity	Dealer	Dealer	Dealer	Dealer

FIGURE 4.1 Competitive bid buying sheet.

One-stop Shopping

The ultimate aim of one-stop shopping is to purchase all products from one supplier, but this is rarely possible. The key to one-stop shopping is, again, careful supplier selection. It is important to determine periodically if the prices you pay are in line with competing suppliers.

One-stop shopping can provide a cost advantage to the purchaser, because the supplier can extend a lower markup over cost when the buyer concentrates purchases. Some institutional distributors with one-stop shopping plans determine par stocks and reduce the purchasing procedure to the ordering function, which can be highly routinized, thus saving valuable management time. Some suppliers also offer extensive specialized expertise that the small operation otherwise could not afford. Large suppliers may hire several product specialists, for example. Most one-stop shopping suppliers offer customers a variety of computerized reports on costs, food usage, and so on. Information in this detail generally is not available to any but the largest food service operations.

The obvious difficulty with one-stop shopping is that the operation engaged in it becomes completely dependent on the supplier. Because the service of the supplier is built into the operation, competitive purchasing know-how can dry up as information from the marketplace on changing costs and availability is screened out. Many operators find that this system places too much faith in an outside agency (i.e., the supplier). Some operators argue that the time-saving aspects make one-stop shopping desirable for small firms; others contend it is exactly the small firm that cannot afford such a system, because, in practice, there probably will not be any systematic review of the suppliers' cost-effectiveness to the buyer. Ultimately, balancing the benefits and the risks of one-stop shopping is the kind of judgment that management must make on the basis of carefully analyzed individual circumstances.

Combination System

There is a buying system that incorporates the best elements of the methods discussed above. This system is designed to gain the benefits of competition among suppliers while minimizing management time commitment by routinizing as much of the purchasing system as possible. Note that an operation must have a fairly large volume of purchases in order to use this system, which involves spreading purchases among a selected group of approved suppliers so as to secure competition in both price and quality.

A limited number of major and minor suppliers are selected for each food group. For instance, a food service operation might utilize three principal meat suppliers and two minor meat suppliers: Companies A, B, and C supply a full line of meats. Company D supplies a specialized product—for instance, low-cost, prefabricated tenderloin steaks—and Company E supplies portion-controlled sausage products.

Company A consistently has been the best supplier from the point of view of quality and price. Companies B and C are acceptable suppliers but generally not as good as A. Companies D and E are specialists who are very competitive on one or a few high-volume items.

The buyer asks A, B, and C for their current prices, which then are recorded on an order list such as that shown in Figure 4.2. If the prices are comparable, the buyer will place the major portion of the order with Company A. Companies B and C are given an order every week or two. Companies D and E are sole suppliers within their specialized product groups—so long as their prices stay in line with the market and the quality of their products is acceptable. (Continuing relationships with three full-line suppliers give the purchaser a source of information on the products and prices of D and E).

Basically, this procedure resembles that used in competitive bidding, except that the food buyer has selected what he or she considers the best three suppliers in the market and deals exclusively with them, except for the few specialized items supplied by D and E.

The number of suppliers is adequate to provide the buyer with much of the available market information as well as the means to "keep the suppliers honest"—a subject we will discuss at some length shortly.

Companies B and C gladly quote their prices, since they receive a substantial volume of business in return. Moreover, they hope to "woo" the facility away from Company A by providing better service. Companies D and E, aware that their prices continually are reviewed are encouraged by that knowledge to remain competitive in order to maintain their high-volume "specialist" position as a supplier. There is an element of competition, even though the field is limited. The buyer can find the best quality and, at the same time, maintain a system of checks on the suppliers and compare the quality of the products received from each.

Instead of written agreements, there are unspoken understandings between the buyer and the suppliers: Each party understands that the individual supplier, in return for quoting prices, will get a certain amount and type of business over a given period. Moreover, the suppliers who receive the largest share of the business are aware of their favored position and know that to maintain that position they must remain competitive in quality, price, and service.

In the example just given, the product discussed is meat, but produce is often purchased by the same method. On the other hand, many operators judge that staple items do not vary enough in price and quality to warrant the expenditure of time and effort involved in soliciting daily bids. Staples often are purchased from a single selected supplier; occasional purchases from other suppliers, however, serve to remind the selected supplier that the buyer is keeping abreast of the market and expects the supplier to remain competitive.

FORWARD BUYING

There are two commonly used methods of forward buying: (1) buying and warehousing product and (2) determining price (or quantity) by contract buying. Today, many firms try to keep a step ahead of the market by attempting to stablize

MEAT QUOTATION LIST
Date: *September 27, 1982*

Item	Quantity Needed	Company A	Company B	Company C	Company D	Company E	Remarks
#1178 Strip steak	4 boxes, 10 lb each	$3.85/lb	$3.95/lb	$3.78/lb	—	—	
#1189 Tenderloin steaks	6 boxes, 10 lb each	4.15/lb	4.23/lb	4.25/lb	3.05/lb	—	
#193 Flank steaks	6 each, 12 lb	3.50/lb	3.60/lb	3.55/lb	—	—	
#109 Rib roasts	12 each, 20 lb each roast	2.95/lb	3.05/lb	2.95/lb	—	—	Yield-test this batch
Pork back ribs	20 lb	3.22/lb	3.25/lb	3.15/lb	—	3.25/lb	
Fresh sausage patties	10 lb	2.20/lb	—	—	—	2.15/lb	
Smoked sausage links	25 lb	2.35/lb	—	—	—	2.35/lb	

FIGURE 4.2 Meat order list. Three companies (A, B, and C) provide a full line of meat products, so they are phoned for competitive bids. Companies D and E are meat specialists whose prices are compared with the full-line suppliers.

their prices for a period of time (commonly, the period of time a firm's prices will run). A firm that sets college board prices a year in advance, for example, needs some guarantee of costs for that period in order to forecast costs accurately. A restaurant, on the other hand, may not be able to change its menu prices as rapidly as food prices change and may use this method to firm up prices for a few months or even a year.

Buying and Warehousing Product

When buying in large quantity, the purchaser first determines the organization's needs. Before approaching suppliers, the purchaser should investigate arrangements for storage of product. Often, on-premise storage space is not available, but freezer or dry storage space usually can be found. (Suppliers sometimes will provide space for quantity purchases and charge a certain amount per pound per month). The purchaser then, approaches suppliers in the area who can supply the product in the quantity and quality needed.

Buying and warehousing usually require payment "up front" (paying at the time you buy). Before buying, the purchaser must compare the savings affected with the cost of interest that would be earned during the period.

Meats and seafoods are the most commonly purchased and warehoused food groups. Small operators frequently take advantage of low prices and stock up. For example, when grocery store chains feature ribs of beef and other front-quarter cuts, there can be an oversupply of hindquarters on the market, which may mean a good buy on steaks for the local small operator. Some buyers, in fact, expect their suppliers to inform them of price breaks so that they can buy ahead.

Contract Buying

Contract buying refers to the establishment of a formal contract between a supplier and a purchaser. Large organizations such as institutional food services, contract food services, and fast food organizations purchase a large percentage of their supplies by contract buying. Although there can be as many types of contracts as there are buyers and sellers, food service operations usually use one of three major types of contract: (1) fixed price contracts, (2) cost-plus contracts, and (3) systems contracts.

Fixed Price Contract This type of contract most often is used by very large (typically governmental) organizations. With this method, the product to be purchased is described in lengthy, detailed specifications given by the buyer to potential bidders, who then submit sealed bids for providing the specified goods. The supplier who offers the lowest bid generally is awarded the contract, provided that the buyer believes that the low bidder really can supply the product at the bid price. Thus, for instance, a large university may buy all of its vegetables from one source for a whole year, or a public school system may sign a contract for milk for one supplier for an entire year or a significant portion thereof. Under such circumstances, obviously, it is essential that a standard product be agreed upon in the contract. The contract provides the government agency, which operates on periodic appropriations, with a definite basis for making budget requests and for setting tax rates or appropriation requests for the period covered.

Cost-Plus Contracts In a cost-plus contract, the buyer arranges to pay a distributor or supplier either a fee or a percentage over the supplier's purchase cost. For example, a fast food company that negotiates directly with a manufacturer for the price of individual packets of catsup must get the catsup packets from the manufacturer to the company's many fast food outlets. The buyer for the company then goes to distributors who are capable of delivering over a wide area and negotiates a cost-plus agreement. The buyer will either negotiate a fee with the distributor for every case of catsup delivered to a unit or for a percent markup (10% is common) of the price of the case of catsup for delivering it.

A "cost-plus" contract also is used by operations determined to get the "top of the market"—that is, the best food products available. In this case, the supplier agrees to provide the highest quality available to the customer at the supplier's own cost plus a predetermined percentage (usually, 10% to 15%). In return, the customer has the right to audit the supplier's books and invoices at any time, to ascertain that the supplier is accurately representing the costs.

Another reason for using cost-plus contracts is to ensure the availability of a product that might be scarce in the market. A restaurant chain specializing in fried shrimp for example, must assure itself of a steady supply of shrimp. Although a long-term fixed-price contract may be ruled out by soaring shrimp costs, a cost-plus contract will ensure the availability of shrimp to the restaurant chain while protecting the supplier from uncontrollable market forces.

Because the supplier determines the base price (before the percent mark-up), cost-plus contracts require great faith in the honesty of the vendor; accordingly, they generally are used only by large companies that can justify the cost of auditing the supplier's books from time to time. Companies that employ cost-plus contracts find that these supplier audits are worthwhile. Not long ago, for instance, one company recovered over $13,000 from a single supplier who had been overcharging.

Systems Contracts A systems contract is a price agreement between buyer and seller for product, with the further stipulation that the seller warehouse and deliver the product as needed. Systems contracts are particularly suited to the purchase of paper products and cleaning supplies. Users of systems contracts claim savings in storage space, reduction in fire insurance rates and risk, and elimination of internal distribution. (A university campus with a number of food service outlets, for example, runs a greater fire risk if paper goods are stored in large amounts on-premise near concentrations of people; the paper supplier's warehouse, on the other hand usually is designed and located to reduce these hazards.)

GROUP PURCHASING

Many food service operations, including those run by health care facilities, schools, and fraternities, have learned to save money on food purchases by organizing or joining group purchasing units. These units may organize on a number of bases: membership in a regional hospital association or council, the proximity of other institutions wishing to participate, or a common religious affiliation or some other allegiance.

The obvious benefit of group purchasing is that it enables a relatively small facility to reap the same cost benefits enjoyed by firms that receive mass-purchasing discounts. For example, a health care facility that purchases 10 cases of apple juice might expect to pay 45 cents for each No. #5 can. But that price might drop to 40 cents per can if the group's purchasing agent were to buy 500 cases. The savings would amount to 60 cents a case—a substantial amount. The annual food savings of the Hospital Council of Western Pennsylvania, a group purchasing unit with a membership of about 80 health care facilities of varying sizes, has averaged between 10% and 15% in recent years. For a 300-bed health care facility with a $220,000 annual food budget, this would amount to a savings of from $22,000 to $33,000 a year. Table 4.4 shows the kind of information on current prices commonly provided to institutions by the group headquarters.

Group members not only can increase their food cost savings but also can tighten their control over group purchasing procedures by designating a representative—preferably someone with purchasing experience—to keep an eye on the group's policies and standards. These representatives collectively can develop purchasing specifications to be used, in turn, by the purchasing agent in obtaining bids or quotations from food vendors. The formulation of these specifications provides an obvious fringe benefit to small health care facilities that previously did not have specifications of their own with which to define the quality of food they require. The membership representatives might also participate in taste panels and can-cutting sessions—activities that encourage more objective and thorough purchasing decisions but are inconvenient and impractical for a single facility to conduct.

The major obstacle to the group purchasing concept is the tendency displayed by some food service managers to favor a certain manufacturer, vendor, or brand of food. Because of these personal preferences, membership representatives occasionally find it difficult to agree on specifications.

The delivery and storage of food bought through a group purchasing plan can be handled either by central storage or by direct delivery. With the central storage method, the vendor delivers the food to a central warehouse; thereafter, the purchasing agent is responsible for transferring the food to the participating institutions. Under this system, the vendor's transportation costs decrease, and that savings is passed along to the purchasing unit. In addition, the purchasing agent is in a good position to take advantage of periodic or seasonal "special buys." The cost of maintaining a large inventory, however, may cancel out the savings in price and transportation.

Under the direct delivery method, the purchasing group specifies that deliveries be made directly to each participating health care facility. (For example, the vendors who supply the health care facilities associated with the Hospital Council of Western Pennsylvania make deliveries once or twice a week to each facility.) When vendors deliver individually, however, they prefer to establish minimum purchase quantities with the purchasing agent.

"KEEPING THEM HONEST"

The process of using competition to ensure the best possible quality, price, and service is sometimes called "keeping them honest." The process sounds a bit hard-hearted—and it is. The best way for supplier and buyer to deal is at arm's length—that is, on a strictly business basis. If you find that a supplier does not meet your specifications, withholding your regular order may provide a strong incentive for him to improve the quality of his product. In fact, company salesmen who earn sizable commissions, as well as company owners who like substantial profits, are not likely to suffer the loss of your business patiently. They will pressure their own employees to remedy whatever problem has cost them your account.

It is possible, however, to overemphasize the keeping-them-honest tactic. You should realize that one supplier's price may be lower on a given day than another's because one supplier has bought more judiciously than the other. This is often true of produce vendors: Produce is largely seasonal, and its availability and price in different sections of the country vary with the time of year. A boxcar of apples, for example, often will head out of Washington state with "East" as its only destination. "Just ship them east," says the seller, "and we'll tell you where to deliver when they reach Chicago." The middleman, or food broker, must (for a commission) find a buyer. Consequently, if a huge number of apples appears on the market at one time, this particular carload may be sold at a bargain price. Vendors who buy these apples will, in turn, be able to offer them to customers at a low price because of their timely purchase.

During some seasons, in contrast, high-quality lettuce is very scarce. Perhaps only one of your regular suppliers will have lettuce that meets your quality standards. If you are eager to maintain the quality of your salads, you may be willing to pay the higher price for the top grade of lettuce. (On the other hand, depending on the operation, there are always limits to the amount you can spend for a particular food product, and you may choose to alter your menu rather than run up your food costs.)

In addition to "keeping them honest," then, buying from a number of vendors also serves to test a supplier's ability as a buyer in the marketplace, where he or she supposedly is an expert. For example, by using the flexible system advocated on page 94, buyers can place most of their orders with companies that provide good service and still can gain access to information about the prices of other

TABLE 4.4 MEAT AND POULTRY PRICING SERVICE

No.	Product	Size	Hanley Green	Johnsons	Fanbord	United Packers	MacPhearson	Slate	Urban
114	Chopped steak—85% C.L., no fillers, no additives, no organ meats, 6 oz, frozen	/lb		1.65					1.14
115	Beef burgers—85% C.L. max., 4% dextrose, no organ meats, binder & spices added, 4% 6 oz frozen	/lb		1.09	0.98	1.13	Chef 1.44		1.05
116	Salisbury steak—85% CL max., 4% dext., no organ meats, binder and spices added, 4% 6 oz, frozen	/lb		1.29	1.12	1.29	1.44	Chef, 4 oz. 1.23	1.05
117	Steak shapes—85% CL max., 4% dext., no organ meats, binder and spices added, frozen	/lb				1.25	1.44		
118	Meatballs—85% CL max., 4% dext., no organ meats, binder and spices added, 32/lb, frozen	/lb	1.25	1.29	1.19	1.29	½ or 1 oz. 1.44	Chef 1.29	1.19

119	Link sausage, beef only—frozen, dom. carton ave 10#, fat max. 30%, 12/lb, 25% shrinkage max., finest quality	/lb	0.89			M.L. 1.35	0.82
120	Farmer sausage, beef.—frozen, dom., carton ave. 12#, fat max. 30%, only 25% shrinkage max., finest quality	/lb	0.84				0.80
121	Link sausage, pork/beef—frozen, dom., carton ave. 10#, fat max. 30%, delinked, 12/lb, 25% shrinkage max., finest quality	/lb	0.89	P.O.C. Special 0.99	0.79	Inst. 0.96	1.01	Chef 0.88	0.78
122	Farmer sausage, pork/beef-frozen, dom. carton ave. 12#, fat max. 30%, 25% shrinkage max., finest quality	/.lb	0.84		0.95	0.79	Inst. 0.96 Devon 0.97	0.94	Chef 0.81	0.75

companies. Thus, buyers can keep their principal suppliers honest while keeping abreast of trends in the market that the suppliers may have missed.

Whenever continually deteriorating service or consistent overpricing indicates the need for a change in major suppliers, the decision should involve senior management.

Buying, then, does not refer merely to placing the order, but rather to the development of a system for deciding which supplier will get the order.

DETERMINANTS OF PURCHASING POLICIES AND PROCEDURES: A SUMMARY

As we have already suggested, the two principal determinants of purchasing policy and procedures are the size and type of the operation. A very large food service organization (e.g., a city school system) may want to purchase on an annual contract basis, whereas other organizations engaging in contract buying may prefer weekly or monthly periods. Operations that must have the very best quality, along with companies that must have a guaranteed quantity of a product (such as a chain of shrimp houses), may choose a cost-plus purchasing arrangement or contract. Most smaller operations do not use the contract buying system, since the size of the contract probably would not justify the expenditure of the bidders' time and energy. Consequently, competitive bidding is the most common method used by medium-sized operations. One-stop shopping may be a reasonable option for small operations.

Ultimately, there are no hard-and-fast rules for determining which system should be used in every instance. As with so many management decisions, the key lies in analyzing the needs of the specific operation and determining the policies and procedures that will best serve the operation.

BEING A GOOD CUSTOMER

A successful buyer is one who recognizes that any transaction is a two-way street. A good buyer, in other words, knows how to be a good and valued customer.

BUYER–SUPPLIER RELATIONSHIP

One of the most important lessons buyers can learn is that purchasing is a business arrangement, both for the supplier and for themselves; it is a relationship based on not favors or friendships, but rather on sound business principles. Customers and suppliers depend on each other. Food services cannot operate without the merchandise, and suppliers must have a market for their goods. Therefore, a satisfactory deal is one that benefits both parties.

Customers, however, need more than simply the product offered by suppliers: They need the suppliers' expertise and their reliable service. To ensure themselves of these benefits buyers should try to be good customers, those whom vendors will value. Reliable vendors will always try to protect their good customers by extending to them the best possible quality, price, and service.

Customers can enhance their value to suppliers in at least three important ways. First of all, they should place orders of a reasonable size. Because delivery services cost money, most suppliers establish minimum size requirements for orders. In other words, the order has to be big enough to make it worthwhile for the supplier to deliver. Buyers should learn these minimum size requirements and try to stay above them. Of course, a good supplier usually will help out in an emergency that requires a rush delivery or a small order, but a customer who rarely asks for small orders is a customer worth keeping—and worth a little extra effort as well.

Second, customers should not place orders too often. In fact, the spacing of orders helps keep them to an acceptable size. Very frequent or small orders indicate inexperience and poor planning on the part of the buyer. If the food service operation is large enough, suppliers may be willing to make frequent deliveries, but they usually will pass the added expense on to the buyer as the price for inefficiency.

The acceptable frequency of delivery varies from place to place and is determined principally by the accessibility of the goods and the distance the supplier has to travel to make deliveries. In large cities, for example, daily deliveries are common. Nevertheless, buyers who do a fairly small volume of business with a supplier should try to place orders only two or three times a week, to minimize the supplier's expenses. In smaller cities served by nearby metropolitan centers, deliveries commonly are made only once or twice a week, or even less frequently, and it may be necessary for the food service operation to maintain a somewhat larger inventory than would normally be desirable. (It is, of course, economically advantageous to keep the inventory as low as possible. Large inventories involve investment, insurance, storage, and spoilage expenses.)

Third, customers should not spread their business among too many suppliers. Wise buyers will allocate their business to a limited number of suppliers who provide acceptable service. Orders occasionally may be placed with other companies, especially if they have something new or interesting to offer but a few suppliers in each food category should receive the lion's share of the business. In some smaller operations, buyers may choose to limit themselves to one-stop shopping or to one supplier in each food category; but where possible, it is wise to have more than one supplier.

SEEING SALESPEOPLE

In some operations, the management sees only those salespeople from regular suppliers. In doing so, however, management deprives itself of expert information regarding new products on the market that may be available from other sources.

Prudent buyers will set aside some time—for instance, two hours once or twice a week—for visits with all salespeople. (The hours chosen usually are the slow ones for the operation). Notice of this policy often is given by a prominently posted sign, such as the one illustrated in Figure 4.3. During these "office hours" the person responsible for purchasing and his or her principal assistants can visit with salespeople about new products, accept samples, and receive any descriptive brochures offered.

This policy has two advantages. First, it allows the purchasing staff to keep up with the most current information on new products. They can also obtain price information from dealers other than the ones from whom they usually purchase; this, in turn, enables them to "keep tabs on" their main suppliers. A second, less tangible advantage to seeing salespeople is that it can help create good public relations. Vendors and their employees are potential customers whose opinion of the operation may be affected by the manner in which they are treated in a business situation. Consequently, it is wise for facilities to maintain congenial business relationships with vendors, even if orders are not placed with them. Such a policy enhances a positive reputation in the community.

ORDERING: ANALYZING THE MENU

Few things are more discouraging than walking into the kitchen on, say, a Sunday morning to hear your cook complain, "We've got a cottage cheese fruit plate on the lunch menu and there's no cottage cheese anywhere in the place." One effective way to avoid a situation like this, and to get a clear picture of your menu requirements, is to break your menu down by course and dish, listing every item served on the menu according to its function. Such a breakdown helps you remember to order everything you need—including coffee, tea, milk, cream, butter, bread, sauces, gravies, garnishes, and condiments. Figure 4.4 illustrates a breakdown of the following selective menu.

ATTENTION VENDORS

Salespersons and other supplier representatives are seen in the Food Production Manager's Office from 2:00 to 4:00 P.M. on Tuesdays and Thursdays. All other visits require an appointment made in advance.

FIGURE 4.3 Prominent sign outside the manager's office indicating hours when salespeople may call.

Tomato juice or
  Seafood Bisque

Roast Breast of Chicken or
  Cheese and Broccoli Quiche

Baked Potato or
  Potatoes, Western Style

Parslied Carrots or
  Stir-fried Zucchini

Tossed Salad or
  Spinach Salad with Bacon Dressing

Chocolate Cake or
  Fresh Fruit Cup

Carrying this analysis one step further, you then gather the appropriate recipes, from which you determine and record all the food products and quantities needed to prepare what is known as a market order. (A sample market order is shown in Figure 4.5.) The amount of each product you would purchase depends on your sales forecast (see Chapter 7).

PAR STOCKS

To simplify the ordering procedure, many operations determine a "par" stock level. The par stock level is the standard inventory level an operation should maintain. Thus, if par for canned peaches is 36 #10 cans and a check of the

Menu Item	Accompaniments and Garnishes
Tomato juice	Lemon wedge, crackers
Seafood bisque	Crackers
Roast breast of chicken	Salt and pepper packets
Cheese and broccoli quiche	Parsley sprig
Baked potato	Sour cream, butter
Potatoes, western style	Catsup
Parslied carrots	
Stir-fried zucchini	
Tossed salad	French and Italian dressings
Spinach salad	Bacon dressing
Coffee	Creamers, sugar
Tea	Lemon wedge, creamers, sugar
Milk	
Chocolate cake	
Fresh Fruit cup	

FIGURE 4.4 A menu breakdown. Correct ordering requires attention to accompaniments and garnishes, as well as to the ingredients on the recipe.

Menu Forecast: Total number of guests 100

Menu Item	Amount to Prepare	Menu Item	Amount to Prepare
Tomato juice	70	Tossed salad	85
Seafood bisque	30	Spinach salad	15
Breast of chicken	55	Bread and Butter	100
Quiche	45	Coffee	60
Baked potato	45	Tea	10
Potatoes, western style	20	Milk Chocolate cake	60
Parslied carrots	75	Fresh fruit cup	40
Zucchini	25		

Market Order For Above Forecast

Meat
    Chicken breasts, 8 oz ea.   55 ea.
    Bacon   1 lb

Dairy
    Sour cream   1 qt
    Swiss cheese, grated   5 lb

Produce
    Baking potatoes   45 ea.
    Carrots   15 lb
    Zucchini   6 lb
    Parsley   1 bu
    Spinach   2 lb
    Fresh fruit mix   2 gal

Groceries
    Seafood bisque   2 #10 cans

Frozen
    Broccoli pieces   2–2.5 lb boxes
    Potatoes, Western style   5 lb
    Pie shells   8 ea.
    Chocolate sheet cake   3/24's

Items on par needed for preparing menu

Lemons	Eggs
Head lettuce	Tomato juice
Tomatoes	Flour
Celery	Salt
Milk, bulk	Pepper
Milk, individual containers	Spices
Butter, 1 lb prints	Coffee
Butter pats	Tea
Coffee creamers, individual	Sugar packets, individual
Salad dressings	Bread
Oil	Crackers
Vinegar	Catsup

FIGURE 4.5 Market order for the selective menu in Figure 4.4. This example also shows how ordering can be simplified if a par stock is maintained. These par stock items are checked and brought up to par so that cooks will not run out. (See discussion on p. 120.)

storeroom reveals only 24 on hand, an order of 12 cans of peaches would be indicated. The par levels generally are based on your experience of the amount of a product used.

The disadvantage of using par stock levels for ordering is that if par levels are not restudied periodically, seasonal variations in volume or shifts in the popularity of an item, for instance, can lead to excessive inventory. For this reason, par stocks often are not used with perishable items. But with staples and supplies, for which perishability is not such a problem, par stock levels do save time in the ordering process.

STANDING ORDERS

Some operations have standing orders for items that are used at a fairly standard rate. Bread and dairy products generally fit into this category. Often the supplier specifies a "use by" date and agrees to take the product back for credit if it has not been used by that date. This procedure eliminates the potential cost of spoilage on these products and saves time for the person responsible for ordering. Where volume varies fairly substantially, standing orders are not effective, because they entail the risk of a run-out or of overbuying. Where volume varies and the supplier has not agreed to take returns of dated merchandise, waste from overstocking is clearly a risk; and even suppliers who have agreed to accept returns may be tempted to violate the agreement if large overstocks occur repeatedly. Since standing orders mean giving up control over a portion of your operation, they should be used only after careful study, and then monitored closely.

INVENTORY LEVELS

The person responsible for ordering may be tempted to order "a little extra" and to maintain a margin of safety in stock levels. The *costs* of inventory are largely hidden and so can be overlooked, but they are actually quite significant.

Capital.   The money tied up in inventory is not available for profitable investment.

Spoilage.   Excess stock of perishable goods leads to product being thrown out as no longer usable—or even worse, being used after it has deteriorated somewhat, leading to a product below the operation's standards.

Labor cost and handling.   The more stock is around, the more handling, cleaning, counting, and so forth is required.

While run-outs of product are intolerable, careful planning of ordering certainly is necessary to avoid the cost of overstocking.

LOGISTICS: PURCHASING IN COMPLEX FOOD SERVICE SYSTEMS[2]

Logistics originally was a military term referring to the activities related to physically moving and supplying armies. Recently, it has come to be used by students of business to refer to similar kinds of business activities: purchasing, shipping, and warehousing, for instance. In a large- or even a medium-sized food service chain,

> Purchasing is one component of a company-wide logistic function in which personal contact is necessarily of less importance than it is in a traditional restaurant. Take as an example a medium-sized fast-food company, which contracts with another company for its logistic function. The second company receives products from the first's suppliers, warehouses them, and distributes them. The first company contracts with an Icelandic company for fish, with a vegetable-oil manufacturer for oil, and so forth.

The financial vice-president of Company A described the purchasing of cooking oil as follows:

> We play the market, short or long. We estimated a 1.7 million pound need for December so last April we decided to buy on the futures market.
> Company C's buyer and our own contract together to buy raw oil. Company C processes it according to our specifications and computes purchase and processing cost to give us a cost per pound.
> On the basis of anticipated need, Company B issues release orders for Company C to ship to Company B. Company B, in turn ships to our stores on need.[3]

Clearly, the centralized purchasing activity of a large company is quite different from that found in the typical food service unit. Purchasing has become highly complex and specialized at the *system level*—that is, for the company as a whole. Although the example given is for a fast food company, it applies equally to large institutional food-service companies.

In the case of the fast food company, in the example just given, purchasing is complex and expert at the system (chainwide) level, but at the individual unit, *purchasing* is not the word we should use. At the unit level, *ordering* is all that is required. Thus, complex food service systems display a contrast between complexity at the companywide level and routinization at the unit level—a contrast we will encounter again in Chapter 6, "Receiving and Storage."

---

[2]For a fuller discussion of this topic see, Thomas F. Powers, "The Emergence of a New Industry. Complex Food Service Systems," Cornell Hotel and Restaurant Quarterly, November 1979, pp. 49–58.

[3]Thomas F. Powers, "The Emergence of a New Industry. Complex Food Service Systems," *Cornell Hotel and Restaurant Quarterly* November 1979, p. 55.

In practice, large firms take advantage of their size to centralize purchasing in a wide variety of ways. Some centralize virtually everything, whereas others are highly decentralized. Some of the principal ways in which large companies use their size in purchasing are listed below, starting with the most centralized technique. Note that purchasing practices vary widely, and that many companies combine several of the techniques listed below.

Commissary Based Centralization. Here all food is prepared centrally and either frozen or chilled and shipped to the units. All nonfood supplies usually are centrally procured and distributed, too.

Central Distribution Center. In this system, virtually all products except fresh and frozen food products are bought centrally and delivered to the operating units. Units buy fresh produce and meat and prepare all food at the unit except foods purchased frozen and prepared from a manufacturer.

Supplier Approval. The company headquarters approves local suppliers or distributors (preferred distribution) and owned units buy only from these suppliers. (Many franchisees also purchase from the franchiser's approved supplier, but generally cannot be forced to do so).

National Contract. Many large companies, including those with a small number of owned units and a large number of franchised units, negotiate directly with food manufacturers. In order to secure favorable access to the large number of units, the food manufacturer—perhaps a coffee company or one that makes frozen apple pies—agrees to a discount on the products it offers for *all* operations affiliated under the franchise. The discount, passed on to the local wholesaler, permits units to achieve substantial savings on many products without any centralized control beyond the national contract agreement. Units are free to take advantage of or ignore the agreement, according to their own best advantage.

It is interesting to note that many large companies do not centralize purchasing beyond the national contract stage, because they find the various costs of centralization are higher than the benefits. Thus, the discussion of purchasing procedures in this chapter applies not only to independent operations but to the units of many chains as well.

SUMMARY

The purchasing activity is one of the key points at which the food service operation interacts with the marketplace. The operation cannot control the market, but it can and must plan how it will deal with the market. To this end, the determination of purchasing policies and procedures is a key management activity.

"Purchasing" covers many activities, which may be divided into buying and ordering. Buying is the management activity of setting policy as to how suppliers will be selected. Ordering is a crucial, skilled routine that determines *how much* of *what* products are needed *when*.

Our principal concern in this chapter has been the management activities related to *buying*. In a general way, we have seen that the choice of supplier is based on considerations of quality, price, and service. Managers measure product quality in terms of excellence but also, very commonly, in terms of the suitability of product to intended use, as measured according to such down-to-earth criteria as size, weight, and market form. Product quality is set out in specifications. Although some operations use very informal and sometimes unwritten "specs," the best management opinion is that written specs should be a part of every operation, especially for high-volume or high-priced items. In most operations, however, quite simple specifications can be drawn up, often from government publications such as IMPS (Institutional Meat Purchasing Specifications). Very large operations, however, find it worth the time and effort to prepare more lengthy specifications based on their particular needs.

The purchasing strategy selected by an operation is based on the needs of that operation as determined principally by the scale of operation—that is, by *size*—and by the customer's needs as interpreted by management in its selection of the *type* of operation. There are probably as many approaches to purchasing as there are operations.

Food service operators either buy on the open market or use a form of forward buying. Competitive bid buying, using selected suppliers, and one-stop shopping are methods of open market buying, whereas contract buying and buying and warehousing product are forms of forward buying. Many sharp operators use a combination of these buying methods to effect savings in every product category.

Our discussion has made clear the importance of information to the purchasing process. Information on the quality and price available in the marketplace is essential to informed and intelligent purchasing. On the other side of the coin, recall that a good buyer learns to be a good and valued customer who recognizes the value of supplier services.

In food service chains, finally, we have noted a split between purchasing activities. Buying often is concentrated at the central office level, where highly specialized expertise is available. At the unit level, purchasing often is reduced to ordering routines, because product specification and supplier selection are taken care of centrally.

Variations in the degree of centralization, however, are very wide. In some companies all products come from a centralized commissary, whereas in others a centralized distribution center handles all but fresh foods. Other companies centralize by using only approved suppliers, with the unit dealing directly—but exclusively—with this supplier. At the other extreme, some large multiunit companies, particularly those with many franchises, leave purchasing largely in the hands of units but negotiate directly with national or regional suppliers of food products to secure price concessions for affiliated units.

KEY WORDS AND CONCEPTS

Purchasing—definition	Combining approaches
Ordering	Forward buying
Buying	Fixed contract
Appropriate quality	Cost-plus contracts
Inspection of supplier facility	Systems contracts
Price	Group purchasing
Yield-testing	Keeping suppliers honest
Drained weight	Being a good customer
Supplier services	Maximize order size
Defining quality	Minimize order frequency
Size, weight, market form	Limit number of suppliers
Specifications	Seeing salespeople
Standards of identity	Ordering
Purchasing approaches	Par stock
Open market buying	Standing order
Competitive bid buying	Inventory levels
Selected suppliers	Inventory costs
One-stop shopping	Logistics

DISCUSSION QUESTIONS

1. Discuss the differences between open market and forward buying.

2. Discuss why product specifications are important in food cost control.

3. You are the owner-operator of a successful family restaurant and have decided to expand and build four more restaurants of the same type over the next five years. During your years of operating, you have found that you have been too busy to spend a lot of time with purchasing. Your strategy has been to select one supplier for each commodity group (meat, produce, groceries, etc.). You think that this strategy has worked well, because your suppliers' prices seem to be competitive, and they often let you know when they have good buys. With five stores to run and less time available for purchasing, however, you wonder how you should organize the purchasing function. An immediate concern is to maintain consistency and the same product mix in all five stores. Discuss some alternatives.

4. Describe the differences in purchasing responsibility between the owner of a restaurant (as in question 3) and the unit manager of a fast food restaurant.

5 DETERMINING PRODUCT QUALITY

Inspection and Grading

Quality Specifications for Meat

Quality Specifications for Poultry

Quality Specifications for Seafood

Quality Specifications for Fresh Produce

Quality Specifications for Processed Foods

Summary

THE PURPOSE OF THIS CHAPTER

In Chapter 4 we described quality as a group of attributes related to the use of the product. We said that "What is needed" defines good quality, and that the needs of the operation with respect to each product should be set out in product specifications that form the basis of communication between buyer and supplier.

In this chapter we turn to the major quality considerations of principal food groups. Whole books have been written on the subject of food quality—indeed, entire books have been devoted to single foods—and we certainly cannot treat this subject in such depth. Nevertheless, this chapter will help you identify the principal considerations in specification writing for most foods.

THIS CHAPTER SHOULD HELP YOU

1. Describe the difference between inspection and grading.

2. Identify and discuss the major quality factors in meats.

3. List and describe the principal grades of meat.

4. Name and describe the major source of information for specifications for meats for food service.

5. Relate quality factors in fish to the market form (for instance, fresh, frozen, or live) in which the product is purchased.

6. List and describe the factors to be considered in preparing specifications for produce.

7. Name the items of information required by law on food package labels and explain their significance.

In studying food quality, first of all identify the products that will be **1.** your principal menu items, **2.** the most expensive foods on your menu, **3.** "signature" items (house specialties), and **4.** those food items that you feel will account for most of your sales dollar. In other words, concentrate on your important food products first—operators should know in depth the quality attributes of the foods they sell. After making this list, you will know which foods to research. This chapter will guide you in identifying key factors. In each food group, we have attempted to identify the information necessary for specification writing. Naturally, some foods are not mentioned, but you should have a general idea of how to go about researching any food product after studying the major food groupings.

INSPECTION AND GRADING

In writing specifications for food quality, you immediately can eliminate much description and still demand attributes that you deem desirable if food is inspected and graded. It is important that you know the difference between inspection and grading.

INSPECTION

In the late 1880s, our food supply was commonly adulterated (unedible filler in sugar and poisonous green dye added to canned peas, for example). Food processing plants sometimes were filthy, and labels on canned foods not only were misleading but often were completely false (ingredient listing on labels was unknown). This situation was brought to the public's attention in Upton Sinclair's popular book *The Jungle,* which focused on the meat packing industry. As a result, a series of food and drug laws was enacted. Today, three governmental agencies inspect food plants and assure us of the cleanliness and safety of processed food products (certainly a primary quality attribute). The Food and Drug Administration (FDA) is responsible for regulating all foods except for red meats, poultry, eggs, and seafoods. The Department of Agriculture (USDA) inspects plants that process meat, poultry, and eggs. Seafood processing plants are inspected by the U.S. Department of Commerce (USDC).

Before inspected foods are offered for sale, they must pass the minimum health and sanitation standards established by these governmental agencies. Included in these standards are the following requirements.

- The food must be processed from raw product that is pure, wholesome, and undamaged.

- The processing plant must be clean.

- The workers must be supervised to ensure sanitary food handling in the plant.

- No harmful preservatives may be used unless they are absolutely necessary, in which case they must be used in minimal quantities and listed on the label.

- The package must not be designed to deceive the buyer, by appearing to contain more than it actually does.

- The label must not make any misleading statements, either directly or by implication.

If you specify an inspected product, therefore, it is unnecessary to specify, for example, that the processing plant be clean or that the food is undamaged when processed.

GRADING

As we have noted, *inspection* determines whether food is fit for human consumption. *Grading,* on the other hand, indicates the quality of the product. The term *inspection* refers to a government activity; *grading* is done both by government agencies and by packers.

Most processing plants are inspected, but not all food is graded. Grade specification eliminates much quality description in specifications, since grades deal strictly with quality attributes. Historically, grading came into being to standardize quality—so that food operators, for instance, could buy food sight unseen but still have a good idea of its quality. Grading has also made it possible for a buyer to purchase foods over great distances and be assured of a certain quality. A USDA Fancy-grade apple, for example, will be mature, not overripe, carefully hand-picked, clean, well-formed, free from defects, and colored as specified for variety. It is unnecessary to include these quality characteristics when you specify a grade.

It should be made clear that the lower grades are perfectly wholesome; they are completely edible, but you must know how to work them into your menu effectively. Inexpensive steak houses, for instance, cannot afford to use choice grade meat; instead, they use the rib eye, loin, and tenderloin muscles from Commercial-grade animals. This meat is less juicy than that of higher grade, but also less costly. Low-grade vegetables may be used in casseroles or soups in which their shape and color are not vital—or when a higher-quality product could not be identified anyway!

Throughout this chapter, we will describe the principal products purchased by food service operators. In addition to describing inspection and grades, we will show the considerations that go into specification writing for each. In other words, we hope to help you sort through product information to develop specifications for your own needs.

QUALITY SPECIFICATIONS FOR MEAT

For the consumer, quality attributes in meat include juiciness, flavor, color (particularly with veal), and (especially today) the amount of fat. But the most important quality factor, as far as most consumers are concerned, is tenderness. The food service operator first of all must satisfy the consumer, but yield, convenience, and labor cost must be considered along with quality aspects. To obtain a tender, juicy, flavorful piece of meat, you must take into account primarily the *age* of the animal, the *fat marbling* of its meat, its sex, and the manner in which it has been fed and exercised. USDA grades designate the age of the animal and the marbling. Inspection, as mentioned earlier, is mandatory for all meat processing plants in the United States, and you can assume that the meat you buy has been inspected by federal or state agencies. The government also provides a grading service to meat packers who wish to pay for it. The USDA has established quality grades for beef, veal, lamb, and pork based principally on maturity (age) and marbling (see Table 5.1). Marbling refers to the fat content of the meaty portion of the carcass (as opposed to the fat cover). Marbling generally appears as flecks of white (fat) within the red meat.

The definitions of the beef grades given below indicate the distinctions among

TABLE 5.1 USDA GRADES FOR RED MEATS

Beef	Veal	Pork	Lamb
Prime	Prime	U.S. No. 1	Prime
Choice	Choice	U.S. No. 2	Choice
Good	Good	U.S. No. 3	Good
Standard	Standard	U.S. No. 4	
Commercial			
Utility	Utility	Utility	Utility
Cutter	Cull		Cull
Canner			

the grades; these distinctions generally can be applied to all four types of animal, allowing for some differences in relative emphasis on the various factors.

U.S. Prime Grade. Beef from young steers or heifers, with liberal marbling. Only a very limited amount of this quality comes to market.

U.S.D.A. Choice Grade. The largest volume of fresh beef available to the consumer, and the grade most commonly used in "white tablecloth" restaurants. It differs from Prime grade only in having less of a fat covering (finish).

U.S.D.A. Good Grade. Beef given this grade has less extensive exterior fat and a higher ratio of lean to fat. It is also from a young animal. It is relatively tender but lacks the juiciness associated with higher fat content.

USDA Standard Grade. Only traces of marbling present, but still from a young animal.

USDA Commercial Grade This and lower grades are from older cattle, particularly cows. Because of the animal's age, only specific cuts are tender. Marbling is limited. Although unavailable to retail market, USDA Commercial grade is available to the institutional trade.

USDA Utility Grade. Meat from older cattle, generally processed into bologna and sausages.

USDA Cutter and Canner Grades. Meat from older cows. Lean and very dark, it is used in processed meat products.

By specifying graded meat, you can specify the age and marbling of the animal. It is more difficult to guarantee tenderness and flavor through grading. Some operators specify meat from only certain processing plants (the number on the grade stamp is the identificaton mark of the processing plant). Another specification used to guarantee tenderness is to stipulate loins and ribs from animals that have been tested with an instrument called a tenderometer. (Tenderness is affected by several factors other than age, such as the amount of exercise and of aging after slaughter.)

PACKER BRANDS
Many meat packers employ their own grade names, which may parallel government grades. Packers attempt to designate the different grades of meat they are selling and to certify quality within their own classifications. (There is no composite list of these private grades or brand names, but individual companies, upon request, will provide buyers with information concerning their own brand names. Because pork is merchandised somewhat differently from other meats, its federal grades have not been widely used. Many cuts of pork, especially those that have been cured and smoked, carry packer brands. Brand names, like grade names, are applied to meat with a roller stamp and a harmless vegetable-base fluid, similar to that used for the inspection stamp, that leaves its mark along the full length of the carcass (or along the cut, if cuts are being graded).

YIELD GRADING OR CUTABILITY GRADING
In addition to federal grading for quality, lamb may be and beef must be cutability-graded. Cutability grading is the inspector's prediction of the percentage of usable meat—rounds, ribs, loins, and chunks—on the carcass. Four factors determine the yield grade.

- The amount of external fat on the carcass.

- The amount of pelvic, kidney, and heart fat present on the carcass.

- The area of the rib-eye muscle at the 12th rib.

- The hot carcass weight.

The USDA cutability grades are numbered 1 to 5, with Grade 1 representing the highest yield or cutability—a very thick muscling with a minimum of fat. The following chart relates the cutability grades to their approximate yields in usable cuts of meat.

Grade	Yield (Percent of Usable Meat)
1	79.8% or more
2	75.2% to 79.7%
3	70.6% to 75.1%
4	66% to 70.5%
5	65.9% or less

Cutability grades permit a buyer in Memphis, for instance, to have a quite specific idea about the quality, in terms of tenderness, juiciness, and flavor, and

112 DETERMINING PRODUCT QUALITY

also the yield that can be expected from carcasses in San Diego or Boston. Since cutability grades apply only to carcasses and prime cuts, and not to portion cuts or fabricated meat, they generally are used by large buyers.

DETERMINING THE CUT

You must decide on the particular cut of meat you desire for your operation. There are two general classifications of cuts for food service: (1) wholesale or primal cuts and (2) institutional cuts. (Every food service student should know these cuts). Figures 5.1 to 5.4 show most of the institutional cuts for beef, veal, pork, and lamb. Our cuts differ from retail store cuts, because we tend to "think big or think little"—that is, we need either large roasts that will serve many persons or portions (steaks and chops cut to serve just one person).

Generally, food services no longer purchase primal cuts of meat, because of the limited use of trim and the fact that a skilled butcher is necessary. We tend to

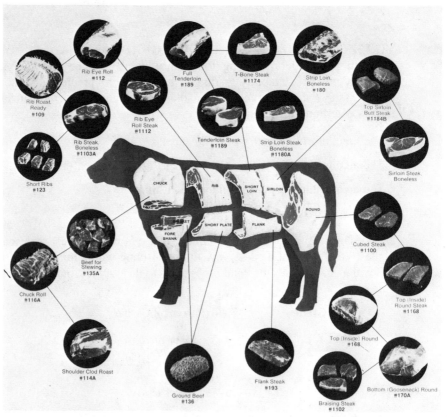

(Courtesy National Live Stock & Meat Board)

FIGURE 5.1 Primal cuts of beef and commonly used food service cuts, with corresponding IMPS/NAMP numbers. (Adapted from J. M. Powers, *Basics of Quantity Food Production,* Photos courtesy National Livestock and Meat Board.)

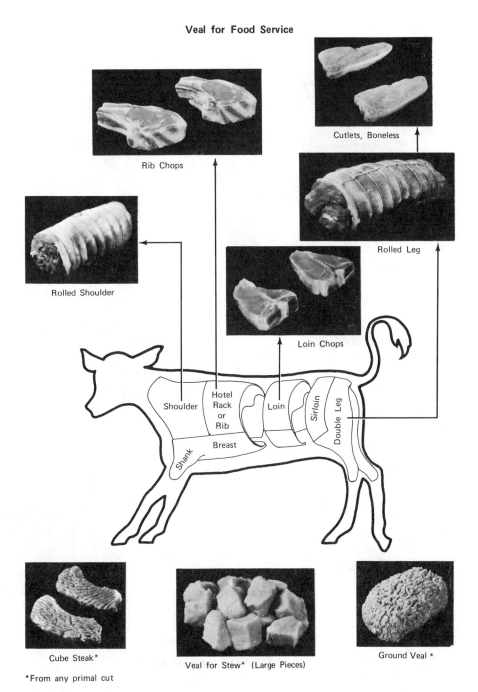

FIGURE 5.2 Primal cuts of veal and commonly used food service cuts. Asterisks indicate products that come from any primal cut of veal. (Adapted from J. M. Powers, *Basics of Quantity Food Production*. Photos courtesy of National Livestock and Meat Board.)

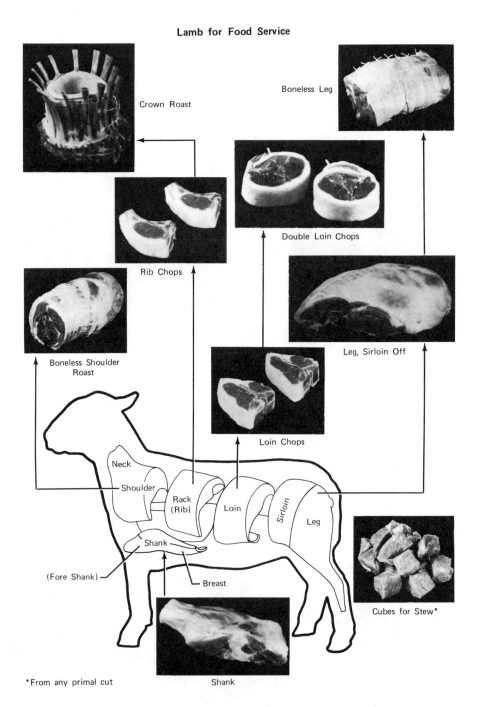

FIGURE 5.3 Primal cuts of lamb and commonly used food service cuts. Asterisks indicate products that come from any primal cut. (Adapted from J. M. Powers, *Basics of Quantity Food Production*. Photos courtesy of National Livestock and Meat Board.)

QUALITY SPECIFICATIONS FOR MEAT

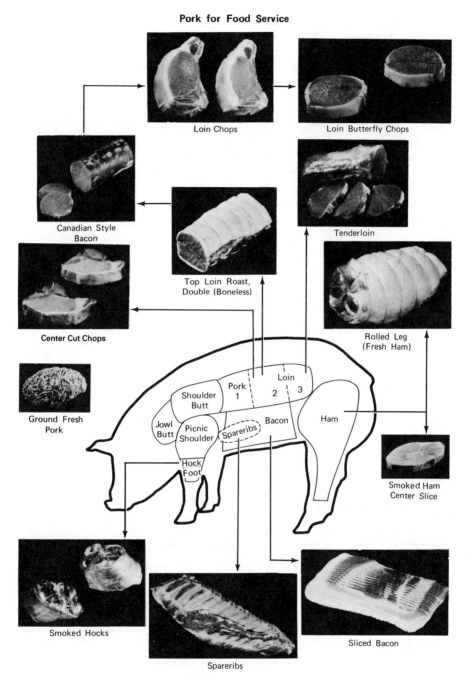

FIGURE 5.4 Primal cuts of pork and commonly used food service cuts. (Adapted from J. M. Powers, *Basics of Quantity Food Production*. Photos courtesy of National Livestock and Meat Board.)

purchase only for specific menu items. For example, if you have roast rib of beef on the menu and purchase a primal rib of beef, you will need to add menu items to utilize the short ribs and extraneous muscles. Operators find that this type of selling detracts from the profitability of the rib roast, and they tend to purchase the roast trimmed and "oven-ready," even though it costs more per pound that way.

INSTITUTIONAL MEAT PURCHASING SPECIFICATION

The purchasing of meat has been greatly simplified by the publication of the National Association of Meat Purveyors' *Meat Buyer's Guide,* which was prepared in conjunction with the USDA. *The Guide* contains standard specifications for institutional meat cuts (known as IMPS or, interchangeably, NAMPS). A standardized numbering system, summarized in Table 5.2, makes the *Guide* easy to use. Numbers in the 100 series refer to standardized cuts such as oven-ready rib or briskets, whereas numbers in the 1000 series refer to portion cuts such as beef cube steak or center-cut pork chops.

General specification information available from the *Guide* can be summarized as follows.[1]

State of refrigeration.

Tying.

Boning.

Steak, chop, cutlet and filet descriptions.

Portion-cut weight or thickness.

Fat limitation for
    Steaks
    Chops
    Cutlets
    Filets

Portion-cut weight tolerances.

TABLE 5.2 NAMP/USDA STANDARDIZED NUMBERING SYSTEM FOR RED MEATS

Meat Products	Standardized Cuts	Portion Cuts
Beef	100	1000
Lamb	200	1200
Veal	300	1300
Pork	400	1400

The Meat Buyer's Guide, National Association of Meat Purveyors, (Tucson. Arizona, 1976).

[1]*The Meat Buyer's Guide,* pp. XIII and XIV.

Portion-cut thickness tolerances.

Patty weight tolerances.

Aged beef.

The *Guide* also provides standard ordering data to be specified by the purchaser.[2] Even more useful, however, are the standard descriptions of institutional cuts and institutional portions, such as the two samples below.[3]

165—Round, Rump and Shank Off, Boneless
This item is the same as Item No. 164 except that it shall be made boneless. The round bone *(femur)* shall be removed as described in Item No. 159. The kneecap *(patella)* and surrounding heavy connective tissue shall be removed. The thick opaque portion of the gracilis membrane shall be removed.

1103—Rib Steaks
Rib steaks shall be prepared from a Rib, Primal-Item No. 103. The short ribs on individual steaks shall be removed at a point which is not more than 3 inches from the outer tip of the ribeye muscle. All muscles above the major ribeye muscle, fat overlying these muscles, the blade bone and cartilage, the feather bones, and the backstrap shall be removed.

SUMMARY
In writing quality specification for meat, you must consider and research the following attributes.

- Grade: quality grade.
- Grade: yield grade for beef and lamb, but only if primal carcasses or cuts are purchased.
- Weight range for roasts and other large pieces of meat.
- Institutional cut needed (IMPS number, when available).
- Weight range for roasts and other large pieces of meat.
- Portion size for individually portioned meats, and weight tolerance.
- Fat tolerance for roasts and portion-controlled meats.
- Thickness of steaks and chops.
- Tenderness tested with tenderometer.
- Aging (beef only).
- Chilled or frozen.

---

[2]Ibid., pp. 43–45, 62–63, 78–79, and 96–98.
[3]"Institutional Meat Purchase Specifications for Fresh Beef Approved by USDA" (USDA, Washington, D.C.), 1975.

QUALITY SPECIFICATIONS FOR POULTRY

Studies have shown that for consumers, juiciness and tenderness are the primary quality attributes of poultry. Tenderness usually is determined by the age (class) of the bird, since young birds generally are more tender than older ones. If poultry is not young, the label should carry the word *mature* or *older,* or some similar term. Juiciness is affected by the length and temperature of cookery and by the finish (fat cover). Juiciness is adversely affected by precooking and reheating—a common restaurant cookery technique. There are processing techniques that actually enhance the juiciness and tenderness of poultry, but these tend to increase the cost per pound. The most tender chicken, for example, is that scalded at a temperature of 123 to 130°F, rather than at the 140°F used in most plants.

Fresh chicken is preferred by many food service operators because of the bone darkening (caused by the dark hemoglobin pigment in the marrow being drawn into the flesh when the chicken is frozen) characteristic of cooked frozen poultry, which has dark and sometimes blood-red flesh around the bone. If you buy in quantity, you may specify that the feed of the chicken not include fish meal, which may impart a distinct fishy flavor to the meat. Finally, the condition of the processing plant and the manner in which it turns over its inventory is critical to quality. Poultry that has been in a cooler for a week at the processing factory will not have a long shelf life in your establishment, and may even have a slight off-flavor even though slime and odor are not detectable when the chickens are received. The choice of supplier is critical, then, if your house specialty is a poultry product.

Poultry processing plants must be visited by state or federal inspectors, so it is not necessary to specify an inspected product. A grade may be specified for chicken, turkey, ducks, geese and squab. The *grade* of poultry is only an indication of quality; it does not guarantee how tender or tasty the bird will be. Grade specifications are based on age, conformation, finish, and number of imperfections. Top-grade birds are likely to be juicier and provide a better yield of meat than lower-quality poultry, because they have more fat covering (finish) and more meat in relationship to bone (conformation). The following grade specifications have been established for poultry.

USDA Grade A. Young, soft-meated birds with well-fleshed breasts and well-developed fat layer.

USDA Grade B. Young, soft-meated birds with fairly well-fleshed breasts; carcasses fairly well covered with fat.

USDA Grade C. Young birds with poorly fleshed breasts and carcasses meagerly covered with fat. Abrasions, discolorations and deformities are allowed.

If you are in doubt about the age of poultry that you buy, the best way to determine maturity on dressed poultry is to examine the breastbone. In a young bird the cartilage, if present, will be pliable and soft, whereas in a mature bird the end of the keel will be hardened cartilage or bone.

When specifications are developed (see Table 5.3), a weight per bird or portion may be specified. Table 5.4 gives a general idea of weight ranges within classes of chicken and turkey. Poultry may be purchased as whole birds, in cut-up pieces, or in parts (quarters or halves). In addition, turkey may be purchased for food service in the following forms: boneless turkey breast, fresh or frozen; turkey roll, cooked and ready to slice, and light, dark, or combination; boneless roast, oven-roasted or water-cooked; individually frozen turkey cubes, cooked. Whole poultry is termed "ready-to-cook" (dressed bird with head, feet, pinfeathers, and viscera removed), in contrast to "dressed" (head, feet, and viscera intact).

In researching poultry products, you will need to focus upon

- Class.
- Grade.
- Weight per bird or portion and tolerance.
- Market form
    Whole or cut up
    Chilled or frozen
- Supplier: processing and shelf life.

TABLE 5.3 SAMPLE POULTRY SPECIFICATIONS

Item	Grade	Purchase Unit	Description
Duckling, Donald brand	USDA Grade A	4 lb each 4 oz tolerance quartered	Ready-to-cook Giblets excluded Send chilled, packaged in ice

TABLE 5.4 CLASSIFICATION OF POULTRY BY AGE AND WEIGHT

Class	Age	Average Weight
Chicken		
Rock cornish hen	5–7 weeks	¾–2 lb
Broiler	9–12 weeks	¾–2½ lb
Fryer	9–12 weeks	2½–3½ lb
Roaster	3–5 months	3½–5 lb
Capon	Under 8 months	3½–9 lb
Stag	Under 10 months	3½–6 lb
Stewing hen or fowl	Over 10 months	3½–6 lb
Cock or rooster	Over 10 months	
Turkey		
Fryer-roaster	16 weeks	4–9 lb
Young hen	5–7 months	8–12; 12–18 lb
Young tom	5–7 months	12–16; 16–20 lb
Old hen	8–15 months	10–20 lb
Old tom	8–15 months	12–30 lb

QUALITY SPECIFICATIONS FOR SEAFOOD

Seafoods include fish, shellfish, and various invertebrates from oceans and fresh waters. The most important quality aspect for seafoods is *freshness*. As soon as seafoods are caught or harvested, their enzyme systems begin to produce undesirable aromatic substances (the "fishy" smell) and spoilage bacteria rapidly multiply, even at refrigerator temperatures. The buyer must know the characteristics of fresh seafoods, and particularly of seafoods that have been filleted or removed from shells. These characteristics can be summarized as follows.

- Fresh whole, drawn, or dressed fish: full, clear eyes, bright skin, tight scales, bright red gills, firm and elastic flesh that does not keep a dent when pressed with the finger, a fresh smell both inside the fish and at the gills, flesh firmly adhering to the bone. The whole fish sinks in water. Packed in ice or moisture-proof wrap.

- Filleted fresh fish: firm and elastic flesh that does not keep a dent when pressed with the finger; a fresh smell. Packed in ice or moisture-proof wrap.

- Frozen fish: evidence of thin coating of ice surrounding fillet or fish portion (called "glaze"), absence of "freezer burn" (characterized by discolored and dry appearance on the surface), absence of ice crystals in the package, no signs of thawing and refreezing (discolored package and freeze burn), little or no odor, undamaged package.

- Fresh live shellfish: must be alive, as indicated by tightly closed shells or movement (crabs and lobsters).

- Shucked shellfish: must be plump and have natural color with clear liquid; fresh odor.

Seafoods are not necessarily federally inspected. The processor pays for inspection services if the company so desires. If you wish to purchase inspected seafood products, therefore, you must specify inspection. Inspected products are statistically sampled for cleanliness, safety, wholesomeness and acceptable quality. Inspected seafoods, therefore, should be fresh and of high quality *at the time of inspection*. (However, it is of utmost importance that you examine the seafoods carefully, to detect mishandling between inspection and delivery to your operation).

Since grading is at the option of the processor, seafood that does not fall into the category Grade A generally is ungraded and sold under packer brands. Grade A is given only to top-quality seafoods—products that are uniform in size, free of blemishes and defects, in excellent condition, and that possess a fresh flavor and odor characteristic of the species. In addition, breading is specified: raw breaded portions must have 75% flesh; fish sticks, 72%; and precooked breaded portions, 65%.

Seafoods are specified by variety and market form (see Figure 5.5). Varieties

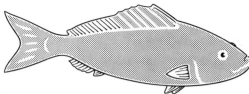

Whole or round fish are those marketed just as they come from the water.

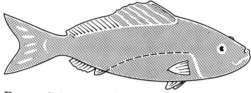

Drawn fish are marketed with only the entrails removed.

Dressed or pan-dressed fish are scaled and eviscerated; usually, the head, tail, and fins are removed. The smaller sizes are ready for cooking as purchased (pan-dressed).

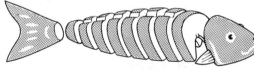

Steaks are cross-section slices of the larger sizes of dressed fish.

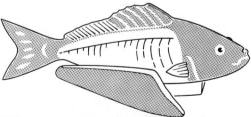

Fillets are the sides of the fish, cut lengthwise away from the backbone. They are practically boneless and require no preparation for cooking.

Sticks are pieces of fish cut lengthwise or crosswise from fillets or steaks into portions of uniform width and length.

Butterfly fillets are the two sides of the fish corresponding to two single fillets held together by uncut flesh and the skin.

Market Forms of Shellfish

Live: Shellfish, such as crabs, lobsters, clams, and oysters, should be alive if purchased in the shell, except for boiled crabs and lobsters.

Shucked: Shucked shellfish are those that have been removed from their shells. Oysters, clams, and scallops are marketed in this manner.

Headless: This term applies to shrimp, which are marketed in most areas with the head and thorax removed.

Cooked meat: The edible portion of shellfish is often sold cooked, ready-to-eat. Shrimp, crab, and lobster meat are marketed in this way.

FIGURE 5.5 Market forms of fish.

of fish generally are classified as freshwater or saltwater and fatty or lean. Seafoods may be purchased in many market forms—fresh, frozen, canned, mild-cured, pickled, dry-salted, and smoked. They are available throughout the country year-round, thanks to quick-freezing, packing, and fast transportation.

In developing seafood specifications (see Table 5.5) you will want to pay particular attention to

- Species or variety.
- Characteristics of freshness.
- Inspection.
- Grade.
- Market form.

QUALITY SPECIFICATIONS FOR FRESH PRODUCE

Although a few operators arrive at the produce market at 5:00 A.M. each morning to choose fruits and vegetables for the day, this procedure is impractical for all but the most dedicated. Many persons also feel that it is unnecessary if buyers can communicate their needs to the supplier—and if the supplier can interpret their needs satisfactorily.

Quality is judged by the individual attributes of the fruit or vegetable, and it is absolutely essential that you research commonly used produce items to find out what these characteristics are. In general, look for the following factors:

Variety. Producers may grow many varieties of a single vegetable or fruit, and the variety chosen may affect the quality of your product. The produce shown in the following list usually requires a specific variety.

TABLE 5.5 SAMPLE SPECIFICATIONS FOR SEAFOODS

Item	Grade	Purchase Unit	Description
Rainbow trout	USDC Grade A	Box of 20 10 oz each Tolerance 1 oz	USDC inspected Dressed with back fin removed head and tail intact Deliver frozen, glazed
Will reject any damaged boxes, signs of freezer burn, absence of glaze, ice crystalization or nonfresh odor.			
Eastern Oyster Shucked	USDC Grade A	Gallon Container 210–300 Count	USDC inspected No less than 95% drained weight Absence of shell particles Deliver chilled, in ice pack
Will reject oysters that have not been freshly shucked, as indicated by plumpness and natural creamy color with clear liquor, and fresh odor.			

Vegetables
Avocado
Beans
Cabbage
Lettuce
Onion
Garlic
Parsley
Peas
Peppers
Potatoes
Summer Squash
Winter Squash
Tomato

Fruits
Apples
Cherries
Figs
Grapefruit
Grapes
Limes
Melons
Oranges
Peaches
Pears
Plums

Maturity. You need to know at what stage in growth a fruit or vegetable should be harvested for optimal quality. Zucchini, for instance, are purchased immature, whereas fully ripened peaches are considered to be the best.

Perishability. You might wish to purchase tree-ripened peaches, but this is impractical unless you are in the center of the growing area, because ripe peaches may bruise without extra care during harvest and transport. Your purchasing decision ultimately will depend upon customer demand. If your customer demands and will pay for tree-ripened peaches, you may specify that they be flown across the country. If your customer is unwilling to pay that cost but wishes to have fresh peaches, then hard-ripe would necessarily be your choice.

Vegetables may be classified by perishability (see Table 5.6). Some vegetables can be held for a long period (onions, white cabbage, carrots and potatoes), whereas others, particularly salad crops and leafy vegetables, are short-lived. Characteristics of produce that has been stored too long include loss of sugar, flavor, and color; wilting or softening; fungal and bacterial rotting; lignification (increase in woody fibers); and with some, growth in shoots and roots.

TABLE 5.6 CLASSIFICATION OF VEGETABLES BY PERISHABILITY

Group	Vegetables	Storage Life
Bulbs	Onions, shallots and garlic	10 months
Root crops	Carrots, parsnips, turnips, beets	6 months
Temperature-sensitive crops	Beans, cucumbers, peppers, tomatoes	Few days to few weeks
Highly perishable	Spinach, lettuce, brussels sprouts, celery, cauliflower, asparagus, peas, sweet corn.	Few days to few weeks

124 DETERMINING PRODUCT QUALITY

Seasonality. You should know not only the availability of produce year-round, but also when the product ripens in your area. Much of our produce can be found on the market year-round, flown in, perhaps, from South America or other parts of the world. Obviously, however, produce is cheapest when it is available locally—and generally, local produce provides the best quality. In the produce trade there is a saying, "The lower the price, the higher the quality"—because local produce is both the best and the least expensive. The annual USDA report *Fresh Fruits and Vegetable Unload Totals for 41 Cities* is a helpful guide to the availability and sources of each commodity, by months.

Size. When specifying size for produce, do not use terms such as small, medium, or large; rather, use *count,* a number that lets your supplier know the exact size of produce. The larger the count number, the smaller the fruit or vegetable, since the count number refers to the amount in a designated container such as a bushel. Figure 5.6 illustrates counts for apples.

Inspection and Grading. About 40% of produce shipments are inspected, with the fee for inspection paid by the purchaser. Produce shipped under packer grades may be monitored more closely, as federal or state standards are quite broad.

Grading. Grades generally are based on size, uniformity of shape, maturity, color, freedom from disease and decay, absence of cuts and bruises, and flavor. Each vegetable has its own grading specification (and may have its own grades). Produce is graded only if it crosses the state lines. Since produce is highly

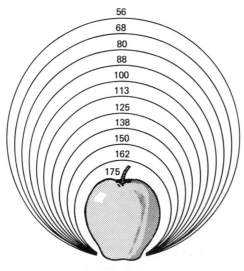

Count per Western Box	Minimum Diameter Size[a]
175	1¼ in.
162	1½ in.
150	1¾ in.
138	2 in.
125	2¼ in.
113	2½ in.
100	2¾ in.
88	3 in.
80	3¼ in.
68	3½ in.
56	3¾ in.

[a]As measured not around girth but from stem to blossom and transversely. *Note:* Federal standards call size 88 or less, *very large;* 96 to 125, *large;* 138 to 163, *medium,*; 175 to 200, *small;* and 216 to 252, *very small.*

FIGURE 5.6 Relationship of count to size for apples. (From Lendal Krofscherar, *Quantity Food Purchasing.*)

perishable, a grade placed on a crate of tomatoes in California may not reflect the condition of the tomatoes when they reach New York. Also, since the grading process itself requires additional sorting and handling, it may, paradoxically, contribute to vegetable deterioration.

Price, Quality, and Availability. In addition to product research, the produce purchaser must keep abreast of market trends. For example, if a drought in a growing area leads to fewer, poor-quality heads of lettuce at a high price, the buyer must be aware of suitable alternatives. If, for instance, other greens are coming in from other growing areas, or cabbage is plentiful, menu changes may avoid customer complaints about quality and reduce costs at the same time.

In writing quality specifications (see Table 5.7) for fresh produce, we generally, include the following attributes.

- Name of vegetable or fruit and variety.
- Grade—federal, state or packer grade.
- Size or count.
- Packaging and weight of package or carton.
- Maturity.
- Market form—packaging, trim, storage conditions.
- Price limitations.

QUALITY SPECIFICATIONS FOR PROCESSED FOODS

Processed foods include the entire spectrum of food groups—produce, meats, dairy products, eggs, beverages, and so on. In addition to canned products, this category includes convenience foods, frozen foods, dried foods, or any food that has been processed in one way or another. Although it is necessary to understand

TABLE 5.7 SAMPLE PRODUCE SPECIFICATIONS

Apples, winesap	U.S. Fancy on delivery	Corrugated container, 40 lb per box	113 count; controlled atmosphere after December; send chilled
Asparagus, green	U.S. no. 1 on delivery	Pyramidal crate holding 12 bunches, 2 to 2½ lb each	Stalk length 7½ to 10½ length; vacuum chilled after harvest; purchase by weight only; send chilled

the quality attributes of each product purchased, we generally need to focus upon the label; inspection and grading; size, count, weight, and specific gravity; and market form.

THE LABEL

The Fair Packaging and Labeling Act, designed to make it easier to make value comparisons, requires that all food package labels provide certain information.

Product name. The legal, usual, or common name of the food.

Variety, style, and packing medium. For example, the label must state if corn is creamed style or kernel, or whether peaches are packed in water, light syrup, or heavy syrup. If a label states "bartlett pear halves," the variety must be bartlett.

Net contents. The label must state the net quantity of the contents, starting with all ounces for weights of one to four pounds and volumes of one pint to one gallon, with fractional volume or fractions of ounces accompanying the appropriate whole units. The listing of the weight in total ounces first makes it easier for the buyer to make cost-per-ounce comparisons of various brands.

Name, Address, and Zip Code for the Manufacturer, Packer, or Distributor.

Additives. Artificial color, flavor, or preservatives must be stated on the label. Many packaged foods could not be produced or would be prohibitively expensive to produce without additives.

Product Standards. The government has developed minimum standards of quality that products should meet. A product can fall below a standard but still be perfectly wholesome, however (e.g., unevenly trimmed pears). The Food and Drug Administration permits distribution of these substandard products, so long as they are clearly labeled as such. Depending on their price and use, such products can be acceptable and, for some uses, a bargain.

List of ingredients. With the exception of products with established "standards of identity," the label must list all ingredients used in the product in descending order of predominance. A product that has a standard of identity contains at least the minimum of each ingredient specified by the government for that product. Mayonnaise and salad dressing are examples of products with standards of identity.

INSPECTION OF PROCESSED FOODS

Before processed foods can be offered for sale, they must pass minimum health and sanitation standards established by the government. The statement "Packed under continuous inspection of the U.S. Department of Agriculture," which may

GRADING OF PROCESSED FOODS

appear with the grade name or by itself, assures buyers that they are purchasing a wholesome product of at least minimum quality, as certified by a federal inspector.

Government grading (USDA) is voluntary and must be paid for by the packer. A government inspector grades products and assigns specific scores based on charts designed for each product. The number of points awarded to the product by the inspector determines the grade it will receive. (see Figure 5.7). Product research will reveal whether or not a product is graded and whether it is practical to specify

---

Score Sheet for Canned Asparagus
Note three standards are indicated: A, C, and substandard.

Number, size, and kind of container
Label
Container mark or identification
Net weight (ounces)
Vacuum (inches)
Drained weight (ounces)
Type
Style
Size or sizes (Spears, tips, and points)
Length of cut
Heads (cut)(percent, by count)

Factors		Score points
Liquor	10	(A) 9–10
		(C) 7–8
		(SStd) [1]0–6
Color	20	(A) 17–20
		(C) 14–16
		(SStd) [1]0–13
Defects	30	(A) 25–30
		(C) [1]21–24
		(SStd) [1]0–20
Character	40	(A) 34–40
		(C) [1]28–33
		(SStd) [1]0–27
Total score	100	

Flavor (A, C, or SStd)
Grade

[1]Indicates limiting rule.

FIGURE 5.7 Sample grade score sheet. (Courtesy of USDA.)

a graded product. Many canned fruits and vegetables, for instance, are graded. There may be a price choice between brand name product and an equally acceptable graded but unbranded product.

SIZE AND COUNT

Individual portions are purchased by size and count. Canned foods for institutional use normally are packed in no. 10 cans and foods such as fruits, olives, and pickles are packed by size and count specified as such. The size and count of a canned product, therefore, directly influences the portion yield, as well as the portion cost. If the standard portion for pear halves is two, the 35-to-40-count no. 10 can will yield 17½ to 20 servings, whereas the 40-to-50-count will yield 20 to 25 servings. Frozen foods may be packed by count: frozen unbaked rolls, breaded items, and cupcakes, for instance, are packed in this way.

DRAINED WEIGHT

The term *drained weight* refers to the actual weight of the product after its liquid content has been drained off on mesh screens for two minutes. The yield of a product, therefore, will vary according to the ratio of vegetable or fruit to packing medium: the more product per ounce of medium, the higher the yield. Since the drained weight of a product does influence its yield, buyers should state their drained weight requirements and test to see that the product equals the drained weight specifications. (In spite of its economic usefulness to a buyer, however, drained weight does not influence the grade of a product.)

SPECIFIC GRAVITY AND DENSITY

For products such as syrups, fruits packed in syrup, catsup, tomato paste and sauce, apple butter, and cream-style corn, specific gravity or density is a measure of water content, and thus a quality measure. (Too much water means a lower quality). A fast method of comparing the density of products is to put equal amounts on blotters and compare the moist rings after two minutes. This test, however, can be influenced by the addition of gums that bind free water and make the product appear denser. (The addition of a gum may be desirable in a product such as pickle relish.) Chemical tests or use of a Brix hydrometer may be necessary if you wish to determine the actual water content of a food.

MARKET FORM

It is necessary to specify the size package needed, and sometimes the packaging material. Can sizes are standardized (see Chart 4 in Appendix 1). No. 10 cans are commonly chosen, but it is costly to purchase this size if only a small amount is used at a time. Generally, case amounts are purchased (six no. 10 cans per case or

QUALITY SPECIFICATIONS FOR PROCESSED FOODS

TABLE 5.8 SAMPLE SPECIFICATIONS FOR PROCESSED FOODS

Item	Grade	Purchase Unit	Description
Peach halves, cling	U.S. Grade A	No. 10 cans, case of 6	Light syrup (14–19° Brix), 35/40 count
Macaroni and cheese	Delicious brand,	Case of 4 full pans	Deliver frozen, no evidence of thawing and refreezing; damaged packages will be rejected

100 individual creamers in a carton). Frozen convenience foods may come in a variety of choices—single serving portions or half-pans of 12 to 24 portions, for instance. If you specify frozen processed foods, you must verify that they arrive in the frozen state. In developing quality specifications (see Table 5.8) for processed foods, you may need to include

- Product name.
- Variety, style, and packing medium.
- Net contents of package.
- Brand name, grade, or quality attributes.
- Additive information.
- Size and/or count.
- Drained weight.
- Specific gravity or density.
- Market form.

SUMMARY

Quality is an elusive term that is sometimes hard to define. One person's fish eggs may be another person's caviar, for instance. In this chapter, we have identified quality attributes that are important in food service. In developing quality specifications, *you* make the decision. You may have simple guidelines or detailed directions for your supplier—it depends upon your needs and the type of operation with which you are involved. One fast food chain has minutely detailed food specifications, whereas another, quite similar chain gives its suppliers only general guidelines. It is most important for you to be able to identify the quality of food delivered to your establishment. Much can happen from the time the product is specified to the time it is received. Hence, product research for each major item on your menu is absolutely essential.

KEY WORDS AND CONCEPTS

Identification of products for research
Inspection of foods
Grading of food
Meat quality attributes
Age
Marbling
Packer brands
Yield or cutability grade
Institutional cuts
IMPS
Poultry quality attributes
Class
Grades
Weight
Market form
Supplier
Seafood quality attributes
Freshness
Glaze
Freezer burn
Species
Inspection
Market form
Produce quality attributes
Variety
Perishability
Seasonality
Size or count
Inspection
Grade
Price, quality
Availability
Processed foods
Label
Inspection
Grading
Size and count
Drained weight
Specific gravity
Density
Market form

DISCUSSION QUESTIONS 1. Which food items for restaurants would call for the most research? Name some food items that would require little or no research before buying.

2. Explain the differences between inspection and grading.

3. Develop a product specification for the following:
(a) Ground beef for a fast food chain.
(b) Chicken pieces for fried chicken restaurant.
(c) Fish sticks for school lunch.
(d) Tomatoes for salad garnish in a luxury hotel.
(e) Canned pineapple chunks for fruit cup in college food service.

4. A purchasing agent made the following statement about product "specs": "In food service we never specify what we want but complain about what we get!" Discuss how you can be sure of getting what you want.

5. A popcorn wagon in a popular theme park has average sales of $1,000 per day. If you were buying popcorn for this operation, how would you go about finding out all you could about popcorn?

6 RECEIVING AND STORAGE

Receiving in a Large Operation

Receiving Control in Smaller Operations

The Logistic Function in Fast Foods

Food Service Storage

THE PURPOSE OF THIS CHAPTER

In the food cost control cycle, receiving and storage are points at which the operation is exposed to waste, theft, and spoilage. Successful management acknowledges that these activities constitute a vital part of control. In large multi-unit operations, receiving and storage may be somewhat simplified at the unit level; In such cases, companywide control procedures achieve control objectives. Thus, reduced control procedures at the unit level may be replaced by inspection of goods before shipment in a supplier's plant.

In this chapter, we will focus first on the receiving activity in a very large operation, which will enable us to detail all the activities involved in receiving. Next, we will discuss how receiving is accomplished in smaller operations and in fast food operations. The next section of the chapter discusses proper storage facilities and procedures, considering how and why storage practices in multiunit companies differ somewhat from those in independent, conventional operations.

THIS CHAPTER SHOULD HELP YOU

1. List the equipment and layout needs for a proper receiving activity.

2. Specify the types of receiving and the advantages of each.

3. Discuss proper receiving procedures.

4. Describe how the receiving function is handled in smaller operations.

5. Explain the proper storage conditions for various kinds of foods.

6. Discuss the changes in receiving and storage practices found in multi-unit operations.

RECEIVING IN A LARGE OPERATION

THE RECEIVING AREA

The location of the receiving department and the space allocated for receiving directly affect the efficiency of delivery handling. Ideally, the receiving area should be located between the service entrance and the storeroom, to control the flow of deliveries into the establishment and to prevent the disappearance or spoiling of merchandise caused by overhandling, oversight, or delays in storing.

RECEIVING EQUIPMENT

To perform efficiently, receiving clerks must have the right kind of equipment. The most crucial item is an accurately balanced set of scales for weighing the merchandise. Scales are quite delicate, and they should be handled with care to ensure that they always record correct weights. In addition to scales, certain other pieces of equipment are needed for efficient receiving operations, including

- A desk, preferably stand-up, at which invoices or delivery tickets can be checked.
- A table, for checking and sorting merchandise before it is transferred to the storeroom.
- A two- or four-wheel hand truck, for moving merchandise from the dock to the receiving area and into the storeroom. (A four-wheel truck can accommodate three to four times as much weight and bulk as the two-wheel type can handle.)
- A dial thermometer, to determine if the proper temperatures have been maintained during the transportation of frozen foods and perishables.[1]

Wire baskets often are used for checking quality and storing produce. Although transferring produce from the original container into a wire basket reveals the quality of all the produce, the transferring process has numerous adverse side effects.

1. The produce is handled yet another time, and may be bruised.
2. The basket allows too much air circulation, which leads to a loss of moisture.
3. Newer shipment containers are designed to extend the shelf life of the produce, and discarding the container is a bad practice.
4. Produce should not be washed before refrigeration, because the moisture accelerates growth of spoilage microorganisms. (Produce should be washed as used.)

For these reasons, we strongly advise against the use of wire baskets in receiving.

THE RECEIVER

Large operations employ at least one full-time receiver, who may have one or more assistants. In this kind of operation, the receiver is a highly trained, responsible person whose job involves not only signing for receipt of the product and moving it to the right storage area, but also inspecting it to ensure that

1. The item received is on order.
2. The weight or count shown on the invoice corresponds to both what was ordered and what was delivered.
3. The quality of the product matches the specifications for that product. Such careful inspection has nothing to do with the integrity of the supplier;

[1]Karla Longrée, *Quantity Food Sanitation* (New York: Wiley, 1967), p. 205.

rather, it is good business practice on the part of management. Mistakes can be made either by the supplier's employees or by employees of the food service operation. Careful checking can eliminate or correct these mistakes.

THE INVOICE

The invoice is the supplier's bill or charge against the food service establishment for merchandise delivered. It is an itemized list of quantities and sale prices. Based on the order that the buyer has placed with the vendor (either by telephone or in writing), it should correspond in detail to the purchase order. Invoices may be handled in various ways, but the following routine is fairly typical of food service procedures.

When the receiving clerk gets the invoice, he or she dates it and then routes it directly either to the purchasing department (if purchasing is a centralized operation), where it is compared to the original purchase order, or to the accounting department (in organizations in which the food service department purchases its own supplies). If, for some reason, an invoice does not accompany the shipment, many operations have the receiver prepare a memorandum invoice (see Figure 6.1), on which the product and amount received is noted. This form takes the place of the invoice until the latter arrives.

METHODS OF RECEIVING

Food service operations generally use one of two basic receiving methods: invoice receiving and blind check receiving. In invoice receiving, the method most frequently used, the receiver checks for quantity and quality and checks the

MEMORANDUM INVOICE No. 1026

Received from ______________________ Date ______________________

QUANTITY	UNIT	ITEMS		

Ordered by ______________________ Received by ______________________

FIGURE 6.1 Memorandum invoice, which may be used in place of a supplier's invoice.

items listed on the invoice against the original purchase order. Some persons argue that although this method is quick and economical, it sometimes can lead to carelessness and indifference on the part of receivers. Because they have the invoice in front of them, they may be tempted to check the merchandise directly from the invoice rather than actually to ascertain weights and quantities and compare them with those recorded on the invoice. Blind check receiving is a more time-consuming method of checking in merchandise that, because of the added expense involved, is practiced by fewer and fewer food service establishments. When this method is used, the receiving person is given a blank invoice or purchase order listing the incoming merchandise by name alone; quantities, weights, and prices are omitted. The receiving clerk must then record all the pertinent information on the blank invoice.

In large operations such as hospitals, university housing and food service, and large hotels, receiving may well be centralized: that is, merchandise and supplies for all the departments, including food service, are received in one central area and then distributed to the appropriate section. In most large operations, receiving is a full-time job.

THE RECEIVING CLERK—ATTRIBUTES AND RESPONSIBILITIES

In choosing a person to fill the job of full-time receiver, you should consider carefully the candidate's ability to perform duties accurately and to work effectively with others. The receiving clerk, once hired, should be carefully trained to work accurately and conscientiously. On-the-job training should be geared to performance of the following functions.

1. Checking the quantity and weight of the incoming deliveries against the purchase order specifications.
2. Inspecting for quality.
3. Recording deliveries received in the daily record.
4. Delivering merchandise to the storeroom or kitchen for storage use.
5. Storing food.

GUIDELINES FOR EFFECTIVE RECEIVING

There are at least six sound receiving practices for conventional food service operations that help reduce the cost and time of handling and minimize the amount of spoiled or misplaced merchandise.

1. The receiver should always be ready to accept merchandise when it is delivered.
2. The receiver should always check the merchandise carefully. This means

checking each delivery for conformity to the quality, price, count, and weight specifications in the original purchase order, and for damage in shipment.

3. Normally, expensive foods—meats in particular—should receive more attention when delivered.

4. The different cuts of meat in a meat order should always be weighed separately, because of the considerable variation in price from one cut to another.

5. Since prolonged exposure to warm room temperatures can cause quality loss or spoilage, the receiver should check and store perishable items first. The quicker all merchandise is stored, the less chance it will become spoiled or be mislaid.

PURCHASE SPECIFICATIONS AND AVERAGE WEIGHT CHARTS

For the sake of efficiency, the receiver should have available a copy of the operation's detailed purchasing specifications. These specifications will help him or her to check quality and quantities more thoroughly, because they provide precise information on such things as the grades, weights, counts, and sizes of the standard units. The purchase specifications for fresh tomatoes, for example, might read: "Tomatoes, fresh, 30 pounds to a lug, $5 \times 5 \times 3$." Such specs could be quite a help when the tomatoes arrive. Charts showing the average weights or merchandise received also help prevent losses.

The receiver should have ready access to charts and purchase specifications. Proper use of these reference tools will

- Eliminate guesswork by the receiving personnel.
- Ensure conformity of the product to the standards of the operation.
- Give the manager a tool for controlling quality from the time the food is received until it is served.

The chart shown in Figure 6.2 indicates the kind of information that might be assembled for a receiver. Note that the information in the chart is determined by the products the operation purchases. Thus, you should expect to prepare such a chart for your operation on the basis of a review of the products you purchase. Local products may be delivered in one type of container, those from distant growing areas in another. Therefore, the chart should also reflect the conditions in effect with your suppliers.

RECEIVING RECORDS

A receiving record, maintained by the receiving clerk, records the date of delivery, unit, quantity, unit price, and total amount for each item received. (See Figure 6.3 for a sample receiving record.) Some operations furnish a copy of the

Apples, red delicious	41–47 lb per box	88 count
Bananas	40 lb cartons	—
Grapefruit, Florida	40 lb cartons	64 count
Grapes, Thompson seedless	Purchase by pound (record exact weight)	—
Oranges, navel	38 lb carton	125's 4 rows 5 × 5 110 Count
Pears, bartlett		
Strawberries	1½ lb per quart	8 quarts per flat
Artichoke, globe	18–24 lb	6 dozen
Asparagus	Purchase by pound (record exact weight)	—
Cabbage	50 lb bags, cello wrapped	25 packages
Celery	60–65 lb crates	—
Lettuce, iceberg	40 lb carton	24 count
Tomatoes	30–32 lb lugs	3 layers, 6 × 6 each layer
(Weight of crate 2 to 2½ lb.)		

FIGURE 6.2 Chart for receiver. Using this chart, a receiver can weigh produce instead of taking a physical count; this saves both the receiver's time and fragile produce.

day's orders in advance to the receiver; this form is then used as a receiving record on which items received are checked off against those ordered. This procedure makes it possible for the receiver to check the invoice against what was ordered for discrepancies as to item delivered, price, quality, and so on (see Figure 6.4).

THE PURCHASE INVOICE STAMP

In larger food services, an invoice stamp designed to suit the needs of the operation is used on all incoming invoices. See Figure 6.5 for (a sample stamp.) The receiver stamps the invoice, dates it, and signs or initials it on the line "Quantity O. K.," to indicate that the correct amount has been received. The invoice is then checked for price approval and sent on to Accounting for approval for final payment.

RETURNING UNSATISFACTORY MERCHANDISE

When the quantity of merchandise received is insufficient or the quality does not conform to the specifications, the receiver prepares a credit memorandum (see Figure 6.6) in duplicate and sends both copies to the office. (One copy is sent to the supplier.)

The receiver's step-by-step responsibilities in returning unsatisfactory merchandise include

Date:							
					Distribution		
Quantity	Unit	Vendor	Item and Description	Unit Price	Extension	Food Direct to Kitchen	Food Direct to Storeroom	Comments

FIGURE 6.3 Example of a receiving record. The receiver, after properly receiving goods, records each item delivered.

Date: _____

Quantity Ordered	Unit	Vendor and Item	Unit Price	Extension	Received	Comments
1	25# bag	Rice - Rex Foods	9.48	9.48	✓	
1 cs.	24/24 oz	Jello, Asst. - Rex	20.40	20.40	✓	
4 ea	5# cans	Tuna - "	6.25	25.00	—	Back Ordered
1 case	case	Mayonnaise "	18.10	18.10	✓	
2	25# bag	Flour - "	6.50	13.00	✓	
2 cases	6 cans	Veg Juice cock - Skyway	3.98	(7.92)	—	one only incorrect charge
4 cases	6 cans	Tomato juice - Skyway	3.50	14.00	✓	
10	1/2 gal.	whole milk - Meadowdale	.85	8.50	✓	
5	1/2 gal	Skim milk	.82	4.10	✓	
300	1/2 pts	2% milk	.17	51.00	✓	

FIGURE 6.4 As goods are delivered, the receiver checks them against the order sent from the purchaser. The receiver checks quantity, quality and unit price.

- Making out a credit memorandum.
- Returning the merchandise immediately.
- Noting on the invoice the reasons for returning the merchandise.
- Notifying the food production manager or food service manager, so that the menu may be changed if necessary.

All correspondence concerning adjustments by the supplier should be handled by the person responsible for purchasing food.

A SUMMARY OF RECEIVING IN LARGE OPERATIONS

Management can ensure maximum control over one of its most valuable assets—the food supply—by maintaining good receiving procedures. These procedures require the following.

Date Rec'd ____________

Quantity O.K. ____________

Prices O.K. ____________

Extensions O.K. ____________

Approved by ____________

FIGURE 6.5 Receiver's stamp.

- Adequate equipment and a convenient place for unloading and checking deliveries.
- The assignment of receiving responsibilities to a competent person.
- Posting specifications and average weight charts for easy reference.
- Supervisory verification of quality whenever the receiver is in doubt about or not qualified to make technical distinctions in grade.

The receiving function involves more than simply a signature on the vendor's invoice: It includes checking all incoming merchandise for quality, quantity,

REQUEST FOR CREDIT MEMO.

Nº 248

TO ____________

____________ DATE ____________

GENTLEMEN:

Please send us Credit Memo for the following:

YOUR INVOICE NO

CLEVELAND HOTEL CO.

BY ____________

FIGURE 6.6 Request for credit memo.

price, count, and weight, as well as for spoilage, damage, or irregularities in appearance. It also involves maintaining tight control over the movement of goods into and out of the delivery area.

RECEIVING CONTROL IN SMALLER OPERATIONS

A review of food service consulting reports prepared over a series of several years by a consulting firm for which one of the authors once worked revealed a startling fact: Every operation that was in trouble had poor (or no!) receiving practices. Although good receiving practices alone will not guarantee a successful operation, poor receiving practices seem linked with poor overall results in food service.

This point is especially applicable to smaller operations, which often argue that they "cannot afford a full-time receiver." This statement may be true, but it does not necessarily follow that because you cannot afford a full time receiver your operation should give up on receiving entirely. The truth is that in many smaller operations, delivery truck drivers simply unload the product and get anyone they can to sign for it. One day it may be the cook, another day the dishwasher. This kind of carelessness is expensive, inexcusable, and unnecessary.

Poor receiving is an outright encouragement to cheating by suppliers. A truck driver may shortweight your operation and sell the "extra" to a friend, or bring it home. Similarly, when one operation checks product and another does not, the good box of lettuce likely will be left with the careful receiver ("to avoid a big hassle," the truck driver will tell you) and the low-quality lettuce dumped at the operation that does not take the trouble to receive it properly. Either in lost product or low-quality product, poor receiving is costly—and since poor receiving can be avoided, it is inexcusable.

Receiving in the smaller operation requires fundamentally the same things as in the larger operation: a place to receive, receiver's tools (including *accurate* scales), a hand truck or other materials-handling equipment (carts, skids, rollers) appropriate to physical layout, qualified personnel, and a predetermined routine against which performance can be monitored.

For small operators, the first step in planning for receiving is to recognize that responsibility for *determining quantity* and *determining quality* can and perhaps should be split. If the chef is assigned the receiving responsibility, a good part of the time he or she will be too busy to do it—and fairly soon, anybody who is handy will be signing invoices.

Counting and weighing can be done by a dishwasher or potwasher. Normal practice where such an employee is responsible for *receiving routine* is to offer premium pay over the rate a dishwasher or potwasher might receive and to use that premium to secure a more intelligent person. The key idea here is to assign the receiver's duties to a position that is not critical to the operation on a minute-to-minute basis. The selected person is then trained: to read invoices; to read scales accurately; to count carefully, to handle frozen products, fresh produce, dairy products, and so on properly; and to report discrepancies to management promptly.

Under these circumstances, quality judgments usually are left to some member of management. The food production manager may not be around to inspect product when it is received, but he or she *can* check the product after it has arrived and, if it is unsatisfactory, contact the supplier to return it or request a credit, or to take some other action. (It might be useful for you to review the concepts related to "keeping them honest" found in Chapter 5.)

Efficient receiving in the smaller operation does require careful planning, organization, supervision, and commitment. But as the authors' own experience in small- and medium-sized operations makes clear, good receiving practices can be achieved (see Figure 6.7).

THE LOGISTIC FUNCTION IN FAST FOODS

In Chapter 4, we discussed briefly how purchasing becomes part of a complex logistic function in large multi-unit chains. Figure 6.8 summarizes logistic function for one company.

As the figure suggests, the Restaurant Company operates at several levels. The Company Headquarters develops highly detailed specifications for products and

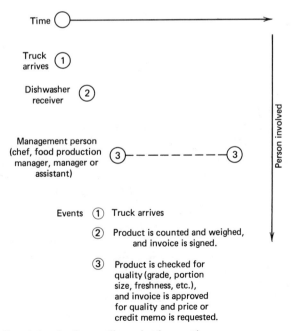

FIGURE 6.7 Receiving in the medium-sized operation.

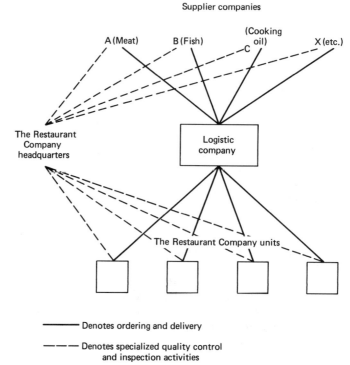

FIGURE 6.8 The logistic function in a multi-unit company.

selects supplier companies to prepare them. The products that these companies (A, B, C, X, etc.) make are inspected on site at the Supplier Company's plant. The Supplier Companies ship product to a Logistic Company, which is in the business of warehousing *all* the products the Restaurant Company uses. Once again, storage criteria such as humidity, temperature, cleanliness, and product handling techniques are monitored by the Restaurant Company at the Logistic Company's central warehouses.

When a Restaurant Company unit wishes to place an order, it does so with the Logistic Company, and that company, which has trucks serving many clients in a territory, ships to the Restaurant Company unit. Because the small shipment to the unit is combined with other shipments, the Restaurant Company saves considerably on delivery costs. The performance of the Restaurant Company unit is analyzed in great detail through both computerized daily reports and frequent visits from field staff. Thus, the unit is subject to tight control and is much less independent than the conventional restaurant. This is why we speak of *restaurant systems:* systems in which the unit is very close, in operating terms, to the regional and central office supervisory staff. Receiving at the Restaurant Company *unit* is very simple. The number of pieces (boxes, bags, crates, etc.) received is checked, usually by the manager or an assistant, against the number of pieces called for on a shipping ticket—and that's it.

A moment's reflection will reveal why the receiving practices outlined here seem so much simpler than what we normally would expect but are still quite in order. Companywide, first of all, a great deal is being done to establish quality standards, and product is monitored from manufacturer to the unit door by expert inspection. Rather than continuous inspection of all products all the time, which would be prohibitively expensive, a statistical sampling technique probably is used to determine the number of expert observations required at each stage. So a very intensive quality control program based on careful specs and continuous sampling *is* at work. Secondly, the unit is very small and relies for its profitability on high productivity of all its employees. Given the companywide quality control program, unit personnel are expected to concentrate on production and service. In these small units, there is virtually no support staff (such as receivers). Moreover, a very few products make up most of each shipment, and those products are highly standardized. Systemwide monitoring makes highly simplified receiving routines acceptable at the unit level in most multi-unit companies.

FOOD SERVICE STORAGE

Our discussion of storage will focus on large-scale operations, but we also will comment on procedures for smaller operations. At the end of the discussion, we will comment specifically on storage in fast food operations.

In the overall operation of food service, storage forms an important link between receiving and production. The quality of the storage system, therefore, directly affects the quality of the product used in food preparation. And storage is vital for another reason: It represents one aspect of the operation where management can exert effective control without appreciably increasing time and personnel costs. In other words, good storage management, in the form of effective controls on **1.** shrinkage, **2.** spoilage, and **3.** pilferage, can help keep down food service costs.

Shrinkage
Loss from shrinkage occurs with meats and produce. As meat is stored, it continually loses weight through drying and—even when cello-wrapped—drip loss. The dry air in most restaurant refrigerators increases this moisture loss. With produce, this shrinkage, in the form of wilting, is even more visible.

Spoilage
Shelf life is the amount of time you can reasonably expect the product to maintain its quality if proper storage procedures are followed. The growth of spoilage microorganisms can be controlled by processing (canning, drying, salting, freezing, etc.), but for unprocessed foods, we must rely upon temperature controls and good sanitation. Lowering the temperature to 40°F (5°C), which represents

normal refrigeration, slows down growth of most spoilage microorganisms. Unnecessary handling increases contamination and thus decreases shelf life, as do unsanitary surroundings.

Pilferage

Most employees do not consider petty pilferage to be wrong, especially when management does not provide clear and explicit policies on pilferage. When employees are allowed free access to storerooms and can come and go through the receiving door, it is easy to take a few steaks, some hamburgers, a can of olives, or other goods home. Another form of pilferage is employee "snacking."

STORAGE CONTROLS

The type and size of the operation, the menu, the number of meals served, the frequency of deliveries, and management policy regarding the size of inventories and monetary investments are major factors in determining the size, combination, and layout of refrigerated storage facilities needed.

Regardless of the type of storage available, the location, layout, equipment, and internal arrangement of facilities all affect the efficiency of the storage operation and the extent to which management can exert its operational controls.

Location. The ideal location for storage facilities is near the receiving area and adjacent to the preparation area.

Layout. Three factors are instrumental in determining the effective layout of storage facilities: **1.** the frequency of use of the various food items, **2.** the space requirements for the storage facilities, and **3.** the characteristics of the items to be stored.

Many operations are not large enough to justify several walk-in refrigerators. In such operations, higher product turnover, careful selection or market form (frozen fish where separate iced storage cannot be provided), and storage of products in airtight packaging materials all can be combined to achieve the maintenance of product quality during storage. Nonfood stores and particularly detergents and cleaning supplies, should be placed in a separate area, away from food supplies.

A final consideration is storage security. High-cost products especially subject to pilferage are often stored in a locked "cage" in the storeroom, in a remote, limited-access storage area, or in a cabinet in the manager's office.

Storing Semiperishable Foods—The Storeroom

Although as a rule semiperishables do not require refrigeration, they do need to be protected from dampness, insects, rodents, and excessive heat. A good storeroom is one that provides optimum internal conditions, is conveniently located, is large enough to handle the anticipated volume of supplies, and is adequately equipped. This type of storeroom is essential for the preservation of groceries and foods not requiring refrigeration.

To provide optimum storage conditions for semiperishable items, the temperature, humidity, and ventilation within the storeroom must be controlled. Although a temperature of 50°F is considered ideal, temperatures up to 70°F are acceptable.

When storage space is available near preparation and service areas, the items used most frequently should be stored nearest the place where they will be used. In many operations, a "working storeroom" is located in or just off the kitchen and bulk storage is located elsewhere. The working storeroom (and working refrigerators) are stocked daily, and open access to them is permitted to all cooks, or to certain designated cooks. The remote storeroom, is usually much less accessible.

The turnover and frequency of deliveries help determine the size and type of storage areas required. If food is received and used daily, for example, a limited amount of space may be adequate. If deliveries are made only weekly or biweekly, however, more storage space will be needed.

Equipment. Generally speaking, the kinds and volumes of foods to be handled and the storage space available will determine the equipment you should acquire. For handling foods, portable equipment—such as hand trucks, semilive skids, or platforms with dollies—is essential.

Internal arrangement. As a general rule, products are stored in "inventory order": that is, in the order in which they appear on the form used to take inventory. This often means that products are stored, by food group, in alphabetical order.

Another factor to consider is the type of food. Ideally, you should have separate walk-ins for meat, fish, dairy products, and produce. Each product group requires a specific temperature for extended shelf life, and transfer of odor is another problem in mixed-storage refrigerators (see Table 6.1).

Humidity is an important but often overlooked factor affecting the quality of foods in the storeroom. For most products, a relative humidity of from 50% to 60% is considered satisfactory. At no time should humidity exceed 70%. As an aid to temperature and humidity control, hot water and steam pipes should be well insulated. Good ventilation, created by natural or mechanical means, can provide clean, fresh air at the required temperature and humidity.

The following recommendations will help you to establish storeroom procedures.

- Store frequently used items where they can be reached easily.

- Stock together foods of the same kind.

- Use the first-in, first-out method. Always move the older stock to the front of the shelves and put the new stock in back.

TABLE 6.1 FOODS THAT GIVE OFF AND ABSORB ODORS[a]

Food	Gives Off Odors	Absorbs Odors
Apples fresh	Yes	Yes
Butter	No	Yes
Cabbage	Yes	No
Eggs, fresh shell	No	Yes
Milk	No	Yes
Onions	Yes	No
Peaches, fresh	Yes	No
Potatoes	Yes	No
Turnips	Yes	No

[a] Robert F. Lukowski, Charles E. Eschbach, and Albert L. Wrisley, Jr., *Using Storage in Food Service Establishments,* Food Management Program Leaflet 4(Amherst, Mass.: Cooperative Extension Service, College of Agriculture, University of Massachusetts, 1968), p. 20.

- Cross-stack such items as potatoes and flour in alternating patterns on skids or racks.
- Store food away from the wall and off the floor. Allow air circulation around product.
- Stack food as high as ease of handling and safety permit.
- Store heavier items close to the floor and lighter items on higher shelves.
- Provide separate storage rooms for nonfood items that give off fumes, such as waxes, soaps, and paint.
- Do not hang wearing apparel in the storeroom.

Storing Perishable Foods—Refrigerated Storage

Two basic types of refrigerated storage are used in food service establishments, depending on the nature of the foods being stored and the temperature range desired: **1.** *normal refrigeration,* in which temperatures from 35° to 40°F (5°C) are maintained; and **2.** *frozen refrigeration,* in which the temperature is maintained at 0° F (−20°C) or lower. These conditions can be provided by both walk-in and reach-in storage boxes.

Normal Refrigeration. As with storeroom facilities, both temperature and humidity should be monitored carefully to provide optimum shelf life for perishable foods. The settings used for specialty refrigerators are listed below.

Normal refrigerator temperature	35 to 40°F	(2 to 5°C)
Produce refrigerator	32 to 35°F	(0 to 2°C)
Mixed meat refrigerator (meat, poultry, fish)	33 to 34°F	(1°C)
Dairy products and eggs	32°F	(0°C)
Poultry	33 to 36°F	(1 to 2°C)
Fish	30 to 34°F	(−1 to +1°C)

Frozen Food Storage. Frozen food storage is energy consuming, particularly in service or cooking areas where reach-in boxes are opened frequently. The walk-in freezer often is located within the walk-in refrigerator, so that cold air lost is not wasted. Most freezers are set at 0°F (−20°C).

Frozen food should be stored (in its original carton) *immediately* after delivery, as fluctuations in temperature can stimulate the growth of sharp ice crystals and damage the product. As with dry and normal refrigerated storage, free air circulation should be allowed around products.

Extending Shelf Life with Good Sanitation Practices

The cleaning of storerooms and refrigerators represents one aspect of a program to extend the shelf life of food. Spoilage bacteria cling to particles of food and multiply on shelving, from which they can be transferred to foods. Fungi frequently are airborne, and they can contaminate products long after a moldy product has been removed. Therefore, sanitation in the storeroom areas should be specified and scheduled. observance of the following rules will help you devise an adequate cleaning schedule.

- Wash refrigerator weekly.
- Place thawing meats on racks above pans.
- Remove spoiled food immediately.
- Sweep storeroom floors daily. Mop the floors with disinfectant. Wash walls, storage shelves, and storeroom equipment on a regular basis.
- Hire professional services for pest control.
- Schedule freezer defrosting when the quantity of food in storage is at its lowest level.
- Periodically call in a competent refrigeration mechanic to check the compressors, condensers, and motors of both refrigerators and freezers.
- Inspect storeroom areas regularly.

Security and Food Storage

Large losses of food through pilferage can be deduced from an increase in food cost or an unusual rise in inventory. However, petty pilferage—the kind employees do not consider as pilferage—is difficult to detect, and storeroom controls must be used to keep it to a minimum.

The physical arrangement and the management of the storage areas can reduce pilferage greatly. In most cases, maximum security storage areas should be identified as such and be equipped with special locks that limit access to a few people. Access to the receiving door should be strictly limited. In most operations, no food should be allowed to go out the back door.

Snacking can be minimized by a management policy of no eating in the kitchen, coupled with scheduled coffee breaks and fair meal policies. A widespread industry approach to employee dining is to allow employees to eat designated foods at a reduced rate and at a specified time—usually just before the meal rush and preferably not in the kitchen.

STORAGE IN FAST FOODS

Whereas larger operations have complex storage facilities, most fast food operators have only limited storage facilities at the unit. Usually, these facilities consist of reach-in refrigerators, a storeroom, and, where frozen food is used, a small walk-in freezer. The simplicity of fast food storage, however, does not mean that these operations ignore good storage design principles. To the contrary, fast food storage is based on two assumptions: narrow product line and high turnover.

It is axiomatic that the number of products for sale to the guest in fast food restaurants is limited, and like products require less variety in temperature and other storage features. Moreover, fast food operations usually are located in areas where reasonably frequent delivery can be expected. Accordingly, the designers can count on a relatively high turnover of product to make large storage space unnecessary.

Remember, too, that whereas storage is a small and relatively simple problem at the unit level, at the system or companywide level, storage can be both extensive and complex, involving either a separate logistics company to handle storage (and related logistics functions discussed earlier) or the large and specialized warehousing that accompanies a company-owned centralized distribution center or commissary.

KEY WORDS AND CONCEPTS

Receiving area	Shrinkage
Receiving equipment	Spoilage
Receiver	Pilferage
Invoice	Storage controls
Receiving methods	Proper facilities
Invoice receiving	Location
Blind check receiving	Layout
Attributes and responsibilities of the receiving clerk	Equipment
	Internal arrangement
Six sound receiving practices	Security
Purchase specs	Storeroom
Average weight charts	Temperature
Receiving records	Humidity
Purchase invoice stamp	Ventilation
Return of merchandise	Refrigerated storage
Credit memorandum	Frozen food storage
Control in smaller operations	Sanitation practices
Logistics function in fast foods	Fast food storage
Storage	

DISCUSSION QUESTIONS

1. You are planning to remodel the receiving area of a large restaurant that has three dining rooms, all of which are serviced from a central kitchen. The existing storeroom is going to be moved to the basement so that one of the dining rooms on the main floor can be enlarged. The basement area had housed a small barber shop, which went out of business. There are two staircase entrances to the new storeoom (ex-barbershop)—one leading directly from the outside and the other leading from a hallway that has access to the kitchen. Discuss the new control problems you will have and how you could solve them. What equipment will you include in your plan? What procedures will you set up for receiving control?

2. A restaurant manager with a chain of hotels has a habit of poking through the garbage every once in a while. Has he lost his marbles? Discuss the merits of his action and how it might help control costs.

3. The chef in a hotel kitchen claims that the amount of food he orders consistently is short. The receiver claims to have checked incoming goods carefully. The general manager is considering switching from invoice receiving to blind check receiving. Would this settle the conflict between chef and receiver? Discuss the merits and disadvantages of this receiving method. Can you think of any other ways to solve the problem?

4. Set up receiving controls for hamburger patties purchased by a large, free-standing restaurant. Discuss the differences in receiving between that restaurant and a fast food operation.

FORECASTING: THE HEART OF PLANNING AND CONTROL

7

Variables in Food Service Forecasting

Some Forecasting Situations

Computerized Forecasting

Fast Food Restaurants

Using Sales Forecasts in Day-to-Day Operations

Using Sales Forecasting in Long-Range Planning

Summary

THE PURPOSE OF THIS CHAPTER

Just what a forecast *is,* varies. A manager who says, "This is a slow season, but the rush starts next week," has made a forecast—although clearly not a very precise one. A supervisor in a fast food restaurant who determines that peak volume during lunch hour will be at 12:10 P.M. and that at that time the operation will have to have, in the bin and ready to serve, 12 large hamburgers, eight cheeseburgers, three fish sandwiches, and so forth, has made a precise but highly specialized forecast.

In this chapter, we will look at the variables that affect food service forecasts. To illustrate how those variables are used in practice, we will look at several specialized kinds of forecasting problems. Finally, we will focus on how managers use forecasting in day-to-day operational planning and in long-range planning.

THIS CHAPTER SHOULD HELP YOU

1. Identify the major variables in food service forecasting.

2. Learn how those variables relate to particular operations.

3. Develop from daily sales data a forecast that can be used to estimate future sales.

4. Become familiar with current computer applications to forecasting in institutional food service.

5. Understand how data from point of sales systems can be used in forecasting.

6. Relate sales reports to production planning.

7. Become familiar with the needs of complex multi-unit systems for longer-range systemwide forecasting.

VARIABLES IN FOOD SERVICE FORECASTING

Basically, a variable is anything that changes. In forecasting, however, we concentrate on identifying and studying those factors that help to predict the likely amount of change in some major variable in the operation, such as food service *sales.* An easy way to summarize these "predicting factors" is under the headings of *time, weather,* and *special conditions.*

TIME

Sales volume varies with time: that is, there are more sales at some times and fewer at others. For instance, the food service department of a hotel likely will be busiest on Tuesdays, Wednesdays, and Thursdays. Sundays, on the other hand, often are the slowest days. The time variable here is the *day of the week*.

Another important time variable is the *hour of the day*. If a hotel coffee shop is open from 6:00 A.M. until 10:00 P.M., the period from 6:00 A.M. to 7:00 A.M. probably would be very slow, as would the periods 9:30 A.M. to 11:30 A.M., 1:30 P.M. to 5:30 P.M., and 8:30 P.M. to 10:00 P.M. until closing. Peaks, of course, occur at the major meal hours: 7:30 A.M. to 9:00 A.M., noon to just after 1:00 P.M. and 6:00 P.M. to 7:30 P.M.

Also, the *season of the year* is almost always an important time variable. The peak seasons for summer and winter resorts are identified by certain months of the year—and certain weeks within those months are busier than others. Thus, operators speak of the "high season" as a part of the season, as well as of off-season months.

Predictions of peak-volume time periods, whether in terms of months or of 10-minute segments, generally are made on the basis of historical records. Daily reports such as that shown in Figure 7.1 provide data that can be summarized for each day of the week. Monthly sales can be compiled from monthly income statements, or weekly sales can be compiled from daily reports. At the other end of the frequency range, hourly register readings such as that shown in Figure 7.2 give a good idea of when peak sales occur during the day.

WEATHER

Notice that the daily report shown in Figure 7.1 calls for the weather on the day being reported. Weather is the second major variable in forecasting. Of course, the seasonal or time dimension cited above often implies something about weather, but such implications are too general. More specific short-term effects of weather on sales include a week with thawing temperatures in a ski resort and a cold spell in July in a summer resort.

What weather means, however, depends to some degree on *where* the operation is and what kind of operation it is. For restaurants in large office buildings, snow or rain outside means good business, because the occupants of the building will not want to go outside. On the other hand, a restaurant down the street, that relies on patrons coming out of nearby buildings for lunch is likely to be badly affected by the same rain or snow. A very hot day may mean good business for an ice cream specialty shop but poor business for an operation specializing in roast beef sandwiches. A beautiful day means better business for restaurants that rely on motorists from a nearby city, whereas a miserable weekend may mean good business for suburban restaurants nearer to people's homes.

VARIABLES IN FOOD SERVICE FORECASTING

RESTAURANT DAILY REPORT

Day _Thursday_   Date _April 4, 1983_
Weather _45°F, Cloudy, Showers_   Unusual Events _R.V. Ross Sales Convention_

SUMMARY OF SALES

	Customers Served	Food Sales	Beverage Sales	Total Today	TOTALS TO DATE This Month	Last Month	This Month Last Year
Dining Room							
Breakfast	68	176.12		176.12	890.35	784.80	663.40
Lunch	215	696.60	68.00	764.60	4,195.00	4,002.65	3,986.23
Dinner	259	1326.08	158.00	1484.08	6,284.28	5,874.25	5,129.00
Total	542	2198.80	226.00	2424.80	11,369.63	10,671.70	9,778.63
Lounge	184		708.40	708.40	2,950.40	2,860.00	2,540.00
Banquet Room	77	962.50	385.00	1347.50	3,250.00	1,120.50	1,250.00
Total	803	3161.30	1319.40	4480.70	17,570.03	14,652.20	13,568.63

CASH SUMMARY

Beginning Balance	12,674	05
Cash Collections	509	03
Other		
Total	13,183	08
Cash Disbursed		
Ending Balance	13,183	08

GUEST STATISTICS

	Check Avg. Today	Check Avg. Last Year
Dining Room		
Breakfast	2.59	2.48
Lunch	3.24	3.21
Dinner	5.12	4.97
Lounge	3.85	3.77
Banquet Room	12.50	9.80

PAYROLL STATISTICS

Meal Period	No. Wait Staff	Avg. Sale/ Wait Staff	Customers Serv/Wait Staff
Dining Room			
Breakfast	3	58.66	23
Lunch	5	152.92	43
Dinner	8	185.51	32
Lounge	4	177.00	46
Banquet Room	4	331.87	19

For General Office:	Date Received:	Approved By:

FIGURE 7.1 Daily report for a restaurant.

The effect of the weather on sales depends on where the restaurant is, who its customers, are and how the customers' preferences are affected by weather. The questions are the important point: By gathering information, you can study business trends as they vary with the weather and thus avoid unnecessary overscheduling of employees and overpreparation of food.

156 FORECASTING: THE HEART OF PLANNING AND CONTROL

```
                                                    Date: _____
STEP 1: Record sales by time of day and daily totals for one week.
                                    Time of Day
              Daily
              Sales    Until    9:00–    11:00–    2:00–    5:00–    After
Day of Week   Totals   9:00A.M. 11:00A.M. 2:00P.M. 5:00P.M. 9:00P.M. 9:00P.M.

Monday        $____    ____     ____     ____     ____     ____     ____
Tuesday       $____    ____     ____     ____     ____     ____     ____
Wednesday     $____    ____     ____     ____     ____     ____     ____
Thursday      $____    ____     ____     ____     ____     ____     ____
Friday        $____    ____     ____     ____     ____     ____     ____
Saturday      $____    ____     ____     ____     ____     ____     ____
Sunday        $____    ____     ____     ____     ____     ____     ____
Weekly Total  $____    ____     ____     ____     ____     ____     ____
```

STEP 2: Add to total for each time period during entire week. Calculate percentage of weekly sales for each time period and percent of weekly sales for each day (for each, weekly total equals 100%).

```
     Percent of Weekly Sales              Percent of sales for the
     for Each Day of the Week             Week, by Time of the Day

Monday        ____%                  Until 9:00 A.M.      ____%
Tuesday       ____                   9:00 to 11:00 A.M.   ____
Wednesday     ____                   11:00 to 2:00 P.M.   ____
Thursday      ____                   2:00 to 5:00 P.M.    ____
Friday        ____                   5:00 to 9:00 P.M.    ____
Saturday      ____                   After 9:00 P.M.      ____
Sunday        ____
Total         100% (Weekly Total)                         100%
```

Additional comments: _____

FIGURE 7.2 Hourly register reading report.

SPECIAL CONDITIONS

Of the wide variety of special conditions, we will limit our discussion to *economic climate, local events,* and *established indicators.*

The Economic Climate

If your operation is located in a large manufacturing center and all the plants are hiring, business is likely to be good. Similarly, if the country's economy is booming, food service sales are likely to be better than average in all operations.

Surprisingly, if the economy softens, food service sales in the market as a whole may stay the same or decline only a little; specific restaurants may lose business, while others will stay even or perhaps gain a bit. This phenomenon reflects the fact that eating out often is a part of a person's life-style that can be changed only with great difficulty: for people who work away from home, it is inconvenient (and often grubby!) to carry lunch to work. In more difficult times, however the consumer may "trade down": that is, patronize less expensive restaurants. For this reason, some restaurants at the upper end of the popular price scale suffer during recessions. The luxury operation, on the other hand, may not be affected by a recession—at least, not until the recession gets deep enough to bring on a cut in expense accounts.

Clearly, judgments about the likely effect of local, regional, or national economic trends are difficult to make—but they must be made. They require a good grasp of who your customers are and of their needs and preferences. The subject is important enough to warrant a concerted effort to keep abreast of the business and economic news of the day.

Local Events

A large convention in your city can mean very high volume, even in a period you normally would expect to be slow. The effect of holidays, however, is less clear. Some restaurants have the kind of menu that makes holidays—even Thanksgiving and Christmas—extraordinarily good days. One such operator, finding that Easter Sunday and Mother's Day were his slowest days, promoted his restaurant as a place to take the whole family, or mother, on those holidays—which now are his best days. On the other hand, a restaurant that is more "just a place to eat" than a place to celebrate may suffer from low volume on a holiday. This is particularly true of restaurants not located on the main highways and thoroughfares, on which a large number of people travel during holidays.

Established Indicators

Many operators have specialized indicators, such as reservations or a hotel house count, on which to base forecasts. A restaurant that suggests or requires *reservations* may be able to forecast business very accurately. In the hotel business, the occupancy (number of rooms occupied) and house count (number of guests in the hotel) normally will permit a precise forecast of breakfast business, and anticipated occupancy will permit a good forecast of dinner volume. As we will see shortly, an even more accurate forecast based on measures similar to occupancy and house count is possible in institutional food services.

SOME FORECASTING SITUATIONS

To this point, we have discussed the major variables on which a sales forecast is prepared. Now, a review of forecasting in particular kinds of operations will provide insight into how forecasting actually is done. At the same time, it will widen our discussion of how the three main variables just reviewed can be used in developing forecasts.

HOTEL FOOD SERVICE: A PREDICTABLE CASE

A hotel's sales volume usually can be predicted fairly reliably. For a hotel catering principally to out-of-town guests traveling on business, for instance, Friday through Sunday is the slowest period. Business improves on Monday night and the hotel likely will be full on Tuesday and Wednesday nights, and very nearly full on Thursday night. The typical hotel week cycle is depicted in Figure 7.3. Not surprisingly, as we noted previously, a hotel's food service business is closely related to the number of guests in the house.

Most hotels can predict breakfast volume almost completely from the house count. The number of guests who do not eat breakfast or who eat breakfast out usually is offset by the number of people who join hotel guests for breakfast or who visit the hotel for breakfast. Lunch and dinner volumes, however, cannot be forecast quite so straightforwardly.

Hotel guests are in town to visit something other than the hotel, and that "something" is likely to take them out of the hotel (unless the goal is a convention and the hotel in question is the headquarters hotel). Because they usually are away from the hotel during the day, hotel guests often are not the principal source of luncheon guests—but that certainly does not mean that hotels should or do suffer from poor luncheon volume. Because most hotels are located near some major activity, are well served by the local transportation system, and have substantial parking available, they often are very popular luncheon spots. But forecasts of hotel luncheon sales have more in common with forecasts for freestanding restaurants (see below) than with those for hotel food service sales at either breakfast or dinner.

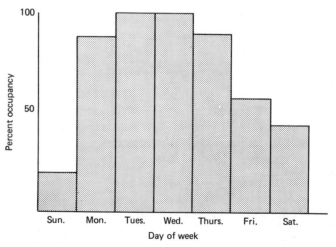

FIGURE 7.3 Typical weekly business cycle for a successful hotel.

Dinner food sales in a hotel cannot be forecast as reliably as breakfast sales can, but they are much more dependent than luncheons on the hotel's occupancy level. For breakfast, convenience of the hotel's dining room and the fact that the meal is fairly standard and simple lead most guests to make the simpler choice and eat in. For luncheon, most guests will eat wherever the business of the day takes them. For dinner, the hotel is once again the most convenient place—but the dinner decision is more complicated. Guests commonly are free of any duties at the dinner hour and so have the time to seek out a restaurant that suits their preferences. Many guests are looking for a way to pass the time when they choose where to eat dinner. Today's restaurant industry, moreover, offers guests the widest possible choice at dinner, ranging from Polynesian to Yankee seafood to Parisian cuisine.

Because the guest's time is freer and the choice wider, many hotel operators feel they can expect, on average, to attract a guest to one evening meal over a three-day stay. Hotels are not content with this kind of average, however; most try to do better, and many succeed. This effort undoubtedly is reflected in the many different kinds of restaurants offered by larger hotels.

From a forecasting standpoint, the dining volume of a hotel presents somewhat less of a problem than that of a freestanding restaurant. A full house almost certainly means a good evening's business, whereas very low occupancy means, at best, a somewhat slower night. The hotel's location, accessibility via mass transportation and highway systems, and ample parking still help to bring in guests from outside the house at dinner as well as at lunch.

Capacity Constraints

Obviously, only so many people can fit into a dining room at any one time, so the first constraint on a forecast is the number of chairs in the room. Since not every chair will be occupied—a single guest takes only one of the two chairs at a table for two, a party of three leaves one chair vacant at a four-top—the number of meals sold at a single seating of a dining room should amount to perhaps 80% of the number of chairs available.

On the other hand, most meal periods extend over several hours. Luncheon guests may turn up at 1:30 P.M. or even later. On a very busy day, or in very popular retaurants, waiting lines may permit a chair to be filled almost immediately after it becomes vacant. In a conventional full-service restaurant, as opposed to a rapid-service operation such as a coffee shop, a very fast chair turn is required to achieve a complete turn in one hour, and so a "turn" of 2.0 would not be likely. A chair turn reflects the average use or occupancy of the seating capacity of a dining area. If, for instance, 200 guests are served during a meal period in a dining room with 100 chairs, chair turn of 2.0 would be achieved. (The "chair turn" concept is not used widely in fast food forecasting).

Figure 7.4 presents a summary of guest count forecasts for a hotel feasibility study.

160 FORECASTING: THE HEART OF PLANNING AND CONTROL

ESTIMATE OF A TYPICAL WEEKDAY FOOD AND BEVERAGE[a]/VOLUME

	Fast Service				Medium-Priced				Supper Club			
		Average				Average				Average		
	Chairs	Check	Turns	Revenue	Chairs	Check	Turns	Revenue	Chairs	Check	Turns	Revenue
Food												
Breakfast	96[b]	$2.10	3.0	$ 605	300	$3.85	2.0	$2310	200	$ 4.50	0.5	$ 425
	104	$2.15	3.0	$ 670								
Lunch	96[b]	$3.25	2.5	$ 780	300	$5.50	2.0	$4125	200	$ 8.50	1.2	$2280
	104	$3.40	2.5	$ 885								
Dinner	96[b]	$4.50	1.0	$ 432	300	$8.75	1.0	$2625	200	$18.50	1.0	$3700
	104	$5.00	1.0	$ 520								
		Food volume		$3892				$9060				$6405
Beverage												
Lunch					300	$1.10	2.0	$ 660	200	$ 2.25	1.2	$ 270
Dinner					300	$1.85	1.0	$ 470	200	$12.00	1.0	$2400
						Total beverage volume		$1130		Total beverage volume		$2670

[a] In restaurants only.
[b] Counter chairs.

ESTIMATE OF A TYPICAL WEEKDAY BAR VOLUME

	Unique Room				Cocktail Lounge				Supper Club-Lounge			
		Average				Average				Average		
Meal Period	Chairs	Check	Turns	Revenue	Chairs	Check	Turns	Revenue	Chairs	Check	Turns	Revenue
Lunch	200	$3.25	1.0	$ 650	100	$3.25	1.0	$ 325	150	$3.25	0.3	$ 135
Dinner	200	$6.00	2.5	$3000	100	$5.50	2.0	$1100	150	$7.85	2.5	$2945
	Total beverage volume			$3650	Total beverage volume			$1425	Total beverage volume			$3080

FIGURE 7.4 Summary of guest count forecasts from a feasibility study.

Banquets
Another forecasting problem faced by hotels is presented by the banquet department. This problem can be solved to a significant degree by requiring that the group making the reservation guarantee a certain number of attendees. Commonly, 90% of the *expected* attendance must be guaranteed. Most banquet departments, however, anticipate the possibility of overattendance and stand ready to serve 5% more guests than forecast—or perhaps 10%, with a relatively small party.

THE FREESTANDING RESTAURANT

A restaurant with no organizational relationship to its location is said to be freestanding. Thus, a restaurant that happens to be located in an office building but is completely independent of any connection (except for the hallway) with that building is considered to be as freestanding as a restaurant that occupies its own building.

"Freestanding" means that the restaurant is on its own. As we have seen, a restaurant in a hotel can depend on the hotel's occupancy for sales. Similarly, a restaurant run by a department store can count on good volume when a big sale is on. The freestanding restaurant, too, is dependent on its environment for its sales, but the relationship is less specific and clear.

Forecasting for freestanding restaurants generally is based on historical records. The most common practice is to record sales daily, noting the number of guests served at each meal and also the amounts of each item sold. The forecaster concentrates on the three factors identified at the beginning of the chapter: time, weather, and special conditions. The process of forecasting begins with a review of last year's business. How does this *time of year* affect the business? Or more simply, how did it do on this day last year?

The Julian calendar in use today is arranged so that any one day of the month (say, the 10th) will fall on the succeeding day of the week in succeeding years. As a result, Tuesday the 10th of a certain month in 1981 has to be compared with either Tuesday the 9th of 1980 or Wednesday the 10th of 1982. Some operators have adopted a 13-month calendar of 28-day "months," in which day 10 of the first period (i.e., the first 28-day "month") always falls on the same day of the week. A calendar for such an operation is illustrated in Figure 7.5.

The next factor to be examined is weather. Weather forecasting is still a chancy business, but such judgments must be made. Will it rain tomorrow? Is the last half of June going to be as warm as the first half? Some restaurant operators go so far as to contract with private weather forecasting firms to get specific forecasts for their immediate area. Whatever the weather expected, it is necessary to estimate the effect of the weather on business. Any of the following lines of thinking would be appropriate.

- Rain is forecast, so everybody will stay in the building. It did not rain on this

162 FORECASTING: THE HEART OF PLANNING AND CONTROL

```
FOUR WEEK              BEAVER FOODS LTD.,           JULY 4, 1982
PERIOD                 1925 DUNDAS ST.,                TO
ACCOUNTING             LONDON ONT.  M5V 1P7         JULY 2, 1983
CALENDAR
****************************************************************************
*         PERIOD ONE         *      PERIOD TWO       *      PERIOD THREE        *
*          WEEKS 1-4         *      WEEKS 5-8        *      WEEKS 9-12          *
*     JULY 4 - JULY 21, 1982 *  AUG 1 - AUG 28, 1982 *  AUG 29 - SEPT 25, 1982  *
*   ----------------------   *  ------------------   *  ---------------------   *
*   S   M  T   W  T   F   S  *  S  M  T  W  T  F  S *  S   M   T   W   T   F  S*
*   ----------------------   *  ------------------   *  ---------------------   *
*       4   5   6   7   8   9  10  *  1   2   3   4   5   6   7  * 29  30  31   1   2   3   4 *
*  11  12  13  14  15  16  17 *  8   9  10  11  12  13  14 *  5   6   7   8   9  10  11 *
*  18  19  20  21  22  23  24 * 15  16  17  18  19  20  21 * 12  13  14  15  16  17  18 *
*  25  26  27  28  29  30  31 * 22  23  24  25  26  27  28 * 19  20  21  22  23  24  25 *
****************************************************************************
              *         PERIOD FOUR         *      PERIOD 5            *
              *          WEEKS 13-16        *      WEEKS 17-20         *
              *     SEPT 26 - OCT 23, 1982  *  OCT 24 - NOV 20, 1982   *
              *   ----------------------    *  ---------------------   *
              *   S   M   T   W   T   F   S *  S   M   T   W   T   F  S*
              *  26  27  28  29  30   1   2 * 24  25  26  27  28  29  30*
              *   3   4   5   6   7   8   9 * 31   1   2   3   4   5   6*
              *  10  11  12  13  14  15  16 *  7   8   9  10  11  12  13*
              *  17  18  19  20  21  22  23 * 14  15  16  17  18  19  20*
****************************************************************************
*         PERIOD SIX         *      PERIOD SEVEN     *      PERIOD EIGHT        *
*          WEEKS 21-24       *      WEEKS 25-28      *      WEEKS 29-32         *
*     NOV 21 - DEC 18, 1982  *  DEC 19/82 - JAN 15/83*  JAN 16 - FEB 12, 1983   *
*   S   M   T   W   T   F  S *  S   M   T   W   T   F  S *  S   M   T   W   T   F  S*
*  21  22  23  24  25  26  27 * 19  20  21  22  23  24  25 * 16  17  18  19  20  21  22 *
*  28  29  30   1   2   3   4 * 26  27  28  29  30  31   1 * 23  24  25  26  27  28  29 *
*   5   6   7   8   9  10  11 *  2   3   4   5   6   7   8 * 30  31   1   2   3   4   5 *
*  12  13  14  15  16  17  18 *  9  10  11  12  13  14  15 *  6   7   8   9  10  11  12 *
****************************************************************************
              *         PERIOD NINE         *      PERIOD TEN          *
              *          WEEKS 33-36        *      WEEKS 37-40         *
              *     FEB 13 - MAR 12, 1983   *  MAR 13 - APRIL 9, 1983  *
              *   S   M   T   W   T   F   S *  S   M   T   W   T   F  S*
              *  13  14  15  16  17  18  19 * 13  14  15  16  17  18  19*
              *  20  21  22  23  24  25  26 * 20  21  22  23  24  25  26*
              *  27  28   1   2   3   4   5 * 27  28  29  30  31   1   2*
              *   6   7   8   9  10  11  12 *  3   4   5   6   7   8   9*
****************************************************************************
*       PERIOD ELEVEN        *     PERIOD TWELVE     *     PERIOD THIRTEEN      *
*          WEEKS 41-44       *      WEEKS 44-45      *      WEEKS 49-52         *
*     APRIL 10 - MAY 7/83    *  MAY 8 - JUNE 4, 1983 *  JUNE 5 - JULY 2, 1983   *
*   S   M   T   W   T   F  S *  S   M   T   W   T   F  S *  S   M   T   W   T   F  S*
*  10  11  12  13  14  15  16 *  8   9  10  11  12  13  14 *  5   6   7   8   9  10  11 *
*  17  18  19  20  21  22  23 * 15  16  17  18  19  20  21 * 12  13  14  15  16  17  18 *
*  24  25  26  27  28  29  30 * 22  23  24  25  26  27  28 * 19  20  21  22  23  24  25 *
*   1       3   4   5   6   7 * 29  30  31   1   2   3   4 * 26  27  28  29  30   1   2 *
****************************************************************************
```

FIGURE 7.5 Thirteen-period calendar.

day last year, and sales were off. We will forecast sales 10% over this day last year.

- The weatherman says we are in for a really hot weekend, and everybody will be out on the road trying to get away from city heat. We should expect our Country Kitchen to have a heavy weekend. Last year the weather was nothing special, so we will estimate that sales will be up 15% for the next three days.
- Well, we got the weather forecast but there is still no snow in sight. I guess we can close down the Skiers' Paradise Room and just run with the coffee shop this weekend.

Finally, special conditions that affect your operation have to be taken into account. If sales are off 5% from last year because of economic conditions—a recession perhaps, or yet still another gas price rise—that fact should alter the forecast much as the weather did in the preceding examples. Similarly, special events such as conventions or football weekends need to be considered. In the case of a big football game or other major attraction, the forecast may be that "we will do all the business we can serve." In that case, physical constraints such as maximum possible chair turn become significant forecast factors.

Forecasting Item Sales

To this point, we have concentrated our attention on forecasting the number of guests to be served in a period. To be useful in operational planning, however, these forecasts have to be turned into estimates of how much of each item will be sold. Once again, we will rely on historical data.

In studying sales, most operators first break them down by major category. For a dinner menu, this procedure might mean an analysis such as the one shown in Figure 7.6. Although this kind of a summary is useful, it is not detailed enough for daily forecasting. First of all, the period in question—one month—is too long. It could well be that desserts are popular on some days but not on others. Even

ROOSTER TAIL RESTAURANT PERIOD ENDING FEBRUARY 28, 19XX		
Total guest count	10,712	100.0%
Appetizers	2,319	21.6%
Entrees	9,943	92.8%
Salads	3,785	35.3%
Vegetables	3,577	33.4%
Potatoes	4,312	40.3%
Beverages	9,914	92.6%
Desserts	5,809	54.2%

FIGURE 7.6 Menu category popularity summary.

more basically, this summary does not offer any way to reflect individual item popularity.

Beyond this point, many operators guess. Actually, a surprising number of operators do not even bother to keep food counts (i.e., a daily tally of the number of portions sold). Common practice, however, is not always a practical guide.

Successful restaurateurs use some form of popularity index. To analyze and then predict any item's sales, they chart day-to-day variations in demand, as well as each item's popularity vis-à-vis other items, whatever the day. The procedure used to make these detailed forecasts varies from one operation to another. The sample analysis we will consider has the advantage of covering the key variables, but it is only one of several possible approaches.[1] Later in the chapter, we will review a much more detailed, statistical approach to forecasting.

Daily Variation

Daily variations may arise for a wide variety of reasons. In the Holiday Restaurant example given in Figure 7.7, the unusually high proportion of entrees ordered on Thursday, for instance, probably reflects the fact that payday for the large insurance company next door falls on that day. Also, management at the Holiday can deduce from the figures for salads that people are more diet-conscious toward the first of the week. It also is obvious that vegetable and potato sales vary with the popularity of entrees on a given day.

	HOLIDAY RESTAURANT SUMMER SEASON				
	Percent of Total Guests Ordering				
	Mon.	Tues.	Wed.	Thurs.	Fri.
Appetizers	8	11	10	14	15
Soups	23	24	29	19	22
Sandwiches	38	39	40	22	34
Entrees	34	32	35	57	41
Salad plates	23	28	25	17	19
Side salads	12	15	17	23	15
Vegetables	9	10	10	14	11
Potatoes	8	10	11	12	10
Beverages	78	79	79	85	80
Desserts	42	45	44	62	57

FIGURE 7.7 Menu category popularity, by day of week (holiday restaurant, summer season).

---

[1] For other approaches to these calculations, see Green, Drake, and Sweeney, *Profitable Food and Beverage Management: Operations* (Rochelle Park, N.J.: Hayden, 1978), pp. 167–169; and Kolschevar, *Management by Menu* (Chicago: National Institute for the Foodservice Industry, 1975), pp. 120–128.

On the day *after* payday, desserts seem to hold up better than entrees do.

The Holiday Restaurant's managers feel the popularity of any one item could vary from day to day on a random basis. Instead of computing popularity on a daily basis, therefore, they summarize their item food counts monthly *by individual item*. They then compute the percentage of a *category's* sales accounted for by each menu item. Thus, out of 12,942 entrees sold, 7,515 were roast round (the featured luncheon item), which has a popularity ratio of 57.3. By contrast, filet of sole sold only 1,450, for an 11.2 ratio. Since entrees remain the same on the permanently printed (hardback) menu at Holiday, this calculation is fairly straightforward. In a restaurant whose menu items change daily, the manager must find a means to reflect those changes. One way to approach this problem is to calculate popularity daily, as is done in Figure 7.8.

HEALTH CARE FOOD SERVICE

From the standpoint of food service forecasting, health care displays several similarities to the hotel situation discussed earlier. Instead of house count (number of guests), for example, the patient census is the forecast determinant. Most hospitals offer some menu selection, and as a general rule, patients indicate their food preferences a day in advance on a form such as that shown in Figure 7.9, allowing accurate forecasts. The process of tallying patient choices can be simplified further by mechanical systems such as that found in Figure 7.10.

Although short-run forecasting for patients is relatively straightforward, virtually all hospitals also have non-patient food services—occasionally a senior staff dining room (an operation much like a small club) and almost invariably a cafeteria for staff and visitors. The cafeteria operation presents many of the same problems encountered in restaurant forecasting, but the total number of guests can be forecast with much more confidence than is the case with most freestanding restaurants.

INSTITUTIONAL FOOD SERVICE

Institutional food service commonly is divided into business and industry (B and I), college and university food service, health care, and school and community nutrition. School and community nutrition normally does not present forecasting problems, whereas B and I forecasting generally resembles that for the non-patient cafeteria just discussed. Total volume generally is quite predictable, as is item popularity, because of the fairly stable population and limited menu selection.

College and University Food Service

The stable population being served makes forecasting more reliable here, too. The shape of the forecasting problem, however, varies somewhat from other types of institutional food service, because of the variety of board plans offered.

Day 1	Percent
Roast beef	55
Fried Chicken	30
Seafood Crepes	15
	100
Day 2	
Stuffed Pork Chop	16
Fried Fish	24
Spaghetti	60
	100
Day 3	
London Broil	20
Fried Chicken	35
Quiche	45
	100
Day 4	
BBQ Pork Ribs	25
Fried Chicken	40
Lasagna	35
	100
Day 5	
Roast Chicken Breast	55
Fried Shrimp	30
Vegetable Frittata	15
	100

FIGURE 7.8 Popularity index of entrees in a cycle menu. This index indicates the approximate percentage of the total guest count that will order each menu item. Note that the positioning of menu items such as fried chicken with different menu mixes affects their popularity.

The earliest board plans simply provided 21 meals per week for a set cost—and indeed, that is still one option found in college food service. The 21-meal package is offered at a very attractive price because of an absentee factor: for instance, weekend meals are less well attended, and many students skip breakfast. Since reliable calculations of the absentee factor are possible, based on experience, the food service manager can offer an attractive package price. Under this package, however, all students pay the full price but only some students eat half or more of the meals (assuming seven weekend meals and five nonweekend breakfasts in a 21-meal week).

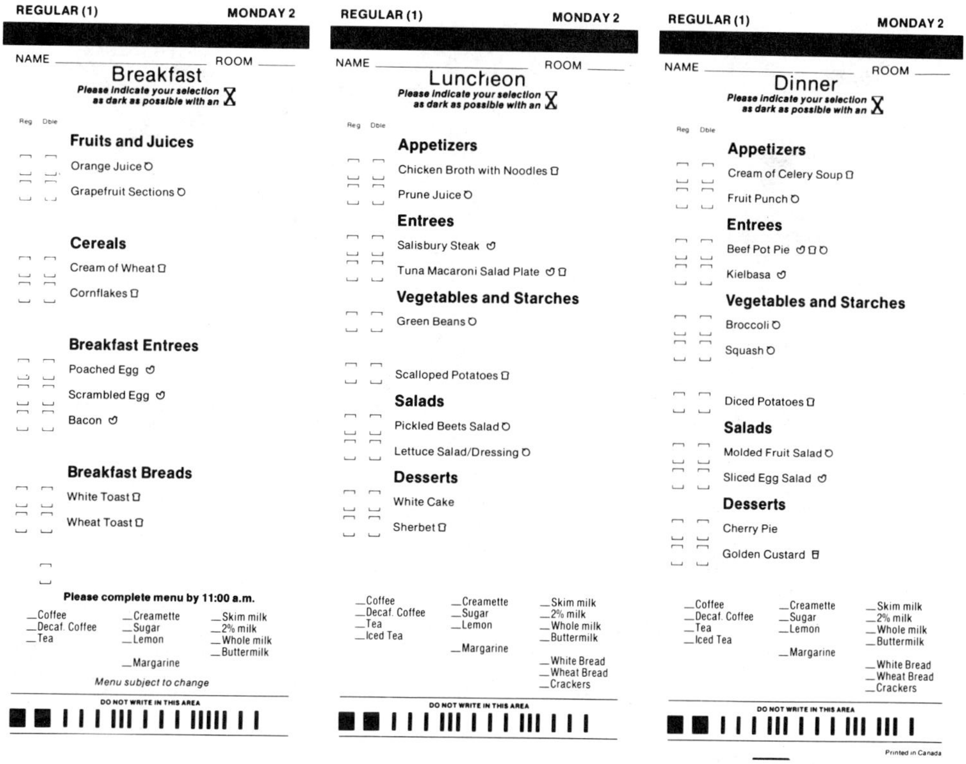
REGULAR (1) MONDAY 2

NAME ROOM

Breakfast

Please indicate your selection as dark as possible with an X

Reg Dble

Fruits and Juices
- Orange Juice
- Grapefruit Sections

Cereals
- Cream of Wheat
- Cornflakes

Breakfast Entrees
- Poached Egg
- Scrambled Egg
- Bacon

Breakfast Breads
- White Toast
- Wheat Toast

Please complete menu by 11:00 a.m.

_Coffee _Decaf. Coffee _Tea _Creamette _Sugar _Lemon _Margarine _Skim milk _2% milk _Whole milk _Buttermilk

Menu subject to change

DO NOT WRITE IN THIS AREA

REGULAR (1) MONDAY 2

NAME ROOM

Luncheon

Please indicate your selection as dark as possible with an X

Reg Dble

Appetizers
- Chicken Broth with Noodles
- Prune Juice

Entrees
- Salisbury Steak
- Tuna Macaroni Salad Plate

Vegetables and Starches
- Green Beans
- Scalloped Potatoes

Salads
- Pickled Beets Salad
- Lettuce Salad/Dressing

Desserts
- White Cake
- Sherbet

_Coffee _Decaf. Coffee _Tea _Iced Tea _Creamette _Sugar _Lemon _Margarine _Skim milk _2% milk _Whole milk _Buttermilk _White Bread _Wheat Bread _Crackers

DO NOT WRITE IN THIS AREA

REGULAR (1) MONDAY 2

NAME ROOM

Dinner

Please indicate your selection as dark as possible with an X

Reg Dble

Appetizers
- Cream of Celery Soup
- Fruit Punch

Entrees
- Beef Pot Pie
- Kielbasa

Vegetables and Starches
- Broccoli
- Squash
- Diced Potatoes

Salads
- Molded Fruit Salad
- Sliced Egg Salad

Desserts
- Cherry Pie
- Golden Custard

_Coffee _Decaf. Coffee _Tea _Iced Tea _Creamette _Sugar _Lemon _Margarine _Skim milk _2% milk _Whole milk _Buttermilk _White Bread _Wheat Bread _Crackers

DO NOT WRITE IN THIS AREA

Printed in Canada

FIGURE 7.9 Hospital patient food order form. (Courtesy of Morris Graphics Limited, Hospitality Division.)

Not surprisingly, students often object to subsidizing other students—that is, to paying for a package that they do not want to use all of. As a result of such objections, colleges now offer a wide variety of board plans, ranging from the 21-meal plan described above to 9-meal plans, 10-meal plans, 15-meal plans, and a wide variety of other specialized "packages." One food service contract company counted 91 different plans available at the campuses they serve. In many cases, several different board plans are available on the same campus. The university at which the authors are employed, for instance, offers students a form of script (a punch card) that can be exchanged for food, just like cash; students may purchase food at any of outlets on campus.

From a forecasting point of view, the variety of board plans available complicates food service forecasting somewhat, but the essential nature of institutional food service forecasting remains unchanged. A known population following a set of common behavior patterns makes predictions here more reliable than any forecasts for full-service commercial restaurants.

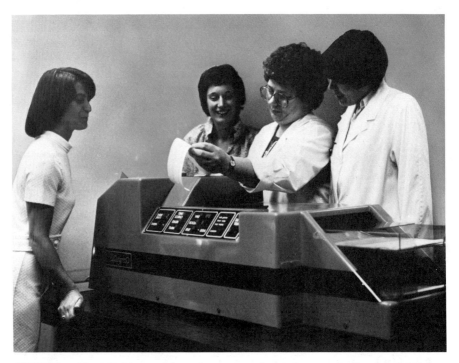

FIGURE 7.10 Machine tallying of menus replaces time-consuming hand tallying. (Courtesy of Morris Graphics Limited, Hospitality Division.)

COMPUTERIZED FORECASTING

The fact that careful forecasting pays for itself by yielding much greater precision indicates that the best model of what all food service forecasting is likely to become in the future can be gleaned from a review of the most advanced practices in today's institutional food service.

Of the several computerized food service management systems developed, one that has been applied in a wide variety of settings is called *Food Operations Computerized Unit Systems,* or FOCUS,[2] which was developed by ARA Services, Inc., in 1973. FOCUS can be applied not only to forecasting but also to "Food Production Control (Chapter 8) and to the monitoring of food cost performance (Chapter 12). Because it is an integrated management system, however, we will summarize FOCUS and its major applications here.[3]

---

[2]FOCUS is a registered trademark belonging to ARA Services.
[3]The discussion of FOCUS that follows here is based on a paper by Charles S. Satterthwait, Jr., "Focus: A Computerized Food Production Planning System for Schools and Colleges," presented to the Operations Research Society of America in November 1975.

FOCUS is designed for use in schools and colleges and has been adopted by institutions with as few as 1300 students. In the late 1970s, the annual operating costs of FOCUS were estimated at approximately $1000 per month, as against operating savings reported by ARA to range between 4 and 10% and to average 8%. The source of these savings will become clear as we discuss the services FOCUS provides.

FOCUS forecasts, on the basis of historical experience, the number of persons who will choose to eat at a given meal. This forecast is said to be acurate within 1%. From the same data, FOCUS computes an acceptability factor, which resembles the popularity index discussed above. Based on a forecasted guest count (see Figure 7.11) and on the acceptability factor, FOCUS forecasts food costs on a weekly basis and per meal, as shown in Figure 7.12. Note that in Figure 7.11 the forecasted number is provided opposite the letters "F/C" (i.e., "forecast"). The unit manager enters the actual number of guests on this form opposite the letters "ACC," and that data is fed back to the computer so it can update its files. In Figure 7.12, direct food cost is the cost of those food items that are portion-counted and recorded. Indirect food cost is food not portion-counted, such as table salt and sugar, fryer shortening, condiments, bulk dispensed milk, and so on.

Given the predicted number of items needed, FOCUS forecasts product needs based on current inventory in the computer's memory and anticipated usage of food products. This forecast is used as a basis for ordering and other management action. The "Short" column in Figure 7.13 indicates items that will be in short supply before the next scheduled delivery and so must either be purchased on an emergency basis or be removed from the menu. The "Surplus" column shows products in inventory that are not committed during current production cycle and so could be used as substitutes for items that are in short supply.

FOCUS prints a production order (see Figure 7.14) that gives the sizes and numbers of portions to prepare. This is a planning tool for the food production manager. The computer prints out recipes for the *exact amount* required by the forecast, avoiding the conventional practice of rounding off to a convenient pan size. Thus, precisely 116 orders of shrimp are to be prepared, according to Figure 7.14, and the recipe printed for the cook's use will produce exactly 191 portions of mushroom gravy.

Figure 7.15 illustrates the benefits of the careful study that computerization makes possible. Notice that in the "Before Menu Analysis" example the relatively high portion cost of chicken is balanced by the lower cost of corned beef hash and cheese blintzes. The balance selected, however, likely will result in a high total meal cost. Analysis with FOCUS' acceptability factor shows that the high-cost item will be very popular and that the "balance" expected will come from two relatively less popular entrees. For this reason, FOCUS forecasts a per patron cost of $0.65. In the "After Menu Analysis" example, the manager, using FOCUS, has balanced the popular chicken dish with two lower-cost items that are considerably more popular. As a result, the forecasted per patron cost is reduced

PATRON COUNT SHEET

100 Week Ending Date 9-19-74

CONTRACT	Fri.	Sat.	Sun.	Mon.	Tue.	Wed.	Thu.	Total
F/C Brk. Act. 101	836	206	176	1288	1035	1033	1176	
F/C Lun. Act. 102	1266	1089	1046	1279	1217	1198	1215	
F/C Din. Act. 103	951	1136	0	1159	1233	1399	1292	
CASH	Fri.	Sat.	Sun.	Mon.	Tue.	Wed.	Thu.	Total
F/C Brk. Act. 104	0	0	0	0	0	0	0	
F/C Lun. Act. 105	0	0	0	0	0	0	1	
F/C Din. Act. 106	0	0	0	0	0	0	2	
OTHER	Fri.	Sat.	Sun.	Mon.	Tue.	Wed.	Thu.	Total
F/C Brk. Act. 107	9	10	9	14	19	19	10	
F/C Lun. Act. 108	22	25	51	37	34	38	25	
F/C Din. Act. 109	11	10	0	13	11	16	12	

Line numbers are to be used for "results" input.

FIGURE 7.11 Weekly forecast of the number of customers per meal. (Courtesy of ARA Services.)

MENU—PRECOST
Week Ending 10-10-74

Forecast direct food cost $9494.91
Forecast indirect food cost $4153.79
Total food cost per forecast patron count $0.641
Direct food cost per forecast patron count $0.446

Direct Food Cost Per Patron

	1 Fri.	2 Sat.	3 Sun.	4 Mon.	5 Tue.	6 Wed.	7 Thu.	Total
1 Brk.	0.212	0.251	0.262	0.134	0.154	0.263	0.098	0.175
2 Lun.	0.349	0.445	0.725	0.378	0.461	0.429	0.464	0.457
3 Din.	0.333	1.558	0.	0.473	0.350	0.580	0.498	0.652
Tot.	0.308	1.001	0.622	0.330	0.327	0.436	0.356	0.446

FIGURE 7.12 Forecast of food cost for a weekly period. (Courtesy of ARA Services.)

172 FORECASTING: THE HEART OF PLANNING AND CONTROL

PURCHASE ORDER
Fish & Poultry Order Group

ITEM NUMBER	ITEM NAME	UNIT	ORDER DATE DELIVERY DATE SHORT	0318 0319	0318 0321	0318 0322	SURPLUS
1028	TKY, PULLED	LB		0	0	0	
1027	TURKEY DRUMSTICKS	LB		0	0	0	
145	CKN,QTRS	LB		0	0	0	
143	TURKEY, WHOLE	LB	−123	34	0	0	
930	CHICKEN, FROZ. DICED	LB		0	0	0	
222	BAKING FISH	LB		0	0	0	3
820	SHRIMP, COOKED IQF P&D	LB		0	0	0	4
1308	CHICKEN, MICROWAVE	BOX		0	0	0	0
1313	ASST HOT HORS DOEUVRES	BOX		0	0	0	30
1249	CHICKEN FAT	LB		0	0	0	
1499	RESERVED LIQUID	QT		0	0	0	
937	CRUMBS GREEN	LB		13	0	0	17
1158	RIND LEMON	TBS		0	0	0	
1160	RIND LIME	TBS		0	0	0	

FIGURE 7.13 FOCUS system forecast of the week's food needs based on customer forecast. (Courtesy of ARA Services.)

COMPUTERIZED FORECASTING 173

```
                    FOOD PRODUCTION ORDER
                          DIN 740914
                      HOT-FOOD DEPARTMENT

WEATHER              SPECIAL CONDITIONS

   F/C PATRONS   1146                              MENU 16301
                                        NUMBER OF PORTIONS
MENU ITEM            PORTION SIZE    TO PREPARE  PREPARED  LEFT OR CC  SERVED
                                                           WHEN OUT

STEAK, 8 OZ, BEEF    1.0/EACH            713
BR. SHRIMP           4.6/LB              116
CHOPPED STEAK        12    OZ            191
LONDON BROIL          4    OZ             36
MUSHROOM GRAVY        2    OZL           191
BAKED POTATO          1    EAC           326
FRENCH FRIED POTATOES 3    OZ           1304
BUT. GREEN BEANS, CAN 3    OZ            727
GLAZED CARROTS, FRESH 3    OZ            258
```

FIGURE 7.14 FOCUS system printout of a production order. (Courtesy of ARA Services.)

174 FORECASTING: THE HEART OF PLANNING AND CONTROL

Before-Menu Analysis			
Item	Portion Cost	Acceptability Factor	Per Patron Cost
Southern fried chicken	0.442	1.350	0.597
Corned beef hash	0.213	0.088	0.019
Cheese blintz	0.150	0.062	0.009
Total		1.500	0.625

After-Menu Analysis			
Item	Portion Cost	Acceptability Factor	Per Patron Cost
Southern fried chicken	0.442	0.947	0.419
Swedish meatballs	0.265	0.176	0.047
Lasagna	0.203	0.377	0.077
Total		1.500	0.543

FIGURE 7.15 Menu analysis. The cost per meal served has been reduced $0.082, while the menu has been improved as evidenced by the patrons' more-frequent selection of the lasagna and Swedish meatballs than the high-cost southern fried chicken. (Courtesy of ARA Services).

to $0.543. Note, too, that the acceptability factor is based on the popularity of the menu item itself *and* on the relative popularity of the menu item with which it is competing. Thus, the acceptability factor for chicken declines when it faces more popular competition.

FAST FOOD RESTAURANTS

Fast food, the fastest-growing segment of food service, presents a special case, because its limited-menu format permits management to focus on a level of detail out of reach of a full-service operation. When all the entrees sold can be summed up in the word *chicken* for instance, far more detail can be handled than when 20 quite different entrees are sold. The old cash register largely has been replaced by the preset electronic cash register (ECR) and the point of sale (POS) systems (see Chapter 3). The automation of data collection and report preparation made possible by this new technology interacts with the simpler menu format to provide management with a depth of forecasting detail that encourages fast food operators to approach planning on an hour-by-hour—and sometimes almost minute-by-minute—basis.

These operations are worthy of extra attention because, as is true of some institutional food service practice, they may reflect what the management of food service operations generally will be like in the not-too-distant future, as more and more menus become simplified and more and better ECR/POS software becomes available to a wider variety of operations.

HOURLY READINGS

Figure 7.16 shows a report that can be produced as frequently as management wishes. These readings permit management to review what labor *was* assigned and what sales totaled—in dollars or in number of customers—in each of charted hours. Note especially "Dollars Earned by Employees Clocked in" and "Labor Cost Percentage This Hour"; these measures of productivity help management quickly to review staffing in order to detrmine where payroll reductions are possible.

PRODUCTION PLANNING

In fast food operations, two factors must be weighed against each other: product quality and speed of service. To secure quality, freshly prepared foods are essential. On the other hand, the need for speed of service to customers in a hurry dictates that in the busiest periods of the day, food be prepared in advance and held. Ideally, a customer should not have to wait more than two minutes (unless the order is a "special"—"no pickles" is the famous example—which in some operations takes a little longer). After a certain time, however, preprepared

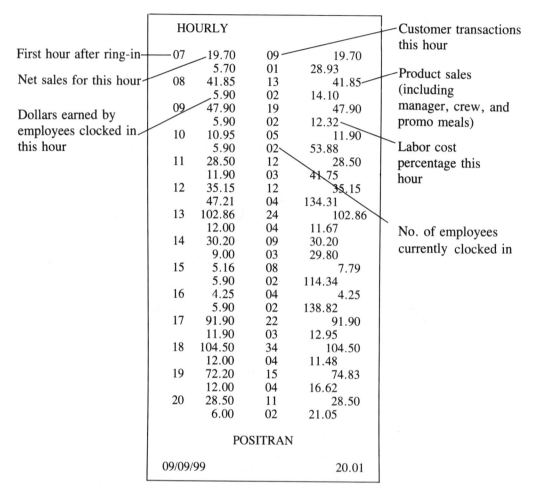

FIGURE 7.16 Hourly sales and productivity report.

product is no longer up to standard—it does not taste so good—and so most operations have a "throw-out policy" under which product can be held ready-to-serve no more than a certain number of minutes. Typical time limits: hamburgers, 15 minutes; chicken, 10 minutes; and french fries, 5 minutes.

Prepreparation of product, then, imposes severe penalties for overestimating demand. Food cost will soar if the equivalent of three or four or five meals is thrown out during each meal period. In some ways, however, an operation incurs an even more serious cost if it does not adhere to its throw-out policy: Faced with stale food, customers will decide to go elsewhere next time.

To show how operators can deal with this problem, we will consider the example of Zoom's Fried Chicken. In this operation, chicken is packaged so that each package of raw chicken ready for production contains the amount that a frier can hold. A work sheet such as that shown in Figure 7.17 is used to collect sales information by hour for each day of the month (from the daily report). Suppose we are concerned with the first hour in a month that has four Mondays, and that we find sales to be as follows.

First Monday	$ 160
Second Monday	142
Third Monday	138
Fourth Monday	176
	$ 616

Dividing by four, we discover that the average sale during the first hour is $154. If the average package of chicken (ready to fry) has a retail value of $14, we can determine that

$$\$154 \div \$14 = 11 \text{ bags}$$

That is, we should expect to prepare 11 bags of raw chicken during the first hour of that day. From data reflecting the sale of other products, in relation to the amount of chicken sold, the manager might estimate, for instance, that for every $100 worth of business, the operation will use

¾ gallon of mashed potatoes.

¾ gallon of gravy.

¾ gallon of cole slaw.

½ gallon of all other salads.

Obviously, these rules of thumb would apply only to a single unit. The sales mix for each store in a chain could be different and would be subject to change according to shifting seasons and changing economic conditions. A production rule of thumb, then, probably would have to be prepared for each store and be revised periodically.

Nevertheless, an operator can use the procedure outlined above to forecast for each day of the month the dollar sales by hour and the number of bags of chicken needed. These dollar and physical units of sale can then be translated into the number of employees required per hour. These calculations can be made for each hour of the day, and a sheet can be prepared for each day of the week using a form such as that shown in Figure 7.18. This kind of planning permits the manager to

1. Offer fresh, high-quality product.

2. Maintain minimum guest waiting time.

3. Avoid excessive waste through too much discarded "old" product.

Worksheet
Hourly Sales—$

Divide Totals by 4 or 5, according to weeks of previous month

Day of Week	10:00 A.M.	11:00 A.M.	12:00 noon	1:00 P.M.
First				
Second				
Third				
Fourth				
Fifth				
Total				
Average Reading				
Pots Needed				

	2:00 P.M.	3:00 P.M.	4:00 P.M.	5:00 P.M.
First				
Second				
Third				
Fourth				
Fifth				
Total				
Average Reading				
Pots Needed				

	6:00 P.M.	7:00 P.M.	8:00 P.M.	9:00 P.M.
First	_____	_____	_____	_____
Second	_____	_____	_____	_____
Third	_____	_____	_____	_____
Fourth	_____	_____	_____	_____
Fifth	_____	_____	_____	_____
Total	_____	_____	_____	_____
Average Reading	_____	_____	_____	_____
Pots Needed	_____	_____	_____	Average sale per bag*

	10:00 P.M.	11:00 P.M.	12:00 P.M.	
First	_____	_____	_____	_____
Second	_____	_____	_____	_____
Third	_____	_____	_____	_____
Fourth	_____	_____	_____	_____
Fifth	_____	_____	_____	_____
Total	_____	_____	_____	_____
Average Reading	_____	_____	_____	*Average sale per bag—see average
Pots Needed	_____	_____	_____	

FIGURE 7.17 Worksheet used to collect hourly sales data.

180 FORECASTING: THE HEART OF PLANNING AND CONTROL

Day _____   ZOOM'S CHIX
Month _____
Average Sale per Bag _____   PROJECTION SHEET

Time of Day	Income	Pots	Trays	Cooks	Packers	Cashiers	Companion Products for this period
7							PACKAGES
8							ROLLS
9							COLE SLAW
10							POTATOES- GRAVY
11							GALLONS
12							GRAVY
1							POTATOES
2							POTATO SALAD
3							BEAN SALAD
TOTAL							BARBQ BEANS

PLAN ON _____ BURNERS _____ TURNS PER HOUR _____ DEGREE GREASE IN J.P. _____

Time of Day	Income	Pots	Trays	Cooks	Packers	Cashiers	Companion Products for this period
4							PACKAGES
5							ROLLS
6							COLE SLAW
7							POTATOES- GRAVY
8							GALLONS
9							GRAVY
10							POTATOES
11							POTATO SALAD
12							BEAN SALAD
13							BARBQ BEANS
TOTAL							

PLAN ON _____ BURNERS _____ TURNS PER HOUR _____ DEGREE GREASE IN J.P. _____

NO	NAME	SHIFT	NO.	NAME	SHIFT	NO.	NAME	SHIFT
1			1			1		
2			2			2		
3			3			3		
4			4			4		
5			5			5		

FIGURE 7.18 Form for calculating the number of employees needed.

USING SALES FORECASTS IN DAY-TO-DAY OPERATIONS

Up to this point, we have focused principally on the forecasting of sales. In the preceding section, however, we saw how that data could be used to forecast product preparation and employee scheduling. We will now look at some other uses managers make of forecasting.

One obvious application of forecasting is purchasing and ordering. If we know what we can expect to sell, we can estimate what amounts of product to order on a day-to-day basis. Forecasting also gives us an objective basis on which to assess inventory levels, not only of food but of paper products, cleaning supplies, and guest supplies. In addition, we have just seen how the forecasting of sales can supply a basis for employee scheduling—a subject that will be treated at length in Chapter 10.

At this point, you should note that the sales forecast provides the basis on which production planning and employee scheduling can rest.

USING SALES FORECASTING IN LONG-RANGE PLANNING

The computer plays a major role in long-range planning in most chains. Either the point of sale terminal *is* a computer terminal, or it can be polled—that is, contacted by a central computer over long-distance telephone wires each day. Such calls give the home office computer access to summary information on the day's business. Each day, then, the control office has fresh data on each unit's operation. Over time, these data are used not only to prepare financial statements but also to prepare forecasts or to update existing long-range forecasts.

Consider a company whose main product is fish purchased at sea from Icelandic fishermen and cooked in oil.[4] The lead time necessary to obtain the fish means that a 10% rise in sales must be communicated quickly to the company's agent in Iceland, so that added stocks can be put into the pipeline. That pipeline must serve—for one company—750 stores located all across North America. Each level of supply—fisherman, processor, and distributor—must gear up its level of activity such that each store can get the extra requirement of product without any sacrifice in quantity.

The smaller operator also can benefit from being able to estimate sales for a longer period of time. Take, for instance, an operator who was doing a substantial steak volume. When given an opportunity to purchase a large quantity of T-bone steaks at an attractive price, he was able to relate the quantity available to his forecasted sales and to determine that it represented about a six-month supply. Feeling that that holding time for a frozen product was satisfactory, he was able to make a substantial saving. In another case, an operator who was opening a new seafood room planned to feature a particular kind of fish and felt that it would hurt his image to run out of that product. A forecast enabled him to purchase a six-month supply, thus ensuring availability of this product. A final example is provided by a small chain that featured shrimp—a food product whose price varies widely from one season to the next. To ensure a steady supply at a predictable price, this company practiced forward buying—that is, they contracted for delivery of product at a set price for a period of 90 to 180 days. The

---

[4]Thomas F. Powers, "Complex Food Service Systems," *Cornell Hotel and Restaurant Administration Quarterly,* November 1979.

security they had with regard to product cost permitted them to mount an advertising campaign that included a published selling price for their shrimp dinners—which was possible only because they knew that they could secure product at a cost that made such a price adequate.

In each of these cases, a "guesstimate" could have been disastrous. The holding of excess inventory, whether in a large multi-unit food service or a single operation, boosts capital costs (the interest lost on money tied up in inventory), storage charges, and the danger of spoilage. On the other hand, a stock-out means product not available for sale or, in the case of forward buying that does not provide enough product, the need to go out on the market and acquire product at a unit cost higher than that available for a larger-quantity purchase. Clearly, long-range forecasting of sales is important enough to warrant careful collection of data that may serve as a basis for forecasting.

SUMMARY

We have seen that the major variables in food service forecasting are basically similar. Time, weather, and special conditions, however, must be considered from different perspectives in different kinds of operations. The predictability and complexity of different kinds of operations—for instance, hospitals and freestanding restaurants—differ widely.

Institutional food service, because it is considerably more predictable, has been the first segment of the industry to make extensive use of the computer in forecasting item demand. The forecasting models in use by institutions, may well offer a taste of things to come in food service as a whole. Clearly, POS systems offer simple access to sales data patterns that can be used in scheduling employees, in planning production, and in purchasing.

KEY WORDS AND PHRASES

Forecast—definition
Predicting factors
Time
Day of week
Hour of day
Season of year
Historical records
Weather
Special conditions
Economic climate
Local events
Established indicators
Reservations

Historical records
Forecasting item sales
Historical data
Food counts
Popularity index
Daily variation
Health-care food service
Patient census
Nonpatient guests
Institutional food service
Computerized forecasting
Fast food restaurants
Hourly forecasts

Forecasting situations
Hotels—meal pattern
Seating capacity
Number of chairs
Chair turn
Banquets
Freestanding restaurant

Dollar sales
Number of customers
Labor cost
Production planning
Time limits
Long range planning

DISCUSSION QUESTIONS

1. What historical data do hotels use to forecast restaurant sales? What other information do they use?

2. If a customer planned a banquet for "around 250" persons in your banquet department, how many guaranteed reservations would you require? How many would you forecast? Discuss the problems that could arise.

3. In which type of food service operation is forecasting most unpredictable? Discuss the strategies you would use to *(a)* increase accuracy or *(b)* live with the unpredictability.

4. Identify a nearby restaurant and determine the maximum number of guests it can serve each meal. First, count the number of chairs and determine the number of "chair turns" per meal. Then, allow for tables that will not be filled completely. Discuss your results. (The manager of the restaurant may be able to help you).

5. What tools are used to forecast quantities of individual items? Discuss the problems involved in predicting item sales.

6. A college food service offers three entree choices at every evening meal, and you have been assigned to develop popularity indices. The first day of the cycle menu features fried chicken, spaghetti, and baked ham, and you have sales data from five previous cycles. Develop a popularity index for each item. Using the percentages developed, forecast how many of each entree you would need if 200 guests were expected. Discuss the effect on your index if steak were substituted for ham.

Cycle	Fried Chicken	Spaghetti	Baked Ham
1	26	104	12
2	38	120	16
3	12	64	8
4	40	114	20
5	24	117	13

7. Study Figure 7.15 and try to schedule this operation more productively. What are the constraints of better scheduling?

8. What data would you use for long-range forecasting?

FOOD PRODUCTION CONTROL

8

The Recipe Kitchen

Portion Control

THE PURPOSE OF THIS CHAPTER

Large factories often have a Production Control Office, which plans how product will move through the plant. Food service establishments are not large enough to warrant a staff devoted to this purpose. This chapter discusses how the production control process is accomplished in food service through advanced planning. The key tools in production control are recipes, method and procedure cards, and marked menus. The majority of the chapter, however, is devoted to the tools and technique of portion control.

THIS CHAPTER SHOULD HELP YOU

1. Relate the recipe kitchen concept to cost and quality control.

2. See leftover control as an advance planning process rather than as a corrective, after-the-fact activity.

3. Recognize the function of portion control and its relation to cost and consumer satisfaction.

4. Identify the major tools for portion control and give several examples of each.

5. Understand the systemwide controls necessary for portion control in fast food.

THE RECIPE KITCHEN

Kitchens can be divided into three categories: those that use standardized written recipes; chef kitchens, which *appear* not to use recipes; and kitchens in which the cooks "do their own thing," without consulting standardized recipes.

A kitchen that uses no recipes has no way of standardizing its product. When Mary makes the meat loaf it tastes one way; when John is on duty, it is quite a different product. The customer, as a result, does not know what to expect. Moreover, management has only a general idea of what its costs are; differing prices might actually be appropriate, depending on whether John or Mary is the cook on duty. Of course, when John or Mary takes another job, the restaurant will have an entirely new kind of meat loaf, depending on who is hired, and this product may be good, bad, or indifferent. Management quite literally has no control over cost or quality.

Chef kitchens *seem* to have no recipes. In a real chef kitchen, with properly trained personnel, however, recipes are part of a tradition and are in the chef's and his skilled cook's heads. Unfortunately, some of the problems encountered with

John and Mary arise here, too, because the recipes are very general and their interpretation and implementation can vary widely from one skilled cook to another. It is highly unlikely that the crabmeat Mornay will not taste good when chefs change, but it is quite possible that it will taste different. Just as quality is likely to remain good while differing in some aspects from cook to cook, costs can vary depending on who is on duty. There used to be considerable debate among food service professionals about the relative merits of the chef versus the recipe kitchen, but chefs and chef-trained cooks have become so scarce that the debate largely has become irrelevant. Chef kitchens are found only in very expensive restaurants—the rest of the food service industry must choose between control or no control, recipe or no recipe.

THE STANDARDIZED RECIPE

The standardized recipe is the backbone of institutional food service, and it is used in most successful full-service restaurants as well. Figure 8.1 illustrates the principal features of a standardized recipe.

- The recipe is written in simple, understandable language.
- The recipe should be presented in easy-to-read form. For this purpose, we advocate the use of large type.
- The recipe uses standard units.

The last point deserves some explanation. A recipe should say, "Add 8 oz diced onion"—not "dice one onion and add." (How much does an onion weigh? That depends on how big it is!) Similarly, measures such as "a handful" need to be translated into standard weights, such as ¼ cup.

A recipe is a full production plan that carries the product from prepreparation to final portioning. In some cases, of course, more than one recipe will be required. For instance, one recipe might cover the making of crepes, another the sauce, and yet a third the combining of crêpes and sauce into a final dish. The point is that *all* the production activity should be specified in writing; nothing should be left to the discretion of the worker if a product standardized in quality and cost is desired.

METHOD CARDS

Another, increasingly common kind of written direction is the Method Card. With the increasing simplicity of menus and greater reliance on prepared-to-order foods in menu planning, a recipe, as a description of a complex production activity, often is no longer necessary. Figure 8.2 shows a method card for fried chicken. Note that although it does not need to deal with the combination of several ingredients, it does cover steps that are to be followed in great detail.

	HONEY GLAZED PORK CHOPS YIELD: 50 SERVINGS SIZE OF SERVING: 1 PORK CHOP, 6 OZ. RAW	
INGREDIENTS	PREPARATION STEPS	UTENSILS NEEDED
2 POUNDS ONIONS EP 1 PINT SOY SAUCE ½ CUP CATSUP 1 QUART WATER 1½ CUPS HONEY 2 TEASPOONS GINGER 1 TEASPOON PEPPER	1. PREPARE MARINADE: CHOP ONIONS. COMBINE SOY SAUCE, CATSUP, WATER, HONEY, ONIONS, GINGER, AND PEPPER.	BOWL SPOON FRENCH KNIFE CUTTING BOARD MEASURING SPOONS MEASURING CUPS
½ POUND SHORTENING 50 EA, 6 OZ. PORK LOIN CHOPS	2. PREHEAT TILTING FRY PAN TO 375°F. HEAT SHORTENING. PLACE CHOPS IN FRY PAN, SINGLE LAYER. BROWN ON BOTH SIDES. TRANSFER TO STEAM TABLE PANS (12/FULL PAN, 6/HALF PAN)	3 FULL PANS 2 HALF PANS SPATULA
½ CUP SESAME SEEDS	3. POUR 1 PINT MARINADE OVER EACH FULL PAN. SPRINKLE WITH SESAME SEEDS. COVER PANS. REFRIGERATE UNTIL READY TO BAKE	MEASURING CUP
	4. BAKE IN BATCHES FOR 40 MINUTES IN CONVECTION OVEN PREHEATED 5 MINUTES TO 300°F. KEEP WARM ON STEAM TABLE. MAXIMUM HOLDING TIME 30 MINUTES	
	5. LEFTOVERS: BAKED CHOPS CANNOT BE REHEATED. HALF PANS OF 6 ORDERS SHOULD BE BAKED AT END OF MEAL PERIOD TO AVOID WASTE.	
	COMMENTS: STEPS 1,2, and 3 CAN BE DONE DAY AHEAD AND REFRIGERATED (COVERED) UNTIL BAKED.	

FIGURE 8.1 Example of a standardized recipe.

FRIED CHICKEN DINNER

FRYER TEMPERATURE: 350°F

1. REMOVE 3 PIECES (LEG, WING, BREAST) OF CHICKEN FROM FREEZER.
2. PLACE IN FRYER BASKET. COOK FOR 12 MINUTES.
3. DRAIN WELL.
4. WHILE COOKING PREPARE CHICKEN DINNER ON HEATED 9" DINNER PLATTER:

   #8 SCOOP COLE SLAW
   1 SLICE TOMATO AND 1 SPRIG PARSLEY GARNISH
   4 OUNCES FRENCH FRIES

5. PLACE CHICKEN ON PLATTER BONE SIDE DOWN.

POINTS TO REMEMBER

COOK CHICKEN TO ORDER EXCEPT DURING BUSY PERIODS. HOLDING LIMIT 10 MINUTES MAXIMUM UNDER INFRARED LIGHT.

DO NOT COOK MORE THAN ONE ORDER AT A TIME. OVERLOADING FRYER CAUSES GREASY, SOGGY PRODUCT.

KEEP CHICKEN IN FREEZER AT ALL TIMES. DO NOT TAKE BAG OUT AND KEEP NEXT TO FRYER.

FIGURE 8.2   Method card for fried chicken.

PROCEDURES

Still other activities, which do not call for a recipe as such, should be under the full control of management. Two examples are worth looking at.

If employees work without specific direction, it is virtually certain that they will arrange their work to suit their own convenience. A busy cook is under a good deal of pressure during a meal and would rather cook all the baked potatoes before the rush. Figure 8.3 shows how a careful management team can ensure that potatoes are baked fresh throughout the meal period, with the guest's taste, not the cook's convenience, in mind.

Figure 8.4 shows another procedure that is vital to quality control. Here, a

```
                    FRED'S STEAK HOUSE
                   BAKED POTATO SCHEDULE

TEMPERATURE: 350°F CONVECTION OVEN: 30 MIN.


   NUMBER OF POTATOES

100 GUESTS  150 GUESTS  200 GUESTS  TIME IN  TIME OUT  COMMENTS
    5           5          10        4:30     5:00     Do not hold longer
                                                       than 30 min.
    5          10          20        5:00     5:30
   25          40          45        5:30     6:00
   30          40          50        6:00     6:30
   25          40          45        6:30     7:00
    5          10          20        7:00     7:30
    5           5          10        7:30     8:00
BEFORE 5:00 P.M. AND AFTER 8:00 P.M., COOK TO ORDER IN MICROWAVE:
3 MIN.
```

FIGURE 8.3 Procedure for baking potatoes in batches throughout the meal period.

chain that puts great emphasis on its specialty fried onion rings feels that the quality of the breading is what gives it the crucial advantage over the competition. The detailed procedure written down in Figure 8.4 permits the chain to achieve the desired results with unskilled cooks.

LEFTOVER CONTROL

One of the major costs in food service arises from overproduction. Leftover food is regarded by employee and customer alike as of secondary quality. And leftovers are combined into a different dish—as when leftover roast beef is used to make roast beef hash, for example—it is almost always a salvage operation in which a full return on product cost is not realized. Because of these drawbacks, leftovers should be kept to a minimum. There are several possible approaches to that goal.

Prepared to Order
The most common solution to the problem of leftovers is to plan a menu in which all or most foods are prepared to order. This, procedure, however, limits both the selection available to guests and the flexibility of production. (Recall that prepared foods are ready to be served; their presence on a menu improves an operation's ability to handle a rush.)

FIGURE 8.4 Procedure card for breading onion rings.

Incorporate Leftovers as a Cost
Some operations plan on a certain amount of leftover food in costing their recipes; they assume the leftovers will be thrown out. The obvious disadvantage to this strategy is that if a competitor can achieve a lower waste factor and lower cost, the looser operation may be undercut on price.

Prepare and Hold
An increasingly common strategy in food service is to prepare foods and hold them under refrigeration. When an order comes in, foods are finished and served. The use of microwave ovens considerably speeds this process.

Frozen foods have been the most common of the prepared foods. Frozen prepared foods, however, generally are prepared by manufacturers and include the manufacturer's labor and overhead costs and profit. Hence, they are expensive. Many operators, moreover, find that the selection available is inadequate and the quality of a standard that is acceptable but generally not excellent.

[1] I. C. I. Sayles and H. A. MacLennan, "Ready Foods: The Application of Mass Production to a La Carte Food Service Using Prepared to Order Food." *The Cornell Hotel and Restaurant Association Quarterly,* August, 1965, p. 21.

Ready Foods

The ready foods concept was first developed during the 1960's[1] for hotels but has since been adopted most widely in hospital and college food services. The system relies on freezing, and a major drawback has been the high cost of the specialized blast freezing equipment needed. Alternatively, the use of conventional freezing equipment to freeze prepared food can cause quality problems, because the slow rate of freezing involved leads to the formation of large ice crystals that destroy tissue and cause flavor and weight loss.

Recent developments in refrigeration, however, may lead to much wider adoption of the ready foods approach. Latent zone (−28°F or 0°C) refrigerators permit the holding of prepared product for up to two or three weeks. In one recent study, Swedish meatballs were chosen for a test. Because of their ingredients, Swedish meatballs are especially subject to flavor loss and microbe growth; but in the study, the meatballs were held for two weeks without any serious deterioration in quality.[2] (Several less-formal tests of the equipment have provided even more encouraging results.) Because Swedish meatballs are especially hard to hold, the study's results are a significant indication of the potential for latent zone refrigeration as a means of expanding the use of ready foods. This development, in turn, would mean a substantial reduction in leftover loss and a major advance in production control.

THE MARKED MENU

If complex menus are to be prepared by several cooks, an operation needs some way of organizing the day's work. One approach to this problem is to use the "marked menu", on which the items are typed double-spaced, to leave room for portion information to be typed in (see Figure 8.5). The cooks assigned to each recipe are noted on the supervisor's copy. Then copies of the marked menus, along with the appropriate recipe, are given to production personnel, and a marked menu is given to pantry personnel (or whoever will be responsible for final plating of the food). The marked menu and recipes can be thought of as a method of management control—or as an organized means of communication. The entire crew—supervisor, cooks, and pantry personnel—work from the same set of directions, and each person is aware of the needs of earlier or later steps in the production process. Marked menus and recipes, therefore, can help develop a team approach to work.

INGREDIENT CONTROL

Another means of organizing the production carries the reliance on recipes a step further by establishing an ingredient room in which all ingredients are measured *before being sent to the kitchen*. The ingredient room staff receives the menu and

[2] J. M. Powers and D. L. Collins-Thompson, "Microbiological and sensory evaluation of partially prepared Swedish meat balls stored in latent temperature zone (−2°C to 0°C)", *Canadian Institute of Food Science and Technology* 15 (4):319–321, 1982.

DINNER MENU

"SEASIDE ROOM"

Fisherman's Choice—Variety of Fresh Seafoods, Fresh Fish, Shrimp, Oysters and Clams

2 pieces   2 ea.   1 ea   2 oz.

Tender Fried Shrimp, Spicy Plum Sauce

7 each   2 oz.

Flounder Stuffed with Almond-Herb Dressing

10 oz.   #12 scoop

Oysters Buccaneer on the Half Shell

6 oysters   1 oz. sauce per oyster

Meetingstreet Crab

6 oz. in shirred egg dish

Broiled Sirloin Steak, Bordelais Sauce

8 oz.   1 oz.

Broiled Petite Sirloin Steak, Mushroom Caps

6 oz.   3 ea.

Served with
Baked Potatoes or Home Fries

1 ea.   #6 scoop

Crispy Green Salad or Cabbage and Carrot Slaw

1 cup   #8 scoop

Freshly Baked Bread and Butter

2 pieces   2 pats

FIGURE 8.5 Example of a marked menu.

sales forecast in advance of production. From recipes, the total amount of raw product required by each menu item is weighed, counted, or otherwise measured. At the start of the production day, this product is issued to cooks.

Since only the amount required is issued, waste is minimized. The practice of limiting issues to recipe amounts also reinforces production personnel's strict adherence to recipes a major *quality control* advantage of ingredient control. Labor productivity also may be improved, since weighing, counting, and other measuring are accomplished by less-skilled—and less-expensive—personnel, leaving to skilled cooks the preparation work alone.

The ingredient control room system is used principally in institutional food service, and particularly in health care. One commercial operator, Morrison's Cafeterias, has long used this approach to food cost and quality control with good success, however.

PORTION CONTROL

All the care taken in planning and production of food can be defeated, however, if food is "dished up" indiscriminantly. If a steak house overportions a 10 oz steak by only ½ ounce, 5% of the product is wasted. Since 5% commonly represents the profit margin of a successful restaurant, the significance of portion control should be obvious.

Portion control also is important in maintaining customer goodwill. Imagine the conversation at a table at which two guests have ordered roast beef and one gets an undersized portion while the other gets an oversized portion. Or consider the reaction of a guest who is served a different-sized portion on a return visit to your restaurant.

Portion control is an important topic that is central to the subject of food cost control. The balance of this chapter, therefore, is devoted to the concepts and tools of portion control, which, along with recipe control, is the backbone of production control.

DETERMINING PORTION SIZE

There are two ways of viewing portion size; from the standpoint of cost and quantity, and from that of guest preference and acceptance. Some types of food service emphasize one view more than the other, but most try to take both factors into account.[3]

---

[3] This section draws on an unpublished paper by Theresa Huber.

Food Cost

In operations that operate on a very tight budget, such as a school food service, cost is the determining factor in portion size. In fact, many young men of high school age find that the standard portion is not enough. But budgeting guidelines are so strict that larger portions just are not possible.

Most institutional food service operations manage to provide adequately for the client's appetite—but only because such low-cost foods as spaghetti, macaroni and cheese, or pork and beans are used frequently. Costs must be held to target in this way because the increases in selling price available to commercial operators usually either cannot be implemented by institutions—or can be implemented only at the end of some contract period. Thus, cost may be the major guiding force in setting portion size here, too.

Guest Satisfaction

For most people, custom and, of course, physiological need determine what size portion is expected and preferred. Most food service operations try to offer portions that are "enough"—that is, that fill the physiological needs and psychological expectations of the guest. Of course, some restaurants specialize in oversized portions, in order to give the guest the feeling that abundance is part of the dining experience there.

Figure 8.6 offers the usual portion sizes for common menu items. There certainly is nothing sacred about these portions; in fact, common portion sizes change as costs change. In the 1950s and 1960s, a 12 or even 14 oz strip of steak commonly would be listed as a lady's steak ("Queen Size"), whereas a 16 or 18 oz strip would be listed as "King Size." Today, the 12 oz strip usually is the largest steak offered on a menu, simply because the price of beef has risen so dramatically. Nevertheless, the information summarized in Figure 8.6 represents current common practice.

Health Care

Portion sizes for the house diet (the menu for guests who are not on special diets) usually offer "enough to eat," perhaps at the lower end of the normal portion range. On the other hand, not only item selection but also portion sizes are affected by special diet considerations.

APPROACHES TO PORTION CONTROL

One approach to portion control is *active*, in that it involves definite action to secure control, such as weighing, counting, or measuring. Another approach is called *passive portion control;* the size of the dish, for instance, may determine the amount of vegetables served—as the bowl determines the amount of salad offered. Both approaches are used in operations of all types, but passive portion control is especially common in such self-service areas as buffets and salad bars.

Soup: Cup—2/3 cup (5 1/3 oz)
         Bowl—1 cup (8 oz)

Vegetables: Green beans, peas, carrots, lima beans, corn—1 serving spoon (3 oz, 3/8 cup)
              Spinach, turnip greens, collards, stewed tomatoes—1/2 cup (4 oz)

              Cabbage—1/6 head

Potatoes: 1/2 cup (#8 dipper) or 4 oz (french fried); size 90 for baked potatoes

Gravies and sauces: 1/4 cup or 2 oz ladle

Salads and Salad Dressings: Dressing—2 level tbsp (1 oz dipper)
                              Greens—3/4 cup for lunch, 1 cup for dinner service

Entrees	*Lunch*	*Dinner*
Roast beef	3 oz	5 to 6 oz
Roast turkey	2 1/2 oz	3 oz
Hamburger patties	3 or 4 oz	
Chopped steak	4 to 6 oz	6 or 8 oz
T-bone steak		12 to 16 oz
Boneless strip steak		8, 12, 16 oz
Rib-eye steak	5 oz	6 or 8 oz
Small filet steak	6 oz	6 oz
Filet mignon		8 to 10 oz
Chateaubriand		16 oz for two persons
Pork chops	4 oz breaded 5 oz broiled	4 to 5 oz Breaded 5 to 6 oz broiled
Lamb chops		4 or 5 oz (2 chops per serving)
Baked ham	3 oz	3 to 4 oz

Desserts: 9 in. pies cut into 7 to 8 pieces
           9 in. cakes cut into 12 pieces
           Puddings—1/2 cup or 4 oz, scoop

Sandwiches: 2 oz meat or 1/4 cup filling   1 tsp mayonnaise,
               2 tsp butter,   3/4 oz lettuce

FIGURE 8.6 Portion sizes commonly used in restaurants.

The first key to successful portion control is the standardized recipe. Such a recipe ensures that portions come from a standard product. A pan of macaroni and cheese cut 3 × 5 (three cuts from front to back of pan and five from side to side) will always yield to same-sized portions[4]—provided that the same recipe is always used. Variation in recipes, however, could reduce or increase the amount of cheese or could result in a thicker or thinner portion if the amount of ingredients varies. Portion control, then, rests on standardized production procedures based on standard recipe and method cards, which include portion size and the means of obtaining it.

A second prerequisite to successful portion control is commitment from top management. In a hotel that was experiencing food cost problems, the general manager walked into the kitchen one day, put on an apron, borrowed a portion scale, and began weighing the julienne of ham, cheese, and turkey. Finding many excessive portions there, he moved on to the sandwich station, which yielded similar results. The food service management's initial reaction to this visit was one of mixed amusement and resentment, but as the G.M. moved systematically through the kitchen and it became increasingly obvious that the hotel's food cost problems were related to overportioning, the reaction changed to one of embarrassed understanding. What the G.M.'s action then and in repeat visits accomplished was not only problem solving but a dramatic demonstration of top management's support of strict portion control procedures. That kind of support, however demonstrated, is essential to good portion control.

Tools for Portion Control

Portion control is a philosophy that should permeate all parts of the kitchen, from purchasing to serving. If management's approach is to insist upon a particular portion size for everything, including a tiny parsley garnish, then it is not likely that expensive meats will be overportioned (or underportioned)—it will be part of each employee's job, and a job done from habit. In this section, we will describe some of the portion control instruments available to food service operators who wish control product throughout the food service system—beginning with the most valuable tool, the portion scale.

Measuring Weight Scales. Of the several kinds of scales used in kitchens today, perhaps the most important is the "over-and-under scale" pictured in Figure 8.7. This scale can be preset for weights in half-ounce gradations. The register quickly and very accurately shows the worker how the portion stacks up against standards. This is a high-speed production piece of equipment used to portion such varied foods as salad meats, sandwich ingredients, and sliced roast meats on the steam table. No kitchen that does any of its own portioning should be without this essential piece of equipment.

---

[4]Remember, though, that a 3 × 5 cut in *different pan sizes* will yield different portions.

PORTION CONTROL **197**

FIGURE 8.7 Over-and-under scale. (Courtesy of Berkel, Inc.)

Notice that for experienced workers, a very common practice, and one that most operators find quite acceptable, is to weigh every third or fourth portion cut. If the portion weight is acceptable, then the next two or three portions are not weighed. If, however, the worker finds that an overportioned or underportioned serving has been cut, every piece must be weighed until the server is sure the cuts are back on target.

Another kind of scale often used in portioning is pictured in Figure 8.8. Because this scale costs far less than the portion scale shown in Figure 8.7, it is favored by many operators. Choosing a scale by its cost—rather than by the cost of the food—clearly is shortsighted. For small portions, first of all, this scale does

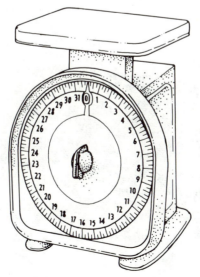

FIGURE 8.8 Portioning scale.

not offer the clearly visible, fine gradation of measurement necessary in portioning an expensive product. Another drawback is that it is a slow piece of equipment to use. If the work being done requires the weighing of a large amount of product (as in portioning roast beef for a large banquet), this delay in itself can be significant. Of equal importance is a tendency of kitchen workers to stop using this kind of scale for portioning as soon as the supervisor's back is turned, presumably because they can feel the scale slowing them down. The high-speed portion scale shown in Figure 8.7 does not have this disadvantage, because it is easy-to-use, accurate, and fast. The scale shown in Figure 8.8 often is used correctly, however, in weighing out ingredients where repetitive high-speed weighing is not called for.

Two other scales deserve mention, although generally they are not used directly to portion a single item for a guest's plate: the baker's dough scale (Figure 8.9) ordinarily is used to measure ingredients in a bake shop. Also it sometimes is used in portioning relatively low-cost baked products where absolute accuracy is not considered necessary. If, for instance, a 4 lb roll of dough should yield 32 rolls, the scale may be used to ensure that the worker starts with exactly the right amount (i.e., 4 lb), and then the baker's experienced eye is used to portion that amount in half, in half again, and finally into the final roll. With expensive breakfast rolls, however, the over-and-under scale often is used to weigh every fourth or fifth roll in the final cut, simply to ensure accurate portioning. Another baker's scale is used to "scale" products into pans. The distinct difference in this scale is that it can be "zeroed" (see Figure 8.10): that is, a pan is placed on the scale, the indicator is set at zero, and batter is then poured into the pan. Say, for example, that your baker has a 40 qt mixer full of cake batter to be portioned equally into eight bun pans (5 lb, 6 oz per pan). Doing this by eye

FIGURE 8.9 Baker's dough scale. These are available in either 8 or 16-pound capacity.

FIGURE 8.10 A scale that can be "zeroed." (Courtesy of Edlund Co., Inc.)

rarely would lead to eight equal pans and probably would result in fewer or more than eight pans! When you zero the weight, it becomes unnecessary to subtract the weight of the pan.

The electronic digital scales that have now entered the kitchen have numerous applications. They generally are equipped with tare weight adjustments (another term for zeroing). Figure 8.11 illustrates a digital scale.

Measuring Volume: Scoops and Ladles. Since everybody has eaten ice cream, the scoop is more or less an American institution. But what people unfamiliar with the back of the house do not realize is that scoops come in a

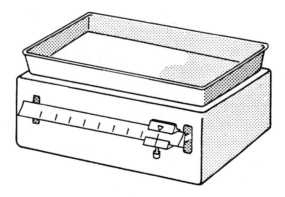

FIGURE 8.11 This digital entrée-weigh scale has programmable presets. It is used for selling foods by weight in, for example, salad bars or "make your own" sandwich operations. (Courtesy of Berkel, Inc.)

variety of shapes and serve many purposes. They are used not only for ice cream but also to dish out such varied products as mashed potatoes, mixed salad ingredients (as in a Waldorf salad), and sandwich fillings (as in a tuna salad sandwich). Other products commonly portioned with the so-called ice cream scoop include croquettes and meat patties, vegetables, muffins, cookies, and, of course, ice cream. Table 8.1 shows the various standard sizes of scoops, the amount of the individual servings, and the number of portions yielded by that scoop from one quart. As a glance at the first and last columns indicates, the "scoop number" is actually a rating formulated according to the number of servings per quart a given dipper will yield.

Figure 8.12 shows different kinds of scoops.

Ladles are used to measure liquid foods such as soups, gravies, and sauces, as well as mixture dishes such as stew and ragout. The ladle size generally is indicated on the handle. Table 8.2 shows the sizes of ladles which are in common use.

Spoons are not, in fact, a portioning tool, but they may be chosen for portioning inexpensive vegetables. Perforated spoons permit excess water to drain before the product is served. Ladles and spoons appropriate to quantity kitchens are shown in Figure 8.13.

Measuring Volume: Dispensers. Condiment dispensers usually are used for semiliquid sauces such as mustard and catsup. They generally have six dial settings that range from 1 to 15 oz (see Figures 8.14 and 8.15).

TABLE 8.1 APPROXIMATE YIELD OF FOOD SCOOPS

Size	Amount of Single Serving	Servings per Quart
No. 6	⅔ cup or 6 oz	6 servings
No. 8	½ cup or 4 oz	8
No. 10	⅜ cup or 3 oz	10
No. 12	⅓ cup or 2.5 oz	12
No. 16	¼ cup or 2.25 oz	16
No. 20	3⅕ tb or 2 oz	20
No. 24	2⅔ tb or 1.5 oz	24
No. 30	2⅕ tb or 1 oz	30
No. 40	1¾ tb or 0.75 oz	40

TABLE 8.2 SIZES OF LADLES

½ oz	6 oz
1 oz	6½ oz
1 ½ oz	8 oz
2 oz	8½ oz
3 oz	12 oz
4 oz	14½ oz
4½ oz	25 oz

PORTION CONTROL 201

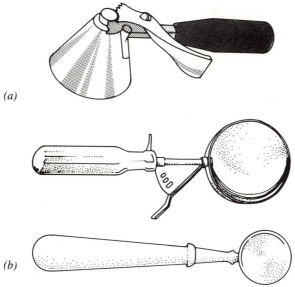

FIGURE 8.12 Scoops used in portion control. (*a*) Spherical scoop. (*b*) Ball scoop, used for fruit or vegetables. Sizes ¼ and ½ in. diameter (used for garnishes), ¾ in. diameter, 1 in. diameter.

Pancake batter dispensers such as the one pictured in Figure 8.16 control pancake portion size as they dispense batter directly onto the grill. This dispenser generally has eight dial settings that range from ½ to 3 oz.

Figure 8.17 shows an adjustable pump that may be used in soda fountain operations or for condiment self-service.

Measuring by Count. Many products are prepared in bulk form and then portioned into several equally-sized portions. The pie and cake markers shown in Figure 8.18 ensure accuracy in portioning.

Similarly, portion-control food slicers are used to portion products on a sheet pan. It is also common to use the experienced eye and hand of the cook to portion products prepared in large pans. Here, as we noted earlier, recipe directons will specify "cut 3 × 5" (meaning three slices from end to end and five slices from side to side) or some other dimension. This practice entails serious risks, however. Although experienced cooks *can* follow the directions, they may not in fact do so. Even experienced cooks must be supervised to some extent, to ensure that care is taken. In the case of inexperienced cooks, a whole pan of product can be ruined by a mistake in untrained judgement. If the inexperienced person does not make the regular cuts the recipe calls for, the result can be unevenly sized portions that cannot be served to the guest.

Portioned Products. Many foods, and particularly meats, come preproportioned. A preportioned steak, for instance, is ready to cook. Other meat products commonly preportioned include hamburger patties and sausage patties.

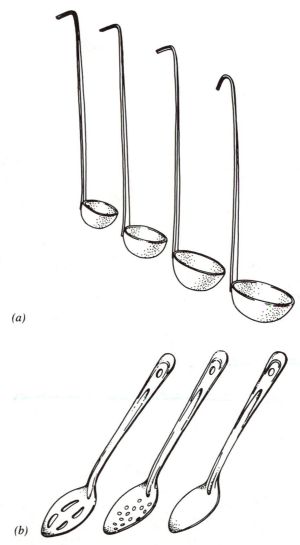

FIGURE 8.13 Ladles and spoons used in portioning. (*a*) Ladles are appropriate for measurement of liquid-based food such as sauces, gravies, soups. The size is indicated on the handle. (*b*) Spoons are available in solid or perforated form. They are not good for exact portion control, but are commonly used for vegetables and potatoes.

Portioned products generally cost more *per pound* than unportioned products, because the labor involved in portioning must be paid for. They are almost invariably a good buy, however, because the meat packer's portioning process is specialized and highly productive. It is thought that freshness is sacrificed when some products are portioned, since, for instance, final portioning of meat in-

FIGURE 8.14 Portion control condiment dispenser. (Courtesy of Server Products, Inc.)

volves cutting that results in fluid loss. Special care in receiving is appropriate with portioned products. If product is purchased *by the pound* and portioned *by the piece,* an error in overportioning by the supplier can result in a serious cost overrun. For example, 2 oz sausage patties that are overportioned by only ¼ oz mean a food cost increase of 12.5% on that particular item. For this reason, spot checks on portion size should be made a part of the receiving process.

FIGURE 8.15 Catsup dispenser for exact portion control. (Courtesy of Belshaw Bros., Inc.)

204 FOOD PRODUCTION CONTROL

FIGURE 8.16 Pancake batter dispenser. (Courtesy of Belshaw Bros., Inc.)

FIGURE 8.17 Adjustable pump for soda fountains. (Courtesy of Server Products, Inc.)

PORTION CONTROL **205**

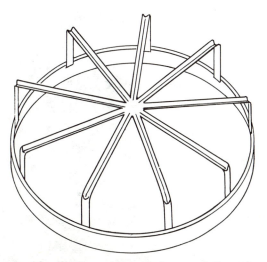

FIGURE 8.18 Pie and cake markers used for dividing a cake or pie into equal slices of a predetermined number, usually 5 to 12.

Using Containers for Portion Control

We noted earlier that active portion control relies on such portioning actions as weighing or measuring final portions. With some products, portion control is completely designed into the production and/or service. (see Figure 8.19). Muffins, for instance, may be sized by choosing from among the various size muffin cups available. Cake and pie pans have a similar effect. The following list, showing the common sizes of muffin pans and cake and pie pans, indicates the wide variation in portion size made possible by different-sized cooking utensils. Various-sized baking utensils are shown in Figure 8.20.

Cup Sizes	Pan Sizes
2 × 1⅛ in.	8 × 1³⁄₁₆ in.
2½ × 1 in.	9 × 1⅛ in.
2½ × 1⅛ in.	9 × 1¼ in.
3 × 1¼ in.	9 × 1½ in.
	9½ × 1¼ in.
	10 × 1⁵⁄₁₆ in.
	10 × 1½ in.
	10 × 1⅝ in.
	10 × 1⁵⁄₁₆ in.

Biscuit, cookie, and doughnut cutters, with differing kinds of edges and oval or round shapes, are available in sizes ranging from ½ to 3 in. in diameter.

Bakewear also is used to control portion size. The selection of china has a

FIGURE 8.19 This operation, not content with allowing the size of the muffin pan ultimately to determine the portion size, avoids variation in portion cost by using a dispenser that measures exact portions. (Courtesy of Belshaw Bros., Inc.)

FIGURE 8.20 The size of the pan influences the portion size and the cost of the product.

major impact on portion size and on the acceptability of portion size. (Too large a dish makes an adequate portion look small.) Common sizes for bakeware include

Custard dishes:	2½, 4, 5, 5½, 6, 7, 9
Shallow oval baker:	3½, 4½, 6, 7, 8, 10, 11, 12, 14, 16, 20
Crab shell:	3
Lobster casserole:	8
Baking shell:	2½, 4½, 5½

Portion Control on the Buffet

Because buffets and salad bars generally offer "all you can eat," they seem to defy portion control. However, some steps can be taken to make this "uncontrollable" form of food service much more susceptible to management direction.

The first step is to select plate, bowl, and side dishes in sizes that will accommodate what you think should be an appropriate portion. More fundamentally, however, is the collection of average-use data. By studying patterns of food use related to the number of guests served, you soon will be able to predict the average food consumption per guest in your operation. This procedure is helpful not only in estimating for preparation but also in determining the selling price of the buffet or of a salad bar.

Similarly, in a full buffet-style service, you cannot control the amount the guest takes, but you can base the price on what an average guest will take. In this way, you can ensure an appropriate relationship between average portion cost and menu price.

PORTION CONTROL FOR FAST FOOD

Portion control for fast food appears to be a simple process at the unit level—and for the most part, it is simple. Most fast food products are preportioned and ready to serve. Some operations, however, do portion their own hamburger or cut frozen fish fillets to portion size. In general, these activities require careful training but present no special difficulty.

On the other hand, to maintain portion size at the plants that supply the units, many companies engage in continuous on-site inspection of the preparation and portioning of product. In fact, as we have noted, receiving is often perfunctory, entailing merely verification of the number of packages. Moreover, many fast food operations do not spot-check weights of preportioned products *unless they have reason to believe there is a problem.*

One chain, for instance, buys fabricated chicken leg product by the pound and portions it by count (i.e., three or five *pieces* are counted out as a portion). Underweight pieces are revealed promptly by the operation's computerized daily food cost report on that item. A daily ending inventory (in pounds) of the store's key items is given to the computer, and sales are registered in the computer directly as they occur. The computer, using a recipe file from its memory banks, compares the number of orders sold with the number of pounds used and provides a daily "efficiency rating" for each of the key food items. When the pieces of chicken leg are undersized, the daily report will indicate that the chicken leg product was underutilized relative to sales.

This underuse percent alerts the store manager, who then checks weights on the product. If underweight products are, indeed, the cause of the underutilization, a report is filed immediately. (Of course, an over weight product—that is, too-heavy chicken legs—would show up on the report as overutilization of product, and also would call for immediate action.) At this point, the Purchasing Department contacts the supplier to remedy the deficiency and, arrange for a credit (if indicated) for improper product shipped.

Portion control in fast food chains, then, includes the fairly simple problem of maintaining portions in the store, which is solved through the use of preportioned products, *and* the problem of policing supplies practices throughout the food service system.

In some contract companies specializing in institutional food service, centralized commissaries produce and preportion products, which are then shipped to units. Commissaries, as noted in the section on receiving, sometime maintain that careful receiving, including the checking of portion sizes, is not necessary, but in the best opinion of experienced unit managers, it is necessary to maintain at least some degree of vigilance regarding the quality and accuracy of portioning. As with *any supplier,* vigilance is especially important when the product is charged to the unit by the pound but portioned by count. Such caution prevents scrimping, however accidental, on guest service, or, conversely, excess food costs stemming from overgenerous portions.

KEY WORDS AND PHRASES

Chef kitchen
Recipe kitchen
Standardized recipe
Method cards
Procedures
Leftover control
PTO
Ready foods
Freezing
Latent zone storage
Marked menu
Ingredient control
Portion control
Determining portion size
Portion control approaches
Portioned foods by the pound
Portioned foods by the piece
Tools for portion control
Weight scales
Dispensers
Pumps
Markers
Pan sizes, standardized
Scoops and ladles
Count
Bakeware
Portion control for buffets
Portion control for fast food
Underuse or overuse percent

DISCUSSION QUESTIONS

1. Indicate how you might accurately ensure portion control for each item on the following banquet menu.

   Grilled steak with mushroom sauce.
   Baked potato with sour cream and butter.
   Asparagus tips.
   Hearts of palm on romaine with vinaigrette dressing.
   Rolls and butter.
   Coffee or tea.
   Coconut cream pie.

2. Identify five procedures that often are not written down in restaurants but that should be to control costs. Develop one procedure from your list.

3. You have no recipe or procedure for making a ham sandwich. Think of ways in which the cost could be altered if you changed cooks.

4. Discuss leftover strategies with regard to PTO and prepared foods.

5. In an ice cream parlor, the manager hires student help to scoop ice cream cones. The students load up the scoop for their friends—and they have many friends. How could the manager control the portion cost in this situation?

6. In your fast food outlet, you portion your own hamburgers from freshly ground beef. At the end of the day, your POS report indicates that you should have used 75 lb of hamburger for the 300 hamburgers sold that day. The ground beef inventory at the beginning of the day was 97 lbs, purchases added 50 lbs and the ending inventory was 79 lb. The report indicates an overuse of 5%. What does this mean? What action should you take? What action would you take if the hamburgers were purchased individually portioned and frozen?

9 PRECOSTING

Accuracy

Handling Special Precosting Problems

Record Keeping for Precosts

THE PURPOSE
OF THIS CHAPTER

Not long ago, before "foodflation," the restaurant operator would figure out menu prices by scribbling costs on a scrap of paper (perhaps a paper napkin) and then multiply by 2 ½ or 3 to get a selling price. In today's competitive atmosphere, such sloppy methodology is simply too risky. Operators know their costs down to the penny (one airline feeder, for example, figures portion costs to thousandths of a cent). Indeed, the entire matter of precosting in some large food services requires a computer that prints out recipes with an up-to-date cost per serving.

Precosting is a necessary management job that can be simplified and systemized. *Speed* and *accuracy* are critical in our busy world. This chapter suggests a system for precosting that will enable you to develop portion costs with exactness and allow you to update your costs rapidly.

Although some fast-food and institutional food services have reduced precosting to a computer routine, this is as yet not the norm in the hospitality industry. The chances are that you will need to precost by hand, and so this chapter approaches precosting from the standpoint of an operation in which precosting is done in that manner.

THIS CHAPTER
SHOULD HELP YOU

1. Determine new food costs with speed and accuracy.

2. Solve the problems inherent in determining costs:
   (a) Weight/measure conversions.
   (b) Weight/volume conversions.
   (c) Counts per purchase unit.
   (d) Yields.
   (e) Trim losses.

3. Make use of a multiplying factor to save time in forecasting.

4. Develop strategies for handling special problems.

ACCURACY

At the outset, precosting can seem like a simple exercise in arithmetic. Take a standard item in many restaurants—a turkey sandwich served with cole slaw. The cost of this sandwich is illustrated below.

214 PRECOSTING

Yield: 1 sandwich

Ingredients	Ingredient Cost
2 oz turkey	$0.263
1 tbsp mayonnaise	$0.018
2 tsp butter	$0.029
1 lettuce leaf	$0.022
2 slices white bread	$0.082
#10 scoop cole slaw	$0.095
2 dill pickle chips	$0.012
½ oz carrot curls	$0.008
1 oz (fluid) cranberry sauce	$.0.053

For food service units, however, going from ingredient to cost can be complicated, even with this simple sandwich. The costs listed above, for example, were determined from the following purchase units and costs:

Fresh turkey: $0.79 per pound.

Mayonnaise: Four 128 oz jars, $18.09.

Butter: 15 lb, $21.00.

Lettuce: carton of 24 heads, $10.25.

Pullman loaves: $0.98 each.

Cole slaw: $3.80 per gal.

Dill pickle chips: 5 gal, $14.90.

Carrots: 50 lb bag, $9.50.

Cranberry sauce: Six #10 cans, $31.44.

Many problems immediately arise: how to convert fresh uncooked turkey to the cooked product; how many leaves of lettuce in a head, or tablespoons of mayonnaise in an ounce; how many slices of bread in a loaf, and so on.

You could guess at the answers, but remember that accuracy is your aim. For this reason, we included Appendix I, which details precosting. The first step in precosting is to convert all ingredients to purchase units. For example, if ingredients are in cups and the purchase unit is in pounds, cups need to be converted to pounds (you could also do it the other way around—it does not matter, so long as each are in the *same* units). This section illustrates how to make these conversions with the help of the charts; the Appendix will be introduced on a chart-by-chart basis.

CHART 1: WEIGHT AND MEASURE CONVERSIONS
The first charts you will need are those for weight and measure conversions. Metric measurements are included in these charts because they increasingly are becoming the international standard, even though you may not need to use them

in your operation. (Canadians use metric measures, and if you buy product in Canada, you will be using metric measure).

We can now begin to solve the mayonnaise problem, for example, by noting, from this chart, that

$$1 \text{ tb} = \frac{1}{2} (.5) \text{ oz (fluid)}.$$

Thus, both the ingredient unit and the purchase unit are put in the ounce units.

Note that in the "List of Common Measures" (Chart 1 in the Appendix) 1 gal is equivalent to 128 oz *fluid*. Fluid ounces are commonly mistaken for weight measure by students, but fluid and weight measures are *not* the same. A fluid ounce is based upon the density of water, and many measures are given in fluid ounces rather than in cups, pints or quarts. In bars, for example, 1 or 2 oz shots of liquor are served, and beer is measured according to 8 or 12 oz mugs rather than 1 or 1 ½ cups. (But to convert a 5 gal keg of beer, you need to know how many glasses of beer to expect from a gallon.)

CHART 2: CONVERSIONS

Chart 2 is probably the most commonly used chart for precosting. In our turkey sandwich, for example, we need two tsp of butter, and butter is purchased by the pound. Chart 2 tells you that there are approximately 2 cups of butter in a pound. Going back to Chart 1 to convert teaspoons to cups, you find that

$$3 \text{ tsp/tbsp} \times 16 \text{ tbsp/cup} = 48 \text{ tsp/cup}$$
$$48 \text{ tsp per cup} \times 2 \text{ cups butter/lb} = 96 \text{ tsp/lb}$$

Note, in using Chart 2, that amounts are based upon the density of the food. Obviously, flour is lighter than, say, honey. (There are approximately 4 cups of flour in a pound, but only 1 ⅓ cups in a pound of honey. Do not confuse these amounts with fluid ounces—students often assume there are 8 oz of flour in a cup when, in fact, there are only 4).

CHART 3: APPROXIMATE YIELDS OF SCOOPS AND LADLES

In restaurants, many foods are prepared or purchased in gallon lots and the cost initially is determined per gallon. Scoops and ladles frequently are used in portioning these goods. Soups, sauces, puddings, rice, mashed potatoes are examples. In our turkey example, a No. 10 scoop of cole slaw is served with the sandwich. The scoop number is equivalent to the number of such scoops per quart. Thus, after referring (if necessary) to Chart 1 for the number of quarts in a gallon, we see that a No. 10 scoop will yield 40 servings per gallon (4 × 10). A portion cost, therefore, requires us to divide the cost per gallon by 40.

In precosting, portion sizes often can be manipulated when the cost of the item is so high that the food service operator suspects there will be price resistance.

216 PRECOSTING

This provides another use for Chart 3. For example, if you are planning to serve a No. 8 scoop of sherbet for a banquet and wondering what the cost would be if you used a No. 10 scoop, you could refer to the charts. Ice creams and sherbets are special problems; they "shrink" when dished, because of the air incorporated in them. Because they are used so commonly, a separate chart for them is included. Thus, we see that a No. 8 scoop will yield 20 to 25 scoops and a No. 10 scoop 24 to 30 servings per gallon.

CHART 4: COMMON CAN SIZES

Again returning to our turkey sandwich example, we see that cranberry sauce is purchased in no. 10 cans. To find out how much this can contains and convert to like units, we consult Chart 4, where we find that there are three quarts in a No. 10 can. Since we need 1 fl oz we also need to consult Chart 1, where we find (under *1A*) that there are 32 fluid ounces in a quart. Thus,

$$32 \times 3 \text{ qt per can} = 96 \text{ fl oz per can}$$

Fortunately, can sizes are standard in the food industry, and it is possible to predict with some accuracy the number of servings—except, of course, for loose items, for which we use the drained weight.

CHART 5: COMMON COUNTS

If you encounter an item for which you need numbers per purchase unit, this chart may help you. For our turkey sandwich, we will find here the approximate number of lettuce leaves in a head, the number of slices of bread in a Pullman loaf, and the number of pickle slices in a gallon. It may seem tedious to go into such detail, but your operation will be more competitive if you know costs to the penny rather than just guess at them. For example, although awareness of the cost of a pickle chip will not make or break a fast food restaurant, that awareness will contribute to profit when millions of sanwiches are sold by the chain. *Every* fast food chain knows the cost of their pickle chips and other garnishes.

CHART 6: APPROXIMATE YIELDS FOR MEAT, POULTRY, AND SEAFOOD

Meats that are purchased fresh, with the bone in, naturally do not yield the same weight as when those that have been trimmed, cooked, boned, and sliced; yet students often nonchalantly divide the cost per pound of fresh by 16 to obtain the cost per ounce. Each individual cut of the animal may have a different yield.

Using Chart 6 with our well-worn turkey sandwich, we find that whole fresh turkey yields only 35 to 45% cooked meat, or 5 to 7 oz per lb purchased. From one pound of fresh turkey, then, we would expect a yield of three turkey sandwiches (average 6 oz per lb and 2 oz per sandwich).

CHART 7: APPROXIMATE TRIM LOSSES IN FRESH PRODUCE
Fresh produce presents the problem that a pound purchased includes peelings and trimmings that will be cut from fresh produce. Chart 7 addresses this problem. The carrot curls with our turkey sandwich can be used as an example: Carrots without tops yield 75 to 82% usable carrots, or 12 to 13 oz per lb; from a pound of carrots, then, we could expect 24 to 26 servings of carrot curls (at ½ oz each).

MULTIPLYING FACTORS
Because of purchase unit sizes, the use of a multiplying factor (MF) will save precosting time—but not the first time through. The savings will come when there is a price change.

The multiplying factor works as follows: If hamburger costs $1.00 a pound and we need 5 lb, the cost of the hamburger is 5 × $1.00, and the multiplying factor is 5. Likewise, if we need half a pound of hamburger, 0.5 × $1.00 will give us the cost—again the multiplying factor is 0.5. If we buy hamburger in 10 lb bags for $10.00, and need half a pound, then 0.05 × 10 will give us the cost; the multiplying factor here is 0.05.

From the example above, the MF is constructed easily when simple units are used. But because we buy by cases, lugs, counts, and many different units, the MF becomes a little complicated to construct at first. Returning to our turkey sandwich, we will construct an MF for several items, to show, step by step, how this procedure works.

There are three steps in developing a multiplying factor and determining ingredient cost:

STEP 1. Put all ingredients and purchase units into the same unit amounts, using the conversion charts.
STEP 2. Divide the amount needed by the amount in the purchase unit. The result is the multiplying factor.
STEP 3. Multiply the MF times the purchase price to obtain the ingredient cost.

To illustrate, using the turkey sandwich:

Turkey

STEP 1. Put all ingredients and purchase units into the same unit amounts
2 oz cooked turkey needed
1 lb fresh turkey yields 5 to 7 oz, (avg. = 6 oz.)
STEP 2. Divide the amount needed by the amount in the purchase unit. The Result is the Multiplying Factor (MF)[1].
2 ÷ 6 (avg.) = 0.3333 MF
STEP 3. Multiply the MF by the purchase price to obtain the ingredient cost.
0.3333 × $0.79 = $0.263 (ingredient cost)

---

[1] Because the purchase units for this ingredient are large, accuracy is obtained by carrying the calculation for the MF to four decimal places.

Mayonnaise

STEP 1. Need 0.5 oz mayonnaise; 512 oz in purchase unit (4 × 128 oz jars/purchase unit)
STEP 2. 0.5 ÷ 512 = 0.0010 (MF)
STEP 3. 0.0010 × $18.09 = 0.018 (ingredient cost)

Butter

STEP 1. Need 2 tsp butter; 1440 tsp in purchase unit (3 tsp per tbsp; 16 tbsp per cup; 2 cups per lb; 15 lb. per purchase unit = 3 × 16 × 2 × 15 = 1440 tsp).
STEP 2. 2 ÷ 1440 = .0014 (MF)
STEP 3. 0.0014 × $21.00 = 0.029 (ingredient cost)

Using these examples, you can compute the MFs for the other ingredients and compare them with our results given in Table 9.1.

As mentioned at the beginning of this exercise, developing a multiplying factor is time consuming the first time you precost a food product. The payoff comes when there is a price change: then, you need only insert the price change and multiply by the MF to obtain the ingredient cost. If there has been a change in the purchase unit, however, then you must develop a new multiplying factor. Table 9.2 provides an example of price revision using the multiplying factor.

KITCHEN TESTING

The charts in the appendix are approximate—the averages of many samples. Food service operators feel it is absolutely essential to kitchen test yields, counts, and sizes to confirm predicted portion costs.

A large food service company, for example, was converting their recipes to computer and hired a food service student from a hotel school to kitchen-test their

TABLE 9.1 TURKEY SANDWICH PRECOST

Prepared by *JMP*
DATE *2/7/83*

Ingredients	Purchase Price	MF	Ingredient Cost
2 oz turkey	79¢/lb.	0.3333	$0.263
1 tbsp mayonnaise	4 128-oz jars, $18.09	0.0010	0.018
2 tsp butter	15 lb, $21.00	0.0014	0.029
1 lettuce leaf	Carton, 24 heads, $10.25	0.0021	0.022
2 slices white bread	1 Pullman loaf, $0.98	0.0833	0.082
#10 scoop cole slaw	$3.80 per gal	0.0250	0.095
2 dill pickle chips	5 gal for $14.90	0.0008	0.012
½ oz carrot curls	$9.50/50 lb bag	0.0008	0.008
1 oz cranberry sauce	6 #10 cans, $31.44	0.0017	0.053
		Cost of 1 turkey sandwich:	$0.582

TABLE 9.2 TURKEY SANDWICH PRECOST REVISION

Prepared by _JMP_
Date _2/7/83_

Ingredients	Purchase Price	MF	Ingredient Cost[a]
2 oz turkey	.89¢/lb.	0.3333	0.297
1 tbsp mayonnaise	4 128-oz jars, $18.09	0.0010	0.018
2 tsp butter	15 lb, $24.00	0.0014	0.034
1 lettuce leaf	Carton, 24 heads, $10.25	0.0021	0.022
2 slices white bread	1 Pullman loaf, $0.98	0.0833	0.082
#10 scoop cole slaw	$3.80 per gal	0.025	0.095
2 dill pickle chips	5 gal for $14.90	0.0008	0.012
½ oz carrot curls	$11.00/50 lb bag	0.0008	0.009
1 oz cranberry sauce	6 #10 cans, $31.44	0.0017	0.053
	Cost of 1 turkey sandwich:		$0.622

[a]To obtain new ingredient costs when there is a price change, multiply the new purchase price by the multiplying factor (MF). It is unnecessary to go through the conversion steps again.

portion costs. The student found that many items did not meet predicted costs. Lasagna, for example, actually cost more than the selling price! Here, the recipes in use had been modified over time by the cooks to "make them better," and they no longer bore any relationship to the original predicted costs. This situation, unfortunately, is not rare.

Another example of why kitchen testing is so critical is supplied by expensive meats. A newly hired purchasing agent for a chain of restaurants found that the company had been purchasing the least-expensive uncooked corned beef on the market. After cooking, however, the yield was less than 25%. He found that the much higher-priced fully cooked corned beef actually was less expensive than the so-called cheapest. Using the conversion yield charts as a guide, you can get some idea of how products _should_ stand up, and what you can expect in yield and trim.

You will find, too, that these charts do not include everything that you will need to make conversions. Often, you will have to go into the kitchen and yield, count, or weigh to obtain a correct portion cost.

HANDLING SPECIAL PRECOSTING PROBLEMS

HIDDEN COSTS

Note in our turkey sandwich example how the cost of the "little" things add up. To obtain accurate portion costs, you must include all costs, particularly those that may not be apparent in the menu item or recipe.

Recipes often do not include accompaniments (sauces, relishes, etc.) and garnishes. Some operators use a set figure (3 to 6% is commonly quoted) for accompaniments, but accuracy requires that you know exactly what will be used and how much the cost per serving is. Another problem is that guests usually are allowed to help themselves to items such as catsup and mustard on sandwiches and sugar and cream in coffee.

Experience is the best way to handle this usage problem. If, for example, you use two No. 10 cans of catsup a week and sell an average of 1000 sandwiches, you can compute the average portion cost of catsup. Occasionally, averages are available if you have no historical data. (Figure 9.1 gives the results of a national poll on the use of sugar and cream in coffee). If it is essential to know the exact portion costs of these accompaniments, techniques for accuracy are available. The most common technique is to use preportioned items such as individual packets of catsup and mustard or of sugar and cream. To control usage, management instructs servers to use a specific number per order (rather than allow customers to take a handful). Another technique is to limit amounts by the serving device used. For example, the size of the salad bowl used on a salad bar limits the quantity the customer can take, as does the ladle size used for the salad dressing.

Other hidden costs to watch for arise from ingredients in recipes that are not mentioned in the ingredient list; examples include breadings, fats for grilling or frying, and seasonings. Usually, these can be identified by reading through the recipe or by observing the preparation of the food.

54% of coffee drinkers use sugar.
40% of coffee drinkers use cream or nondairy creamers.
6% of coffee drinkers use artificial sweeteners.
28% of coffee drinkers have a second cup.

FIGURE 9.1 Results of national coffee poll. *Source*: Gallup survey, 1970.

SEASONAL PRICE CHANGES

The prices of some foods, particularly produce and meats, change frequently. For example, if you are setting the price of a salad and lettuce has jumped in price from $7.00 to $20.00 a carton in several weeks, what price should be used for the purchase cost? Here it is helpful to review the past history of price fluctuations and set the purchase cost based on an average price. The purchase price of a carton of lettuce, for example, might be averaged as follows.

Month	Average Price
January	$ 5.50
February	$ 5.50
March	$ 6.00
April	$ 7.00
May	$ 8.00
June	$ 7.50
July	$ 7.50
August	$ 8.50
September	$ 9.00
October	$12.00
November	$ 8.50
December	$ 7.50
Average Purchase Price for Year	$ 7.71

When setting menu prices for the next period, operators today build in an inflation factor based on previous price increases and market analysis predictions for the next year. In the case of contract feeders, menu prices are often set as much as a year in advance, and they must build an inflation factor into their costs.

FAT USAGE

Deep-fat-fried foods are a special problem, because the portion cost must include the cost of the fat. The amount of fat absorbed is an insufficient measure, because when a vat of fat deteriorates to a certain point, it must be discarded. The cost of fat for frying one order of food, therefore, is determined by studying fat usage. First, the amount of fat added to an empty fryer is measured. Then, both the number of orders fried and the additional fat added are recorded until the fat is discarded. Table 9.3 illustrates this procedure.

WASTE FACTOR

Because animal and plant products have a certain degree of inconsistency and deviate somewhat from the standard charts, a waste factor generally is used in determining portion costs as a cushion. Also, no operation is immune from error. Precosting must take into account a certain unavoidable amount of waste, from product being overcooked, a plate or tray of product being dropped on the floor, or product being consumed by employees against the rules. The waste factor is determined by the type of operation. Operations with an extended menu (such as cafeterias) find it necessary to use a higher waste factor than that used by a limited-menu operation (such as fast food). The frequently used industry figure is 10%, but many operations strive to keep the waste factor under 5%, and many fast food operators operate with significantly lower unavoidable waste allowances.

TABLE 9.3 STUDY OF FAT USAGE

	Amount of Fat Added to Fryer	Number of Orders Fried
Day 1	50 lb	160
	12 lb	
Day 2	10 lb	140
Day 3	10 lb	140
Day 4	15 lb	200
Day 5	10 lb (fat discarded at end of day)	120
Total	107 lb	760 orders
Cost of fat @ $0.60/lb	($0.60 × 107 = $64.20)	
Cost of fat per portion; fried: $64.20 ÷ 760 = $0.085/serving		

222 PRECOSTING

RECORD KEEPING FOR PRECOSTS

We strongly suggest that you maintain a record keeping system separate from your recipe file for raw food costs. This is a managerial control system. A readily available file box containing costs written on index cards may well work. It also is important to date costs, so that when you recost, you will know how long it has been since you last costed the recipe.

Frequently, large operations are able to place price changes into a computer's memory banks and let the computer determine the cost per serving. Although the chapter assumes the computer is *not* available, you may be interested in the example of such a computer determined precost, shown in Figure 9.2, which builds yields and trim factors into the costs.

KEY WORDS AND PHRASES

Precosting
Speed and accuracy
Weight and measure conversions
Weight-to-volume conversions
Scoop and ladle yields
Can yields
Common counts
Yields for meat, poultry, seafood
Trim loss for produce

Multiplying factor
Three steps
Kitchen testing
Hidden costs
Seasonal price changes
Fat usage
Waste factor
Record keeping

DISCUSSION QUESTIONS

1. Discuss why it is important to know product costs with accuracy.

2. Discuss how product perishability affects product cost.

3. If the restaurant down the street sells steak at a profit for $4.00, does that mean that your restaurant could do the same? Discuss the parameters necessary before this would be true.

4. Discuss why fast food chains must know to a fraction of a cent the cost of every food ingredient and condiment.

5. How would you set up a fat usage study? How would you analyze results?

6. Discuss why kitchen testing is critical after a preliminary estimate of product cost.

RECORD KEEPING FOR PRECOSTS

```
11/26/80                                                    UNIVERSITY OF MISSOURI MEDICAL CENTER
PAGE 0001                                                   DEPARTMENT OF NUTRITION AND DIETETICS
RECIPE CODE NO: 430773         RECIPE NAME: SPANISH RICE                    STD
                               NC INGREDIENTS: 7                            DINNER OR SUPPER STARCH
NUMBER CAFE SERV:  50          NUMBER PT. SERV:  50         BATCH SIZE: MIN:  50      ADVANCE PREF CODE: 1
PER/CAFE SERV:  5.5 OZ         WT/FT. SERV: 160 GM                      MAX: 200      RECIPE YIELD: 18.10 LBS

  INGRED                         NUTR              PRE-PREP    QTY     COST/   PREP    CKD     CKD    E.F.    SUB       ADV    ADV   PREP
  CODE   INGREDIENT NAME         CODE   QTY UNIT   YIELD      AP LBS  INGR    YIELD   YIELD   WEIGHT YIELD  INGRED     WITH   PREP   STEP  CD
1 41459  RICE                    1872   2.50 LB    0.99       2.52    0.456   0.99    2.94    7.27   0.99   00000       9      1      1    3
2 32808  TOMATOES                2283  128.00 OZ.  0.99       8.08    3.522   0.99    0.99    7.84   0.99   00000       9      1      2    3
3 32255  GREEN PEPPER            1546   1.25 LB    0.80       1.56    0.595   0.99    0.99    1.22   0.99   00000       9      0      3    3
4 35645  PIMENTO                 1610   2.50 OZ    0.95       0.16    0.074   0.99    0.99    0.15   0.99   00000       9      0      4    3
5 43435  SALT                    1963   1.50 OZ    0.99       0.09    0.005   0.99    0.99    0.08   0.99   00000       9      1      5    3
6 04057  BACON                   0126   1.50 LB    0.99       1.51    1.629   0.99    0.60    0.88   0.99   00000       1      0      6    3
7 33626  ONION                   1413   1.00 LB    0.99       1.01    0.275   0.99    0.85    0.84   0.99   00000       9      0      7    3

                                                  TOTAL FOOD COST       6.556   CAL REC YIELD  18.28 LBS   PERCENT DIFFERENCE   0.0
SUGGESTED SELLING PRICE FACTOR  4.0
SUGGESTED SELLING PRICE   $0.52                   COST CAFE SERV        0.131   CAL WT/CAFE SV  05.8 OZ   PERCENT DIFFERENCE   5.0
ACTUAL SELLING PRICE      $0.95                   COST PT. SERV         0.131   CAL WT/PT. SV 166 GM     PERCENT DIFFERENCE   3.0

NUTRIENT COMPOSITION/PATIENT SERVING

CAL    PRO    FAT    SEA    UFA1   UFA2   CHO    FIBER   CHOL   CALC   PHOS   IRON   SODIUM   POTAS   VIT-A    THIA   RIBC   NIAC   VIT-C
       GM     GM     MG     MG     MG     GM     GM      MG     MG     MG     MG     MG       MG      I.U.     GM     GM     GM     GM
142.   4.8    4.4    1.     2.     0.     20.9   0.7     6.     23.    63.    1.4    367.     264.    784.     0.2    0.07   1.7    29.
```

FIGURE 9.2 Computerized precosting.

PRODUCTIVITY ANALYSIS AND PAYROLL CONTROL

10

Productivity in Food Service

Categories of Payroll Costs

Tools for Analyzing and Controlling Payroll

Scheduling

Organizing for Productivity

Ratio Analysis

Point of Sales Systems and Productivity

THE PURPOSE
OF THIS CHAPTER
Productivity measures how much is obtained for a given cost: for instance, how many meals per manhour or how many guests served per employee. Productivity is important to food service managers because of increasing wages and because good employees—at any cost—are scarce. For these reasons learning how to plan for productivity is crucial.

In this chapter, we will review the productivity outlook in food service and study the tools managers use to control payroll costs, which amounts to the same thing as controlling productivity. Finally, we will study the means of organizing food service, to ensure that our productivity planning is put into practice.

THIS CHAPTER SHOULD HELP YOU
1. See payroll control in the broader context of productivity in food service.

2. Identify the major kinds of payroll costs.

3. Tell the difference between marginal improvements in payroll, which are the proper function of operative management's attention, and gross changes in productivity, which require a change in the operation's way of doing business.

4. Identify and know the uses of the major payroll-control tools.

5. Know the pitfalls as well as the positive factors involved in overtime and in part-time scheduling.

6. Understand the need for an overall organizational plan to manage for productivity.

PRODUCTIVITY IN FOOD SERVICE

That payroll costs have been increasing is such common knowledge that we almost hesitate to restate the obvious. When the Fair Labor Standards Act became law in the United States, the minimum wage was 40 cents and food service was exempt from the act. Since that time, the minimum wage has climbed steadily and in 1966 the U.S. hospitality industry came under the provisions of the act. Clearly, there has been no halt in the rise in this floor under wages in the intervening years.

Another floor under wages is income from various governmental sources available to people who are not working, such as unemployment compensation and welfare benefits. Although these programs are aimed at supporting those who temporarily cannot find work or are unable to work, they also have made available to some potential workers the choice of receiving without working,[1] approximately what the entry-level worker in our industry earns.

The hourly rate for food service workers has been rising steadily since 1958, when that data first became available. But so has the hourly rate for all other workers. In fact, the rate of increase has been about the same for food service as for the economy in general. Food service, however, suffers from a crucial handicap in terms of productivity.

Two common measures of productivity in food service are the number of guests served per employee hour and the dollar sales per employee hour. In terms of sales per employee hour, productivity in eating and drinking establishments in the United States has been increasing at an average annual rate of 1% since 1958. In the same period, however, productivity in the private economy rose at an annual rate of nearly 3%.[2] As a result, unit labor costs have been rising much more rapidly in food service than in the private economy as a whole.

Any manager must have a variety of skills, but perhaps the single most desirable skill for the generation now joining management ranks is an ability to enhance productivity. This skill involves, among other things, the ability to use the appropriate tools for planning and controlling labor costs on a day-to-day basis. Secondly, it involves an understanding of the factors that affect productivity in organizational planning.

CATEGORIES OF PAYROLL COSTS

Payroll costs fall into two basic categories: fixed and variable. Cost planning for productivity requires different considerations for each of these categories.

FIXED PAYROLL COSTS

There is a minimum number of workers without which your business could not open. Included in this basic crew are management and supervisory personnel and the minimum number of hourly production and service workers required to serve the operation's lowest volume level at acceptable standards of quality. Planning for the fixed crew involves studying possible combinations of duties so that the basic crew does, indeed, require the *minimum* number of workers.

A more subtle problem in planning for the basic crew is that management will be tempted to cut below *real* requirements. A common temptation is for management to take over a significant share of the worker's duties, replacing an hourly worker with a manager "who will get paid anyway." Well, a manager *can* wash

---

[1] For fuller discussion of this issue, see Thomas F. Powers, "Labor Supply, Payroll Costs, and Change," *CHRAQ* May 1974, p. 9–12.
[2] R. B. Carnes and Horst Brand, "Productivity and New Technology in Eating and Drinking Places," *Monthly Labor Review,* Sept. 1977, p. 9.

dishes—but he or she cannot very well do so and also, for instance, check portion size or oversee guest service. Quality standards must be maintained during minimum volume levels, too.

VARIBLE COSTS

The simplest example of a variable-cost employee is a banquet waitress. If the standard of the house for a simple banquet is one server per 30 banquet guests, then a banquet of 60 guests requires two servers, and one of 90 guests, three servers. The challenge in scheduling these employees lies in having adequate production standards so that an appropriate number—neither too few nor too many—of variable employee hours can be scheduled to cover needs (see below).

Of course, *perfect* variability *cannot* be achieved; a banquet of 100 guests in the example above would not mean 3.3 servers, for the simple reason that servers do not come in that kind of unit! For this reason, some variable costs, such as payroll, often are referred to as step variables, or mixed costs.

Step Variables

Say that a restaurant has three dining rooms, each with a capacity of 45 guests, and a minimum of two employees on duty per room. When sales volume is expected to exceed the capacity of one room, such an operation will not have the smooth increase that a perfectly variable cost would imply. One evening, 45 guests might be served in one room by two servers. If 60 guests show up the next night, however, the restaurant would have to open a second room, and that would mean a step, or jump, in servers from two to four. Productivity would change from 22.5 guests per server to 15 guests per server, in order to maintain the operation's quality standards in guest service.

The step points—that is, the points at which increases in labor are needed—usually are clear, and so forecasting labor costs in a stepwise fashion need not present any special difficulties.

The term *mixed costs* refers to costs with both fixed and variable elements. Some payroll situations (minimum crew size plus increases to match sales volume increases) fit this description, but it also applies to a wide variety of other costs—particularly utility costs. Mixed costs are discussed in Chapter 14, which is concerned with budgeting and longer time periods. This chapter concentrates on the concepts and tools used in shorter-run payroll planning.

PRODUCTIVITY LEVELS

One problem with planning to reduce costs is that some managers seem to think that they should aim for the ultimate reduction—to zero. In practice, obviously, there are limits to how much productivity improvement is possible or desirable. The most basic limitations are those of human capacity and endurance: there are limits to how fast a server can move or how fast a cook can cook.

Table 10.1 suggests where some limits may lie.[3] Notice that it takes about 2 ½ times as many employee hours to serve a hundred guests in a luxury restaurant as it does in a family restaurant or cafeteria. Fast food establishments, in turn, can serve twice as many guests per employee hour as can family restaurants. So to double productivity, for instance, we would need to *change the kind of operation*. To put it another way, a gross change in productivity requires major *system* change.

An example may be helpful here. If a hotel were to introduce new bus carts in its coffee shop and improved methods in the dish room, the resulting change in productivity in handling sorted china, glass, and silver might well be important and significant—but it would be only a *marginal change*. On the other hand, if the space occupied by coffee shop were remodeled into a limited-menu snack bar with complete self-service, management could expect a *gross change* in productivity.

It would be pleasant to think that major improvements in productivity were possible. But in fact, *gross changes* in productivity require a change in business strategy; that is, in the way we do business and that involves decisions by the management or owners.

In the balance of this chapter, we will concentrate not on gross improvements such as a doubling of productivity but on *marginal productivity improvements* such as might be achieved by climinating 5 or 10% of the labor hours in an operation over a given period. These marginal improvements in productivity are the proper focus of *operating* management's attention.

TOOLS FOR ANALYZING AND CONTROLLING PAYROLL

In this section, we will examine productivity standards briefly, consider techniques used in employee scheduling, review methods of payroll budgeting that relate hours worked to dollar sales volume, and finally, examine the scheduling problems and benefits that result from part-time and overtime scheduling.

TABLE 10.1 LIMITS TO PRODUCTIVITY

Food Service Type	Direct Labor Hours per Hundred Guests
Luxury restaurants	72.3
Family restaurants	20.7
Cafeterias	18.3
Fast food	10.5

Source: Agricultural Research Service

[3]For a fuller discussion of the data discussed here and summarized in Figure 10.1, see Thomas F. Powers, "The Impact of Productivity on the Service Restaurant," *Cornell Hotel and Restaurant Association Quarterly,* February 1974.

PRODUCTIVITY STATISTICS

The most common single productivity statistic in the hospitality industry is the payroll cost percentage, which can be found by dividing payroll dollars by sales volume.

$$\frac{\$ \text{ Payroll}}{\$ \text{ Sales volume}} = \text{Payroll cost percent}$$

This is a sound *long-range* budgeting tool, because in order to reach profit targets (or a breakeven or subsidized-loss target in nonprofit organizations), major cost groups such as food cost, payroll cost, and other direct operating costs must relate to sales.

On the other hand, payroll costs and selling prices may not display a stable relationship. In times of inflation, both change rapidly. Also, sales dollars do not necessarily indicate the amount of work that is to be done. In the hotel business, for instance, August commonly is a poor month, and so the sales department, in order to get *some* business, often quotes lower prices for banquets that can be scheduled in August. In December, on the other hand, when the banquet department is crowded, it is likely that only the more expensive end of the banquet menu will be quoted to prospects. Thus, a banquet of 1000 guests dining on fried chicken in August can be compared to a banquet of 1000 guests dining on beef Wellington in December. For the banquet department, the labor hours required might be the same, but we can safely guess that the sales dollars are quite different, indeed.

Standard Times

One means of setting performance standards is time-and-motion analysis, under which an experienced worker is asked to do a job according to an approved procedure. Sometimes the job itself is studied and improved in this process. What finally emerges is a standard expressed as the time it takes a trained worker to do a specific job under appropriate conditions.

Although time and motion is a helpful measure, it presents several problems for food service. Time and motion analysis was developed for use in studying repetitive manufacturing tasks, but in food service, much of the work is based on customer demand. The ideal time it takes to accomplish a task is a useless standard unless it can be assumed the worker will be called on to repeat the task as many times as reasonably possible each hour. If business is slow, the worker may be paid to stand and wait! (When we discuss scheduling, we will consider this question from a different standpoint.) Standard times for frequently repeated jobs (setting up a dining room, cleaning and closing down a dish machine, mopping a specific area, etc.) are useful planning tools, but for much of the planning food service managers must do, this kind of information is neither available or useful.

Unless there are chronic and expensive problems, time-and-motion studies, usually are not cost-effective management tools in food service.

OUTPUT STATISTICS

A more commonly used measure of productivity relates employee hours to units of guest service. The standard, alluded to earlier, of one server per 30 guests at a banquet is a good example of a useful payroll planning tool.[4] Statistics may be accumulated more generally, to show the number of covers (i.e., guests) served per cook, server, bus employee, and dishwasher.

The use of these measures, of course, assumes that the work is done at a reasonable level of output. A lack of good standards can result from a lack of critical thinking. Some years ago, for instance, a new hotel chain, determined in its early days of operation that a maid could clean between eight and nine rooms. As the company grew, expanding into different labor markets and drawing on a pool of more experienced managers, that standard later was raised to 12 rooms per maid-day. Today, the standard in that company is 14 rooms per maid-day. Output statistics not only need to reflect not just what has been done but also must be based on a reasonable standard of efficiency.

There are very few, if any, *standard* output expectations in the food service industry, because of variations in the menu in use, the kind of service offered, the physical plant in which work is done, the level of sales, and so forth. Even within a single company, output per worker may vary from unit to unit as a result of factors such as those just cited. Accordingly, it became essential to develop standards appropriate to the many types of food service operations.

SCHEDULING

The heart of payroll control is scheduling. Sometimes, when an operation is at minimum crew size, paying an employee to "stand and wait" is unavoidable, but proper scheduling is *the* tool to hold wasted payroll dollars to a minimum. As one authority on food service productivity, speaking of that most efficient of food service operations, fast food, noted,

> The main opportunity to improve productivity and to reduce costs in fast food restaurants lies in developing tighter schedules based on production requirements. . . .[5]

Two of the most important tools used in scheduling are the operations needs chart and the bar chart schedule.

---

[4]Note that depending on standards of service, complexity of menu served and price charged this measure of productivity may be much higher or much lower in this example.

[5]John F. Freshwater, *Labor Requirements and Operating Costs in Fast Food Restaurants* (Washington, D.C.: Agricultural Research Service, 1975), p. 38.

Operations-Needs Chart

Figure 10.1 charts the ideal needs for a department made up of a receiver, dish and pot washers, and clean up personnel. The positions are listed at left, and the hours of the day are listed across the top. The lines indicate the hours at which work needs to be done. At this point in the analysis, we need not worry about minimum or maximum worktime spans; we will concentrate on needs.

Bar Chart Schedule

People will not always work the exact hours management would prefer. In the second step in this process, we add names to the job titles and schedule people according to what *is* possible. Accordingly, we have assumed that we can identify scheduled hours during which there is no real need for employee coverage. We then pay special attention to these hours, doing everything possible to

1. Minimize the number of excess hours scheduled.

2. Identify incidental duties (such as wall washing, silver burnishing, and inventorying in the department studied).

In translating the information on needs into the schedule found in Figure 10.2, we have followed some useful conventions for preparing a bar chart schedule. Notice

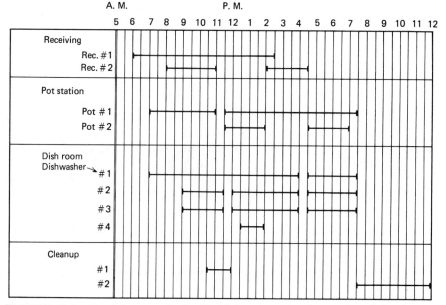

FIGURE 10.1 Operations-needs chart for dishroom, pot station, and receiving department.

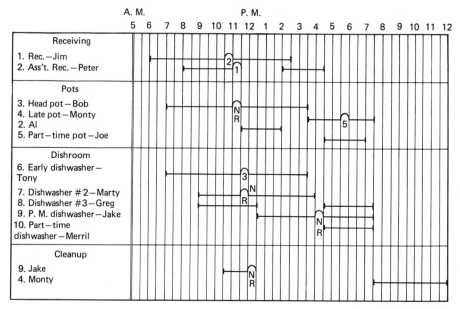

FIGURE 10.2 A bar chart schedule.

that down the left-hand side we have listed each position with a brief job title such as receiver, potwasher and part-time potwasher. We have put a person's name beside each of these positions, and each position is given a number. In some cases, the schedule is interrupted by a small loop with a number or some letters under it. The loop indicates the lunch break period (any employee working eight hours has to have at least a half-hour lunch break), and the number under the loop refers to the number of the person on the schedule who is to relieve the position. The letters *NR* mean "no relief."

For instance, the receiver, Jim, is relieved by his assistant, Peter, from 10:30 A.M. to 11:00 A.M. Jim comes back from his lunch break and relieves Peter from 11:00 A.M. to 11:30 A.M. Notice that the numbers under the loops correspond to the person who is doing the relieving, and that the loop indicates when that position is expected to receive relief. Also note that on this schedule we have used two partime workers: Joe works in the pot station from 4:30 P.M. to 7:00 P.M., and Merril becomes the third person in the dish room from 4:30 P.M. to 7:30 P.M.

Another, more detailed example of scheduling is presented below.

The Green Room

Let us assume that a hotel has a 120-chair dining room called the Green Room. Management has found that adequate service coverage can be provided during the Green Room's busy periods by assigning 30-chair stations at breakfast and 20-chair stations at lunch and at the evening meal. Management has arrived at some scheduling rules informally, as a result of feedback from the waitresses. (These rules might also be based on legal wage-and-hour law restrictions, work rules in a union contract, or written company policy.)

> *Scheduling Rules.* Part-time workers are guaranteed four hours, minimum, at a single meal. If a part-time worker works two meals, a minimum of six hours is guaranteed. The maximum time between split shifts will be no more than two hours, and the maximum span of a split-shift day will be no more than 10 hours.

In Figure 10.3, in which just *needs* are outlined, we see that a minimum of one waitress is required from the time the Green Room opens, at 6:00 A.M., until one hour after it closes, at 9:00 P.M. A second waitress is required at 6:30 A.M., a third at 7:00, and a fourth at 7:30. Because of late breakfast diners, two waitresses are needed through the end of the breakfast meal, at 11:00 A.M. Volume falls off by 9:00 A.M., however, and drops even further by 9:30, so a fourth waitress is needed only until 9:00 and a third until 9:30.

Two waitress can cover the start-up of lunch, until 11:30 A.M., but a third is needed to deal with early lunch customers at 11:30, and two more are needed by 11:45. At noon, all stations must be covered, so a sixth waitress is required. By 1:15 P.M., the biggest part of the rush is over, and as the chart indicates, one waitress can then go off duty, with three more to follow 15 minutes later. From 2:15 P.M., one waitress can cover until the cocktail hour begins at 4:30. The *day of the week* we are looking at is Friday, on which occupancy in the hotel generally is poor, so the evening meal will be fairly light. A third waitress, however, is needed from 5:30 P.M. to 7:30 P.M.. Two must be on duty until the Green Room closes, at 10:00 P.M.

Management now must create a schedule to meet these needs. Figure 10.4 shows one means of covering those needs with five full-time and two part-time (less than eight hours) waitresses. Note that the schedule contains a position number at left, as well as the waitress's name

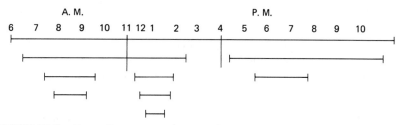

FIGURE 10.3 Green Room operations need.

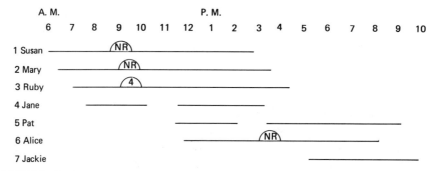

FIGURE 10.4 Green Room waitress schedule for Friday.

Susan opens the Green Room. Business is very slow from 6:00 to 6:30, so she manages to set up the room (water, coffee, butter and cream to side stands) during this period, too, and does not need to start before the opening. She has a meal break from 9:00 to 9:30, but since only three waitresses are needed at this hour, no relief is scheduled. Susan works the luncheon meal, going off duty at 2:30, after eight hours of work.

Mary comes on at 6:30 and works until 3:00, with a half-hour meal break from 9:30 until 10:00 without assigned relief, since only two waitresses are needed at that hour.

Ruby comes on duty as breakfast volume picks up at 7:00. She too, is a "breakfast and lunch girl," working a full day, until 3:30. Her meal break comes from 9:30 to 10:00, and she is relieved by Jane—otherwise, the crew level would fall below two. (Note that this means that Jane takes over Ruby's station but leaves any tips for Ruby.).

An alternative would be to delay Ruby's break until after 10:00 A.M. In this case, management chose to schedule coverage for the break from Jane so that all three girls could be on duty together from 10:00 until 11:30, during which time the dining room side work (filling sugar and pepper shakers, cruets, etc.) is done. Although these "chores" do not require all of the time scheduled here, management has found that if one waitress goes on break, the other two feel that they do more side work, and complain. *Our point* in mentioning this is that the schedule can and should reflect not just the basic needs of the operation but also other factors, such as those bearing on morale.

Jane is a split-shift, part-time employee. Since she is off from 10:00 to 11:30, there is no need to schedule a break for her. Although she need not remain on duty as late as she does in the afternoon, the scheduling "rules of the game" guarantee her six paid hours.

Pat is a full-time, split-shift waitress who works lunch (11:30 to 2:00) and dinner (3:30 to 9:00). No relief need be scheduled for a split-shift employee here.

Alice is a full-time "lunch and dinner girl" who works from 12:00 until 8:00, and Jackie is the "choring girl," a part-timer.

Management could expect complaints from other girls that Alice's shift is the best, because she works when tips are best. Alice does not come on until lunch is in full swing; she works the cocktail hour; and she goes off duty right after the dinner rush, at 8:30. She is the oldest employee in time of service, however, and has earned the best shift through seniority. (Personal factors count, once again, in common-sense scheduling).

In summary, a schedule should arise from detailed analysis of the needs of each day of the week and be based on both the operation's needs and whatever groundrules for scheduling are appropriate. Schedules should reflect not only needs and rules, but also, to the extent possible, factors such as employee morale, seniority, and other "personal" factors needed to make people work together.

The Weekly Schedule
A weekly posted schedule lists the days off for each employee, notes who relieves that person on his or her day off, and identifies, daily and by job position, the hours for each job. Figure 10.5 presents an example of the weekly posted schedule for a small kitchen. Note that names of the position and of the person in that position, together with the number from the bar chart schedule, are placed on the margin at the left of the page. The days of the week are listed across the top, and a grid is drawn to provide a block for each person and each day. The working hours for all the regular employees are listed, together with their names and days off. *Person relieved by* is indicated in the appropriate block. Although this department has only four positions to fill, the schedule lists six people. Olga works as a full-time relief cook and Alice rounds off the relief work, working three days a week.

The uses of a document like this are twofold. First of all, with the operation's need chart, this schedule helps the manager graphically to analyze the work needs. Even for such a small group as this, it is virtually impossible to hold all the possible combinations in your head. By treating this schedule as a draft document at first, you, as a manager, can try all the various combinations to find the one that holds payroll dollars to a minimum and is acceptable to the people working for you. Moreover, the week's schedule, properly planned, ensures that coverage of each station for each day of the week matches forecasted sales for that day.

Secondly—and this holds true for the bar chart schedule as well—written schedules constitute an important communication tool. They should be posted prominently where every employee can see them. This is a necessary step in holding every employee responsible for being at work at the times designated. At the same time, it is important that schedules be planned and posted far enough in advance to give employees the time they need to plan their own schedules.

Guide Hours Analysis
Another way of approaching scheduling is to determine what the *allowable* payroll is, given a payroll target. One way of doing this is the guide hours method. To compute guide hours for an operation, five steps are necessary.

	MON.	TUES.	WED.	THURS	FRI.	SAT.	SUN.
1. SALADS 6:00–2:30 Jane						OFF Alice	OFF Alice
2. EARLY COOK 6:00–2:30 Mary						OFF Olga	OFF Olga
3. LATE COOK 10:00–6:30 Louise				OFF Olga	OFF Olga		
4. BAKER 6:00–2:30 JoAnn	OFF Olga	OFF Alice					
5. COOK'S RELIEF Olga	Baker 6:00–2:30	OFF N.R.	OFF N.R.	L. Cook 10:00–6:30	L. Cook 10:00–6:30	E. Cook 6:00–2:30	E. Cook 6:00–2:30
6. P.T. RELIEF Alice	OFF N.R.	Baker 6:00–2:30	OFF N.R.	OFF N.R.	OFF N.R.	Salads 6:00–2:30	Salads 6:00–2:30

FIGURE 10.5 Weekly posted schedule.

STEP 1.   Given a forecast of a week's (or some other time period's) sales and a target labor-cost percentage, the maximum dollars needed to meet the payroll target can be computed.

Assume: Sales of $15,000 and a labor cost target of 30%.
Then, total payroll must be no more than $4,500.

STEP 2.   From records of the operation (and with critical judgement of the performance the records indicate), determine the percent of the payroll required for each payroll section.

Assume: Cooks   33%
Service   40%
Dish, pot, receiving and cleanup 27%

STEP 3.   Apply these percentages to the total allowable payroll to determine the dollars available for each payroll section.

Cooks $1500
Service $1800
Dish, pot, etc. $1200

STEP 4.   From records, determine the current average hourly rate by payroll section.

Assume: Cooks $5.00
Service $1.50
Dish, pot, etc. $3.00

STEP 5.   Dividing the average wage (Step 4) into the dollars available per section (Step 3), compute the number of hours that can be scheduled in the week, given the sales forecast.

Cooks   300 hours
Service   1200 hours
Dish, pot, etc.   400 hours

At this point, the actual schedules can be compared with what would be allowed under the guide hours.

The major use of guide hours arises when payroll exceeds the percentage targets. It is important to see that the outcome of the guide hours analysis is *not* a schedule, but a means of evaluating a schedule. If the guide hours fall substantially below what was actually scheduled, several possibilities need to be considered. Schedules may have gotten "loose" in a period of high volume, for instance, and management may have been reluctant to cut back. For whatever reason, the present schedules *may* have more employee coverage than is needed. Another possibility is that wage rates have crept up but menu prices have not been adjusted. Possibly, too, a brief seasonal "valley" in sales volume has been reached and the laying off of employees to reach the target might result in the loss of valuable, trained workers who will be needed again shortly, when volume moves back up to normal.

Guide hours are an aid to analysis—not a substitute for it. Enlightened management will use this tool as a basis for discussion of schedules with the supervisors responsible for the various departments and schedules—not as a rigid guideline. We might even say, in this age of participative management, that the guide-hours figures provide a useful basis for negotiation with department heads and supervisors when schedule revisions are necessary.

SPECIAL CASES: PART-TIME AND OVERTIME

The use of part-time workers often is seen as a solution to high labor costs, whereas overtime usually is seen as a cause of high labor costs. In fact, both scheduling strategies can either cause problems or provide solutions to wage cost difficulties, depending on how carefully their use is planned and implemented.

Determination of the "employer mix" of part-time and full-time employees requires both judgement and experience in a specific labor market and operation.

Part-Time Employees

If a restaurant does a very large luncheon volume but much less dinner business, it clearly cannot afford to schedule all its waitresses for both meals. An ideal solution is to hire waitresses who want to work just during the luncheon meal. There are many other possible examples of the productive use of part-time workers. In health care, it is common to schedule a preparation crew that will finish work between 3:00 P.M. and 5:00 P.M. and to bring in a part-time crew to physically deliver the evening meal to patients. Most college food service operations use part-time student employees in a variety of jobs during the meal hours, relying on a smaller full-time crew for the basic food preparation. Because of the extreme peaks and valleys in their business day, fast food operations have maximum flexibility in the hours employees are scheduled, and they use part-time employees to acheive this goal.

The problems that arise from part-time scheduling have to do with cost and reliability. Although a part-time worker costs less per day than a full-time person in the same job would cost, there are some hidden costs. First of all, if extensive training is required, the training cost looms as a large overhead cost. Turnover among part-time workers is common, and if turnover *is* experienced where there is a significant training need, then the training cost can become prohibitive. Along with turnover, another problem encountered with part-time workers is absenteeism. A part-time worker probably is not earning his or her main income in the part-time job. Married women who work part-time probably are contributing to the family's income, but the main source for that income comes from the full-time paycheck of the husband. Consequently, her "full-time" job of homemaker could take preference. The same is true of persons working a second job: the full-time job commonly will take precedence. Finally, students often make exams (or vacations) a priority over a part-time job; this proclivity can make them unreliable if hiring and scheduling is not done with considerable care. In general, it is clear that problems can emerge if special care is not taken in the selection and scheduling of part-time workers.

A common strategy in fast food is to hire students and to build the crew mostly on part-time employees. Operators use a large number of part-timers and limit the hours they work quite severely. This tactic gives management a large crew from which to draw if some workers prove unreliable. Reliable employees are rewarded with better and longer hours. Since the training cost is low for these employees, turnover presents less of a problem.

Overtime

Overtime can present problems because of the need to pay time-and-a-half, a drawback we will discuss shortly. First, however, we should note that overtime *can* be a solution. If an extra half-hour of dish room coverage is required at the end of an eight-hour shift, it obviously makes sense to bear the penalty of time-and-a-half rather than to try to schedule somebody for such a short time. And if an additional four hours is needed in a job that requires skill and significant training, it probably is more cost-effective to schedule the same worker and pay the overtime rate. Finally, when an emergency threatens to disrupt service to guests, supervisors need to be able to schedule overtime to maintain quality standards.

Overtime becomes a problem when poor planning results in stopgap use of this device—when every day seems to bring an emergency. Then, the time-and-a-half paid for overtime is the kind of waste that literally can bankrupt an operation. For this reason, most managers have strict overtime controls.

Overtime Authorization. The most common overtime control measure is a rule that only relatively senior personnel can authorize overtime. In a large hotel, "senior personnel" might mean the department head who has profit (or cost) responsibility for the department or activity. In many operations, however, the manager or his principal subordinates may be the only persons allowed to approve overtime. A form like that shown in Figure 10.6 often is used to make a record of the overtime authorization. This form serves the dual purpose of requiring an authorization in writing and of documenting the reason for overtime, which can be analyzed at the end of the payroll period.

```
                    Thundercreek Inn
                  Overtime Authorization

Name _____        Date_____
Department _____        Overtime Hours Authorized_____
Reason


                                   Approved _____
```

FIGURE 10.6 Overtime authorization.

ORGANIZING FOR PRODUCTIVITY

In reviewing an organization's staffing, we must consider the special problems and opportunities of each group of employees. We will look first at some of the problems of scheduling managment, and then turn our attention to food production, service, and utility workers.

SCHEDULING MANAGEMENT

A key problem in determining the hours management will work frequently is referred to as "management presence." There must be a person in charge, one who can make decisions and accept responsibility. In a large operation whose sales volume will support shift managers, this need presents less of a problem. It is very common, however, to find situations in which a single manager must cover a long stretch of hours. The most common strategy employed in such a case is to identify lead employees—in fast food, often called crew chiefs—who can accept responsibility for routine responsibilities such as opening and closing an operation.

The lead employee responsible for opening must unlock secure areas, set up the cash register, and see that other workers are in place and that the operation is running smoothly in what is generally a low-volume period. The lead employee at closing has analagous assignments plus the responsibility of assuring the cleanliness of the operation. The responsibilities these employees undertake may seem routine, but they certainly are central, involving as they do cash handling, access to pilferable items, and sanitation. Clearly, whenever lead employees are given this kind of responsibility, they must be selected with great care from among experienced employees.

Another problem very common to food service is the overscheduling of managers. The fact is that managers are human, too. A good manager *can* work very long hours for a period of time; after a while, however, it almost seems that the longer the manager works, the less is accomplished. The manager wears out, and gradually quality begins to slip and costs begin to rise.

Whereas full-time hourly workers generally work between 40 and 44 hours, a work week of 50 to 56 hours is common for managers. So the food service business *is* a long-hour business for many managers and supervisors. But when managers or supervisors consistently are scheduled at 60 hours per week or more, it is common to see management productivity and morale decline. Overwork is one of the most common causes of turnover in food service, especially among managers and supervisors.

COORDINATING SHIFTS

In larger operations that operate on more than one shift, management presence is not such a difficult problem, but coordination of shift responsibilities is. Where this factor is not attended to, feuds can break out between shifts and morale and performance will drop all around.

Consider a situation in which the day shift opens the operation, serves breakfast and luncheon, and is relieved around 3:00 P.M. by an evening crew that serves dinner and has responsibility for "cleanup and close up." This arrangement makes good sense—but it also can go badly wrong. The evening crew may feel that the day shift "leaves everything in a mess for us to clean up"—which might be true. The day crew may say that "things are never clean or in order when we come on duty and we have to spend half our time doing the cleaning up." From this kind of disharmony, an operation can get to the point where each crew hides "its" equipment from the other.

This is by no means a hypothetical situation. To avoid this kind of intershift conflict, shift supervisors sometimes are scheduled to overlap by as much as an hour or two. An alternative is to schedule a senior manager who is closely involved in operations to overlap both shifts; each shift supervisor then reports directly and daily to the senior manager, who schedules frequent meetings between the supervisors.

In summary, management presence for responsible decision making and security is necessary during all hours of operation, although lead employees may bear much of this responsibility in smaller operations. Moreover, managers who consistently overschedule themselves are likely to find themselves less effective. Finally, coordination between shifts in a multishift operation is essential to morale and to the upholding of quality and cost standards.

FOOD PRODUCTION

In staff planning for food production, the best place to start is with the menu. If you know what has to be produced and what equipment layout is necessary, you can identify a basic crew for low-volume periods. Planning then takes account of increases in volume through the specializing of station assignments at higher-volume periods. On a very busy day, for instance, a luncheon crew may have a lead cook who is responsible for roasts, sauces and gravies, and soup and who also helps out, as needed, as a working supervisor during the rush. In addition, the steam table may be staffed by two people, and there one person apiece may be given charge of salads, sandwiches, and desserts. On a very low-volume day, this crew of six might be reduced, as shown in Figure 10.7, to two people or held at some intermediate step. The analysis needed identifies the basic crew and then specifies the number of people to be added at varying levels of volume. In very large operations, such as theme parks, detailed written schedules for the food service staff commonly are worked out at several levels of volume, and, when a week's sales forecasts become available, staffing assignments are made according to the predetermined plan. At peak volumes, part-time employees commonly are used, whereas the basic-crew needs are usually filled by full-time employees.

SERVICE EMPLOYEES

A serious problem that arises with tipped employees has to do with *early and late hours*. If volume is low during these times, the employee may not earn as much per hour in tips as do those who work during the busier periods. The ideal situation is to have an opening waitress who prefers the early hours, so she can get off early. In some cases, however, it is necessary to provide extra compensation, usually on the grounds of the extra responsibility of a lead employee. Similar considerations apply to the closing waitress.

Another problem arises between meals, when a substantial staff may be available to wait on few, if any, guests. Careful planning of side work can help fill

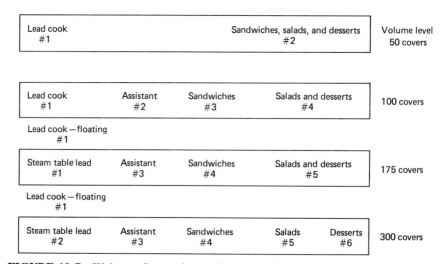

FIGURE 10.7 Welcome Inn station assignments—lunch.

up this time, but logically, this is the time when the crew size should be reduced as much as work rules, employee hours, and company policy permit.

An important area for supervisory attention is the server-kitchen relationship. Because of the potential for friction, work rules covering this interchange should be specific—spelling out, for instance, how the server may "call" an order and how the production worker should notify the server when the order is ready for pickup. Many operations schedule a supervisor in the order and pick up area during peak volume hours to avoid problems between dining room and kitchen staff.

Self-Service
In recent years, one of the major means of improving employee productivity has been the move to self-service. In fast food, the server has been completely eliminated (as has long been true in cafeterias). Many full-service restaurants, however, now have introduced self-service salad bars—and sometimes dessert tables—which enable the waitress to carry a larger station and the restaurant to manage with fewer waitresses without slowing service. Note, however, that self-service reduces labor but does not do away with it entirely. Guest pickup areas must be carefully maintained, with a view both to keeping an adequate supply of foods on hand and to maintaining a general appearance of neatness and sanitation. This means that one or more employees must be assigned to servicing the guest pickup area.

UTILITY WORKERS
As with the preparation staff, the dish-room, pot-washing, and cleanup crew need to be planned with volume variations in mind. Opportunities for combining jobs among these relatively unskilled workers often occur during low-volume periods. Slack time in the back of the house should be anticipated, and recurring jobs such as wall washing, silver burnishing, and other special cleanup tasks should be identified and planned for these periods.

POINT OF SALES SYSTEMS AND PRODUCTIVITY

In Chapter 3 we discussed the impact of POS systems on payroll control. At this point, it is useful to review the principal functions POS systems can fulfill in staff planning and payroll control. Most POS systems offer a time-clock feature that permits employees to log in and log off work on the system, with the POS automatically indicating the time (see Figure 3.28). At the end of the shift and at the end of the day, summary reports of employee hours worked, by employee, can be taken from the master terminal. The system also will store this information on a period-to-date basis, which simplifies payroll computation.

244 PRODUCTIVITY ANALYSIS AND PAYROLL

A POS system also will convert time-clock data to costs and provide a report summarizing both hours worked and dollar costs. Figure 3.29 provides an example of such a report. Productivity reports such as that shown in Figure 3.30 give periodic summaries of productivity by hour or half-hour time segments. These reports provide an ideal basis for preparing and reviewing operations-needs charts and daily schedules.

Finally, special productivity data such as that found in the waiter tracking report (Figure 3.25) and the selective sales itemizer (Figure 3.27) permit management to review the productivity of individual employees.

KEY WORDS AND PHRASES

Fair Labor Standards Act
Minimum wage floor
Productivity—definition
Number of guests/employee-hour
Dollar sales/employee-hour
Categories of payroll costs
Fixed costs
Minimum number of workers
Variable costs
Mixed costs
Productivity levels
Gross change in productivity
Marginal productivity improvements
Tools for analyzing and control
Payroll cost percent formula
Standard times
Output statistics
Scheduling
Operations-needs chart
Bar chart schedule
Split shifts
Full-and part-time scheduling
Weekly schedule
Guide hours analysis
Payroll target
Five steps to determine guide hours

Evaluating schedules using guide hours
Part-time employees
Turnover
Training cost
Absenteeism
Overtime
Overtime authorization
Organizing for productivity
Lead employees
Coordinating shifts
Overlapping shifts
Food production staffing
Start with menu
Basic crew for low volume
Service employees
Side work
Self-service
Utility workers
POS productivity controls
Time clock
Shift reports
Summary hours worked
Dollar costs
Waiter tracking
Selective sales itemizer

DISCUSSION QUESTIONS

1. What are minimum wage rates? Discuss how they affect costs throughout a hotel organization.

2. Discuss how you could affect a gross change in productivity.

3. A young chef's dream is to open a *haute cuisine* restaurant. Discuss

the productivity he might expect. What employee hour estimate could he use for 100 guests?

4. Determine the payroll cost percent for one day at "The Inn," given that

Joe worked six hours @ $4.00/hr.
Nancy worked eight hours @ $3.50/hr, plus one hour overtime at time-and-a-half.
Pat worked four hours @ $3.50/hr.
Sales for the day totaled $950.

5. Design an operations-needs chart for a restaurant for which you have worked or for your favorite restaurant. Then, schedule employees using a bar chart. Discuss the problems you encounter in doing this.

6. Use the five steps outlined in the chapter to determine guide hours for the following restaurant operation:

Sales per week: $21,000.
Labor target cost: 27%.
Percent of payroll:
    Cooks, 35%
    Service, 40%
    Utility, 25%
Average hourly rate:
    Cooks, $6.00/hr
    Service, $3.50/hr.
    Utility, $3.50/hr.

Discuss how these guide hours should be used and how they could be misused.

7. According to a restaurant manager, "The best staffing plan can be ruined when my employees don't show up for work." Discuss the problems currently associated with staffing and productivity in the food service industry.

AN INTRODUCTION TO FOOD COST CONTROL

11

An "Ideal" System

A Critical Review

Conclusions

THE PURPOSE OF THIS CHAPTER

If we think for a moment about just what a restaurant or other food service operation is, the problem of control becomes apparent. Food service is, among other things, a system that transforms valuable products from one form into another. A restaurant transforms into a hamburger, for instance, raw beef and bread in the form of a bun. In a more complex operation, many *raw foods* are transformed into a variety of *meals.*

The primary aim of food cost control is to assure that the product purchased in the raw state is actually converted to a meal and that it is sold to a customer. Secondly, food cost control should be used to identify when "mysterious disappearance" of product has taken place—and to do so in a way that helps managers identify the cause of disappearance.

In this chapter, we will examine the traditional food cost control system as one "ideal" and coherent approach to food cost control. We will also analyze the weaknesses and disadvantages of the traditional system. In the *next chapter,* we will build on the understanding of a control system developed here by examining the principal kinds of control techniques actually in use in modern food service.

THIS CHAPTER SHOULD HELP YOU

1. Define control in terms of a food cost control system.

2. Trace the traditional control system's unbroken chain of control.

3. Criticize the traditional control system in terms of its accuracy and the cost of control.

4. State where the traditional system is still used.

AN "IDEAL" SYSTEM

The word *ideal* has more than one meaning. It can refer to a "standard of perfection"—a notion that probably fit the traditional system of control when it was introduced over 50 years ago. If not a "perfect" system of control, the traditional system was the next best thing to it. Today, this system is still widely *studied* as *the* system of food cost control, but in practice it is used principally in clubs and in large hotels and hospitals.

Our interest in the traditional system also relates to a second meaning of *ideal*—that of symbolizing an idea. The idea we wish to review is that of an unbroken chain of control: from the receipt of a valuable food product through the transformation of that food product to a meal, its sale to the guest, and the deposit of funds in the bank (or acceptance of a guest charge).

What we do and do not mean by *control* needs to be clarified. A car is said to be under control as long as the driver is "in charge" of its speed and direction. The

248 AN INTRODUCTION TO FOOD COST CONTROL

car is "out of control" in a bad skid or when the steering breaks down. We have a somewhat different meaning in mind when we speak of *control* in food cost control. The function of the food cost control system is more passive than that of the driver of the car. At the end of the control cycle (a day, a week, or a month) the control system tells us how much we have used, permits us to trace the process of use of product through the operation, and tells us how much we received from the guest in cash or charges, at the end of the process. Examination of Figure 11.1 will aid us in tracing this process of unbroken control.

FROM VENDOR TO STOREROOM TO KITCHEN

Food is received from the vendor's truck at the receiving entrance of the operation, and an invoice for the foods received is forwarded for payment to the accounting department. Under the traditional cost control system, most of the food then goes to the storeroom, and its dollar value is reported on the receiving report and posted to the cost analysis sheet (Figure 11.2). Most food received results in an increase in the inventory value of the storeroom. As food is needed in the kitchen, it is requisitioned by the kitchen and issued by the storeroom; the requisition (Figure 11.3) is also posted to the cost analysis sheet. This issue reduces the storeroom's inventory value. In some operations the requisition form is referred to as a Food Issues Slip.

Some products, however, are issued directly to the kitchen. These so-called direct issues, usually products that will be used up on the day they are received, such as produce. Another kind of product in this category is flour. If a 100 lb sack of flour is received, it is not practical to take it into the storeroom and break it down into five 20-pound containers and issue one of these per day. Instead, the flour goes directly to the bake shop and is either charged in its entirety to food cost on the day issued or, less commonly, charged to food cost on some kind of average-use basis—for instance, 20 pounds per day.

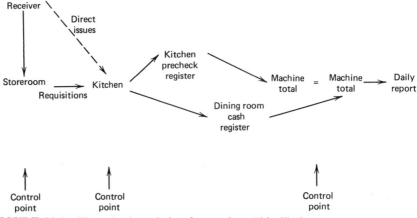

FIGURE 11.1 The unbroken chain of control: an "ideal" view.

FIGURE 11.2 The dollar value of food received is posted on the cost analysis sheet.

FOOD REQUISITION

Date _____

ARTICLE	QUAN.	PRICE	AMOUNT

_____
Department Head

FIGURE 11.3 A food requisition is made by the kitchen and sent to the storeroom, where the storeroom clerk fills the order and posts the requisition on the cost analysis sheet (Figure 11.2). (Courtesy of the Copley Plaza.)

FROM KITCHEN TO SERVICE

Food is prepared in the kitchen, and in the traditional system, just as the kitchen requisitions food from the storeroom (or has it "direct issued"), the kitchen issues food only upon presentation of a guest check as a requisition. One way to enforce this system is to have the waitress pick up food from the cooks and then have the tray inspected by a food checker, who assures the accuracy of the waitress's check and validates each item to be charged by ringing it up on the check.

Because a food checker represents a substantial addition to the payroll, an alternative system called prechecking commonly is used. In this system, the waitress rings up her check on the precheck register before ordering from the cook and presents a copy of the machine-validated check as a requisition to the cook. (Figure 11.4 shows a waitress at a precheck machine.) Notice that whether the guest check is run through a food checker's register or a precheck register, the value of product requisitioned by the dining room from the kitchen now becomes part of a *machine total:* that is, as each check is rung, the individual charge is printed on the guest check and also contributed to a machine total that can be read at the end of each shift. The total food requisitioned by the dining room from the kitchen should be equal to the total in the kitchen checking register (or registers). Figure 11.5 summarizes the process of control from the kitchen in the traditional system.

Referring back to Figure 11.1, we can now trace what appears to be the unbroken chain of control through several control points.

1. All food received should be accounted for by an increase in the storeroom inventory or by a direct issue to the kitchen.

2. The storeroom inventory should reflect receipts minus issues: that is, every change in storeroom totals should be accounted for by invoices or by issues.

3. The kitchen's efficiency should be reflected by the day's food cost: that is, the food used, expressed as a percent of sales for the day, should meet the food cost target for the operation.

4. The machine total for requisitions from the kitchen by servers should equal the

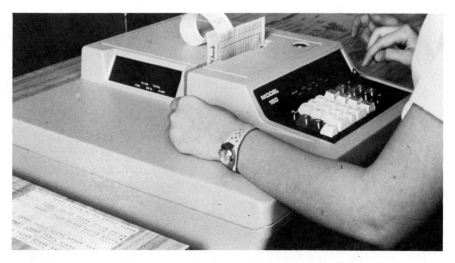

FIGURE 11.4 Precheck station. (Courtesy of Data Terminal Systems.)

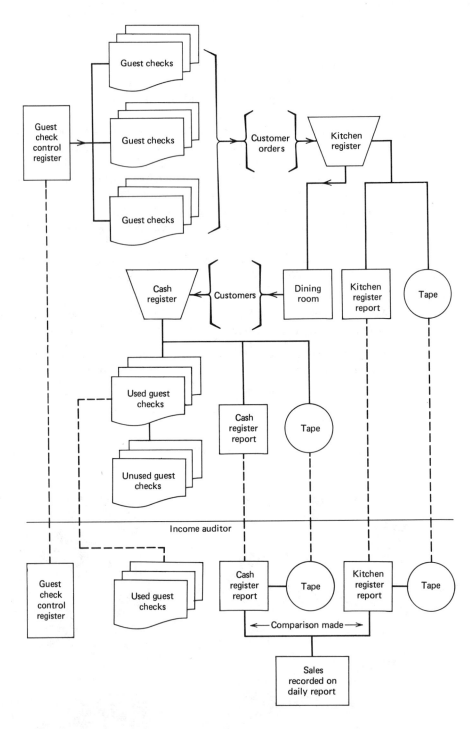

FIGURE 11.5 Summary of the process of control in the traditional system. (Adapted from Horwath, Toth, and Lesure, *Hotel Accounting*.)

machine total for sales recorded by the cashier, and these two totals should be reflected in the total automatically prepared for management in the daily report.

In this system, then, control means the ability to determine whether something went wrong and, if so, where. The controls can be likened to the sensory perception of the driver of the car referred to earlier. Management action is necessary to correct discrepancies in performance, much as the driver can alter speed or direction as he or she observes the progress of the car along the road.

We called this an "ideal" system, indicating that it symbolized the *idea of the unbroken chain of control*. But *ideal* can also mean "a mere mental image." As we review the problems the traditional system of food cost control presents to today's food service industry, we may decide that in some ways the traditional system may offer the "image" of daily food cost control, but only at considerable expense. In practice, it seems to offer, at best, month-to-date control with daily figures that provide the uncritical with an illusion of control.

AN ILLUSTRATION OF THE SYSTEM

Most operations today use a simplified system such as that in use at Boston's Copley Plaza Hotel. Shipments of meat, fish, poultry, and produce are received daily and move to the kitchen as direct issues, charged to food cost on the day received. Receiving activity is summarized in a receiving report (Figure 11.6). Some foods, such as canned foods and staples, are sent to the storeroom, issued as needed, and charged to food costs as issued. Figure 11.7 illustrates the movement of product in the Copley Plaza system and how product is charged to food cost.

FIGURE 11.6 Receiving clerk's daily report. (Courtesy of the Copley Plaza.)

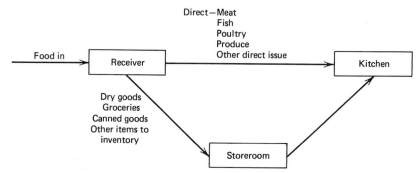

FIGURE 11.7 Movement of product in Copley Plaza system.

The daily cost (Figure 11.8) is not perfectly accurate, because the direct issue items on one particular day may be intended for the following day's business. For this reason, management focuses principally on the month-to-date (MTD) food cost summary shown in Figure 11.9. "Direct issues" can be posted from the receiving clerk's daily report (Figure 11.6), and "Store Room Issues" represents the total of the day's requisitions. Where items are purchased from petty cash, they are shown as "Sundry Purchases." Transfers of alcoholic beverages from the bar are listed under "Beverage for Cooling." Notice that in order to simplify the system's operation, categories of food cost such as those shown in Figure 11.2 are eliminated, and food cost is treated as a single total.

Credits to Food Cost

The largest factor here is employee meals. Many operations use a standard figure based on government guidelines. In the operation used as an example here, employee meal checks are collected and credited to total food cost at a standard percentage of the selling price for the food actually consumed. In either case, the logic is that food cost should reflect the cost of *food consumed* by guests, and that an appropriate amount should be deducted from food cost and charged to employee compensation, so that real costs incurred can be reflected accurately.[1]

Other credits include the cost of food used by management to entertain guests (charged at menu price times a standard food cost percent) and the cost of food (such as garnishes for drinks) transferred to the bars.

A number of other adjustments and computations are made on a monthly basis,

---

[1] Practice in the industry *does* vary. Some operations furnish food to employees at a reduced price, whereas others charge employees the full menu price for food consumed. Some operations do not credit employee meals to food cost. Whenever employee meals are furnished as part of compensation (and often when they are furnished at a reduced price), the food employees are allowed to consume is limited by rules laid down by management.

THE COPLEY PLAZA
DAILY FOOD COST

DAY: _____
DATE: _____

	TODAY	TO DATE
GROSS COST:		
STORE ISSUES		
DIRECT PURCHASES		
SUNDRY PURCHASES		
BEVERAGE TO FOOD		
TOTAL		
CREDITS:		
EMPLOYEE MEALS		
ENTERTAINMENT CREDITS		
FOOD TO BEVERAGE		
TOTAL		
NET COST OF FOOD:		
FOOD SALES:		
FOOD COST %:		

Form # 120 8007HPC

FIGURE 11.8 Form for computing daily food cost. (Courtesy of the Copley Plaza.)

THE COPLEY PLAZA
COPLEY SQUARE, BOSTON, MASSACHUSETTS 02116

MTD FOOD COST   DATE _____

SALES: _____

GROSS COST:

    DIRECT ISSUES: _____
    STORE ISSUES: _____
    SUNDRY PURCH: _____
    BEV FOR COOKING: _____

    TOTAL: _____

CREDITS:

    EMPLOYEE MEALS: _____
    ENTERTAINMENT: _____
    FOOD TO BEV: _____

    TOTAL: _____

NET COST: _____   COST % _____

cc: F. Prevost
    J. Lever
    L. LeBlana
    R. Redmond
    W. Heck

TELEPHONE (617) 267-5300   OPERATED BY HOTELS OF DISTINCTION, INC.

FIGURE 11.9 Form used to compute month-to-date (MTD) food cost summary. (Courtesy of the Copley Plaza.)

these adjustments are reflected in Figure 11.10. Notice that the food inventory is divided into food held in the storeroom and food that is in the production area (i.e., the kitchen). Some purchases for a particular operation (Whimsey's) are accounted for separately. As in many hotels, cooks receive a certain amount of beer daily as a part of their compensation ("Cooks' Beer").

Credits include meals provided as promotion, sales at cost (stewards' sales), cash sales to employees, and revenue from sales of discarded grease. Note that under summary of storeroom issues is a summary of transactions that indicates the difference between the issues accounted for by requisitions (book issues) and the actual change in the storeroom inventory based on physical inventory. As long as this error is relatively small, it can be tolerated; if it becomes large, however, a breakdown in control, or substantial theft, or very probably both, is indicated. Also note that at the bottom of the page, the used guest checks can be compared against unused checks still in the server's possession and checks that are presented for payment. If a server uses a check to requisition food, presents it to the guest, is paid, and then pockets the money, the check will be missing at the end of the shift—alerting management.

In the next step, guest checks reflecting customer orders are run through and posted in the kitchen register or prechecking machine. The validated check is used as a requisition and will be reflected in the kitchen register report. The other copy is presented to and paid by the customer, and is reflected in the dining room register report. At the end of the day, a comparison between the cash register report and the kitchen register report establishes whether all food taken out of the kitchen has been charged to a customer.

As a practical matter, there are often discrepancies, caused by human error, in the storeroom balance. Either these discrepancies are reported as a "store difference,"[2] or a very expensive tracing process must be undertaken. Thus, on a routine basis, serious discrepancies arise in the daily food cost.

A CRITICAL REVIEW

The traditional food cost control system is intended to give management an unbroken chain of control and to summarize results daily for management review and action. We need to question, first of all, just how well this system does what it sets out to do. Next, we need to review the cost of such a system in the context of potential savings. We also need to determine whether there is any need for this much information. Finally, we will review those situations in which the traditional system is still used. (In Chapter 12, we will see how the basics of this system have been adapted by many food service operators.)

---

[2]Ernest B. Horwath, Louis Toth, and John D. Lesure, *Hotel Accounting,* 4th ed. (New York: Ronald Press, Wiley, 1978), p. 189.

258 AN INTRODUCTION TO FOOD COST CONTROL

RECONCILIATION OF FOOD COSTS
HOTEL COPLEY PLAZA LOCATION BOSTON, MA MONTH _____

Sales
   Total Food Sales $_____

   Less; Rebates   _____

    Net Food Sales $_____

Costs
   Opening Storeroom $_____
     Inventory
   Opening Production   _____
     Inventory
   Total Opening Inventory $_____

Whimsey's Purchases   _____

Storeroom Purchases   _____

Direct Purchases   _____

  Total Purchases $_____

Beverage to Food   _____

Cooks Beer   _____

  Total Charges $_____

Less
   Closing Storeroom $_____
     Inventory
   Closing Production
     Inventory   _____

   Total Closing Inventory $_____

Credits: Food to Bars   _____
         Gratis to Bars   _____
         Mgr. Req.   _____

FIGURE 11.10 Form for computing food cost for the month, including a number of adjustments to cost that are unique to this hotel. (Courtesy of the Copley Plaza.)

Promotion
  Expense—Manager
            Sales Staff
            Other   _____
                             _____

Steward Sales   _____
Cash Sales-Employee Meal   _____
Guest Supplies   _____
Grease Sales   _____

Total Credits $_____

Total All Credits $_____
Cost of Food Consumed $_____
Less: Cost of Employee
  Meals   _____
Net Cost of Food Sold   _____

Summary of Storeroom Issues   *Inventory Turnover*
Kitchen—Main $_____   Dollar Inventory at
        Staff   _____   Par $_____
                                  Physical Inventory   _____
Food to Bars   _____   Inventory Over/Short _____
Steward Sales   _____   Actual Inventory   _____
Other   _____   Turnover   _____
Total Book Issues _____   Total of Returns   _____
Total Actual Issues _____   Corrections for Month _____
Storeroom Over or
  Under   _____

FIGURE 11.10 *(Continued).*

ACCURACY

Difficulties involved in the implementation of the traditional system practically ensure that *any single day's food cost* is not reported accurately. First of all, recall that according to the concept of direct issues, food intended for use on the day received is sent directly to the kitchen. It seems unlikely, however, that precisely the amount received will be used; the unused balance will be stored in the kitchen and used the next day. Similarly, the sacks of flour mentioned earlier will be used over some period of days. And yet all of this food will be charged on the day received. Direct issues, then, can distort the daily food cost—often seriously.

HOW UNBROKEN IS THE CHAIN OF CONTROL?

We have already noted that the storeroom balance is often inaccurate, and that this reduces the real effectiveness of the system. We might also note that because no single-day cost is likely to reflect perfectly the day's real cost, management seldom watches the single-day costs. Since only the person who computes the daily cost usually looks closely at that figure, the "control" over performance in the kitchen provided by this system—at least on a daily basis—breaks down. Thus, the unbroken chain is really an *illusion*.

In some ways, this illusion of control can be more dangerous than a lack of control. An unsophisticated manager who receives lengthy reports full of very detailed figures may be lulled into thinking that "we have a fine control system," and thus assume that costs really *are* under control. In practice, however, control consists of taking corrective action—and a series of reports containing more or less inaccurate figures does not seem to provide the best basis for management action.

THE COST OF CONTROL

The traditional cost control system was developed when labor was relatively inexpensive, but times have certainly changed. When a cook requires food under the traditional system, a requisition must be prepared and approved by a supervisor. All of this activity—preparation of the requisition, finding the supervisor to approve, the review and approval of the requisition by the supervisor—costs money. After the requisition has been presented at the storeroom, it must be posted. Requisitions, in turn, must be added up and appropriate totals entered on the daily report. Then, the highly detailed daily report must be typed, and management must take time to review the report.

In one club the authors studied, we estimated that club management was spending the equivalent of 10 percentage points on its food cost solely to maintain the cost control system and its supporting records. In this case, the cost of control clearly exceeded any benefit the control system might provide.

Since the *daily* figure probably is relatively meaningless (except in fast food, as we will see in Chapter 12), we might ask whether there is any real reason to prepare it. Some advocates of the traditional system may reply that while the daily figure is not accurate, after a few days the variations cancel themselves out and the month-to-date figures become meaningful. It is this figure that most operators, in fact, focus on.

The question, of course, is whether management would not best be served by awaiting the day's results and *then* compiling the cost for the period to date. In Chapter 12, if fact, we will see that most full-service food operations do compute food cost periodically over a period great enough to cancel out random variations but short enough so that serious problems cannot persist for protracted periods. In practice, as we will see, reports should contain only the information management can use.

USES OF THE TRADITIONAL SYSTEM

The traditional system is used in one variation or another mainly in three kinds of operations: large hotels, hospitals, and clubs.

Large hotels often have several different kitchens. For instance, the main kitchen may serve a coffee shop and fine dining room, whereas the banquet department may have a separate kitchen, or at least a separate area within the main kitchen, A specialty room, such as a rib room, may prepare its own food, too. Under these circumstances, a formal issues system helps separate costs so that the relative efficiency of each operation can be measured.

Notice, however, that where there is a single food *preparation* area but many *service* areas, the system probably achieves much less. Food is issued not to one dining room or another or to the banquet department, but to the kitchen. Under these circumstances, the problem is not to trace food from storeroom to preparation, but to trace it from preparation to the service area. Since many products will be prepared jointly for several operations, the measurement problem is complex, and a cost accounting system that perfectly reflects the transfers may be more costly to administer than is dictated by the savings it leads to.

In health care, it is common to have a central purchasing department that buys, receives, and stores all products for all departments. Under these circumstances, an issues system is necessary to separate the dietary department's costs from other departments. From the dietary department's point of view, the central purchasing department operates as if it were a single supplier. This is really a quite special case.

Finally, the traditional system is used in *private clubs*. An accountant once pointed out to the authors that there is an interesting rationale for using the system in clubs. "Clubs," he said, "are run by committees of members who usually know absolutely nothing about food service. The only thing the house committee or the budget committee knows for certain is that food service costs a lot. It's natural for them to think that some of this cost may be the result of theft. While the traditional system of food cost control doesn't always really improve management's control, it is a highly visible system that assures members that food is not being stolen.

Since, under the circumstances, it makes members reponsible for overseeing the club's management more comfortable and gives them a talking point in dealing with other members complaining about the club's costs, it's probably worth the cost of the system."

CONCLUSIONS

At a time when clerical employees were not paid very well, the traditional system served to keep track of valuable food products as they were transformed from raw food into meals sold to guests. The system is very expensive in today's labor market, however. Moreover, it is too cumbersome for most operations, even though it is still used in clubs and in large hotels and hospitals. Our review of this system has been helpful, nevertheless. It has shown us what a control system *should* accomplish. In the next chapter, we will look at some of the principal approaches to food cost control in use today. One thing that we will find is that with the advent of computerized POS systems and simplified menus, many of the traditional system's goals vis-à-vis highly specific product control are again becoming realistic. The way in which those goals are pursued, however, has changed significantly.

KEY WORDS AND PHRASES

Food cost control	Prechecking
Identify mysterious disappearance	Kitchen register report
An ideal system	Dining room register report
Unbroken chain of control	Daily food cost
Vendor–storeroom–kitchen control	Accuracy
Cost analysis sheet	Single-day food cost
Direct issues	Cost of control
Kitchen-to-service controls	Uses of traditional system
Food checker	

DISCUSSION QUESTIONS

1. Discuss the key control points in the traditional food cost control system.

2. Discuss the time involved in preparing the control forms advocated for the traditional food cost control system. Identify which person in the organization would be responsible for executing each form.

3. Discuss the problems inherent in maintaining a daily food cost.

4. Contact a food service operation, such as a large hotel or club, that uses the traditional system. Find out which parts of the system they use and discuss how they interpret results.

5. What is mean by an "unbroken chain of control?"

12 MONITORING PRODUCT COST PERFORMANCE

Measures of Food Cost

Taking Remedial Action

THE PURPOSE OF THIS CHAPTER

In Chapter 11, we examined a control system based on an unbroken chain of control from the receiving of raw products to the sale of meals. That system is very expensive to implement, and it turned out, the "unbroken chain" was more an idea than a fact.

In restaurants with simplified menus and POS systems, control systems actually can track an operation's main products by the piece or the ounce, by using computers instead of expensive human labor. Many full-service restaurants, however, have complex menus. Although software for computerized control systems for these operations is available, it is expensive both in terms of software purchase and adaptation cost and of the management time required to adjust to and use the new control systems. Many successful full-service restaurants have adopted a philosophy of control we might call key factor monitoring. Rather than monitoring each key product, management chooses key points in the system for monitoring and studies individual products only when a problem is detected.

Even where POS systems are available, much of product cost control is based on the implementation of specialized control systems such as yielding and special-issues systems. Such physical approaches to control as lock and key systems are important, too.

THIS CHAPTER SHOULD HELP YOU

1. Know the steps in the process of actually computing a food cost.

2. Understand how simple computerization can improve the efficiency of the food cost computer process.

3. Be familiar with common specialized controls.

4. See guest check control as a part of the total system of control.

5. Describe a course of action to determine the cause of food cost averages.

MEASURES OF FOOD COST

In restaurants, food cost generally is computed as a total dollar cost and stated as a percent of sales. Food cost, very simply, is the cost of food used up in the operation during the period in question. In institutional food service, food cost often is stated as "ration cost" or "food cost per patient day."

MECHANICS OF FOOD COST CONTROL

The Purchase Ratio

One measure of food cost is the *purchase ratio,* which is simply food purchases divided by food sales. Underlying the purchase ratio is the assumption that virtually all the food purchased in the period has been used up in the period. This assumption sometimes is valid. For instance some food service operations receive nearly all their food from a commissary in regular, periodic shipments that are gauged to the unit's use. For example, if a restaurant received a weekly commissary order valued at $2000 and sales for that week were $6000, the purchase ratio would be 0.33. The ratio of 0.33 should remain fairly constant—if sales were to increase to $6500, then the commissary delivery should be around $2150. To be used as a control figure, the inventory in the restaurant must remain about the same each week at the time of delivery.

Most operations, however, are not that uncomplicated. They commonly receive orders each weekday from a variety of suppliers, and inventory variations can be substantial. For instance, large deliveries may be received on Thursday and Friday to stock up for weekend business, so purchases for those days can be heavy. But the sales related to those purchases occur on Saturday and Sunday, and if the accounting period ends on Friday, the value for purchases will be overstated for the period ending Friday and the value for sales overstated for the period beginning Saturday. Such distortion makes a purchase ratio meaningless at best and dangerously confusing at worst. For this reason, most operations adjust their food cost computations for inventory change.

Food Cost Adjusted for Inventory Change

Food cost adjusted for inventory change can be determined by fitting the appropriate information into the form of the equation:

Beginning Inventory plus Purchases minus Ending Inventory equals Cost

or

$$BI + P - EI = C$$

Beginning Inventory

The beginning inventory for one accounting period is the ending inventory for the one preceding it. Inventories taken for formal accounting purposes theoretically should be taken as of midnight on the last day of the month, so that the ending inventory as of midnight, June 30, for example, would also be the beginning inventory as of 12:01 A.M. on July 1. In practice, however, inventories often are taken in the afternoon between lunch and the evening meal, when there is some overlap of supervisory personnel and a lull in the operation's business.

Purchases

The monetary value of purchases—that figure used in the food cost equation—is calculated from the total suppliers' invoices accompanying the food received for the period. A summary of all the invoices that have been approved for payment during a period usually is maintained in a daily purchase journal such as the one shown in Figure 12.1.

Ending Inventory

For food cost to be determined, the ending inventory for the accounting period must be computed. This process involves simply counting the food items on hand and multiplying the number of items by the cost of the items.

The *food cost percentage* involves stating the food cost as a percent of food sales.

$$\frac{\text{Food cost}}{\text{Food sales}} = \text{Food cost percent}$$

The food cost percent is then used both as a budgeting tool and as a measure of performance.

In institutional food service, where often there is no real "sales" figure, food cost is stated as a ratio cost or food cost per person per day. In health care, for instance, the total food cost for the period is divided by the number of patients served during that period. The resulting figure, the food cost per patient day, is used as both a budgeting figure and a control figure: that is, budgets and other financial plans are prepared on the basis of a projected cost per patient day and the actual cost subsequently is measured against the budgeted cost to determine whether goals were met or not.

Frequency of Computation

Many operations compute food cost on a monthly basis, because the time involved in inventorying is considerable. The time saved by infrequent inventories, however, is often lost when trouble arises. If food cost is out of line, the amount of data accumulated during the month—both sales and purchases—is unwieldy, and variations can be lost in the large numbers accumulated for sales and purchases. Moreover, a costly practice (overportioning or theft) can develop and grow to serious proportions in 30 days. By the end of the month, a large, hitherto undetected loss can be incurred. There is then no way to reverse the loss. More-frequent inventories and cost computations can catch unfavorable trends early, when they can be reversed with a minimum of cost.

On the other hand, too-frequent computations involve considerable outlay of management time, and where dollar totals are small, relatively minor random errors in counting and cost can throw calculations off and mandate time-consuming recounts and recalculations.

			Categories														
Date	Vendor	Invoice No:	I	II	III	IV	V	VI	VII	VIII	IX	X	XI	XII	XIII	XIV	XV
8/23/73	Capitol	32518	77.68		79.80												
8/23/73	Portion Pack	68742		96.00													
8/23/73	Patts	15208				65.08											
8/23/73	Penn Dairy	59247									27.80						
8/23/73	Penn Dairy	59248								58.75							
8/23/73	J. Haugh	24501							175.44								
8/23/73	Juniata	47805						125.10				24.00					
8/23/73	Confair	12375											48.00	52.25			

Key to categories
I. Meat
II. Fish
III. Poultry
IV. Fresh Fruits and Vegetables
V. Frozen Fruits & Vegetables
VI. Canned Fruits and Vegetables
VII. Groceries
VIII. Milk and cream
IX. Butter
X. Bake shop and desserts
XI. Beverages
XII. Dining room condiments and dressings
XIII. Eggs
XIV. Cheese
XV. Miscellaneous

FIGURE 12.1 Daily purchase journal.

In the authors' own experience, a 10-day inventory period has proved satisfactory. Many large food service companies, however, require submission of a calculated food cost on a weekly basis. Other periods commonly encountered range from 5 to 15 days. On the other hand, as we will see shortly, fast food operations compute food cost (for their principal food items) daily.

Taking the Physical Inventory
As a first step, it is necessary actually to count the items on hand. In many food service operations, everything is counted, no matter how small the quantity on hand. This process is extremely time-consuming, and it is not always worth the time to be so precise. Accordingly, the inventory category called the *working inventory* receives special treatment. *The working inventory* includes food that has gone to a cook station in the the kitchen and is being used in preparation, food that has been prepared for service that day, and food that has been returned to the main storage area as leftovers. Working inventory remains fairly constant, and its value is generally minor. As a rule, it is either not counted in the interest of saving management time, or some constant estimate of its value is added to inventory each time.

To facilitate the work of the inventory team, as well as the cooks, foods are stored in the storeroom in alphabetical order by product group, and their locations remain fairly constant. Once the plan of the storeroom has been established, inventory forms conforming to the layout of goods on the shelves are prepared. These forms generally are arranged so that it is possible for the inventory recorder to proceed without having to flip back and forth among the pages.

Inventory should be done taken carefully and methodically. The inventory team often is made up solely of management personnel and should always include at least one member of management who is in charge. Upon entering the storerooms, the team should begin to the immediate left of the door, counting first the top shelf, then moving down to the bottom of the first set of shelves. Next, the team should move clockwise to the adjacent set of shelves, beginning at the top and, again, working to the bottom. In this way, the team will proceed systematically through the storeroom. This systematic approach is much more accurate— and timesaving—than is skipping around as items are found, seen, or thought of.

To record the inventory, one member of the team "calls"—that is, counts the number of items and then repeats the name and count to another person, who enters the notations on the inventory form. If, by chance, an item is located in two or three different places or is found in more than one storage area, a plus (+) is entered after the first number and the number of the second count is placed after the plus; all plusses are totaled at the end of the inventory. Figure 12.2, an inventory summary sheet, illustrates how the inventory is taken and totaled.

Once the items on hand have been counted, the next step in calculating the ending inventory figure is to price the inventory. Inventory pricing often involves the use of a price book—a looseleaf notebook containing a separate page for each

Stock No.	Unit	Item	Total	
02119	cs	Sugar, ind.	3	3
02120	lb	Sugar, powdered	3+2	5
02121	5# bx	Sweet roll mix	10+2	12
02122	5# cn	Syrup, dark Karo	5	5
02123	5# cn	Syrup, white Karo	4	4
02124	gal	Syrup, maple	3	3
02125	2 oz	Tabasco, sauce	22+6+7	35
02126	lb	Thyme, rubbed	2	2
02127	#10 cn	Tomatoes, whole, canned	6	6
02128	cans	Topping, Rich's	10	10
02192	gal	Vinegar, distilled	3+1	4
02130	gal	Vinegar, wine, red	2+3	5
02131	4# bx	Wafers, vanilla	3	3
02132	gal	Worcestershire sauce	2+3+4	9

FIGURE 12.2 Inventory summary sheet.

inventory item, including the supplier's most recent invoice cost. (Some operations, however, use the supplier's invoice itself.) Since the price book must be updated constantly for accuracy it is almost never correct for all the items it lists. (If you cannot update all of the items regularly, at least update the costly items or those whose prices change frequently.)

Once the inventory has been priced, it must be extended and footed. Extending simply refers to multiplying the total count on hand by its cost. Footing means adding up an inventory page or adding up the entire inventory. Figure 12.3 illustrates the form typically used when extending and footing are done by hand.

Category	Item	Unit	Quantity	Unit Price	Extended Value
Fresh Fruit	Apples, red delicious 113's	Carton	1/2	$5	$2.50
	Apples, baking				
	Bananas	Carton	40 lb	$4	$4.00
	Blueberries				
	Cherries				
	Grapefruit	Carton	1/2	$3.50	$1.75
	Grapes, emperor				
	Grapes, Thompson seedless				
	Lemons	Carton	1/3	$8.00	$2.67
	Limes				
	Melons, cantaloupes				
	honeydew				
	watermelon				
	Nectarines				
	Oranges, navel	Carton	1	$8.50	$8.50
	Oranges, valencia	Carton	1/4	$8.00	$2.00
	Peaches				
	Pears				
	Plums				
	Strawberries				
	Tangerines				
	Other:				
				TOTAL VALUE	$21.42

FIGURE 12.3 Inventory calculation.

Categorized Food Costs

Some operations segregate the food cost into separate categories, in order to facilitate analysis of food cost variances. Figure 12.4 and 12.5 illustrate food cost reports using a 14-category system. The advantage of a categorized system in full-menu operations such as are found in institutions and complex-menu restaurants, is that a variation in total food cost can be traced through the categories and usually can be isolated more easily.

The disadvantage of categorizing food cost is that every invoice must be broken down into appropriate categories—a fairly time-consuming clerical process. Moreover, it has been the authors' experience that major food problems almost invariably are traced to the categories made up of the most expensive menu items—usually meats, occasionally desserts. The categorized food cost is popular with many full-menu operators, however.

Computerizing the Inventory Process

As Chapter 3 pointed out, restaurants using POS systems—and particularly limited-menu operations—generally use an automated inventory report as a part of their routine functioning. We will study the use of that kind of report shortly. Limited computerization, however, is available very inexpensively from computer service bureaus, and one function that can be computerized is the inventory computation.

We have noted that at least one member of management should be in charge of the inventory team, indeed, the assignment of two members of management to the team is not uncommon. Thus, inventorying necessarily uses expensive management time. Some operations compound this time commitment by assigning a manager to extend and foot the inventory. This is a very expensive use of management time. Even if a clerk is used to perform this computation by hand, expensive employee time is used unnecessarily. Any computer service bureau listed in the Yellow Pages can extend and foot an inventory, using a computer program such as the one provided in Appendix II. In addition to the inventory count (using a form like that shown in Figure 12.1), the service bureau must be supplied an input summary (see Figure 12.6) and item price updates. The resulting report should include a page of inventory for each category, such as is shown in Figure 12.7, and a summary food cost, such as is shown in Figure 12.8.

STANDARD FOOD COSTS

A standard cost system involves developing a "bill of materials" (i.e., a recipe) for each product and comparing the amount of food used with the amount that ought to have been used, given actual sales. Although such a control system technically is possible for full-menu operations such as institutional food service and for full-menu restaurants, the use of such systems is not widespread in such operations. In light of the menus in question and of the variety of items and

Period Ending

No.	Category Description	3/10	3/20	3/31	4/10	4/20	4/30
1	Meat	14.5	14.0	15.0	14.8	13.1	15.0
2	Fish	2.8	3.2	2.7	2.8	3.1	2.7
3	Poultry	1.4	2.1	1.6	1.3	1.8	1.6
4	Fresh fruit and vegetables	3.1	2.8	3.6	2.5	2.1	3.6
5	Frozen fruit and vegetables	0.4	0.5	0.4	0.7	0.5	0.4
6	Canned fruits and vegetables	1.0	1.4	1.0	1.1	1.3	1.0
7	Groceries	2.2	2.2	2.1	1.7	2.1	2.1
8	Bake shop and desserts	3.4	3.6	3.3	3.5	3.7	3.3
9	Beverages	1.5	1.7	1.2	1.9	1.4	1.2
10	Soup Bases	0.2	0.1	0.1	0.1	0.1	0.1
11	Dining room condiments & dressings	1.0	1.0	1.4	1.0	1.0	1.4
12	Milk & cream	2.8	3.1	3.3	3.3	3.0	3.3
13	Butter and cheese	1.5	1.6	1.2	1.5	1.5	1.2
14	Eggs	1.2	1.4	1.2	1.3	1.4	1.2
T	Overall food cost	37.0	38.7	38.1	37.5	36.1	38.1

FIGURE 12.4 Food cost reports, using a 14-category system.

		Period Ending					
No.	Category Description	3/10	3/20	3/31	4/10	4/20	4/30
1	Meat		14.3	14.5		14.0	14.3
2	Fish		3.0	2.9		3.0	2.8
3	Poultry	Same	1.7	1.7	Same	1.6	1.6
4	Fresh fruit and vegetables		2.9	3.2		2.3	2.7
5	Frozen fruit and vegetables	as	0.5	0.4	as	0.6	0.5
6	Canned fruit and vegetables		1.2	1.1		1.2	1.1
7	Groceries	3/10	2.2	2.1	4/10	1.9	2.0
8	Bake shop and desserts		3.5	3.4		3.6	3.5
9	Beverages	on	1.6	1.5	on	1.6	1.5
10	Soup bases		0.1	0.1		0.1	0.1
11	Dining room condiments and dressings	ten-day	1.0	1.1	ten-day	1.0	1.1
12	Milk and cream		3.0	3.1		3.1	3.2
13	Butter and cheese	Inventory	1.6	1.4	Inventory	1.5	1.4
14	Eggs		1.3	1.3		1.4	1.3
T	Overall Food Cost	37.0	37.9	37.8	37.5	36.9	37.1

FIGURE 12.5 Food cost percentage, by category (month-to-date).

	FOOD COST REPORT		
		Input Summary Period Ending	30 SEP 19XX
Category		10–Day	Month–to–Date
I. Meat	Beginning inventory purchases	$195.35 842.65	$215.00 2864.15
II. Fish	Beginning inventory purchases	165.55	32.65 564.98
III. Poultry	Beginning inventory purchases	122.69 275.46	168.55 1124.25
IV. Fresh fruits and Vegetables	Beginning inventory purchases	101.50 247.55	78.63 976.07
V. Frozen fruits and Vegetables	Beginning inventory purchases	65.44 179.85	82.14 698.73
XII. Desserts	Beginning inventory purchases	63.21 145.36	86.52 512.78
XIII. Soup bases	Beginning inventory purchases	25.87 53.45	21.08 210.95
XIV. Miscellaneous	Beginning inventory purchases	23.12 39.50	45.60 205.10
	Total food cost	$4084.24	$11,762.01
	Sales	$11,844.00	$35,050.00

FIGURE 12.6 Computer input summary form (14-category cost).

ingredients—soups, salads, breads, and entrees ranging from beef bourguignonne to tournedos Rossini or meat loaf to roast turkey, not to mention mashed potatoes, dressing, and gravy—the complexity of the task and the difficulty of interpreting results is easy to grasp.

In limited-menu restaurants, however, the problem of standard costing is less complex, and the POS applications we studied in Chapter 3 can make the implementation of a standard cost system into a fairly simple routine. In one popular fish specialty chain, for instance, 95% of the fast food cost is accounted for by just eight items in the food inventory. In this restaurant, not only is a food cost computed daily, but product use accounted for by sales is compared to actual use measured on the basis of a physical inventory of those key items. Variance is then measured in physical units as well as dollar costs, in a report such as that shown in Figure 12.9. In this chain, indeed, just as fish usage is measured in pieces, chicken or hamburger waste is accounted for in pieces or patties in fast food restaurants featuring those items.

In a full-menu operation, a great amount of detail would be required to assess

MONITORING PRODUCT COST PERFORMANCE

PERIOD 11-21 to 11-30

LOC	GRP	CAT	ITEM #	DESCRIPTION	ON HAND	UNIT COST	EXTENDED COST
1	01	06	1001	ANCHOVIES, CANNED	25.00	.60	15.00
1	01	06	3002	CATFISH	9.00	1.35	12.15
1	01	06	3005	CRAB MEAT, KING	10.00	5.85	58.50
1	01	06	4006	DEVILED CRAB	.25	6.84	1.71
1	01	06	6007	FLOUNDER, WHOLE	5.00	3.00	15.00
1	01	06	6933	FLOUNDER, FILET	10.00	1.77	17.70
1	01	06	11932	KITCHEN INV	1.00	25.00	25.00
1	01	06	12011	LOBSTER, FLORIDA	9.00	2.55	22.95
1	01	06	12014	LOBSTER MEAT	3.00	5.73	16.11
1	01	06	12014	LOBSTER TAIL	6.00	7.20	43.20
1	01	06	13015	MAR HERRING, JAR	7.00	2.40	7.20
1	01	06	15016	OYSTERS BREADED	1.00	6.60	6.60
1	01	06	15017	OYSTERS SHELL	3.24	51.54	167.50
1	01	06	19020	SCALLOPS	13.00	7.00	91.00
1	01	06	19021	SHRIMP BREADED	12.00	4.38	52.56
1	01	06	19022	SHRIMP GREEN	15.00	3.42	51.30
1	01	06	19023	SHRIMP MEAT	15.00	2.85	42.75
1	01	06	19024	SHRIMP PDQ	21.00	4.62	97.02
1	01	06	19025	SNAPPER, RED	5.00	2.07	10.35
1	01	06	20029	TUNA FISH #10	3.00	6.36	19.08
1	01	06	20935	TROUT, BONELESS	19.00	2.97	56.43

	10-DAY PERIOD	MONTH TO DATE
BEGINNING INVENTORY	$ 685.65	$ 790.95
PURCHASES	1,409.00	3,323.79
ENDING INVENTORY	829.11	829.11
FOOD COST	1,265.54	3,285.63
FOOD SALES	24,337.30	82,140.75
FOOD COST %	5.2%	4.0%

FIGURE 12.7 Category cost printout—fish.

the final use of each menu item. Reviewing all that information would be time-consuming and expensive. The alternative approaches discussed below focus attention on costly, high-use items. In a limited-menu operation, however, only a few items need be scrutinized; this makes a daily food cost computation *feasible and useful*.

We should note, however, that the daily total food cost computed in fast food is a standard cost: that is, the standard recipe is multiplied by the number of items

MEASURES OF FOOD COST 277

	10-Day Period	Month-to-Date
Beginning inventory	1062.96	1273.28
Beginning purchases	439.87	1293.12
Ending inventory	1116.59	1116.59
Food cost	386.24	1449.81
Food sales	1237.95	4488.73
Food cost percent	31.2%	32.3

FIGURE 12.8 Summary food cost.

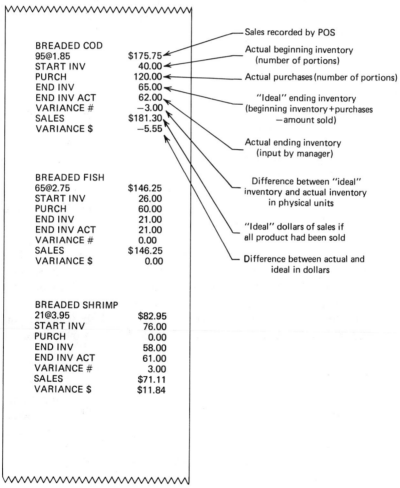

FIGURE 12.9 The variance in physical units, as well as in dollar costs, for a fish specialty chain.

sold (usually by the computer or microprocessor) to yield a food cost figure that represents the expected results, or standard cost. This "full" cost in most operations is *confirmed by a full inventory of all food products* only monthly, or even less frequently. The daily physical inventory for computation of actual use to compare with expected or standard use of product typically is confined to the small number of high-cost items (as a rule, meat, fish, poultry, and dessert) that make up 80 to 95% of the food consumed in the operation.

SPECIALIZED CONTROLS

Controls have been developed to suit the special needs of the many different operations found in today's world of food service. We will discuss those controls that have been applied widely. These specific controls not only are useful in themselves—they also serve as useful illustrations of the logic of special control system development.

Yielding

The first specialized control we will study is yielding—which actually is not new to us, since we studied yields in Chapter 9. Yielding can be seen as a kitchen operating control—a continuous check on expensive foods. Certain meats can be designated for yielding, to ensure that the yield anticipated when determining the cost will indeed be that cost.

Valuable meats may pass through several stages of processing. For instance, a primal cut of meat must be trimmed before it is cooked and portioned. Figure 12.10 illustrates the assignment of market values to the trimmed portion of a primal rib of beef. Where there are several steps in the production process, it is common to compute a yield after each step in the process, in order to determine the amount of shrinkage at each point. This type of yielding also is useful in comparing two different ways of purchasing the same product as the examples illustrated in Figures 12.10 and 12.11 demonstrate.

Figure 12.10 depicts a yield chart for the primal rib, which originally weighed 28 pounds. The boneless rib roast is removed from the primal cut along with usable short ribs, ground meat, and stew meat. It is then necessary to assign values to each by-product before computing the value of the rib roast. Thus, in our example, market values of $1.45 a pound for short ribs and $1.49 a pound for ground and stew meat are assigned. Since the bones and fat have no value to this operator, no value is assigned to them. The value of the roast then is determined by adding the value of the usable by-products and subtracting that sum from the total cost of the primal rib ($50.12 − $16.27 = $33.85).

After cooking, the roast weighs 6 ½ lb, and an additional 0.5 lb is lost during carving. The roast is divided into sixteen 6 oz portions at a cost of $2.11 each.

$$\$33.85 \div 16 \text{ portions} = \$2.11$$

DATE: 9-3-82
ITEM: Primal rib of beef
WEIGHT: 28 lb
TOTAL COST: $50.12   AT $1.79 per lb.
Number: 1

Product Yield	Weight	Percent Weight	Market Value per pound	Total Value
Rib roast boneless	11 lb	39	$3.08	$33.85
Short ribs	3 lb	11	1.45	4.35
Ground beef and/or stew meat	8 lb	29	1.49	11.92
Bones and fat	6 lb	21	no value	0
Total	28 lb	100		$50.12

Rib of beef, boneless

Weight before cooking	11 lb	Number of usable portions: 16	
Weight after cooking	6 lb, 8 oz	Cost per oz: 0.353	
Loss in cooking	4 lb, 8 oz	Cost per portion: $2.11	
Loss in carving	8 oz	Percent yield (raw:cooked): 54.51%	
Usable meat	6 lb		
Portion size	6 oz		

FIGURE 12.10   Yield chart—primal rib of beef.

Comparing the two types of rib, you will notice that even though the boneless rib costs $2.95 per pound, as against the $1.79 per pound of the primal rib, the cost per serving of the boneless rib is less than that of the bone-in rib. (There is also less labor involved in preparing the boneless rib for serving, since much of the difficult trimming was eliminated when the round was butchered.)

Going a step further, we then compare the yields from the two rib roasts with

Date: 9-3-82
ITEM: Rib of beef, boneless   Number: 1
WEIGHT: 12 lb
TOTAL COST: $35.40   AT $2.95 per lb

Product Yield	Weight Lb. Oz.	Percent Weight	Market Value Per Pound	Total Value
Rib, boneless	12 0	100	$2.95	$33.40
Total	12	100	. . .	$35.40

Rib of beef, boneless   Cooking Loss

Weight before cooking	12 lb	Number of usable portions: 18
Weight after cooking	7 lb, 12 oz.	Cost per oz: $.314
Loss in cooking	4 lb, 4 oz.	Cost per portion: $1.96
Loss in carving	12 oz	Percent yield (raw: cooked) 58.3%
Usable meat	7 lb	
Portion size	6 oz.	

FIGURE 12.11 Yield chart—roast boneless rib of beef.

expected yields from the yield chart (Chart 6, Appendix I), and find that the expected yield from boneless rib of beef is between 55 and 60 % and both fall within this range.

Special Issuing

A very common practice in food service is to segregate valuable products and develop for them a specialized means of monitoring use. In one hotel the authors operated, for instance, a significant part of dinner sales was accounted for by steaks, a high-cost item. The steaks were kept in a separate refrigeration area, to which only management had access. At the start of the evening meal, steaks were issued to grill personnel according to the day's forecasted sales. If more steaks were required during the meal, the restaurant manager or her assistant made a second issue. Duplicate guest checks were used in the dining room, and the servers handed in one copy of the check (usually called a "dupes" for "duplicate") with their order. The grill cook saved his copies and at the end of the evening turned them into the manager on duty, together with any leftover steaks. Steaks accounted for on "dupes" plus steaks not cooked were expected to total to the issue—with no "mysterious disappearance."

Similar issue procedures can be used for other valuable products, such as live lobsters, as well as for expensive desserts. As with the daily inventory procedures used in fast food, the special issuing procedure is intended to *focus attention and the control process on the limited number of valuable products that make up a large part of the cost of food consumed.*

Perpetual Inventory

If a POS sytem is used, a perpetual inventory in effect, is maintained automatically: that is, each item received is recorded as an increase in inventory on hand, and each sale is recorded as a decrease in product on hand. At the end of the day, as we indicated earlier, product actually on hand is compared with the amount expected to be on hand if standard costs had been achieved perfectly. The difference or variance is automatically highlighted for cost control, and total inventory printout becomes a useful guide for ordering. In fact, reorder points often are included in the computer program, and reorder items and amounts automatically indicated on the inventory report.

Whenever this process requires hand posting, however, it is too prodigal of labor to use for reorder purposes. Experienced food supervisors can estimate the amount of product on hand from a visual inspection of the storeroom and refrigerators almost as quickly as they could by examining a series of inventory cards, and without laborious hand posting. Perpetual inventories sometimes are maintained, however, on a few very expensive items in a way that mirrors the special-issues systems discussed above. Figure 12.12 provides an example of a perpetual inventory card used to keep track of the use of beluga caviar.

Keys and Locks

All too often, control is thought of as something specialized and written down. It is useful to remind ourselves that in practice, control is part of a management process—something that managers *do*. The simple step of putting locks on doors and refrigerators, for instance, can be an important control process in itself.

Many operations use the planning of storage arrangements and access to storage as a part of the control process. For instance, food for the day's use may be readily accessible to the kitchen, but other products can be stored in another, remote area which is accessible only under management supervison. This *limited-access storage* also may be used to keep especially valuable products that

Caviar, beluga—2 oz									
Received					Issued				
Date	Rec'd From	Qty.	Unit Price	Amt	Date	Issued to	Req. No.	Qty.	Balance Qty. Amt.

FIGURE 12.12 Perpetual-inventory card.

are not being used for a given meal—as for instance, in the steak-issue example discussed earlier.

Since keys have a way of getting lost—only to be found by a dishonest employee—some operations use variable combination locks. The combination on these locks can be changed as frequently as management wishes, and new combinations distributed to appropriate management staff.

Guest Check Control

Food pilferage or loss in production is a problem in the receiving, storage, and production process, but unfortunately the risk of pilferage does not stop there. A dishonest server, if given the opportunity, may charge a guest for the food and pocket the money—or even go so far as to give the guest food without charging for it, on the understanding that an especially good tip will be forthcoming. Two means of avoiding this problem are prechecking and guest check control.

Prechecking. When a server has taken an order, he or she proceeds to a specially designated register and enters the order. With older equipment, the order is written out by hand while the dollar value is machine-printed. As a rule, where prechecking is enforced, numbered checks are used (Figure 12.13) and a machine-validated (i.e., printed) "dupe" must be handed in in order to obtain an order. One of the major conveniences of POS systems to workers and guest alike is its clear, legible machine printing of both item name and price.

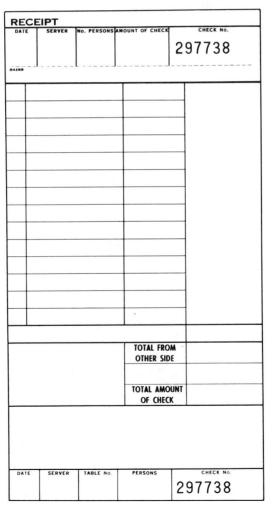

FIGURE 12.13 Example of a numbered guest check.

At the end of the meal, the dollar total on the precheck register should equal the amount of cash and charges recorded on the dining room cash register. If there is a serious discrepancy, all "dupes" can be collected and compared with guest checks. Since both check and "dupe" have the same printed number, any discrepancies between what was issued by the kitchen to servers and what was paid for by guests should be readily detected.

Operations that use duplicate checks should require each cook to turn in all "dupes" received at the end of each meal. If "dupes" are randomly spot-checked against product used at a particular station, discrepancies in yield can be determined. If the spot checking and follow-through on discrepancy are well known, the possibility of collusion between server and cook is less likely, because it will be seen to be risky.

Since prechecking requires multipart guest checks, specially designated precheck registers, and a significant time commitment on the part of servers and supervisors, it is a moderately expensive process. For this reason, prechecking usually is used only where the value of the food sold warrants such care. Many smaller operations, in which everything takes place under the watchful eye of the owner, do not precheck. Note, however, that prechecking reduces this aspect of supervision to the level of operational control, and thus allows management to be concerned less about routine problems.

Check Control. In manual systems, checks are signed out to servers, often on a check-issue sheet such as that shown in Figure 12.14.

As checks are paid, they are sorted by the cashier first according to server and then numerically according to check number. If individual checks are issued at each meal, unused checks are turned in at the end of the meal, and checks used and checks remaining are reconciled. If a server is charged with a book or block of checks, a record of the starting and ending numbers for each day can be used to achieve the same effect.

SERVERS' SIGNATURE BOOK				
SERVER NO.	GUEST CHECK			SERVERS' SIGNATURE
	From	To	Closing No.	

FIGURE 12.14 Check-issue sheet (from Horwath, Toth, and Lesure, *Hotel Accounting*).

Where POS systems are in use, check tracking reports can be used. One such report indicates which checks are out at any given time during a meal, and another reveals which checks have not been turned in at the end of the meal.

TAKING REMEDIAL ACTION

Frequent routine computation of food cost can be likened to an early warning system. As long as there is no problem detected on the food cost front, management can concentrate its attention on other problems, such as employee morale and guest satisfaction. When a rise in the food cost percent indicates that there is a problem, swift action must be taken to determine exactly what product's usage is out of line. This information is automatically available in the inventory variance report (see Figure 3.22) in a POS system, but the same kind of information can be derived by hand with limited effort. We refer to this process as the physical analysis of use.

PHYSICAL ANALYSIS OF USE

Generally, a significant variation in cost results from consistent, particular activities by one or more persons. These actions include overportioning, cooking too fast (excess shrinkage), purchasing the wrong product (excess trim loss), and pilferage. The key is to find out what is wrong—*fast*.

Recall the equation for computing food cost,

$$BI + P - EI = C$$

and remember that it can apply to pounds (or other measures of count or weight). Refer back to your inventory for beginning inventory in physical units—say pounds. Tally amounts on current invoices to determine purchases—in pounds—and enter the most recent ending inventory, again in pounds. Usage can now be compared with actual tallies of food sold, taken from guest checks.

This food count process usually is done routinely by the cashier for all appetizers, entrees, and desserts. Where an ECR or POS with appropriate preset keys is available, these tallies are given automatically.

Since a serious discrepancy in food cost likely has arisen from waste of an expensive and heavily used product, physical analysis of use generally is performed only for high-volume, high-cost menu items. An important advantage of frequent inventories is that purchases need be tallied from only a limited number of invoices. The whole process—assuming that only a few expensive, high-use items need be studied—is really very simple and can ordinarily be handled quite informally. In fact, the authors usually have been able to complete the process in 10 or 15 minutes—often on the back of an envelope!

286 MONITORING PRODUCT COST PERFORMANCE

KEY WORDS AND PHRASES

Key factor monitoring
Measures of food cost
Mechanics of food cost control
Purchase ratio
Food cost adjusted for inventory
$BI + P - EI = C$
Beginning inventory
Purchases
Ending inventory
Food cost percentage
Food cost divided by food sales = food cost percent
Food cost per person per day
Frequency of computation
Physical inventory
Working inventory
Counting
Calculating inventory value
Extending

Footing
Computerized food cost
Categorized food cost
Extending and footing via computer
Standard food costs
Variance
Specialized controls
Yielding
Special issuing
Perpetual inventory
Keys and locks
Limited-access storage
Guest check control
Prechecking
Check control
Taking remedial action
POS inventory variance report
Physical analysis of use

DISCUSSION QUESTIONS

1. You are the manager of a fast food restaurant unit. Your daily inventory variance report indicates that the evening shift "lost" (cannot account for) 30 hamburgers. During this shift, 400 hamburgers were sold. Discuss what you should do. (It may be helpful to identify ways this loss could have occurred). Would you be concerned about a loss of two hamburgers?

2. A lawyer and an interior decorator with no food service experience are building a restaurant in a shopping center and have consulted you for advice. They want you to devise a food cost control system for them. Discuss a "key factor" monitoring system that would be relatively inexpensive but would give them the control they needed.

3. Your food cost has risen three points and you are taking remedial action. You have identified three items for physical analysis of use: roast beef, steaks, and chicken. First, you collect data—inventory figures and invoices recording purchases during the period. You also tally sales (your operation uses a simple cash register, and you need to go through guest checks for sales figures). This data is summarized below. Determine if there are problems with any of these items, and discuss what remedial action you would take.

Item	Beginning Inventory	Purchases	Ending Inventory	Sales
Steak (8 oz)	2 boxes (20/box)	5 boxes	1 box	115
Chicken (Quarters—12 oz. ea)	30 lb	100 lb	10 lb	95
Roast beef (3 oz portions—yield, 60%, each roast, 15 lb)	1 roast	3 roasts	1 roast	80

4. Discuss how numbered checks can be used to control food costs.

5. Discuss the differences between a purchase ratio and a food cost adjusted for inventory.

6. Determine the food cost value when:

   Value of beginning inventory is $ 2000.
   Value of purchases is $10000.
   Value of ending inventory is $ 1500.

Determine the food cost percent when sales are $35,000 for this period.

13 CONTROLLING BEVERAGE COST

Overview

Purchasing

Receiving and Storage

Precosting and Pricing

Production Control

Monitoring Beverage Costs

Automation

THE PURPOSE OF THIS CHAPTER

Alcoholic beverages play two important roles in food service operations. First of all, they appeal to the customer. A cocktail or an aperitif before dinner, a dinner wine with the meal, and a cordial or dessert wines after the meal enhance the relaxation that should accompany the dining experience. Alcohol is an important part of the social ritual that accompanies dining. In a cocktail lounge, where dining is secondary or where food may not even be served, alcoholic beverages are the center of a relaxation attraction. And from the point of view of revenue, alcoholic beverages produce operating profits that are as much as 50 to 100% greater than the profits from typical food sales. Thus, beverage operations are an important source of profit and an important inducement to guests to patronize a particular operation. Beverage and bar management is a complex subject,[1] and our focus in this chapter will be on the subject of controlling beverage costs.

THIS CHAPTER SHOULD HELP YOU

1. Understand beverage cost control as another aspect of product cost control.

2. Identify the major factors of importance in the purchasing, receiving, and storing of alcoholic beverages.

3. Use standard drink recipes and standard glassware as the heart of beverage production control.

4. Identify the principle means of monitoring beverage costs and know how they are used.

OVERVIEW

Beverage cost control is essentially another form of product cost control. Although the preceding chapters focused exclusively on food products, the principles of product cost control developed earlier apply to alcoholic beverages as well. Because the product cost and profit potential of beverages are so significant, however, and because the specifics of their controls are sufficiently different, a separate chapter dealing with this application of product cost control is warranted.

In some very large banks, gold is stored in a "bullion room." Not surprisingly, security and control procedures related to this bullion room are extraordinarily

---

[1] For a fuller discussion see Gus Katsigris and Mary Porter, *Pouring for Profit: Profitable Bar Management* (New York, Wiley, 1982).

tight. In many ways, alcoholic beverages are the bullion of food service: the product is costly and readily subject to pilferage (and, unlike gold, to consumption by the people who are supposed to be "guarding" it). For this reason, beverage control occupies an important place in the literature of food service management.

As with all controls, however, it is important to keep beverage control systems in perspective. The term *cost-effectiveness,* as applied to controls, means that the value of the prospective loss to be prevented must be greater than the cost of avoiding the loss. Some control systems involve a great deal of paperwork, and employees and supervisors concerned with beverage control can spend hours chasing errors in complicated computations instead of concentrating on real cost problems. In the discussion that follows, therefore, we will express some reservations.

PURCHASING

A much more limited number of products and a higher degree of standardization,[2] compared to foods, makes the purchasing of beverages far more straightforward. In some jurisdictions, the state or province is the only agency allowed to sell liquor. Very commonly, wholesalers have exclusive franchises for geographical areas. All in all, then, supplier selection usually is limited and rarely presents a problem. Thus, purchasing largely is reduced to the ordering function described in Chapter 4.

There are three basic product categories (although more complex classification schemes are possible):

Distilled spirits include bourbon, Canadian, Scotch, and American blend whiskies; gin; rum; brandy; liqueurs; and cordials.

Malt beverages include common beer and ale, as well as hock, porter, and stout.

Wine is made from fermented fruit, especially grapes. The alcohol content of dinner wines usually ranges from 10 to 12%. In fortified wines, such as sherries and ports, the distilled spirits added boost the alcohol content to up to 20% by volume.

In discussing purchasing, we noted earlier that quality is determined by function. A similar principle applies in beverage inventory policy involving "well whiskey," the availability of "call brands," and the general question of how extensive a wine list should be.

"Well whiskey" is the product poured when the guest orders a cocktail without

---

[2]Imported wines are an exception. Whole books have been written on wines, which often comprise the subject of an entire course. Such complexity is beyond the scope of this text.

specifying a liquor brand. Most operations select a Scotch, a bourbon, a Canadian, a blend, a gin, and a vodka for the "well." These bottles, which are kept in the most convenient part of the bar work area (usually in what are called speed racks), are the distilled spirits highest in dollar volume sold. Operations in which cost and selling price are the major concerns use less-expensive "well" brands, whereas operations whose customers are more interested in quality than in price may choose better-known or higher-quality brands that are most costly.

"Call" brands are brands specified by a guest when ordering. Some operators feel disgraced if a customer orders a brand that they do not have in stock. Increasingly, however, operators are rationalizing inventories to emphasize a reasonable selection of major brands, rather than trying to have "one of each," no matter how obscure the product. If the beverage inventory includes 10 bottles of very slow-moving product, with an average cost per bottle of $20, the capital cost of holding those bottles on the shelf for one year is $20 if interest rates are at 10%, and $30 if they are at 15% (see Figure 13.1).

Similarly, most operations try to offer a limited selection of wines, usually featuring a domestic wine in the categories of red, white, rosé, and sparkling wines. A slightly more complicated wine menu may offer a limited selection of imported wines. French wines and German whites were once virtually the only

FIGURE 13.1 "Well" brands electronically dispensed (interfaced with POS system) and 16 call brands, manually dispensed. (Courtesy of Autobar Systems Corp.)

imported wines offered by restaurants. In recent years, however, the quality of superior Italian wines has come to be recognized, and these wines have become available more widely in North America. Increasingly, Italian dinner wines are listed with French and German wines or supplant them altogether on restaurant wine lists featuring imports. Of course, superior North American wines are the backbone of many wine lists.

At the other extreme, some restaurants choose to develop a very extensive list of wines in an effort to offer a distinctive dining experience and to appeal to guests' interest in the romance—and snob appeal—of wine. Although such a policy has often proven successful when properly carried out, nothing irritates a wine customer more than a fancy wine list that turns out to be a list of items the restaurant is out of. Since a large wine inventory is expensive in terms of interest on the capital tied up, as well as in space and management time to oversee timely reordering, the decision to opt for an extensive wine list should only be made on the basis of careful calculation of its cost-effectiveness. Once a wine list is established, the rule of inventory policy must be: do not run out.

One measure of inventory size is the stock turn (a ratio produced by dividing average beverage inventory for the period into total beverage purchases). According to an authoritative estimate, "The beverage inventory should be turned over about once every three months in an average first class restaurant."[3] The same authors suggest that "where the supply of liquors and wines is good and if large stocks of foreign wines are not needed, operators can maintain a turnover rate of once every 45 days or less." Thus, an average stock turn of between four and eight times per year is a reasonable expectation. A *monthly* stock turn, however, will serve most operations as a better yardstick, because months reflect seasonal variations. When there are significant sales in more than one group of alcoholic beverages, it may be appropriate to compute separate stock turns for each major group (for instance, beer, wine, and liquor).

RECEIVING AND STORAGE

Receiving of beverages is not complicated. The receiver need make no quality judgements and must simply be sure that the goods listed on the invoice actually have been received in good order. Since one or more bottles in an apparently sealed case occasionally are broken (or removed) in transit, it is important to check that cases actually are full. One way to do this speedily is to weigh each

---

[3]Eric F. Green, Galen G. Dale, and F. Jerome Sweeny, *Profitable Food and Beverage Management: Operations* (Rochelle Park, N.J.: Hayden, 1978), p. 237.

case received and compare the weight to a chart of standard case weights prepared for that purpose. Needless to say, liquor should never be left unattended in the receiving area.

STORAGE

The two principal concerns in regard to storage of alcoholic beverages are security and temperature. Storage also has its own set of controls in some operations, and certain basic procedures are dictated by the nature of the product and by its packaging.

Security

Recalling the "bullion room" analogy, we can quickly see why liquor storage requires great attention to security. Because alcoholic beverages are easy—some would say too easy—to consume, minor pilferage is a constant hazard. Major theft is also a potential problem, because of the product's high dollar value, compactness, and ease of resale. Faced with the likelihood of "mysterious disappearance," most operators limit access to the liquor storage area. The most common practice is to give only one person in an operation keys to the main storage area (although this is not practical in very large operations). That person is charged with filling requisitions during his or her duty day for the various areas that require product during that day.

Storage areas at the bars, in turn, are always locked except when in use, and a bartender commonly must call in a supervisor to unlock the underbar cabinets and refrigerated storage areas at opening. At the close of business, all liquor invariably is locked away in cabinets.

Temperature

No alcoholic beverage should be stored where it is likely to become hot—in a room with heat pipes that are not properly insulated, for instance. A warm, dry atmosphere will dry the corks in the bottles and thereby promote evaporation of product. With product costing $1 per ounce or more, evaporation can be expensive.

The problem of dry corks is even more severe with wines, because as air or microorganisms enter the bottles, the wine can begin to oxidize or ferment, which eventually can sour whole bottles. For this reason, wines with corks should be stored on their sides. All wines should be stored in a cool room, preferably one that remains at "cellar temperature" (around 60°F). White and sparkling wines must be chilled before service but may not be stored for more than a week under refrigeration. Wine generally is chilled in a 40°F refrigerator. Wine generally is stored in bins that are numbered, to facilitate filling requisitions and inventorying. Because many guests are self-conscious about pronouncing the foreign names of wines, it is a common practice to provide the bin numbers along with the names on wine lists and to encourage guests to order by bin number.

Bottled beer may be stored at room or cellar temperature until chilled for service, but draft beer should be maintained at a temperature between 40° and 50°F. At lower temperatures, beer becomes flat; above 50°, the product becomes "wild"—that is, very foamy—when drawn.

Storage Control

To facilitate ordering, a *par stock* level and a reorder point often are developed for liquor inventory items. Generally, the main storeroom par is that amount sufficient to cover usuage between deliveries plus a margin for error. The par stock will vary, therefore, not only from operation to operation but from item to item within an operation, depending on availability. A common practice is to maintain a bin card for each item in inventory (see Figure 13.2). The amount on hand can be compared with the par stock as a fast guide to ordering. Bin cards are useful in ordering when the amount on hand is so large that a quick visual inspection is not possible. (You can tell at a glance if there are eight bottles on hand; if there are supposed to be 80, you will have to count them.)

Bin cards have other control functions. They form a record of issues by bar (see "Issued to Bar No." columns in Figure 13.2), although if there is more than one bar, that record should be available from the requisition. Perhaps more importantly, bin cards also tell the person in charge of the liquor storeroom how much there *should be* in each bin. If the amount on hand differs from the bin card total, the manager in charge of the liquor storeroom (or the storeroom keeper, in very large operations) knows there is a problem. Even in this case, however, we suggest that the benefits of that control be weighed against the effort involved. If storeroom access is limited and restricted properly, as we have advocated, in most operations the person inspecting the bin card *should be* the only person who can remove

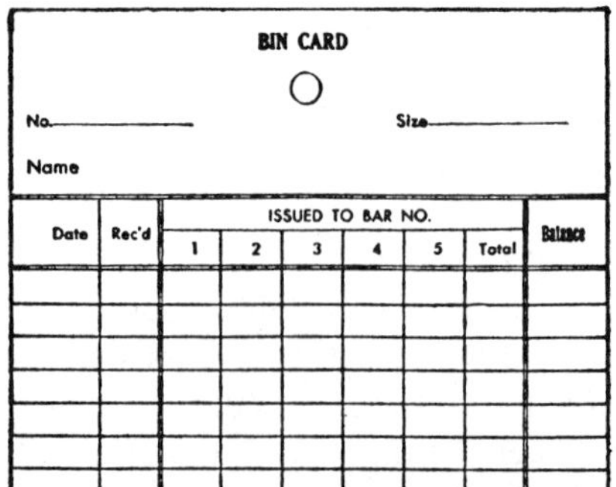

FIGURE 13.2 A bin card commonly is maintained for each item in inventory. (From Horwath, Toth, and Lesure, *Hotel Accounting*.)

liquor—or enter the storeroom at all. Under these circumstances, if you find that a bin card total is out of line with the amount of product actually on hand, what you probably are looking at is your own clerical error; but since that fact is hard to accept, a good deal of effort goes into trying to trace the discrepancy. Where more than one person has access to the storeroom, bin cards have a clear control function; but where proper limits on access can be and are maintained, the bin card's control function is at least open to question. They are, however, helpful in reordering where inventory size warrants their use for that purpose.

Another reorder and control form frequently used in large liquor storerooms is the perpetual inventory. The bin card, properly maintained, is actually a perpetual inventory—but it is kept in the storeroom by whoever is responsible for that secure area. A perpetual inventory normally is maintained by a different person, and so provides a check on the person responsible for the storeroom. (There is no justification for allowing the storeroom manager to keep both bin cards and the perpetual inventory.)

A perpetual inventory does take time and effort to maintain by hand, and hence it is an expensive control device. Modern POS systems, however, can be programmed to maintain perpetual inventories automatically. This kind of equipment has so many control advantages that it is being installed in most large operations today. Where a POS system is available, the inventory function is a major advantage. To be useful, however, the POS inventory figure must be compared regularly to an actual physical inventory.

PRECOSTING AND PRICING

The precosting of beverages is much simpler than the precosting of food, but the approach developed in Chapter 9 still applies. As with food precosting, our approach depends on standard recipes; the difference is that with drinks, there is no need to deal with shrinkage or trim loss. There should be little or no shrinkage with liquor, although some operations allow a small margin for unavoidable error and minimal evaporation. Figure 13.3 provides a chart from which you quickly can obtain a drink cost if you know the case cost. It is important, however, to be sure to include in the cost the mixers and garnishes (cherries, orange slices, lime wedges, etc.), and some very simple yielding is called for in computing, say, the cost of one orange slice.

The pricing of spirits and beer generally is based on cost plus a standard markup: for instance, four times cost, to achieve a 25% pouring cost (i.e., product cost for a specific drink or group of drinks.) Very commonly, however, the pouring cost for specific products differs. For instance, the pouring cost for cocktails generally ranges between 25 and 30%. Bottled beer usually is priced to yield a 40% product cost, whereas draft beer commonly yields a 20 to 25% cost. Wines are commonly priced to yield a 50% cost. All of the above cost percentages are subject to local competition, however.

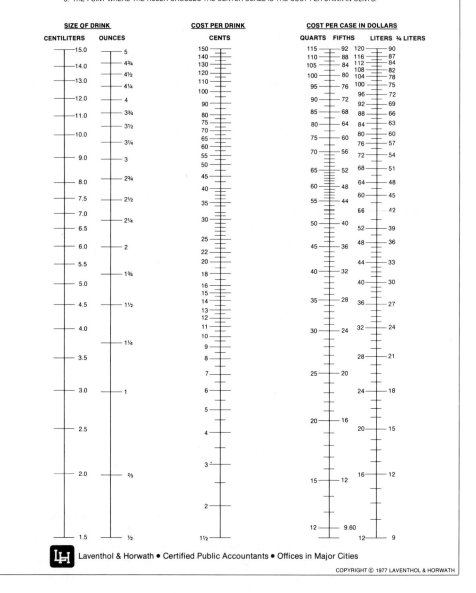

FIGURE 13.3 Cost-per-drink chart. (Courtesy of Laventhol & Horwath.)

Wine pricing strategy sometimes varies from the standard percentage markup. Operations that seek to promote wine as an accompaniment to dining often base prices on cost plus a standard dollar markup. This results in a significantly lower menu price that is particularly noticeable for imported wines. The markup is intended to cover costs over product costs, such as the carrying charges for inventory (interest and space), labor, glassware, and profit. Since very little additional labor cost is involved in the sale of a bottle of wine and the overhead costs generally are the same for all wines regardless of product cost, this pricing strategy is a rational approach to building sales volume in imported wines through competitive pricing.

PRODUCTION CONTROL

As in food production control (see Chapter 8), the key tools to bar operations planning are carefully prepared lists (i.e., menus and standardized recipes). Equally important is the use of standard portioning devices in the form of jiggers, shot glasses, and standardized bar glassware. A useful device that can take the place of the shot glass or jigger is the gravity-fed dispenser, which, when attached to a bottle, measures *and* pours only the measured amount when the bottle is upended.

STANDARD RECIPES

Standardized recipes for drinks are necessary to guarantee quality to the customer and on-target cost performance to management. A first basic policy decision concerns the size of the standard drink—that is, the "shot size." The alcohol served with a highball such as a Scotch and soda provides the simplest example. In such a drink, the shot size commonly ranges from 1 ounce to 1½ oz. Some bars, in an attempt to keep prices as low as possible, serve a ⅞ or even ¾ oz shot, whereas other operations serve only "double" (i.e., 2 to 3 oz) drinks. A second decision involves selecting recipes (or formulas, as some prefer to call them) for mixed cocktails. Here, most operations use the same portion of alcohol as is used in highballs; major exceptions include martinis (which may contain from three to five or more parts gin or vodka to one part dry vermouth) and manhattans (usually, three parts whiskey to one part sweet vermouth).

From the wide variety of cocktail recipe books available, management should adopt and strictly enforce one standard set of recipes.[4] Recipes should specify more than the alcoholic part of the drink: correct use of ingredients such as sugar (powdered for most cocktails) and juice (generally fresh frozen) in the recipe amount is absolutely essential.

---

[4]The reader is referred to Katsigris and Porter, *The Bar and Beverage Book,* p. 440, for one such list.

Free Pouring
Many experienced bartenders insist that they can pour every bit as accurately without a shot glass, and that they can work faster without the intermediate step of measuring. Some suggest, too, that customers resent the use of the shot glass because it looks "stingy." Most operators, however, reject these arguments.

First of all, although highly experienced bartenders probably *can* free-pour accurately, the first question that arises is whether they *do* pour accurately all the time: an off night or an extra busy period (or a heavy-tipping customer) could result in overportioning. The time involved in measuring ingredients really is not significant.

Moreover, and unfortunately, cheating both the house and the customer is a common problem in beverage operations. With free pouring, for instance, it is much easier to short-pour drinks for a customer who has had several drinks and whose taste buds may not be overly sensitive. After a few such drinks have been served, the bartender knows there is a "balance" of liquor on hand but already accounted for that can be sold for cash, with the bartender pocketing the money. The use of standard procedures, such as jigger-measured liquor (see Figure 13.4) and the issuance of a printed receipt with each drink, or some other form of prechecking, will not eliminate this danger, but it will help reduce it.

STANDARD GLASSWARE

Selection of glassware that fits the drink size helps ensure standard drinks. It is most important to use glassware that presents the standardized drink in a manner that is inviting and appealing to the customer's eye. Moreover, standardized glassware provides one means, particularly with cocktails, to hinder overpouring. When selecting glassware, also consider its durability and the likelihood that it can be replaced (i.e., that the line will not be discontinued).

MONITORING BEVERAGE COSTS

Beverage cost most commonly is monitored by the computation of a dollar beverage cost for a certain period based on purchases adjusted for inventory change. Two other approaches, which involve relating physical units of inventory to dollar sales, are the so-called ounce-control system[5] and the potential-sales-value control system.[6]

---

[5] For further discussion of this topic, see Carl H. Albers, *Food and Beverage Cost Planning and Control Procedures* (East Lansing, Mich.: The American Hotel and Motel Educational Institute, 1974), p. 115; and Charles Levinson, *Food and Beverage Operations* (Englewood Cliffs, N.J.: Prentice-Hall, 1976) pp. 67–68.

[6] For further discussion of this topic, see Green, Drake, and Sweeny, *Profitable Food and Beverage Management: Operations,* pp. 251–253.

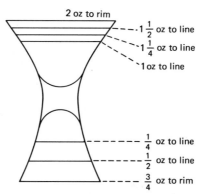

FIGURE 13.4 Metal jigger with quantity lines. This is a flexible, accurate, high-speed tool for a trained bartender. For instance, to mix a 5-to-1 martini, you measure $\frac{1}{3}$ oz of vermouth (between the $\frac{1}{4}$ and $\frac{1}{2}$ oz lines) with the small end; then flip and measure $1\frac{2}{3}$ oz (between $1\frac{1}{2}$-oz line and 2-oz rim) of gin.

TOTAL DOLLAR USE

The most common approach to bar cost control is to determine the dollar value of liquor actually used. The formula used is one we have seen before:

$$BI + P - EI = C \text{ and } C\% = C/S$$

that is, beginning inventory plus purchases minus ending inventory equals the dollar beverage cost, and that cost divided by sales equals the beverage cost percentage. The beverage cost achieved is compared to a target budgeted cost figure, which should be based on careful precosting and on a realistic estimate of the sales mix between drinks. Most operations compute costs monthly, but a 10-day or weekly inventory period is preferable. Costs for individual bars usually are commonly computed on a daily basis.

Bar-Issues Systems

Operations that have more than one bar normally issue beverages from the central liquor storeroom on the basis of requisitions. These issues can be treated like "purchases" in the above equation. The frequent (even daily, as we have noted) inventorying of an individual bar can be accomplished fairly quickly, because of the modest amount of stock involved. If bar costs are computed frequently for individual bars within an operation, those computations can serve as the control device, and monthly calculation of the overall operation's beverage cost will be quite adequate.

The beverage cost may vary from one unit in a property (particularly a hotel) to another. For instance, a cocktail lounge without entertainment will have lower prices and thus a higher beverage cost percent than will an operation with

FIGURE 13.5 This automatic dispenser measures glasses, mugs, and pitchers of beer, and keeps count of each. (Courtesy of Autobar Systems Corp.)

entertainment. Banquet customers often are billed by the bottle, at a substantially lower price than the same liquor would bring in in a regular bar. So-called full-bottle sales also occur in hotel room service. Where this variation in bar costs within an operation is in effect, the need for separate computation of costs should be obvious, because the overall bar cost cannot be evaluated properly without information on the individual revenue center's cost performance.

Figure 13.6 shows a combination form that both documents an individual bar inventory and can be used as a requisition documenting the issue of beverages to an individual bar. Figure 13.7 shows a daily-beverage-cost form for an individual bar.

Bottle Issue and Empty Bottle Exchange

Dishonest bartenders can easily bring their own bottles to the bar, pour drinks from them, and pocket the proceeds of the sale. This scam leaves the bar cost unaffected—and the loss potentially undetected. For this reason, operators commonly mark bottles with a stamp or decal as they are received into the main liquor storeroom. Empty bottles with the proper stamp or decal must accompany the requisition from each bar. This method ensures that only the approved amount of product is in inventory at each bar and minimizes the chance of an unnoticed "partner" working the bar.

OTHER APPROACHES

The "ounce" control and the potential-sales-value control systems both relate the physical amount of product used (i.e., ounces, fifths, or liters) to the dollar sales. Each of these systems can accommodate the issue to bars, banquet departments, and other use centers.

The *"ounce" method* is based on an analysis of actual sales. The amount of product that should have been used according to standard recipes for these sales is calculated and compared to the amount actually used in a given day. Abstracting sales by hand is a time-consuming activity, but this information is available routinely from a POS system. Comparisons of physical use with standards is an automatic part of the daily report in most POS systems.

The *potential-sales-value control system* sets a sales value on each bottle of liquor. The sales value is based on an abstract of actual sales for a period, to account for different pouring costs for different drinks. The amount of liquor used is thus expressed in terms of the potential sales value for that liquor compared to the actual sales experienced in the period. This system can also be programmed into a POS system.

Both of these procedures focus attention on the physical variance (in ounces, etc.) between what has been used and what should be used for a given amount of sales. When used in conjunction with a POS system, these procedures are more-or-less "free" by products of the POS system. If computation by hand is the rule, the time required to maintain them may outweigh the savings they make possible.

COPLEY PLAZA HOTEL
BAR INVENTORY AND REQUISITION

BAR _____   DATE _____

Size	Description	Qty.	Cost	Size	Description	Qty.	Cost	Size	Description	Qty.	Cost
	SCOTCH				**RUMS**				**BITTERS**		
A100	BAR SCOTCH			E100	BAR RUM			G100	ANGOSTURA		
A101	BALLENTINE			E101	BACARDI WHITE			G101	GRENADINE		
A102	BUCHANAN			E102	MEYERS			G102	ROSES LIME JUICE		
A103	CHIVAS REGAL			E103	TEQUILA WHITE			G103	FERNET BRANCA		
A104	CUTTY SARK			E104	TEQUILA GOLD				**BEER**		
A105	DEWARS			E105	MT. GAY			I100	BUDWEISER		
A106	J & B				**BRANDIES**			I101	HEINEKEN		
A107	JOHNNY WALKER BLACK			F100	BAR BRANDY			I102	MICHELOB		
A108	JOHNNY WALKER RED			F101	COURVOISIER			I103	MILLERS		
A109	USQUEBACH			F102	HENNESSY ***			I104	LITE		
A110	HAIG & HAIG			F103	MARTEL VSOP			I105	SCHLITZ		
A111	GLENLIVET			F104	REMY MARTIN VSOP			I106	BECKS		
A112	GLENFIDDICH			F105	METAXA			I107	ST. PAULI GIRL		
A113	JOHN JAMESON			F106	HENNESSY VSOP			I108	MOLSON		
	CANADIANS & RYES			F107	MARTELL CORDON BLEU			I109	GUINESS		
B100	CANADIAN CLUB			F108	REMY NAPOLEON			I110	BASS		
B101	SEAGRAMS VO			F109	FUNDADOR				**MINERAL**		
B102	BAR RYE			F110	DELAMAIN			J100	TAB SPLIT		
B103	SEAGRAMS 7			F111	HENNESSEY XO			J101	TONIC SPLIT		
B104	SEAGRAMS CROWN ROYAL			F112	REMY LOUIS XIII			J102	SODA SPLIT		
B105	SOUTHERN COMFORT				**CORDIALS**			J103	GINGER SPLIT		
	BOURBONS			H100	AMARETTO			J104	COKE SPLIT		
B107	OLD FORESTER 86			H102	B & B			J105	SEVEN-UP SPLIT		
B108	OLD GRANDAD 86			H103	W. MENTHE			J106	FRESCA SPLIT		
B109	BAR BOURBON			H104	G. MENTHE			J107	SCHWEPPES BITTER SPLIT		
B111	JACK DANIELS			H105	DRAMBUIE			J108	PERRIER SPLIT		
B112	WILD TURKEY							J109	TONIC QT.		

302

C100	VODKA		H106	GRAND MARNIER		J110	GINGER QT.
C100	SMIRNOFF		H107	KAHLUA		J111	SODA QT.
C101	GORDON'S		H108	TIA MARIA		J112	SEVEN-UP QT.
C102	ABSOLUT		H109	GALLIANO		J113	COKE QT.
C103	BAR VODKA		H110	WHITE COCOA		J114	PERRIER QT.
C104	STOLICHNAYA		H111	DARK COCOA		J115	EVIAN QT.
	GINS		H112	COINTREAU			COPLEY WINE
C105	GORDON'S		H113	COFFEE BRANDY		K100	RED
C106	BEEFEATER		H114	APRICOT BRANDY		K101	WHITE
C107	TANQUERAY		H115	CREME DE CASSIS		K102	ROSE
C108	BAR GIN		H116	ANNISETTE			
C109	BOMBAY		H117	BENEDICTINE			PLAZA WINE
			H118	BLACKBERRY BRANDY		K103	RED
	APERITIFS		H119	YELLOW CHARTREUSE		K104	WHITE
D100	DUBONET RED		H120	GREEN CHARTREUSE		K105	ROSE
D101	DUBONET BLONDE		H121	CHERRY HERRING			
D102	COMPARI		H122	CHERRY BRANDY		K106	CHAMPAGNE
D103	DRY VERMOUTH		H123	SAMBUCA			
D104	SWEET VERMOUTH		H124	PERNOD			
D105	LILLET		H125	PEACH BRANDY			
			H126	SLOE GIN			
	PORT & SHERRY		H127	TRIPLE SEC			
D106	ROBERTSON'S No. 1		H128	CRANBERRY BRANDY			
D107	TIO PEPE		H129	MANDARINE NAPOLEON			
D108	HARVEY BRISTOL CREAM		H130	KIRSCH			
D109	HARVEY DRY		H131	IRISH MIST			
D110	DRY SACK		H132	GINGER BRANDY			
D111	HAWKERS AMONTILLADO		H133	APPLE JACK			
D112	HAWKERS CREAM		H134	PIMM'S CUP			
			H135	WILD TURKEY LIQUEUR			

INVENTORY TAKEN BY: ISSUED BY: RECEIVED BY:

FIGURE 13.6 Form for bar inventory and requisition. (Courtesy of the Copley Plaza.)

THE COPLEY PLAZA
DAILY BEVERAGE COST

OUTLET: _____

DAY: _____

DATE: _____

	TODAY	TO DATE
LIQUOR ISSUES:		
BEER ISSUES		
SODA ISSUES		
HOUSE WINE ISSUES		
FOOD TO BEVERAGE		
BEVERAGE TO FOOD(–)		
ENTERTAINMENT CREDITS (–)		
TOTAL BAR ISSUES		
BAR SALES		
BAR COST % :		
BOTTLE WINE ISSUES		
BOTTLE WINE SALES		
BOTTLE WINE COST% :		
TOTAL BEVERAGE ISSUES		
TOTAL BEVERAGE SALES		
BEVERAGE COST % :		

Form # 122 8007HPC

FIGURE 13.7 Form for computing daily beverage cost. (Courtesy of the Copley Plaza.)

AUTOMATION

Several systems now on the market actually can measure and pour the appropriate amount of liquor for a drink; the bartender then mixes the liquor with other ingredients (see Figure 13.8). One of these systems is controlled by preset keys on a cash register. When a key is depressed, a signal is sent to a minicomputer that controls an automatic dispensing mechanism. The proper amount of liquor is poured, and at the same time the transaction is automatically recorded by the computer and added to the sales and inventory totals. In such systems, liquor is stored in a back-bar area and connected to a dispensing head.

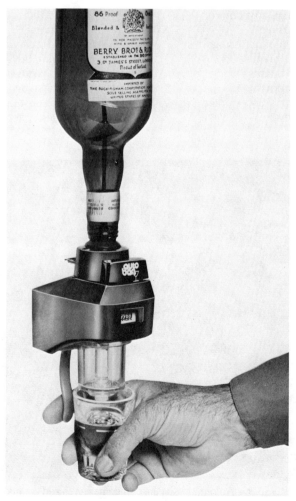

FIGURE 13.8 Each shot is both measured and counted as it is dispensed. (Courtesy of Autobar Systems Corp.)

306 CONTROLLING BEVERAGE COST

Another type of mechanical-control device is one that is attached to the top of each bottle and that both controls the amount of beverage poured and counts each shot as it is dispensed (see Figure 13.9).

Automated bars and mechanical controls are becoming increasingly common where there is a large volume of traffic and a relatively impersonal atmosphere, such as in an airport cocktail lounge. At the other extreme, a private club or expensive lounge or restaurant is less likely to use such devices, because of their impersonal nature and because they give the bar the appearance of being stingy.

KEY WORDS AND PHRASES

Beverage cost control
Purchasing
Three product categories
"Well" brands
"Call" brands
Stock turn
Receiving and storage
Security

Standard recipes
Free pouring
Standard glassware
Monitoring beverage costs
Total dollar use
Dollar beverage cost formula
Beverage cost percentage
Bar-issues systems

FIGURE 13.9 Automatic dispenser that measures and counts each drink. (Courtesy of Autobar Systems Corp.)

Temperature
Storage control
Par stock Level
Reorder point
Precosting
Production control

Bottle issue and empty bottle exchange
"Ounce" method
Potential-sales-value control system
Automation

DISCUSSION QUESTIONS

1. Follow beverages through a restaurant from purchase to service and identify the key control areas. Discuss what could go wrong at each stop along the way.

2. Discuss what steps you would take if your beverage cost percentage suddenly went up by several points.

3. Discuss how you feel about "free pouring" and what alternatives could be used.

4. Discuss the differences between the bottle issue system, the "ounce" method and the potential-sales-value control system. Which system would you suggest if a number of different drinks with varying percent markups were produced from a single bottle of liquor.

5. A large metropolitan hotel has one freestanding bar and also serves drinks in two on-premise restaurants. Presently there is a liquor storeroom, and stock requisitions go from the storeroom to each beverage serving area. The operators are considering putting a wine bar in an unused basement area, and they have hired you to set up their control system. Identify the controls that would be necessary. Discuss why the beverage cost percentage could vary among the beverage serving areas.

BUDGETING FOR FOOD SERVICE OPERATIONS

14

Introduction

The Budgeting Process

Cost Behavior

The Basis for Budgeting

Budget Planning Participation

Performance Responsibility

THE PURPOSE OF THIS CHAPTER

In previous chapters, we have been concerned with planning and control in very specific ways, such as control of food or payroll cost, or we have focused on specific components of the control cycle, such as purchasing, receiving, and storing. In this chapter and the next, however, we will concentrate on planning and control in the operation as a whole. In many ways, these chapters will help you to put together the pieces of the control cycle and to see the operation's process as an interactive whole.

THIS CHAPTER SHOULD HELP YOU

1. Understand the budget planning process.

2. Describe the major forms of cost behavior as they relate to food service.

3. Know the principle bases on which budgets are drawn.

4. Describe a cash budget.

5. Comprehend the importance of participation by subordinates in budget planning.

6. Describe the allocation of responsibility for performance in responsibility accounting.

INTRODUCTION

Budgeting is not "free." It requires a great deal of effort to prepare a budget—and even more to live up to it. The benefits of budgeting do, however, far outweigh the costs. First of all, without a budget, the business has no realistic profit (or nonprofit) objectives. To say that an organization has a 10% profit goal (or intends to hold subsidies to 30%) in itself is meaningless. To accept this goal as a realistic one, we need to know what the intermediate steps are: What will the food cost be? What will the payroll cost be? How will these costs vary from month to month? As a budget emerges, we will have a complete statement of subgoals that will lead to the achievement of our overall goal. A budget, first and foremost, then, is a set of interrelated goals and the financial plans for achieving them.

Implicit in the first advantage of budgeting is a second. When the period planned for is finished, we need to compare operating results with some objective standard, and the best standard is our own, carefully planned budget. To the degree that realistic budgeted results have been achieved, the operation is to be congratulated. Perhaps more importantly, the fact that target results are not being attained in the budget period can become apparent early enough to allow corrective action to be taken or the budget to be revised. A budget, then, gives management both a basis on which to determine if operating results are acceptable and the means to analyze and correct for error.

The budget is also a useful tool for the communication of goals within the organization. To the degree that all levels of management have been involved with the budgeting process, it amounts to an agreement between superior and subordinate as to what results are expected.

Finally, a budget makes other kinds of financial planning possible. Firms have debts that must be paid or expansion plans that must be financed. The operating budget gives top management the information necessary for this kind of planning.

THE BUDGETING PROCESS

The budgeting process generally begins with an estimate of sales volume, which often is based on such estimates of physical volume as guest count or the number of patient meals. Expected physical volume (e.g., guest count) multiplied by expected average check by category of meal (breakfast, lunch, dinner, coffee shop, dining room) provides a basis for estimating total dollar sales. On the other hand, a total dollar volume estimate may be the most reasonable first step where guest counts are expected to remain constant and price changes are known. In general, past-dollar-sales volume provides a better basis for estimating future sales in an ongoing, fairly stable situation. Organizations undergoing change are more likely to build up from guest count and average sale to total sales volume, which is absolutely essential in preparing projections for a new operation. (In Chapter 7, we discussed the specialized forecasting problems of several different kinds of operations, and you may wish to review that chapter at this point.)

The sales volume estimate, however, is a necessary starting point, because much of the rest of the budget is based directly on it and all of the budget is affected by the level of sales forecasted. Once the sales forecast is ready, operating-expense and capital-expenditure estimates can be prepared.

BUDGET REVISIONS

The first draft budget almost never represents the final document. As discussions with department heads and supervisors progress, the budget is refined. Moreover, once the budget is completed and the operating year is underway, conditions may change sufficiently to warrant revising the budget.

If costs or sales levels are altered dramatically, it is better to prepare a revised budget with realistic targets based on new conditions than to work with a document as central to management as a budget that is outdated. The notion of revising budgets to meet changed conditions applies to *all* parts of the budget process.

VARIABLE BUDGETS

In some cases, it is best to budget on the basis of several levels of sales volume. For instance, if you prepare a budget for a ski resort in July, you cannot know what snow conditions will prevail during the season, or whether the resort will have a poor or good or even great season. In this circumstance, budgets can be constructed for each of several assumptions. The effect of above-average sales volume would be twofold: whereas dollar costs will be higher, those costs expressed as a percent of sales will be lower and profit, both in dollars and as a percent of sales, should be higher. In the next section, we will review this procedure more carefully, but for now, note that for most cost groups, higher sales will not result in a directly proportionate rise in expenses. The cashier, host or hostess, chef, and manager—to name just a few positions—all can handle a larger number of guests without a significant increase in the operation's cost.

Conversely, when sales volume is lower than normal, most expenses cannot be reduced beyond a basic level and costs, as a percent of sales, rise while profits fall. The question of variable budgets logically leads to a consideration of ways to group costs according to the way they behave when sales volume varies. An understanding of cost behavior will help us to understand better the subject of budget preparation.

COST BEHAVIOR

This concept is sometimes referred to as the cost-volume-profit relationship, because as sales volume rises or falls, cost and profit relationships change. At the extremes, some costs are *fixed,* regardless of profit, whereas others are *variable* and rise or fall in company with sales. In between these extremes are other cost-volume-profit relationships, including *mixed* and *step variable* costs. These four categories are useful concepts not only in budgeting but also in any cost control effort.

FIXED COSTS

As long as a business is in operation, some costs will go on regardless of sales volume; these costs, principal among which are capital costs, are referred to as *committed fixed costs*. Costs assumed to be fixed because of management decisions are referred to as *programmed fixed costs.*

Committed costs include interest on debt (set at a percent of the principal outstanding), real estate taxes (set at a dollar value based on the value of the property), and fire insurance (which is also, for the most part, related to the value of the property). These other committed costs, such as franchise taxes, license fees, and personal property taxes, are based on values that are not affected by sales volume.

In some instances, rent is a fixed cost; it is increasingly common, however, for rent to have a fixed component and a component based on volume. A lease may specify, for instance, that rent is $30,000 per year plus 1 percent of all sales over $300,000.

Another fixed cost is depreciation and amortization. Depreciation is an accounting charge that "writes down" the value of an asset over its useful life. Amortization refers to a similar charge that reduces the value of a leasehold or improvements to a leasehold. In fact, no cash changes hands at the time these charges are made; the cash has already flowed, at the time of purchase. For instance, if an operator purchases a lease and pays the person giving up the lease $25,000, then that leasehold is listed as an asset in the company's books of account and is written down over the life of the lease. If the lease lasts 10 years, then each year an amortization of $2500 is entered on the books, to reflect the fact that 10% of the leasehold purchased has been used up. Improvements to a leasehold would, similarly, be amortized over their useful life or the life of the lease, whichever is shorter. (Note that rent also must be paid each year, but that this is a cash transaction in the accounting period and has no accounting relationship to amortization.)

Similarly, a building purchased for, say, $1 million is depreciated over what is assumed to be the building's useful life—say, 40 years. The cash transaction has already taken place, but the business shows on its books an annual depreciation of $25,000—reflecting the accounting recapture of funds that already have been expended. Because depreciation (and, to a lesser extent, other noncash entries) distorts the cash flow of a business, some operations prepare a separate "cash budget" to reflect cash transactions only.

From an accounting standpoint, depreciation and amortization are fixed by the cost of the asset and its life, and thus are *committed fixed costs*. Since they are noncash transactions, however, they require special budgetary treatment, which we will take up in the section on cash budgeting.

Programmed fixed costs are set by management decision for the period of the budget. The marketing budget and the manager's salary, for instance, are fixed as the result of management planning. If a disastrous year ensues, marketing costs might be reduced on an emergency basis to save the business—or, if the business has sufficient cash, marketing may be stepped up to a higher level in an attempt to recoup sales. In a bad year, the owners might decide to discharge some or all of its managers and hire a less expensive management team. Alternatively, in a very good year a manager might receive other offers of employment, and the owners might raise his or her salary to keep a good manager. In either case, this budget item *could* change. Our point is that although programmed costs are *treated as fixed costs,* in extraordinary situations they could be subject to change.

Absorption

Since fixed costs are set in absolute dollar amounts, a rise in sales volume means an improved relationship between sales and fixed costs. Lower sales alter that relationship for the worse. It is common to speak of the "absorption" of these and other relatively fixed overhead costs. With improved volume, a business experiences overabsorption (higher profit), whereas with poorer sales, fixed costs are underabsorbed and profit is lowered.

VARIABLE COSTS

The best example of a variable cost is product cost, such as food or beverage cost. Logically, for every portion sold, one unit of food is used up. A variable cost is one that *varies directly with sales*. Other variable costs are guest supplies, laundry and linen rental, and china, glass, and silver.

Relevant Range

Even variable costs do not always vary at the same rate as sales. Food cost provides a good example. A minimum number of errors and bad luck befalls any kitchen: a pan of vegetables burns up, a cake is dropped, a steak is overcooked. A small increase in such errors may occur as volume grows, but experience suggests that with proper staffing, they can be held to a minimum. Because this kind of error is, relatively speaking, a fixed cost associated with having a kitchen in operation, the dollar amount looms larger as a percent of sales at lower volume levels. Thus, at sales between $25,000 and $30,000 per month, food cost might be budgeted at 32.5%. This budgeted figure is valid only over the *relevant range* (i.e., $25,000 to $30,000); at double that volume, a cost of 32.3%, for instance, might be expected. Careful examination of the records of an operation will help you to determine the correct range of a budget estimate for each variable cost.

MIXED COSTS

In manufacturing, labor is treated as a variable cost, but food service features a large fixed element in labor cost. In Chapter 10, we noted that the minimum crew needed to open a restaurant is much like a fixed cost and that, in fact, mixed costs are those that have a fixed and a variable component. Another mixed cost is that for energy, for which there is a minimum charge for connection to the power system as well as a charge above some minimum level for use. We noted earlier that rents often contain both a fixed and a variable element, and that franchise fees, too, commonly are mixed costs.

STEP VARIABLE COSTS

In Chapter 10 we used as an example of step variable costs a banquet department in which a server must be added for each 30 banquet guests. In budgeting for this operation as a whole, however, we more likely would be concerned with major volume swings such as are experienced in resorts or restaurants near (or in) convention hotels. At a minimum volume level, only one dining room may be in operation and a single bar may serve as both service bar and a cocktail lounge. As the season picks up, whole dining rooms may be opened and additional service bar staff added. In some ways, the notion of a step variable cost is similar to the concept of a relevant range, and it also has elements of the idea of mixed costs: that is, a minimum crew is required at each level of volume, at which level the cost is more or less fixed, with additional units required for higher-volume periods.

Step variable costs are more common in short-range budgets, such as those covering a week or a month. The concept also is more likely to be used in budgeting for a time period that is close to the time of budgeting (next week, next month) than for a time period that is some time off (this month, next year), because the detailed information for estimating a step variable cost normally is not available far in advance.

THE BASIS FOR BUDGETING

Two common bases for budgeting are industry statistics and past performance. Both are useful, but neither can be used alone. Ultimately, however, a properly constructed budget should be based principally on standard costs.

Historical performance provides a good starting point. By studying performance in past years, we can determine the level of sales during a particular period and the cost relationships at that level of sales volume. Unfortunately, history has errors and luck built into it. An operation does not want to repeat past errors; it cannot count on past good luck repeating itself.

Industry studies[1] offer another useful tool, but they have some pitfalls. You will not know, for instance, whether the conditions found in the sample of operations on which these studies are based apply to your own operation. Industry studies do suggest the limits of what is possible, however. They provide some help in budgeting for a new operation and form one useful means of comparing an independent operation with some outside reference group.

Chains and franchise organizations disseminate operating results to their own units. And in a chain, average performance probably will be determined on the basis of detailed studies of various locations and sales volume levels. Industry averages such as those shown in Figure 14.1 provide a useful starting point for independents.

---

[1]Food service operating statistics for conventional restaurants are published annually by the National Restaurant Association and the accounting firm of Laventhol and Horwath, in *The Restaurant Industry Operations Report*. Operating statistics for specialty restaurants and for fast food are published annually in *Nation's Restaurant News*. Operating statistics for hotel food service are published annually by the accounting firms of Harris Kerr Forster and Co. *(Trend of Business in Hotels)* and Laventhol and Horwath *(U.S. Lodging Industry)*.

THE USE OF STANDARD COSTS

Although the study of past performance provides a reasonable basis for starting the budget process and industry (or chain or franchise group) statistics provide a useful background for review, the best bases for budgeting are the results management expects to achieve on the basis of careful planning for each cost.

Standard Product Costs

The basic determinant of what product costs *should be* is the sales mix. In food sales, for instance, the food cost percent often is lowest for the breakfast meal. Steaks, on the other hand, commonly have a higher food cost than other entrees (although that is balanced by a lower labor cost). The food cost that should be targeted, therefore, is a function of the food items you expect to sell and the proportion of each of these items or groups where the standard food cost differs among the items or groups.

For example, a restaurant in a northern city found demand for hearty prepared dishes such as beef stew, ham loaf, and roast turkey was heaviest during winter, whereas salads and fruit plates were much more popular during the summer months. Let us make some assumptions regarding this operation.

	Proportion Sold		
	Salads	Mixture Dishes	All Other
Fall	35%	35%	30%
Winter	20	50	30
Spring	35	35	30
Summer	50	20	30

and

Sales Group	Food Cost
Salads	35%
Mixture dishes	30%
All other	32.5%

Given these assumptions, food cost should vary as follows

Season	Food Cost
Fall	32.50%
Winter	31.75%
Spring	32.50%
Summer	33.25%

	All Restaurants			
	Ratio to Total Sales		Amount Per Seat	
	1980	1979	1980	1979
Sales				
Food	78.7%	78.2%	$6,125	$4,934
Beverage	25.9	24.8	1,751	1,404
Total Sales	100.0%	100.0%	$7,514	$6,158
Cost of Sales				
Food[a]	38.3%	38.4%	$2,617	$1,863
Beverage[a]	25.0	24.2	408	341
Total Cost of Sales	36.3%	35.6%	$2,836	$2,182
Total Gross Profit	63.7%	64.4%	$4,678	$3,976
Other Income	1.1	0.9	85	52
Total Income	64.4%	65.0%	$4,731	$4,031
Controllable Expenses				
Payroll	24.3%	25.9%	$1,748	$1,591
Employee Benefits	4.8	6.0	362	402
Direct Operating Expenses	5.1	5.0	383	300
Music & Entertainment	1.4	1.9	87	96
Advertising & Promotion	2.4	1.7	188	100
Utilities	2.6	2.3	184	132
Administrative & General	4.5	5.1	311	277
Repairs & Maintenance	1.7	1.8	124	100
Total Controllable Expenses	45.9%	47.8%	$3,330	$2,884

Income before Occupation Costs	18.5%	17.1%	$1,401	$1,125
Occupation Costs				
Rent, Property Taxes and Insurance	7.8%	6.7%	$ 540	$ 376
Interest	2.1	0.8	98	40
Total Occupation Costs	7.2%	5.8%	$ 478	$ 323
Income before Depreciation	11.4%	11.4%	$ 923	$ 799
Depreciation	2.1	1.8	138	$ 106
Restaurant Profit	9.3%	11.1%	$ 783	$ 735

*a*Ratios based on individual department sales.

FIGURE 14.1 Industry averages for a sampling of California restaurants. (From "California Restaurant Operations," Laventhol & Horwath, Certified Public Accountants, Los Angeles, Cal., 1981.)

Given the accurate precosting and sales counts provided routinely by today's POS systems, the historical information from which such forecasts can be prepared should be readily available.[2]

Projecting Labor Costs

As a "rough and ready" measure, labor costs sometimes are budgeted as a percent of sales based on historical data. With changing wage rates, as well as changing labor requirements arising from menu and service change, this approach is more rough than ready for today's food service world.

The best basis for projecting labor costs is an employee schedule much like the one discussed in Chapter 10. Naturally, the names of the people are not included, but schedules for various levels of sales volume should be prepared and revised on the basis of experience. When budget planning begins, these schedules should be reviewed and updated, and then costed at current wage rates. Thus, the budget for wage costs should be based on the actual anticipated operating needs of the operation.

---

[2]For a detailed discussion of a more formalized approach to the forecast and evaluation of food cost, see "Precost, Precontrol Food Accounting System" in E. F. Green, G. G. Drake, and F. J. Sweeney, *Profitable Food and Beverage Management: Operations* (Rochelle Park, N.J.: Hayden, 1978), pp. 190–200.

OTHER DIRECT OPERATING COSTS

Unless one of these costs is unusually significiant, most operators project other direct operating costs (such as linen, china and glassware, cleaning supplies, etc.) as a percent of sales. If one of these costs looms large, however, specific budgeting procedures should be considered for products in that cost group.

Capital Costs

Capital costs are based largely on investment made by ownership, and management cannot control the level of these costs. From a budgeting standpoint, since virtually all of these costs (except the volume provision on rent in a lease) are fixed, they present no special problems in budget preparation. We cannot suggest, however, that operations managers can afford to ignore these costs. Unless the margin of income over operating expenses is sufficient to defray capital costs, the business soon will be without a location.

CASH BUDGETING

A detailed cash budget involves the determination of when cash will be received and paid out. Thus, sales for cash in a period are shown as a cash receipt in that period, but, depending on how fast charge customers and credit card companies pay, *charge sales* may be shown as a cash receipt in the next accounting period. Cash budgets also recognize items, such as prepaid expenses, that do not affect cash in the period. They also adjust for depreciation and amortization, which are shown as noncash items that can be added back to profit to compute cash flow. A cash budget also recognizes any unusual cash payments, such as annual insurance premiums, and includes payments made on the principal of a loan. These transactions will not show up on regular accounting statements.

Detailed examination of cash budget construction normally takes place only in an accounting or finance course. Figure 14.2, however, shows a common means of estimating cash flow that is adequate for most operational needs. The estimate converts the operation's "Statement of Income and Expenses" by recognizing noncash expenses and adding them to profit to obtain a "Total Cash Flow In." This rough cash budget then recognizes any cash payments not shown on the "Statement of Income and Expense," such as mortgage payments.

BUDGET PLANNING PARTICIPATION

The budget process generally starts with a single individual—in a small operation, perhaps the general manager or one of his or her principal assistants. The budgets of larger organizations may begin in the accounting department. When computerized budgeting is used, a companywide budget, including a first-draft budget for every unit, may be prepared by the comptroller on the basis of a computer simulation reflecting assumptions about the coming year's operation. Budgets, however, are intended to achieve results that only *people* in the organization can deliver, and so managers and supervisors at all levels should participate in the budget process.

The cost of involving all levels of the organization in the budgeting process comes down simply to time and effort. The time necessary to make the computations needed to draw up a budget, or to revise a draft budget prepared by somebody else, is substantial. As the process moves down the line in the organization, the effort required to achieve real involvement increases, because the process may not be understood at the supervisory level, and managers may have to take time to explain the process and what it means.

On the other hand, if the *process* of budget development has the real support of management, the benefits of involving subordinates in budgeting can be substantial. First of all, people at the operating level are familiar with many details that higher-level or staff people may not be aware of. A budget that has been reviewed carefully by operating personnel has a better chance of avoiding overlooking small but important details.

Perhaps even more important, the involvement of subordinates in the budget process, if based on two-way communication about goals and performance expectations, is likely to draw commitment and support from those same people as the budget year unfolds. If, in a real sense, the budget is *their budget* as well as the comptroller's or general manager's, they are likely to feel responsible for achieving the results to which the budget commits the organization.

PERFORMANCE RESPONSIBILITY

Responsibilty for results lies at several levels in the organization. We will discuss four levels of responsibility and authority: the investment center, the profit center, and the revenue and cost centers.[3] The process of gathering budget and performance data around these levels commonly is referred to as *responsibility accounting*.

INVESTMENT

The responsibility for achieving a return on the owner's or stockholder's investment characteristically is accorded to top management. If profits are adequate in the light of reasonable operating performance standards but inadequate in terms of return on investment, top management must decide whether or not to change the nature of the business. This is more than a budgeting decision, although such a decision certainly should include consideration of one or more budgets.

---

[3]For a more detailed discussion of responsibility centers and responsibility accounting, see Clifford T. Faye, Richard C. Rhoads, and Robert L. Rosenblatt, *Management Accounting for the Hospitality Service Industries*, 2d ed. (Dubuque, Iowa: W. C. Brown Co., 1976), pp. 392–400.

	Income Statement	Comments	Cash Budget Changes
Sales	$62,510		
Cost of sales	22,171		
Gross profit	40,339		
Controllable expenses			
Salaries and wages	17,815		
Related payroll expense	2,672		
Total payroll and related expenses	20,487		
Direct operating expenses			
Uniform	250	(1)	250
Laundry and linen rental	501		
China, glass, and silver	499	(2)	499
Cleaning supplies	249		
Guest supplies	125		
Misc. direct operating expenses	998		
Advertising	2,688		
Utilities	1,875		
Administrative and general	1,687		
Repair and maintenance	937		
Total controllable expense	30,296		
Profit before occupancy costs	10,043		
Occupancy costs			
Rent	2,500		
Interest	625		
Municipal taxes	875	(3)	875
Depreciation	1,250	(4)	1,250
Total occupancy costs	5,250		
Profit before income taxes	4,793		
Provision for income taxes	2,515	(5)	2,515
Net profit after taxes	2,278		
Add: total noncash entries	5,389		5,389
Total cash flow from operations	7,667		
Less: mortgage payment	2,500	(6)	
Net cash flow	5,167		

> *Comments*
>
> 1. Uniforms in this operation are purchased every two years and written off over 24 months. This expense item reflects a write-off of these assets, not a cash payment in the period.
> 2. China, glass, and silver are purchased from time to time. The monthly entry is based on estimated breakage. This figure is corrected on the basis of inventory annually. This expense does not reflect a cash payment in the period.
> 3. Municipal taxes are paid in advance, annually. This item reflects $\frac{1}{12}$ of the taxes that have already been paid and do not affect cash in this period.
> 4. Depreciation represents a write-off of plant valued at $100,000 over an estimated 25-year life. Depreciation does not reflect a cash payment in the period.
> 5. Income taxes are paid quarterly on the basis of estimated profit. This item does not reflect a cash flow in this month, but will involve payment of three months' estimated taxes next month.
> 6. Mortgage payments on a $600,000 mortgage written off over 20 years do not appear as an expense, but they do constitute a cash payment during the period.

FIGURE 14.2 Jolly Trader Restaurant cash-flow estimate June, 19XX.

One interesting example of this kind of change occurred when a large metropolitan hotel recently changed ownership. The hotel had a fast-service coffee shop that achieved the best operating percentages of any food service unit in the hotel and had a good operating profit margin. One of the new owner's first actions, however, was to close this operation and replace it with a very fine cocktail lounge—which had a much higher check average and hence achieved a higher return on the owner's investment.[4]

PROFIT CENTERS

Operating management usually finds that the investment decisions have already been made by the time it arrives on the scene. The owners, or top management representing the stockholders, have determined what the business is to be. Within this framework, senior operating management is responsible for the proper relationship between sales and cost—that is, for the general profitability of the operation. As a rule, senior operating management is responsible for preparation of the budget for the overall operation, and its performance is evaluated on the basis of profit-before-capital-costs.

---

[4] We are indebted to Mr. William Heck, senior vice-president of Hotels of Distinction and general manager of the Copley Plaza Hotel, for this example.

The amount of real authority at this level of the organization varies with the size and type of the organization. Some managers have broad authority to change menu items sold, menu prices, rates of pay for employees, suppliers, and so forth; they have virtually complete control of their budget. In other units, particularly chains, menus and prices are set nationwide, suppliers are identified centrally, and even pay scales largely are determined by company policy. In the latter case, the managers' work really is limited to the effective utilization of resources. In both cases, however, managers are evaluated (and, probably, compensated) according to profits achieved. And in both cases, budgeting responsibility for profit lies with senior operating management.

REVENUE AND COST CENTERS

At the department level, the number of variables under the control of the department head may make it impractical to set up profit as a budgetary goal and as a means of evaluating performance. For instance, a catering manager who is responsible for booking and supervising banquets can be expected to participate in budgeting through the estimation of sales and may be evaluated principally on the level of banquet sales achieved. On the other hand, a chef probably will participate in budgeting food cost and be evaluated on the basis of food cost performance. The person who must agree to a budget for a revenue or cost center is the department head or supervisor responsible for that unit of operation.

TIME PERIODS[5]

Just as budget responsibility is related to level of management, the time period for which managers are expected to budget is a function of the organizational level that does the planning.

Long-range planning begins with the setting of organizational goals. Properly, this is the work of top management. Those levels of the organization with responsibility for investment centers—and in the case of large, complex units such as hotels, for profit centers—accept responsibility for long-range planning, which invariably encompasses more than one year and commonly is based on 5- or 10-year forecasts.

The *operating plan* extends for one year. Major changes in facilities, services, or the nature of the business are not possible over that period, so the operating plan focuses on the efficient use of resources. The operating plan commonly is the focus of unit managers and their senior subordinates.

The *achievement plan* focuses on the immediate future. Once an annual budget is prepared, it will be broken down into monthly budgets. (In fact, where volume varies substantially from one month to the next, the annual budget probably will

---

[5]Adapted from Fay, Rhoads, and Rosenblatt, *Managerial Accounting for the Hospitality Industry* (Dubuque, Iowa: William C. Brown Co., 1976) pp. 411–412.

be a summary of monthly budgets.) Because of the nature of the department head's responsibilities, he or she can most usefully focus on the current month. This monthly budget includes departmental sales forecasts and plans for payroll and other cost performance. As the working tool for department level planning, it should serve as a key aid to communication between the unit manager and department heads. Moreover, a summary of departmental achievement plans provides unit managers with a useful frame of reference for reviewing their own performance. (Figure 14.3 shows the three levels of planning horizon for a hotel.)

BUDGETING IN LARGE ORGANIZATIONS

As noted earlier, budgeting in large organizations is a complex, companywide process that commonly involves computer simulation of operating assumptions for the coming year. Though the full complexity of this process is beyond the scope of this text, it is useful to note that the operating budget often is integrated

---

A. *Long-Range (Strategic) Plan*
   Forecasted by years for three to five years into the future; revised and updated annually.
   1. Proforma income statements.
   2. Proforma balance sheets.
   3. Capital expenditure budgets.
   4. Source and application of funds projections.
   5. Cash projections.
B. *Annual Profit (Operating) Plan*
   Prepared for the forthcoming year.
   1. Sales forecast.
   2. Proforma departmental profit projections.
   3. Administrative and general expense budget.
   4. Advertising and promotion budget.
   5. Heat, light and power budget.
   6. Repairs and maintenance budget.
   7. Proforma income statement, and balance sheet.
   8. Capital expenditure budget.
   9. Source and application of funds projections.
   10. Cash projection.
C. *Achievement (Monthly) Plan*
   Prepared for the forthcoming month.
   1. Departmental sales forecasts.
   2. Departmental payroll budgets.
   3. Proforma departmental profit projections.
   4. Proforma income statements.
   5. Cash projections.

FIGURE 14.3 (The three levels of planning horizon for a hotel. Adapted from Faye, Rhoads, & Rosenblatt, *Managerial Accounting for the Hospitality Industry,* p. 413.)

TABLE 14.1 BUDGET PREPARATION TIME TABLE[a]

Time	Activity
November 1982	Estimate construction of new stores for parent and franchises.
January 1983	Set targets for store construction.
April 1983	Store construction committed. Estimate capital needs. Develop draft operating budgets centrally for each store and for each region and district by computer. These are to be "rolled down" to region and district for reaction, critique, and revision.
July 15, 1983	First pass operating and capital budgets ready for year beginning July 1.
October 1983	Finalized budget, based on field interaction and computer sensitivity analysis, is printed; it includes capital needs for construction of new stores and for improvements to existing stores, as well as operation budgets for each store.

[a] Adapted from Thomas F. Powers, "Complex Food Service Systems," *Cornell Hotel and Restaurant Administration Quarterly,* November 1979, p. 58.

into the company's overall financial plan. Table 14.1 provides an example of the budgeting process in a large fast food company.

KEY WORDS AND PHRASES

Planning for whole operation
Profit objectives
Budgeting—definition
Objective standard
Budgeting process
Estimate of sales volume
Estimate of physical volume
Budget revisions
Variable budgets
Grouping costs
Cost behavior
Cost-volume-profit relationship
Fixed costs
Committed fixed costs
Cash budget
Programmed fixed costs
Absorption
Variable costs
Costs varying directly with sales
Relevant range
Mixed costs
Step variable costs
Basis for budgeting

Historical performance
Industry studies
Standard costs
Projecting labor costs
Schedules for levels of sales
Other direct operating costs
Capital costs
Cash budgeting
Estimating cash flow
Statement of income and expenses
Total cash flow in
Budget planning participation
Involvement of supervisory personnel
Performance responsibility
Investment
Profit centers
Revenue and cost centers
Time periods
Long-range planning
Operating plan
Achievement plan
Budgeting in large organizations

DISCUSSION QUESTIONS

1. You have been asked to prepare a budget for a lake resort whose business is highly dependent upon weather conditions. Discuss why you probably would include levels of sales volume. Discuss how costs usually respond to various levels of sales volume.

2. What costs would you include in preparing a budget? Discuss where you would find the figures you use, and their accuracy.

3. The comptroller of a large hotel has completed the budget for the coming year and presented it to the general manager, who had not seen it. After review, the G.M. tells the comptroller that the budget will not work and orders him to redraft it. Discuss what might have happened and what the comptroller may have failed to do.

4. Which personnel in a food service operation are most affected by a budget plan? For each employee identified, discuss the level of responsibility for budget achievement.

15

EVALUATION AND DECISION MAKING IN FOOD SERVICE OPERATIONS

Introduction

Ratio Analysis

Decision Making and Strategic Planning

THE PURPOSE OF THIS CHAPTER

In the final analysis, management has to look at the results: "How did we do?" The evaluation of operations, good, bad, or indifferent, underlies a key operating decision: Shall we continue as we are, or are corrective measures needed? In operations, evaluation is a decision-making tool.

Management must also make periodic, one-time decisions as to whether to expand, purchase new equipment, lease or buy, etc. This chapter summarizes the most common decision-making tools required by operating management.

THIS CHAPTER SHOULD HELP YOU

1. Understand managerial control as a process.

2. Identify the key ratios for the analysis of operating and financial health.

3. Perform the computation necessary to determine these ratios.

4. Become familiar with common decision-making tools for
(a) Investment decisions
(b) Key decisions

5. Be able to use breakeven analyses to determine levels of sales volume that permit either bare survival or adequate profit.

INTRODUCTION

Evaluation of operations is recurrent: this kind of "scorekeeping" lies at the heart of operational control and managerial control—concepts we explored in Chapter 3. Operational control, you will recall, is procedural and based on rules; a good example is the cashier's report. Managerial control, on the other hand, requires judgment—as, for instance, in dealing with payroll cost that has become excessive. In operational control, very little decision making is required; the procedure tells the employee what to do.

In this chapter, however, we are concerned with judgment and decision making—that is, with managerial control. The fundamental decision is that outlined in Figure 15.1. In analyzing the operation with respect to a key variable (food cost or payroll cost, for instance), the manager first wants to know if performance is on target. If it is, then he or she moves on to other variables; more time always must be devoted to employee and guest satisfaction. If, on the other hand, a problem arises in connection with that variable, then corrective action must be taken. This process, the identification and solution of problems, comprises the heart of a manager's work.

328 EVALUATION AND DECISION MAKING IN FOOD SERVICE OPERATIONS

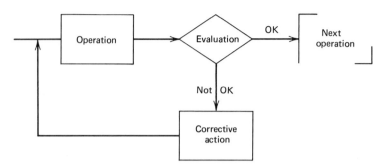

FIGURE 15.1 The managerial control process.

In this text, we have focused largely on the tools available for dealing with particular potential problem areas such as purchasing, receiving, and storing or for solving specific problems—cost problems, for instance. Just as, in Chapter 14, we moved from specific areas to a concern with planning for the overall operation by considering the budget process, we now must consider how to evaluate the operation from an overall standpoint. Along with comparison of operating results and budget, a common tool used by operating management in such evaluations is ratio analysis.

RATIO ANALYSIS

A *ratio* expresses the relationship of two variables. The relationship is expressed in the form of one variable stated in terms of the other.

THE ARITHMETIC OF RATIOS

A quick review of what ratios are, how they are computed, and what they mean may be helpful here. We can begin with a *simple ratio*. If there are 1000 apples and 100 people, then the ratio of apples to people is

$$\frac{1000 \text{ apples}}{100 \text{ people}} = 10 \text{ apples per person}$$

As is clear from this example, a ratio is computed by dividing one variable by another. Ratio analysis tells us something more than the raw numbers (in this case, 1000 apples and 100 people) involved in a real situation. If people are hungry, we know how many apples are available for each. We could compute that there is 1/10 of a person per apple, but that would just be arithmetic, not meaningful information.

Ratios also can be presented as *percentages*. A percentage is computed by dividing the base number—that which we wish to take as the standard comparison—by a number that we want to express *in terms of* the base number. Thus, if in a study of the popularity of apples, only 50 out of 1000 people studied are found to dislike apples, we can say that

$$\frac{50}{1000} = 0.05, \text{ or } 5\%$$

of the sample disliked apples. The decimal proportion 0.05 is multiplied by 100 to convert the ratio from a decimal proportion to a percent.

Another common use of ratios is to determine *turnover*—that is, the relationship of use or consumption of an asset by some using or consuming person, group, or function. If five pinball machines are needed to satisfy a group of 20 students in a recreation room, the turnover ratio could be computed as

$$\frac{20 \text{ students}}{5 \text{ machines}} = 4 \text{ students per machine}$$

This becomes useful information if the number of students using the area increases to 100; in such a case, we know we will need 20 more pinball machines to permit this turnover to continue at the same rate.

Finally, it often is useful to express performance or needs on a per-unit basis. If 1000 guests use 750 paper napkins, then

$$\frac{750}{1000} = 0.75 \text{ napkins used per guest}$$

This could be a useful figure in preparing a budget for paper supplies use. Figure 15.2 summarizes the four common kinds of ratio used for analysis in food service.

The situation: In a snack bar that serves 200 people per day, 20 cans of soft drinks are sold. An inventory of 100 cans is maintained in the cooler. Fifty straws, served only with soft drinks, are used every day.

Simple ratio:	$\frac{20 \text{ cans}}{200 \text{ people}}$	= 0.1;	one in 10 people have a soft drink
Percentage:	$\frac{20 \text{ cans}}{200 \text{ people}}$	= 0.1 × 100 = 10%	of the people have a soft drink
Turnover:	$\frac{100 \text{ cans in inventory}}{20 \text{ cans per day}}$	= 5;	that is, the soft drink inventory will turn over every 5 days
Per unit:	$\frac{50 \text{ straws}}{20 \text{ soft drinks}}$	= 2.5;	that is, 2.5 straws are used, on average, for every soft drink

FIGURE 15.2 Common uses of ratios.

OPERATING RATIOS

Analysis of Sales

There are several ways of using ratios and percentages to review sales performance, as examination of Figure 15.3 will make clear. The first point to be made about the data given in the figure is that there has been a dramatic change in the *distribution of sales* between food and beverages. Food sales in dollars have increased only slightly, but beverage sales, which carry a higher profit, have increased, as a percent of sales, by 6.6 percentage points.[1] The dollar sales amount for beverages has increased nearly 41%.

	19×5 (dollars)	19×4 (dollars)	19×5 (percent)	19×4 (percent)	Percent Change
Sales					
Food	763,819	751,707	68.5	75.1	+ 1.6
Beverages	351,003	249,235	31.5	24.9	+ 40.8
Total Sales	1,114,822	1,000,942	100.0	100.0	+ 11.3
Cost of sales					
Food	295,598	287,152	38.7	38.2	+ 2.9
Beverages	91,612	63,056	26.1	25.3	+ 45.3
Total cost of sales	387,210	350,208	34.7	35.0	
Gross Profit					
Food	468,221	464,556	61.2	61.8	+ .7
Beverages	259,391	186,178	73.9	74.7	+ 39.3
	727,612	650,733	65.3	65.0	+ 11.8
Operating expenses					
Payroll and related expenses	314,380	308,290	28.2	30.8	+ 2.0
Advertising and promotion	21,182	21,020	19	21	+ .7
Other operating expenses	120,401	112,106	108	112	+ 7.4
Total operating expenses	455,963	441,416	409	441	+ 3.3
Profit before occupancy costs	271,649	209,317	24.4	20.9	+ 29.8
Occupancy costs					
Depreciation	86,001	85,080	7.7	8.5	+ 1.1
Insurance	9,143	8,006	.8	.8	+ 14.2
Interest	12,443	13,101	1.1	1.3	− 5.0
Total occupancy costs	107,587	106,187	106	106	+ 1.3
Profit before provision for income taxes	164,062	103,130	14.8	10.3	+ 59.1

FIGURE 15.3 Sans Souci Restaurant—comparative statement of income and expense.

[1]Note that the difference between food sales as a percent of total sales—that is, between 75.1 and 68.5—is 6.6, and that a difference computed between percentages in this way is reported in *points*—the result of simple subtraction.

The average sale per guest (which cannot be readily determined from Figure 15.3) is another means of analyzing sales. At Sans Souci, the following changes have taken place.

	19X5	19X4
Food-only average sale	$12.21	$12.02
Beverage-only average sale	$ 5.61	$ 4.00
Total average sale	$17.82	$16.02

Another means of measuring sales is the average sales per seat. Given that Sans Souci has a seating capacity of 140 chairs, the average sale per seat has increased from $7150 in 19X4 to $7963 in 19X5.

Sales could also be broken down in terms of average sale per guest by meal period (i.e., for lunch and for dinner), and check averages might be computed by meal for food, beverage, and total sales. We have used the terms *check average* and *average sale per guest* interchangeably here, but another meaning of check average is "the average of the total of all checks." Since parties may differ in size from one check to another, this average of check totals is not particularly meaningful, and the preferred statistic is the average sale per guest, sometimes called the "average cover."

Product Costs

The customary way of portraying product cost is as a percent of sales. Note that in Figure 15.3 the food cost is stated as a percent of food sales and the beverage cost as a percent of beverage sales. For this reason—because the bases of those two cost percentages differ—the two percentages cannot be added. Rather, total product cost is computed as a percent of total sales. We saw in the previous chapter that the best means of evaluating these cost percentages is to compare them against budget, but that it is also useful to compare performance with past years and with industry averages.

Labor Cost

Labor cost percentages can be compared with the previous year's performance, but, once again, the best means of evaluating performance is against budgeted labor cost. Assisting in this comparison are such statistics as number of employee hours per guest, dollar sales per employee, and number of guests per employee-day. The employee-hour per guest information can usefully be broken down on a per-meal basis.

Prime Cost

Although some operators focus on product cost and others principally on labor cost, most operators are interested in the joint performance of those two costs. Product cost plus labor cost is referred to as prime cost. The prime cost for Sans Souci in 19X5 was 62.9 percent, down from 65.8 in 19X4.[2]

---

[2] Prime cost is arrived at by adding the total cost of sales (i.e., food cost and beverage cost) to payroll and related expenses. In this case, 34.7% + 28.2% = 62.9%.

Profitability

The most common measure of profitability is profit as a percent of sales. This is the usual criterion by which an operation's manager's performance is measured, although a fairer criterion is profit before occupancy costs (i.e., capital costs that the operating manager cannot control) as a percent of sales.

From the point of view of ownership, the most significant measure of profit is profit as a percentage of invested capital—that is, the return on investment.

$$\text{Return on investment} = \frac{\text{Net profit after income taxes}}{\text{Average stockholder's (or owner's) equity}}$$

This is a concept to which we will return.

Growth Ratio

Sans Souci has had a healthy increase in total sales but a phenomenal increase in profit, largely because of the increased sales of beverages, which have a higher profit margin. Growth ratios may be computed as follows.

$$\frac{\text{Year 2} - \text{Year 1}}{\text{Year 1}} \times 100 = \text{Growth percent}$$

$$\frac{\$1,114,822 - \$1,000,942}{\$1,000,942} = 0.113 \times 100 = 11.3\%$$

Growth can be computed usefully for sales and profits but also may be informative when applied to sales by category (food, beverage, etc.)

Activity Ratios

The classic hospitality-industry activity ratio is hotel occupancy, a figure that often is used to forecast hotel food and beverage sales. In food service, a common activity ratio is the seat turn—that is, the number of guests served in relationship to the restaurant's capacity.

$$\frac{\text{Number of guests}}{\text{Capacity (number of chairs)}} = \text{Seat turn}$$

If, for one meal, 125 guests are served in a room having 95 chairs, the chair turn is

$$\frac{125}{95} = 1.32 \text{ turns}$$

This ratio commonly is calculated separately for each meal.

Another common activity measure is the stock turn, which is computed

$$\frac{\text{Total product cost}}{\text{Average inventory}} = \text{Stock turn}$$

If a restaurant's average monthly food inventory is $2300 and food cost in the month is $8500, then the stock turn is

$$\frac{\$8500}{\$2300} = 3.7 \text{ turns per month}$$

This ratio indicates the average speed with which inventory is being used. If the stock turn is low relative to previous performance or comparable operations, the operation may be carrying larger inventories than necessary, which could mean excessive spoilage of perishable product, interest lost through the tying up of excess capital in inventory, commitment of extra space to storage, and interest lost on capital unnecessarily tied up in inventory.

THE FINANCIAL HEALTH OF A FIRM

Ratios also can help you to assess the financial health of a company. Some common measures of financial performance are liquidity ratios, accounts receivable and accounts payable turnover, debt-to-equity ratios, and ratios used in assessing a company's stock's performance. Although they are not used in evaluating the performance of food service operations, these ratios are familiar to financially literate managers. We include them here as a further indication of the many uses of ratios as analytical tools in business. Ratios in this section will be computed on the basis of Figures 15.3 and 15.4.[3]

Liquidity, or solvency, is measured by the relationship of current assets to current liabilities. The most common measure is the *current ratio*.

$$\text{Current ratio} = \frac{\text{Current assets}}{\text{Current liabilities}}$$

$$\frac{\$75,447}{\$35,319} = 2.14$$

This ratio is used to state the number of times current liabilities are covered by current assets; the current ratio here is 2.14. A variation of the current ratio is the

---

[3] We have deliberately refrained from indicating what a "healthy" ratio is, because of the great variety encountered in the hospitality industry. For instance, it was once common to think of 2:1 as a healthy *current ratio,* and some people still quote that figure. More commonly, a healthy current ratio in our industry is said to be 1:1—that is, current assets equal to current liabilities. On the other hand, the authors once were employed by a very successful company that made deliberate use of short-term debt and generally had a current ratio of 0.25:1—that is, 25¢ of current assets to every dollar of current liabilities. The definition of "health," in this area, involves analytical judgements rather than rules of thumb.

Current Assets			**Current Liabilities**	
Cash		$ 25,411	Accounts payable	$ 24,041
Accounts receivable		32,009	Accrued expense	3,278
Inventory			Note payable, less than 1 year	8,000
Food	$ 12,618			
Beverage	5,409	18,027		
Total current assets		75,447	Total current liabilities	35,319
Fixed Assets			Long-term liabilities	
Leasehold	174,422		Note payable	78,000
Less: amortization	9,873	164,549		
			Total liabilities	113,319
Leasehold improvements	42,000		Capital stocks	50,000
Less: accrued amortization	3,419	38,581	Retained earnings	115,258
Total fixed assets		203,130	Total capital stocks and retained earnings	165,258
Total assets		$278,577	Total liabilities and capital	$278,577

FIGURE 15.4 Sans Souci Restaurant—balance sheet.

acid-test ratio, which sometimes is called the quick ratio, because the assets measured are cash and other assets that can be turned into cash quickly.

$$\text{Acid-test ratio} = \frac{\text{Cash + Marketable securities + Accounts receivable}}{\text{Current liabilities}}$$

$$\frac{25{,}411 + 0 + 32{,}009}{35{,}319} = \frac{57{,}420}{35{,}319} = 1.63$$

Stability and Leverage Ratios

These ratios assess the degree to which the ownership of a company is financing its own business and, conversely, the degree to which outside financing is relied upon. A company with little debt is thought to be less subject to outside control; a company that is using outside funds is said to be leveraged—that is to be using the leverage of borrowed funds to operate its business. The most common measure of stability and leverage is the ratio of debt to equity.

$$\text{Debt to equity} = \frac{\text{Debt (total liabilities)}}{\text{Equity (capital stock plus retained earnings or net worth)}}$$

$$\frac{\$113{,}319}{\$165{,}258} = 0.686 \text{ or } 68.6\%$$

Other measures include equity to total assets,

$$\text{Equity to total assets} = \frac{\text{Equity}}{\text{Total assets}}$$

$$\frac{165{,}258}{278{,}577} = 0.593 \text{ or } 59.3\%$$

and debt to total assets,

$$\text{Debt to total assets} = \frac{\text{Total liabilities}}{\text{Total assets}}$$

$$\frac{\$113{,}319}{\$278{,}577} = 0.407 \text{ or } 40.7\%$$

Stock Analysis Ratios

Because an increasing number of hospitality firms are publicly owned, it is useful to know the three most common ratios used in assessing a stock's outlook and performances. Since a share of stock is basically a claim on ownership, investors assess the share of earnings that can, in effect, be purchased with a share of stock by computing the earnings per share of common stock (EPSC):

$$\text{EPSC} = \frac{\text{Net profit after tax}}{\text{Number of shares of common stock issued}}$$

If a publicly traded company has 250,000 shares outstanding and earns $1,250,000, then

$$\text{EPSC} = \frac{\$1,250,000}{250,000} = \$5 \text{ per share}$$

The *price/earnings ratio* reflects the value the market puts on a company's earnings. A high price/earnings ratio (i.e., a higher stock price relative to earnings) reflects optimistic assumptions by investors, whereas a lower price/earnings ratio suggests the market regards the stock as more risky.

$$\text{Price/earnings ratio} = \frac{\text{Current market price per common share}}{\text{Earnings per common share}}$$

If the stock in the EPSC example were trading on the stock market at $50, then its price/earnings ratio would be 10.

$$\frac{\$50}{\$5} = 10$$

Some stocks are bought because of the dividend they pay. For such stocks, the stock's yield is significant.

$$\text{Stock yield} = \frac{\text{Annual dividend per common share}}{\text{Current market price per share}}$$

If the stock paid an annual dividend of $4 per share, its yield would be

$$\frac{\$4}{\$50} = 0.08 \text{ or } 8\%$$

DECISION MAKING AND STRATEGIC PLANNING

Evaluations of an operation's operational or financial health largely are made on the basis of periodic reports, such as those that emerge from an analysis of an income statement or the more detailed studies on which payroll and food cost performance evaluation are based. Performance evaluation essentially is repetitive; the same tools are used each month (or week or quarter or year) to analyze the results of essentially similar operations.

Another set of decisions managers must make are *not* repetitive. The purchase of a new dish machine and expansion of the business are examples of decisions that involve us in collecting data that will support these unique kinds of decisions. Similarly, decisions on whether to lease or purchase linen or to make or buy pastry products require special tools of analysis. This subject is dealt with in considerable depth in accounting and finance courses. Our treatment will stick to fundamentals.

INVESTMENT DECISIONS

The Green Glade Restaurant began as a small country inn. Good food, friendly service, and pleasant surroundings all combined to help "The Glade," as its employees called it, grow. The growth was very satisfying to its owner, but it presented some real difficulties, one of which involved dirty pots. As food volume grew, potwashing, which initially was part of the dishwasher's duties, came to require three full-time employees who earned $4 per hour. Howard Connally, the Glade's owner, considered investing in a mechanized pot machine. He was quite sure he could reduce his potwasher staff to two, but the pot machine would cost $12,000, including installation. He was surprised but pleased to find that one of the ancient sinks the potwashers had been using had antique value when an antique dealer offered him $100 for it.

We can use this example to illustrate the elements of an investment decision. An investment of $12,000 offers a savings of 33% of the Glade's potwashing labor. Mr. Connally can approach his decision by determining how long the savings will take to pay off the investment cost. This approach involves computing the *payback period*. Alternatively, Connally can determine the rate of return the pot-machine investment will earn. To compute either of these measures, he must first compute the *net investment (NI)* and the *operating savings (OS)*.

$$NI = \text{Installed cost of pot machine} \qquad \$12{,}000$$
$$\text{Less: salvage value of "antique" sink} \qquad \underline{100}$$
$$\$11{,}900$$

OS = Reduction in potwasher labor, 40 hours × $4 = $160 per week

To compute the payback period, he must divide the *investment* by the *operating savings*.

$$PB = \frac{NI}{OS} = \frac{\$11{,}900}{\$160} = 74.375 \text{ weeks}$$

From these calculations, Connally sees that he can recover his investment in about a year and a half. (Notice, though, that the answer his calculations gave him was expressed in terms of weeks, since the problem was set up in weeks.)

To compute his rate of return, Connally must divide his *operating savings* by his *net investment*. Because rates of return usually are stated in terms of annual interest rates, the *OS* must be converted to annual terms, or ($160 × 52 weeks) $8320. The rate of return, therefore, is

$$ROR = \frac{OS}{NI} = \frac{\$8{,}320}{\$11{,}900} = 0.70 \text{ or } 70\%$$

After comparing this rate of return with the 12% he would have to pay the bank on a loan to purchase the pot machine, he decided to make the purchase. If we wish to adjust our *ROR* calculations to reflect the interest cost, we can assume that the $12,000 is borrowed on a two-year note. The interest (at 12%) of $1440 would be deductible from *OS*, and the *ROR* after interest costs would be

$$ROR = \frac{OS}{NI} = \frac{6880}{11900} = 0.58 = 58\%$$

MAKE OR BUY

A common investment decision involves the question of whether to make or buy a product. A small French restaurant served French pastries that were purchased daily from a nearby bakery for 60 cents apiece and sold in the restaurant for $1.00. The owner found he could hire a very good pastry cook for $6.50 per hour on a part-time basis, and that she could make the pastries the operation needed in three hours a day. He also found that he could purchase the ingredients for the pastries for 20 cents per serving. He summarized his option as follows.

Buy Pastries			Make Pastries	
Sales	50 @ $1.00	$50.00		$50.00
Food cost	50 @ $0.60	30.00	50 @ $0.20	10.00
		$20.00		$40.00
Labor cost		—	3 hours @ $6.50	19.50
To profit		$20.00		$20.50

In order to make the pastries, renovations to the kitchen and new equipment would require an investment of $2500. He felt he could continue to sell 50 portions of the product for the indefinite future. Since his restaurant was open 250 days per year, he was sure he could save $125 per year. Thus,

$$ROR = \frac{OS}{NI} = \frac{125}{2500} = 5\%$$

The owner quickly saw that the operating savings did not justify the change.

We should pause to note, however, that the numbers may provide only a part of the answer. In the case we have just examined, many restauranteurs would *interpret* the numerical outcome to mean they *should* make their own pastries—not because of the savings themselves, but because a fresh and potentially higher-quality product could be made on-premise at such a modest cost. The fact that the restaurant *could* say honestly on its menu, "We make our own pastries," would be more important to such operations than the *ROR* would be. In any case, however, knowledge of the financial impact of such a quality decision is essential.

BREAKEVEN ANALYSIS

The Glade's continuing success led Mr. Connally to consider the addition of a cocktail lounge. After conversations with a contractor, he estimated the cost of his new lounge at $85,000.

To determine the point at which the new lounge will break even, he must calculate the point at which sales revenue will exactly cover fixed and variable costs—the point at which the operation will neither suffer a loss nor earn a profit.

$$\text{Sales} = \text{Fixed costs} + \text{Variable costs}$$

In this case, Connally assumes that the payroll for bartenders and waitresses for the operation will amount to $820 per week and that the bar cost is 28%. To just cover the operating costs, he computes as follows.

$$\text{Sales} = \$820 + 28\% \text{ of sales (let } X = \text{sales)}$$
$$X = 820 + 0.28$$
$$0.72X = 820$$
$$X = \$1138.88$$

Notice that if 28% of sales goes for variable costs, then 72% remains to cover fixed costs and profit. This—the revenue remaining after variable costs—is referred to as the contribution margin.

Simple coverage of cash operating costs is not enough, of course. Mr. Connally's accountant indicates that he can write off (i.e., depreciate) the new cocktail lounge over a five-year period. Connally decides to add enough to the fixed costs to cover a weekly depreciation charge of 260 weeks × $327 = $85,020. Thus, fixed costs, including depreciation and operating costs, amount to $820 + $327 = $1147.

If sales equal X,

$$X = \$1147 + 0.28X$$
$$0.72\,X = \$1147$$
$$X = 1593.10$$

340 EVALUATION AND DECISION MAKING IN FOOD SERVICE OPERATIONS

Another way of looking at this problem is to begin with what we know and what we need to know (indicated below by "?").

	$Cost	Percent
Sales	?	100
Variable cost	?	28
Contribution margin	?	72%
Fixed cost	$1147	
Profit	-0-	

Note that we begin with sales as 100% and with variable costs and contribution margin required to break even stated as percents. Having determined the relationships from the information provided, we can determine the level of sales required to break even. We know that to break even, the contribution margin must exactly cover the amount of fixed cost. Therefore,

$$\text{Breakeven sales} = \frac{\text{Fixed costs}}{\text{Contribution margin percent}} = \frac{1147}{0.72} = \$1593.10$$

However we decide to set up the problem, we can check our results following the format we just used.

Proof

Sales (100%)	1593
Variable cost (28%)	446
Contribution margin (0.72%)	1147
Fixed costs	1147
Profit	-0-

After some consideration, Connally decides that he wants to earn an annual return of 20% on his investment: that is, he wants total revenue to cover his fixed costs plus $17,000 per year, or roughly $327 per week. This means that total sales have to provide $1474 (i.e., $1147 + 327) after variable costs, to cover fixed costs and the minimum profit goal.

$$X = \$1474 + 0.28X$$
$$0.72 X = \$1474$$
$$X = \$2047$$

Used in this manner, the breakeven formula can be adapted to calculate the sales required to produce a desired profit.

Setting up the problem in the alternative way we used before,

Sales	?	.100
Variable cost	?	.28
Contribution margin	?	.72
Fixed costs	$1147	
Profit	$ 327	

then,

$$\text{Sales necessary to produce the desired profit} = \frac{\text{Fixed costs plus profit target}}{\text{Contribution margin percent}} = \frac{\$1147 + \$327}{0.72} = \$2047$$

Once again, we can check our results.

Proof

Sales (100%)	$2047
Variable cost (28%)	573
Contribution margin (72%)	$1474
Fixed costs	1147
Profit	$ 327

In order to understand how breakeven analysis is used, it is helpful to see *how it aids management judgement*. Let us assume that The Glade's proposed lounge will sell drinks at an average of $2. Given the dollar sales (approximately $2050) necessary to provide the desired profit, Connally must sell 1025 drinks per week. Assuming that his operation is open six days a week, Connally must sell an average of about 171 (170.8) drinks a day. Further assuming that an average guest in his restaurant has two drinks in the bar, he needs just over 85 (an average of 85.4) guests per day. It is much easier to judge whether sales goals such as these are reasonable or not than it is to evaluate an investment of $85,000 in isolation from supporting analysis. Breakeven analysis, then, is intended to help managers make an orderly statement of the facts regarding a decision and to reduce the assumptions necessary to a decision to manageable levels.

We should note that the week's time period was chosen for convenience in using the analysis. Had it been more convenient, we could have made the time period one year.

X = Annual fixed costs + Profit, or (52 × $1474) = $76,648 + 0.28$X$
X = $76,648 + 0.28$X$
0.72 X = $76,648
X = $106,455

Alternatively,

	Cost	Percent
Sales	?	100
Variable costs	?	28
Contribution margin	?	72
Fixed costs	$59,644	
Profit	$17,004	

and,

$$\frac{\text{Fixed costs} + \text{Profit}}{\text{Contribution margin percent}} = \frac{\$76,648}{0.72} = \$106,455$$

Proof

Sales (100%)	106,455
Variable costs (28%)	29,807
Contribution margin (72%)	76,648
Fixed costs	59,644
Profit	17,004

Connally's target volume, expressed in annual sales volume, is $106,455.

When approximations suffice, it sometimes is helpful to perform the breakeven analysis graphically, as shown in Figure 15.5. On the vertical side of the graph,

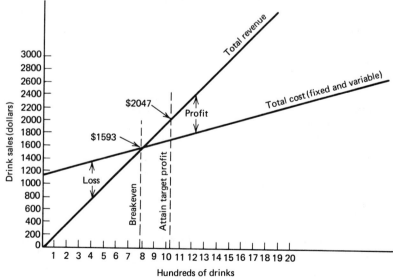

FIGURE 15.5 Graphic breakeven analysis for Sans Souci.

we enter dollars. Across the bottom of the graph, we enter units of sale. A sales line is drawn through several points. (At $2 per drink, 100 drinks equal $200 in sales, 500 drinks equal $1000 in sales, etc.). Next, a total-cost line is constructed. Since fixed costs will go on whether or not there are sales, we begin to draw our cost line at the level of fixed costs (i.e., even when no drinks are sold), or 1147. We know that total cost equals fixed cost plus variable cost. In our example above, some values for total costs would be

Number of Drinks   **Total Cost**
- 0 drinks = $1147 (Fixed cost only)
- 400 drinks = 1371 (Fixed cost $1147, plus variable cost at 28% × $800)
- 1000 drinks = 1707 (Fixed cost $1147, plus variable cost at 28% × $2000)

Plotting these points on Figure 15.5, a line can be drawn to intersect the sales line. Notice that this chart provides the same results as our earlier calculation: approximately 797 drinks with a value of about $1593 mark the point where the sales revenue and cost lines intersect—that is, the breakeven point. At a volume of approximately 1023 drinks with a value of about $2047 per week, we reach our target profit of $327 per week.

KEY WORDS AND PHRASES

Evaluation of operations
Managerial control process
Key variable
Ratio analysis
Percentages—how to compute
Common uses of ratio
Simple ratio
Percentage
Turnover
Per unit
Operating ratios
Analysis of sales
Distribution of sales
Average sale per guest
Average sale per chair
Average sale per guest by meal period
Check average
Average cover
Product costs
Labor cost
Prime cost
Profitability
Return on investment formula

Growth ratio computation
Activity ratios
Chair turn
Stock turn
Financial health of a firm
Liquidity
Current ratio
Acid-test ratio
Stability and leverage ratios
Ratio of debt to equity
Equity to total assets
Debt to total assets
Stock analysis ratios
EPSC
Price/earnings ratio
Stock yield
Payback period
Net investment
Operating savings
Rate of return computation
Make or buy
Breakeven analysis

DISCUSSION QUESTIONS

1. To ensure that you understand how to determine ratios, calculate ratios for the following fast food restaurant example. (It may help to refer to Figure 15.2.) Sandy's chicken restaurant serves 500 persons per day, and an average of 350 orders of fried chicken is sold daily. Cole slaw is ordered by 200 of the guests who order chicken. An inventory of 400 orders of fried chicken is maintained in the cooler. Calculate

Simple ratio: ratio of chicken to persons served per day.
Percentage: percent of guests ordering chicken.
Turnover of chicken.
Per unit: how much cole slaw is used, on average, for every order of chicken.

Discuss how useful each of these calculations is to management.

2. As manager of the Fishfare restaurant, you are comparing last year's sales with this year's figures. Determine the percent change in sales: average sale, food-only in 19X3 was $4.63; in 19X2, it was $4.52. How would you interpret the results if *(a)* average sale was a check average or *(b)* average sale was average guest cover?

3. Sales for Fishfare in 19X3 were $1,290,000, down from $1,340,000 in 19X2. How would you compute a growth ratio for the restaurant?

4. What is the dinner chair turn in the Fishfare if there are 75 chairs, and an average of 180 are served every evening? Discuss what this means.

5. The Fishfare carries an average monthly inventory of $1600, and sales for the month are $24,000. Determine the stock turn. Another Fishfare unit in the same city carries a stock turn of 10. Discuss the possible causes.

6. You were just hired as president of a chain of ailing restaurants. You have been told that you may need to close some of the units. Identify the information you will need from each unit and how you will analyze this information.

APPENDIX 1
precosting

CHART 1 WEIGHT AND MEASURE CONVERSIONS

1A

Metric	U.S. (Amer.)
2000 ml (2 liters)	1 gallon (128 oz fluid)
1000 ml (1 liter)	1 quart (¼ gallon, 32 oz fluid)
250 ml	1 pint (16 oz fluid)
125 ml	1 cup (8 oz fluid)
50 ml	1 tablespoon (½ oz fluid)
25 ml	1 teaspoon
15 ml	½ teaspoon
5 ml	¼ teaspoon
2 ml	
1 ml	

1B / 1C

Weight and Measure Conversions	Metric Conversions
3 teaspoons = 1 tbsp	1 liter = 33.8 oz
16 tablespoons = 1 cup	1 fluid oz = 29.6 ml
2 cups = 1 pint	1 ounce (mass) = 28.3 g
2 pints = 1 qt	1 pound = 454 g
4 cups = 1 qt	1 inch = 2.54 cm
4 quarts = 1 gal	1 cubic centimeter (cc) = 1 ml
2 tablespoons = 1 oz fluid	
16 ounces = 1 lb	

1D

Metric Conversions for Recipes and Precosting

American	Metric (exact)	Metric (rounded)[a]
¼ teaspoon	1.2 ml	1 ml
½ teaspoon	2.5 ml	2 ml
¾ teaspoon	3.8 ml	3 or 4 ml
1 teaspoon	4.9 ml	5 ml
1 tablespoon	14.8 ml	15 ml
¼ cup	59.1 ml	60 ml
⅓ cup	78.9 ml	80 ml
½ cup	118 ml	125 ml
⅔ cup	158 ml	160 ml
¾ cup	177 ml	175 ml
1 cup	237 ml	250 ml
1 pint	473 ml	500 ml
1 quart	946 ml	1000 ml
1 gallon	3.79 liters	4 liters

[a]Rounding usually is not recommended when recipes are converted to metric units and then increased (say, 10 times). For recipe conversion, rounding to the closest measure should be done after the recipe has been increased. Kitchen testing is recommended for metric recipe conversion.

CHART 2 VOLUME/WEIGHT CONVERSION CHART

Food	Volume of 1 Ounce	Volume of 1 Pound	Weight of 1 cup (ounces)	Weight of 1 Cup (Grams)	Volume of 1 Kilogram
Allspice	4½ T	1 qt	4	110	2.2 L
Almonds		3 c	5⅓	150	1.5 L
Apples, whole		3.113 ct			6–7, 113 ct.
Apples, diced		3 c	5½	150	1.5 L
Applesauce		2 c	8	260	1095 ml
Apricots, dried		3 c	5½	150	1.5 L
Asparagus, fresh		10–20 stk			20–40 stk
Asparagus, canned		2½ c	6	190	
Avocadoes, whole		2 med			4–7 med
Avocadoes, peeled, diced		3 c	5½	152	
Bacon, raw		20–25 sl			40–50 sl
Bacon, fat		2 c	8	220	1 L
Baking power	2 tbsp	2½ c	6	168	1250 ml
Bananas, whole		2–3 med			5–6 med
Bananas, diced		2–2½ c	6½	150	1–1.25 L
Barley, pearl	2 T	2 c	8	224	1 L
Beans, green, fresh		1 qt	4	110	2 L
Beans, kidney, dry		2⅔ c	6	175	1.325 L
Beans, lima, dry		2½ c	6½	180	1.25 L
Beans, navy		2¼ c	7	200	1.1 L
Bean sprouts		1 qt		110	2 L
Beef, cooked, diced		3 c	5½	150	1.5 L
Beets, fresh		2–3			5–6
Beets, fresh, cooked		2½ c		180	1.25 L
Blackberries		2–2½ c		180	1–1.25 ml
Blueberries, fresh		2¼ c	5	140	1.25 L
Bran, dry		1½–2 qt	2	56	3–4 L
Bread crumbs, soft		2½ qt	2	45	5 L
Bread crumbs, dry	¼ c	1 qt	4	110	2 L
Bread, (see Bread, Chart 7)					
Brussels sprouts		1 qt	4	110	2 L
Butter	2 tbsp	2 c	8	225	1 L
		45 pats			100 pats
Cabbage, shredded		5⅓ c	3	150	2.5 L
Cantaloupe		1 med			2 med
Carrots, grated, raw		1 qt	4	110	2 L
Catsup, tomato		1¾ c		255	875 ml
Cauliflower, med		1 head			2 heads
Celery, diced		1 qt	4	110	2 L
Celery, whole		½–1 stk			1–2 stk
Cereals					
Bran flakes		12 c.	1⅓	37	6 L
Cornflakes		16 c	1	25	8 L
Cracked wheat (uncooked)		3 c	5⅓	150	1.5 L
Oatmeal, uncooked		5⅓ c	3	80	2.6 L
Farina, uncooked		3 c	5⅓	150	1.5 L
Ground wheat, uncooked		3 c	5⅓	150	1.5 L

CHART 2 VOLUME/WEIGHT CONVERSION CHART *(Continued)*

Food	Volume of 1 Ounce	Volume of 1 Pound	Weight of 1 cup (ounces)	Weight of 1 Cup (Grams)	Volume of 1 Kilogram
Puffed rice		27 c	½	13	3.5 L
Puffed wheat		32 c	½	12	16 L
Rice flakes		13 c	1¼	32	6.5 L
Cheese					
American, grated		2½ c	6½	180	1.25 L
Cottage		2¼ c	7	200	1.12 L
Cream Cheese		2 c	8	225	1 L
Cheese slices		1 slice	16 slices		35 slices
Cheddar, shredded		3 c	5⅓	150	1.5 L
Cherries, fresh, pitted		3 c	5⅓	150	1.5 L
Cherries, glace		2½ c	6½ oz	180	1.25 L
Chicken, cooked, diced		3 c	5⅓	150	1.5 L
Chives, frozen	½ c	2 c	2	55	4 L
Chick peas (garbanzos)		2 c	8	225	1 L
Chocolate	1 sq	16 sq	8 sq	225	35 sq
Chocolate chips			6.25 oz		
Cinnamon	4 tbsp	1 qt	¼ oz	110	2 L
Citron		2½ c	6½	180	1.25 L
Cloves, ground	3½ tbsp	3¾ c	4½	120	1.9 L
Cocoa	4 tbsp	1¼ qt	4 oz	100	2.5 L
Coconut, shredded, dried		4½–7 c		65	2.5–3.5 L
Coffee, ground	5 tbsp	5 c	3¼	90	2.5 L
Coffee, instant	½ c	2 qt	2	55	4 L
Corn, canned, drained		2 c	8	225	1 L
Corn meal		3 c	5	118	1.5 L
Cornstarch	3½ tbsp	3½ c	5	120	1.75 L
Corn syrup		1½ c	11	300	750 ml
Crabmeat		5⅓ c	3	85	2.65 L
Cracker crumbs		6⅓ c	2¼	70	3.2 L
Cranberries		1 qt	4	100	2 L
Cucumbers, med		3			6–7
Cucumbers, sliced, med		3 c		150	1.5 L
Currants, dried		3 c	5¼	150	1.5 L
Dates, pitted		2¾ c	6	165	1.4 L
Dates whole		45 whole			
Eggs, dry, whole	¼ c	2 c	4	108	1 L
Eggs, hard-cooked		2 c	4 eggs	225	1 L
		8–10 eggs			18–22 eggs
Eggs, whites		2 c	7 to 9	225	1 L
Eggs, whole		8–10 eggs	8 oz (4–5)	225	1 L (18–22)
Eggs, yolks		24–26	12–14	225	52–57
Figs, dry		3 c	5⅓	150	1.5 L
Flours, cake, sifted	5 tbsp	4–4¾ c	3½	110–140	2–2.25 L
Flour, rye		5–5⅔ c	3⅓	150	2.5–2.75 L
Flour, all purpose	¼ c	4 c	4	110	2 L
Flour, whole wheat		3–3¼ c	5⅓	120	1.5–1.6 L
Gelatin, unflavored	3 tbsp	3 c	5	160	1.5 L
Gelatin, flavored	2 tbsp	2⅓ c	7	200	1.2 L
Grapes, seeded		2¾ c		150	1.4 L

CHART 2 VOLUME/WEIGHT CONVERSION CHART (Continued)

Food	Volume of 1 Ounce	Volume of 1 Pound	Weight of 1 cup (ounces)	Weight of 1 Cup (Grams)	Volume of 1 Kilogram
Grapefruit sections		2 c		225	1 L
Ham, ground		2 c	8	225	1 L
Hominy, pearl		3 c	5⅓	150	1.5 L
Honey		1⅓ c	12	338	650 ml
Horseradish, prepared		1 qt	4	110	2 L
Ice cream		3½ c	6	135	1.7 L
Jam		1⅓ c	10.5	315	650 ml
Jelly		1⅓ c	10.5	315	650 ml
Lard		2 c	8	220	1 L
Lemons		3–4			7–9
Lemon Juice	½ lemon	2 c	8	240	1 L
Lemon Peel	4 tbsp				
Lentils		2¼ c	7	200	1.12 L
Lettuce, average head		1 head			2 heads
Macaroni, dry		4½ c	3½	98	2.25 L
Marshmallows		80 whole			175 whole
Mayonnaise		2 c	7¼	225	1 L
Margarine	2 tbsp	2 c	8	226	1 L
		45 pats			100 pats
Milk, whole		2 c	8	244	1 L
Milk, evaporated		1⅞ c	9	250	930 ml
Milk, dry, regular		1 qt	4	110	2 L
Milk, dry, instant		5¾ c		75	2.85 L
Milk, sweet, condensed		1½ c	11	330	750 ml
Molasses		1⅓ c	11	328	650 ml
Mushrooms, fresh		7 c	2¼	65	3.5 L
Mushrooms, canned		2 c	8	220	1 L
Mustard	5 tbsp	5 c	3¼	90	2.5 L
Noodles, dry		3 qt	1¼	72	6 L
Nuts, chopped		1 qt	4	110	2 L
Nutmeg, ground	3½ tbsp	3½ c	4½	125	1.75 L
Oil, vegetable		2¼ c	7	200	1.1 L
Onions, chopped	2 tbsp	2 c	8	225	1 L
Onions, dry, chopped		3 c	5⅓	150	1.5 L
Orange juice		2 c	8	225	1 L
Paprika	4 tbsp	1 qt	4	110	2 L
Peaches		3 med			6–7 med
Peanut butter		1¾ c	9	248	875 ml
Pears, fresh		3 med			6–7 med
Pecans		4 c	3½	110	2 L
Pepper, ground	4 tbsp	1 qt	4	110	2 L
Peppers, green, chopped	3 tbsp	3 c	5	150	1.5 L
Pimentos		2¼	7	200	1.1 L
Pineapple slices, canned		8–12 sl			18–26 sl
Pineapple juice		2 c	8	225	1 L
Pork, ground		2 c	8	225	1 L
Potato chips		4–5 qt	¾–1	22–30	8–10 L
Potatoes, white, cooked, diced		2–3 med			5–7 med
Potatoes, instant, flake		4½ c	3½	100	2.25 L

CHART 2 VOLUME/WEIGHT CONVERSION CHART *(Continued)*

Food	Volume of 1 Ounce	Volume of 1 Pound	Weight of 1 cup (ounces)	Weight of 1 Cup (Grams)	Volume of 1 Kilogram
Prunes, cooked		3 c (no juice)		150	1½ L
Prunes, dried		2½ c	6½	180	1.25 L
Pumpkin, canned		2 c	8	220	1 L
Raisins, seedless		3 c	5⅓	150	1.5 L
Rice, raw		2 c	8	191	1 L
Rice, cooked		2 qt	2	37	4 L
Rhubarb, ½ inch pieces		1 qt	4	110	2 L
Salad dressing		2 c	8	220	1 L
Salad oil		2 c	8	220	1 L
Salmon, canned		2 c	8	220	1 L
Salt	1½ tbsp	1½ c	10½ oz	300	750 ml
Sausage, bulk		2 c	8	220	1 L
Shortening, hydrogenated	2⅓ T	2¼ c	7	200	1.1 L
Shrimp		3⅓ c	5	125	1.65 L
Soda	2 tbsp	2⅓ c	7	200	1.15 L
Spaghetti, dry		1 qt	4	110	2 L
Spinach, fresh cooked		2½ c	6½	180	1.25 L
Spinach, raw		4 qt loose		30	8 L loose
Squash, summer, pulp, cooked		2½ c	6½	180	1.25 L
Squash, winter, pulp, cooked		2¼ c	7	200	1.125 L
Starch, pregelatinized		3½ c	5	130	1.75 L
Strawberries, crushed		2 c	8	225	1 L
Strawberries, fresh		3 c	5⅓	150	1.5 L
Sugar, brown, light pack	2½ tbsp	2¾ c	6	220	1.4 L
Sugar, confectioners (10 X)	3 tbsp	3 c (sifted)	5½	176	1.5
Sugar cubes		96 cubes			210 cubes
Sugar, granulated	2 tbsp	2 c	8	200	1 L
Syrup, corn		1½ c	11	300	750 ml
Sweet potatoes, cooked, mashed		2¼ c	7	200	1.125 L
Sweet potatoes, canned		2 c	8	225	1 L
Tapioca, instant		2½ c	6¾	180	1.25 L
Tapioca, pearl		3 c	5⅓	150	1.5 L
Tea		6 c	2 to 3 oz	75	3 L
Tomatoes, canned		2 c	8	225	1 L
Tomatoes, fresh, diced		2½ c	6½	180	1.25 L
		3 med			6 to 8 med
Tomato, juice		2 c	8	225	1 L
Tomato puree		1¾ c	8½	249	875 ml
Tuna fish, canned		2 c	8	225	1 L
Vanilla wafer crumbs		5 c	3¼	90	2.5 L
Veal, ground		2 c	8	225	1 L
Vinegar		2 c	8	225	1 L
Walnuts, chopped		1 qt	4	110	2 L
Weiners		10–12			22–26
Yeast, dry	¼ c	1 qt	4	110	2 L
Yogurt		2 c	8	244	1 L

CHART 3 APPROXIMATE YIELDS OF SCOOPS AND LADLES

Scoops (Number (#) Means Number of Scoops per Quart or Liter[a])

	U.S. Measure	U.S. Measure	Metric—Rounded (Volume Measure)
[b]#60	1 tablespoon	½ ounce	15 ml
[b]#40	1½ tablespoons	¾ ounce	25 ml
#30	2 tablespoons	1–1½ ounces	35 ml
[b]#20	3 tablespoons	1¾–2 ounces	50 ml
#16	¼ cup	2–2¼ ounces	60 ml
#12	5 tablespoons	2½–3 ounces	80 ml
[b]#10	6 tablespoons	3–4 ounces	100 ml
[b]#8	½ cup	4–5 ounces	125 ml
#6	⅔ cup	6⅔ ounces	165 ml

Ladles (Volume Measure)

Ounces	U.S. Measure	ml—Exact	ml—Rounded
1	2 tablespoons	29.6	30
2	¼ cup	59.2	60
4	½ cup	118.4	125
6	¾ cup	177.6	175
8	1 cup	236.8	250
10	1¼ cups	296	300
12	1½ cups	355.2	350

Ice Cream All Flavors	Scoops/Gallon
# 40	72–90
# 30	60–75
# 24	48–60
# 20	40–50
# 16	36–45
# 12	28–35
# 10	24–30
# 8	20–25

[a]Ice cream poses a special problem, because it loses air and shrinks when scooped. A special chart for these yields is included.

[b]Metric scoops

CHART 4 COMMON CAN SIZES

Can size	Amount (Liquid Measure)		Uses
	Metric	**American**	
6 oz	175 ml	¾ c	Frozen juices
8 oz	240 ml	1 c	Fruits and vegetables
No. 1 (9 oz)	300 ml	1¼ c	Condensed soups
No. 300 (13½ oz)	400 ml	1¾ c	Specialty foods such as pork and beans, cranberry sauce
No. 2	590 ml	2½ c	Vegetables, fruits, juices
No. 2½	825 ml	3½ c	Large cans of fruits; some vegetables such as pumpkin
32 oz	950 ml	1 qt	Frozen fruit juices
No. 3 cylinder (46 oz)	1.36 L	5¾ c	Vegetables and fruit juices
No. 5	1½ L	1½ qt	Nuts
No. 10	3 L	3 qt	Institutional-size container; one can of vegetables will serve about 25 persons

Substitutions

1 # 10 can = 7 #303 cans
5 #2 cans
4 #2½ cans
2 #5 cans

CHART 5 COMMON COUNTS OF SELECTED FOODS (APPROXIMATE)

Food Item	Count (American Units)
Anchovies	13 oz can—80 average
	20 oz can—170 average
Apples, spiced rings	85/#10 can
Apples, whole, 113 count	3/lb
Apricot halves	75–85/#10 can
Apricot halves, small	110–150/#10 can
Apricots, whole	50/#10 can
Asparagus, fresh	10–20 stalks/lb
Avocadoes, whole	2 medium/lb
Bacon, raw	20–25 slices/lb
Bananas, whole	2–3 medium/lb
Beans, green, whole	240/#10 can
Beets, tiny, whole	125–150/#10 can
Breads—measured without end crusts	
1¼ lb loaf (565 gm)	19 slices, ⅝ in. thick (1.6 cm)
1½ lb loaf (680 gm)	24 slices, ⅝ in. thick (1.6 cm)
2 lb loaf (900 gm)	24 slices, ½ in. thick (1.3 cm) Pullman loaf
2 lb loaf (900 gm)	36 slices, ⅜ in. thick (1 cm)
3 lb sandwich loaf (1.36 kg)	44 slices, ½ in. thick (1.3 cm)
3 lb sandwich loaf (1.36 kg)	56 slices, ⅜ in. thick (1 cm)
Butter	45 pats/lb
Cantaloupe	1 medium/lb
Carrot sticks, 3 in.	150/lb
Cauliflower	1 medium head/lb
Celery sticks, 3 in.	150/lb
Celery, whole	½–1 stalk/lb
Cherries, halves	550/half-gallon
Cherries, sweet	240–260/#10 can
Cherries, whole	200/half-gallon
Clams, butter, shucked	100–200/gal
Crabapples	55/#10 can
Dates	45/lb
Eggs, hard-cooked, sliced	1 egg yields 6 slices
Figs, kadota, canned	110–120/#10 can
Garlic, fresh	15 cloves/pod; 15 pods/lb
Grapefruit sections, fresh	200/gal
Grapes, red	65/lb
Grapes, white, seedless	85/lb
Lemons	3–4/lb
Lettuce, average head	1 avg head/lb
Lettuce, leaves for sandwiches	20 leaves
Melon balls, frozen	24/lb
Mushrooms	25 large/lb
	40 medium/lb
Olives, black pitted, whole	430/#10 (varies—check container)
Olives, black colossal, whole	156/#10 can
Olives, stuffed, whole	Size 60/70[a] "super colossal" 170/gal
Olives, stuffed, whole	70/80 "colossal" 196/gal
Olives, stuffed, whole	80/90 "jumbo" 222/gal
Olives, stuffed, whole	90/100 "giant" 248/gal

CHART 5 *(Continued)*

Food Item	Count (American Units)	
Olives, stuffed, whole	100/110 "mammoth"	275/gal
Olives, stuffed, whole	110/120 "extra large"	300/gal
Olives, stuffed, whole	120/130 "large"	327/gal
Olives, ripe (green)	Size 132 super colossal	132/#10 can
Olives, ripe (green)	156 colossal	156/#10 can
Olives, ripe (green)	198 jumbo	198/#10 can
Olives, ripe (green)	228 giant	228/#10 can
Olives, ripe (green)	288 mammoth	288/#110 can
Olives, ripe (green)	338 extra large	338/#10 can
Olives, ripe (green	404 large	404/#10 can
Onions, cocktail	160/pint	
Onions, green	11/bunch	
Oysters		
Eastern	150–200/gal	
Pacific	64–240/gal	
Olympia	1600–1700/gal	
Oranges, mandarin sections, canned		
Orange sections, fresh	250/gal	
Parsley	30 sprigs/bunch	
Peaches, halves	35–40/#10 can	
Pears, halves	35–40/ 40 to 50 per #10 can	
Pickles		
Dill chips, slices	700/#10 can	
Spears	65–70/#10 can	
Gherken	150–175/#10 can	
	250–500/#10 can	
Pineapple slices (rings	52–66/#10 can	
	8–12 slices/lb	
Pineapple, chunks	232–290/#10 can	
Plums, purple	65–90/#10 can	
Plums, gage	45–55/#10 can	
Prunes, large stewed	45/#10 can	
Radishes	30/lb	
Scallops, bay	500/gal	
Scallops, sea	150/gal	
Shellfish–see individual species		
Shrimp, headless	Raw, Peeled, Deveined	Cooked, Peeled, Deveined
Extra jumbo, 16–20 count[b]	20–25/lb	31–40/lb
Jumbo, 21–25 count	26–31	41–60
Extra large, 26–30 count	32–38	61–90
Large, 31–35	39–44	91–123
Strawberries, fresh	300/flat	
Tomatoes	3 med/lb	
Tomatoes	5–6 slices/tomato	
Tomatoes, cherry	300/flat	
Weiners	10–12/lb	

[a]Count per pound.
[b]Shrimp generally are ordered by this count, which refers to number per pounds of headless shrimp.

CHART 6 APPROXIMATE YIELDS FOR MEAT, POULTRY AND SEAFOOD

	Percent Yield (Cooked)	Average Cooked Yields per Pound (Boneless), in Ounces
Beef		
Chuck roll	55	9
Chuck shoulder clod	60	9½
Corned beef brisket (boneless)	50–60	8–9½
Flank steak, trimmed	67–75	10–11
Ground beef (no more than 30% fat)	73	11½
Ground beef (no more than 25% fat)	75–76	12
Knuckle	65	10–11
Rib, oven-prepared	35	5–6
Rib roast, boneless	55–60	9–10
Round, bottom, gooseneck	78	12½
Round, (bone-in), rump and shank off	34	6
Round, top (inside), boneless	55–65	9–11
Rump	35–40	6
Sirloin, top butt, boneless	70	11–11½
Sirloin butt, boneless	58	9
Pork		
Ground	60–73	9½–11½
Ham, fresh, bone-in (leg)	54	8½
boneless	68	10½
Ham, smoked, bone-in, sliced	67	10½
boneless	77	12
Loin, bone-in	50	8
boneless	77	12
Shoulder, picnic, bone-in	48	7½
boneless	64	10
Sausage	48	7½
Spareribs	26	4
Veal		
Ground	65–70	10–11
Leg, cutlets, boneless	70–75	11–12
Leg, bone-in	49	8
boneless	60–70	9–11
Lamb		
Ground	68	10½
Leg, bone-in	45–50	7–8
boneless	70	11
Shoulder, bone-in	57	9
boneless	73	11½

CHART 6 *(Continued)*

	Percent Yield (Cooked)	**Average Cooked Yields per Pound (Boneless), in Ounces**
Variety Meats		
Heart	35–40	5½–6
Liver	65–70	10–11
Tongue	50	8
Precooked meats (slicing loss)		14-15
Poultry		
Chicken, whole	34	5–6
breasts with ribs	53	8
breasts without ribs	55	8
drumsticks	42	8–9
thighs	45	7
Hen, stewing	34	5–6
Turkey, whole or halves	35–45	5–7
breast quarters	45–51	7–7½
breast, whole	51–58	8–9
boneless roast or roll		
cooked	92	14½
uncooked	70	11
leg quarters	43–48	6½–7½
Seafoods		
Crab, blue	10–18	1½–2½
Crab, dungeness	22–26	3½–4
Fish, whole, dressed (see also species, below)		
Fillets (species variation)	64	10
Lobster, New England (American)	25	4
Lobster, spiny (tails only)	46	7
Shrimp, in shell, headless	50	8
raw, peeled	56	9
Fish	**Percent Yield, Whole Dress to Fillets**	**Yield in Ounces (Raw)**
Bluefish	52	8
Bass	40	6
Cod	31	5
Flounder	40	6
Haddock	48	7½
Halibut	59	9
Mackerel	54	8½
Perch	36	5½
Pollock	45	7
Pompano	52	8
Salmon	65–75	10–12

CHART 7 APPROXIMATE TRIM LOSSES IN FRESH PRODUCE

	Percent Yield	Yield (E.P.) from One Pound (A.P.), in Ounces
Apples, peeled and cored	70–76	11–12
Asparagus	49–56	8–9
Avocado	60–75	10–12
Banana	68	11
Beans, green or wax	84–88	14
Beans, lima, in pod	39	6
Beets, no tops	76	12
Blueberries	84–92	13–15
Broccoli	61–62	9–10
Brussels sprouts	74–77	12–13
Cabbage, green	79	13
Cantaloupe, without rind	50–60	8–9
Carrots, without tops	75–82	12–13
Cauliflower, untrimmed	31–45	4–5
trimmed	95	15
Celery	71–75	11–12
Chard	77	12
Cherries, pitted	79–89	13–14
Cranberries	96–97	15
Cucumbers, pared	95	15
unpared	72–73	12
Eggplant	75–81	12–13
Endive, chicory, escarole	74–75	12
Grapefruit, sectioned	47–48	7–8
Grapes, seedless	94	15
Honeydew, without rind	56–60	8–10
Kale	74–81	12–13
Lemons, juice	43	7
Lettuce, iceberg, untrimmed	69–74	11–12
Lettuce, leaf	67	11
Mushrooms, whole	97	15
Okra	78–96	12–15
Onions, mature	76–89	12–14
Oranges, juice	50	8
Oranges, sectioned	56–57	9
Parsnips	84–85	13
Peaches	76–80	12–13
Pears	67–78	11–12
Peas, green, in shell	27–38	4–6
Peppers, green	78–82	12–13
Pineapple	48–52	8–9
Plums	93–94	15
Potatoes	76–84	12–13
Potatoes, sweet	75–81	12–13
Rhubarb, leaves off	86	14

CHART 7 APPROXIMATE TRIM LOSSES IN FRESH PRODUCE *(Continued)*

	Percent Yield	**Yield (E.P.) from One Pound (A.P.), in Ounces**
Radishes, with tops	60–63	10
without tops	90	14–15
Rutabagas	77–85	12–14
Spinach, untrimmed	67–74	11–12
cello-packed	92	14–15
Squash, Acorn, peeled	66	10
seeded	88	14
Squash, hubbard	58–66	9–11
Squash, summer	83–98	13–15
Squash, zucchini	83–98	13–15
Strawberries	84–87	13–14
Tomatoes	86–91	14
Turnips	80	12–13
Watermelon, cubed and seeded	36–46	5–7

Uses for Chart 7

If recipe calls for "edible portion" (EP) amount, obtain "as purchased" (AP) amount by

$$EP \div \text{Percent yield} = AP$$

To determine EP amount when AP amount is given:

$$AP \times \text{percent yield} = EP$$

Column 3 is useful for determining the cost per serving quickly when recipes or portion sizes are given in pounds and ounces. Example: If carrots are $1.36 per pound, what is the cost of a 3 oz serving? An approximate yield of 12 to 13 oz per pound will produce four servings per pound, or $0.09 per serving.

APPENDIX 2
fortran program[1]

PURPOSE OF SYSTEM

This system is designed to give inventory cost analysis reports at 10-day and monthly intervals for a restaurant or snack-bar business. The report gives the amount, unit cost, and extended dollar value of each item on hand. For each group and category of merchandise the beginning inventory, purchases, ending inventory, cost of sales, and ratio of cost to sales are shown.

The inventory data can be subdivided according to location, group, and category. Location refers to the physical location of the restaurant. Group divisions are basic sections within the restaurant, such as food sales, bar sales, and novelty items. Categories further subdivide items within a group: for example, the categories meat, poultry, and vegetables within the group "food sales."

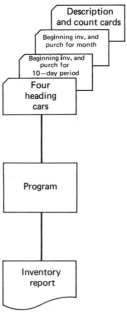

FIGURE A2.1 System flowchart.

---

[1]This program may be "ready to run" *only* in the computer on which it was designed. Although it probably will not run as it is written on any other computer, it can serve as a model for adaptation by a local programmer at minimal cost.

PROGRAM SET-UP, RUN, AND ERROR CONDITIONS

Program set-up is as follows:
1. Computer operating system cards.
2. Program deck.
3. Input cards.

The basic data file unit consists of a set of cards for a category, as follows:

(a) Four header cards, with the proper location, group and category numbers; and item numbers 00001, 00002, 00003, and 00004. Typically, card 1 would contain the restaurant location name; card 2, the merchandise group name; card 3, the category name; and card 4, the date of report.

(b) Beginning inventory, purchases, and "sales (group)" figures for the category for the 10-day period. This card has item number 00005.

(c) Beginning inventory, purchases, and "sales (group)" figures for the category for the month. This card has item number 00006.

(d) Interleaved item description cards and item count cards. The description and count cards pertaining to a given item must have the same item number, and the description card must precede the item card. There must be only one description card per item, and there should be only one count card per item. For these cards, item numbers may be assigned as desired, beginning with number 00010.

The interleaving of description and count cards can be done on a card sorter. Stack the cards so that all description cards are together at the front of the stack, followed by all the count cards. Then begin sorting at the low-order position of the item number, and continue sorting on successive columns down to column 1. After the run is completed, the count cards can be pulled out of the deck by sorting on column 80. All cards except count cards should be blank in column 80, and they will fall in the reject hopper, ready for use in preparing the next run.

The above sequence 3*a* through 3*d* may be repeated for the different categories within a merchandise group, and for groups within a restaurant location, for as many locations as desired.

4. A blank card must be the last card of the complete input deck.

There are no special running instructions. Use a standard carriage control tape with Channel 1 punched for top-of-form skip. The only output is printer output.

Error conditions are as follows.

1. If the input file is out of sequence, the program will skip to top-of-forms and print "FILE OUT OF SEQUENCE, CARD READ WAS," followed by the information on the last card read and terminate.

2. If the program encounters either a duplicate item description card or a count card not preceded by a description card having the same sequence number, the card encountered will appear as a detail line in the report with "ERR" printed to the immediate right of the line. Such cards should be removed or corrected, but they will not affect the report totals.

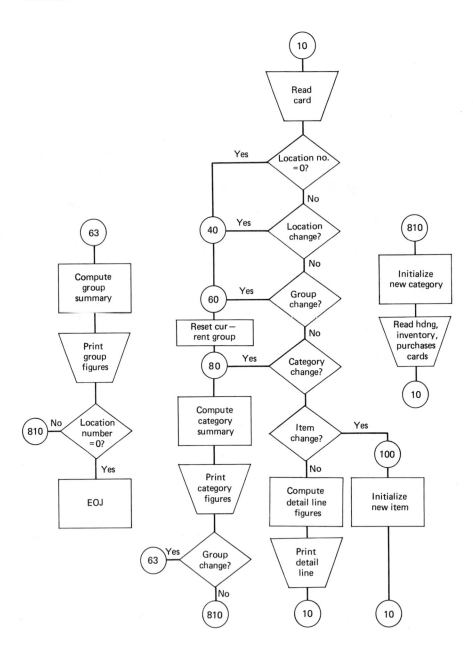

FIGURE A2.2 Program flowchart.

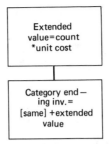

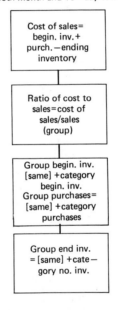

For both month and 10—day totals:

FIGURE A2.3 Detail of "Compute Detail Line Figures" block.

GLOSSARY OF PROGRAM ABBREVIATIONS

A	=	Temporary storage of information from input cards until type of card is assembled.
ALFA	=	Temporary storage of alphanumeric information from cards.
ALFAS	=	Temporary storage of alphanumeric information from cards.
B	=	Same use as A.
BI10	=	Category beginning inventory, 10-day period.
C	=	Same use as A.
CATCR	=	Current category number.
CATEI	=	Category ending inventory.
CS10	=	Category cost of sale, 10-day period.
CSMO	=	Category cost of sales, month.
CSR10	=	Category cost/sales ratio, 10-day period.
CSRMO	=	Category cost/sales ratio, month.
EXTVA	=	Extended value.
GPEI	=	Group ending inventory.
GRPCR	=	Current group number.
GRPSW	=	Program switch set to 1 when a group change occurs.
ICAT	=	Category number as read from input card.
ICC	=	Stores column 80 code from input cards.
IGRP	=	Group number as read from input card.
ITM	=	Item.
ITMCR	=	Current item number.
LINCT	=	Line Count
LINRE	=	Lines remaining (short of 33) per page.
LOC	=	Location number as read from input card.
LOCCR	=	Current location number.
PBI10	=	Group beginning inventory, 10-day.
PBIMO	=	Group beginning inventory, month.
PPR10	=	Group purchases, 10-day.
PPRMO	=	Group purchases, month.
PUR10	=	Category purchases, 10-day.
PURMO	=	Category purchases, month.
SGP10	=	Sales (group) figure, 10-day.
SGPMO	=	Sales (group) figure, month.
TLLIN	=	Number of title lines read from header cards.
TLSAV	=	Storage area for title lines until printing.
UNICO	=	Unit cost.

```
/ JOB
LOG DRIVE    CART SPEC    CART AVAIL    PHY DRIVE
  0000         0001          0001         0000
// XEQ ON

// FOR
LIST SOURCE PROGRAM
IOCS(CARD,1403 PRINTER)
HEADER CARD (ICP)



PAGE    2                HEADER CARD (ICP)

      INTEGER GRPCR,CATCR,GRPSW,SMMSW,TLLIN
      DIMENSION ALFA(10),ALFAS (10),TLSAV(4,10)
      DATA BLNK/'   '/
      CATEI=0.0
      LINCT=0
      LOCCR=0
      GRPCR=0
      CATCR=0
      ITMCR=0
      PBI1O=0.0
      PBIMO=0.0
      PPR1O=0.0
      PPRMO=0.0
      GPEI=0.0
   10 READ (2,1000) LOC,IGRP,ICAT,ITM,(ALFA(I),I=1,10),A,B,C,ICC
 1000 FORMAT(I4,I3,I2,I5,10A4,3F8.2,1X,I1)
   13 IF (LOC) 11,40,11
   11 IF (LOC-LOCCR)200,12,40
   12 IF (IGRP- GRPCR)200,14,60
   14 IF (ICAT-CATCR)200,16,80
   16 IF (ITM-ITMCR)200,20,100
C     EVERYTHING THE SAME -- THIS SHOULD BE A COUNT CARD.
C     IF SO, ACCUMULATE CATEGORY ENDING INVENTORY AND PRINT DETAIL LINE.
C     IF NOT, IT MUST BE A DUPLICATE MASTER ITEM CARD. CHECK COL 80 TO
C     FIND OUT, AND IF IT IS GO PRINT SAME AS FOR COUNT CARD WITHOUT
C     ITEM CARD. DO NOT SAVE THE INFORMATION FROM THIS CARD.
   20 IF (ICC)21,107,21
   21 EXTVA=A*UNICO
      CATEI = CATEI + EXTVA
      IF(LINCT-33)26,23,23
   23 LINCT=0
      WRITE (5,2054) ((TLSAV(I,J),J=1,10),I=1,4)
 2054 FORMAT (1H1,25X,10A4,/, 3(1X,25X,10A4,/,))
      WRITE (5,2055)
 2055 FORMAT( 1H0,18X,40X,9X,5X,4HUNIT,1X,8HEXTENDED,/,
     1  1X,29H LOC GRP CT   ITEM DESCRIPTION,29X,4X,5HCOUNT,5X,4HCOST,
     1    4X,5HVALUE,/)
   26 LINCT=LINCT+1
      WRITE (5,2010)LOC,IGRP,ICAT,ITM,(ALFAS (I),I=1,10),A,UNICO,EXTVA
 2010 FORMAT (1H ,I4,I4,I3,I6,1X,10A4,3F9.2)
      GO TO 10
C     LOCATION CHANGE -- LOC. NUM. DIFFERENT - ASSUME NEW GRP AND CATEGORY
C     NO ASSUMPTION NECESSARY ON ITEM.
C     PROCEDURES IDENTICAL TO THAT FOR GRP CHANGE, ALSO RESET LOCCR.
   40 GO TO 60
C     GROUP CHANGE -- LOC. NUM. SAME - ASSUME NEW GRP AND CAT.
C        NO ASSUMPTION NECESSARY ON ITEM.
C        PROCEDURES REF. AS IN CATEGORY CHANGE --
C           1) SAME
C           2) SAME,ALSO RESET IGRPCR, AND PRINT GROUP SUMMARY INFO.
C           3) SAME
C           4) SAME,ALSO NEW GROUP SUMMARY INFO.
C           5) SAME, ALSO RESET GRPSW=0 IN CATEGORY ROUTINE
   60 GRPCR=IGRP
      GRPSW=1
      GO TO 80
   63 WRITE(5,3000) ((TLSAV(I,J),J=1,10),I=1,4)
```

```
PAGE   3                 HEADER CARD (ICP)
 3000 FORMAT (1H1,25X,10A4,/, 3(1X,25X,10A4,/,),1H0,25X,11X,
     1    18HGROUP SUMMARY DATA)
      CS10= PBI10 +   PPR10 - GPEI
      CSMO =   PBIMO +  PPRMO - GPEI
      CSR10 = 0.0
      CSRMO = 0.0
      IF (SGP10 - 0.0) 64,65,64
   64 CSR10 = CS10/ SGP10 * 100.0
   65 IF (SGPMO - 0.0) 66,67,66
   66 CSRMO = CSMO/ SGPMO * 100.0
   67 DO 300 I=1,33
  300 WRITE (5,3070)
 3070 FORMAT (1X)
      WRITE (5,2020)   PBI10, PBIMO, PPR10, PPRMO,GPEI,GPEI,CS10,CSMO,
     1      SGP10, SGPMO
      WRITE (5,2026) CSR10,CSRMO
      PBI10 = 0.0
      PBIMO = 0.0
      PPR10 = 0.0
      PPRMO = 0.0
      GPEI  = 0.0
      IF (LOC) 812,811,812
  811 WRITE (5,3010)
 3010 FORMAT (1H1, 10HEND OF JOB)
      CALL EXIT
  812 GO TO 810
C  CATEGORY CHANGE -- LOC AND GRP NUMS SAME.
C       NO ASSUMPTION ON ITEM.
C     PROCEDURES --
C           1) WHAT WE SHOULD HAVE JUST READ IS THE FIRST OF A NEW SET OF
C              TITLE CARDS. ITM SHOULD = 1.
C           2) RESET ICATCR, SET ITMCR=0.  ACCUM ON GROUP BASIS 10-DAY AND
C              MONTH BEGINNING INVENTORY, PURCHASES, ENDING INVENTORY,
C              COMPUTE COST OF SALES AND COST/SALES RATIO.
C           3) SKIP TO NEW PAGE AND PRINT NEW FIRST LINE OF TITLE, READ AND
C              PRINT THREE MORE LINES. CHECK ITEM NUMS ON THESE CARDS AND
C              THE ONE IN STEP 1) ABOVE - IF TOO FEW CARDS OR OUT OF
C              ORDER, TRY TO RECOVER.
C           4) READ SUMMARY INFO FOR THIS CATEGORY. CHECK ITEM NUMS ON THE
C              SUMMARY CARDS -- IF WRONG OR MISSING ABORT JOB.  THERE
C              SHOULD BE 2 CARDS, 2 FIGURES EACH, I.E., BI AND PUR FOR
C              10-DAY AND MONTH (CARDS WITH ITM NUMS 5 AND 6,RESP.).
C           5) GO READ.
   80 CATCR = ICAT
      ITMCR=0
      SMMSW=0
      IF(LOCCR) 83,810,83
   83 CS10 = BI10 + PUR10 - CATEI
      CSMO = BIMO + PURMO - CATEI
      CSR10 = 0.0
      CSRMO = 0.0
      IF (SGP10 - 0.0) 866,867,866
  866 CSR10 = CS10/ SGP10 * 100.0
  867 IF (SGPMO - 0.0) 868,869,868
  868 CSRMO = CSMO/ SGPMO * 100.0
  869 LINRE=33-LINCT
      DO 310 I=1,LINRE
  310 WRITE (5,3070)
      WRITE (5,2020)   BI10,BIMO,PUR10,PURMO,CATEI,CATEI,CS10,CSMO,
     1      SGP10, SGPMO
 2020 FORMAT(1H ,25X,21X,28H10 DAY PERIOD  MONTH TO DATE,/,
     1    1H0,25X,22HBEGINNING INVENTORY     ,F11.2,F15.2,/,
     2    1X,25X,22HPURCHASES               ,F11.2,F15.2,/,
     3    1X,25X,22HENDING INVENTORY        ,F11.2,F15.2,/,
     4    1H0,25X,22HCOST OF SALES           , F11.2,F15.2,/,
     5    1X,25X,22HSALES(GROUP)            ,F11.2,F15.2)
      WRITE (5,2026) CSR10,CSRMO
 2026 FORMAT (1H0,25X,22HRATIO OF COST TO SALES,F11.2,F15.2)
      PBI10 =  PBI10 + BI10
      PBIMO =  PBIMO + BIMO
      PPR10 =  PPR10 + PUR10
      PPRMO =  PPRMO + PURMO
      GPEI  = GPEI + CATEI
      IF (GRPSW-1)810,63,810
  810 TLLIN=0
      LINCT=0
      BI10 = 0.0
      PUR10 = 0.0
      SGP10 = 0.0
```

PAGE 4   HEADER CARD (ICP)

```
      BIMO = 0.0
      PURMO = 0.0
      SGPMO = 0.0
      WRITE (5,2025)
 2025 FORMAT (1H1)
      DO 804 I=1,4
      DO 804 J=1,10
  804 TLSAV(I,J) = BLNK
   81 IF (ITM-1) 803,86,84
   84 IF (ITM-5)86,88,93
   86 WRITE (5,2040) (ALFA(I), I=1,10)
 2040 FORMAT (25X,10A4)
      TLLIN = TLLIN + 1
      IF ( TLLIN-4)801,801,803
  801 DO 802 I=1,10
  802 TLSAV( TLLIN,I) = ALFA(I)
  803 READ (2,1000) LOC,IGRP,ICAT,ITM,(ALFA(I), I=1,10), A,B,C,ICC
      GO TO 81
   88 BI1O = A
      PUR1O = B
      SGP1O = C
      GO TO 803
   93 IF (ITM-6) 84,94,13
   94 BIMO = A
      PURMO = B
      SGPMO = C
      CATEI = 0.0
      GRPSW = 0
      LOCCR = LCC
      WRITE (5,2055)
      GO TO 10

ITEM CHANGE -- LOC, GRP, AND CAT NUMS SAME.
   SHOULD HAVE JUST READ AN ITEM CARD.
   MAY HAVE READ COUNT CARD W/O ITEM CARD.
     PROCEDURES --
         1) RESET ITMCR, SAVE ALFA, A, AND B
         2) CHECK COL. 80 FOR COUNT CARD.
              IF NOT COUNT CARD THEN SHOULD BE, AND IS ASSUMED TO BE, AN
              ITEM CARD, SINCE IMPOSSIBLE TO TELL OTHERWISE.
              IF COUNT CARD, PRINT AS IS WITH ZERO UNIT COST AND EXTVAL.
              PRINT THIS WITH INDICATION OF ERROR
         3) GO READ.
  100 ITMCR = ITM
      IF(ICC) 107,105,107
  105 DO 103 I=1,10
  103 ALFAS (I) = ALFA(I)
      UNICO = A
      EXTVA = B
      GO TO 10
  107 IF (ICC-0) 109,108,109
  108 ICC = 0
  109 WRITE (5,2050) LOC,IGRP,ICAT,ITM,(ALFA(I), I=1,10),A,B,C,ICC
 2050 FORMAT (1H ,I4,I4,I3,I6,1X,10A4,3F9.2,1X,I1,3HERR)
      LINCT = LINCT + 1
      GO TO 10
  200 WRITE (5,3022) LOC,IGRP,ICAT,ITM, (ALFA(I), I=1,10), A,B,C,ICC
 3022 FORMAT (1H1,31HFILE OUT OF SEQ, CARD READ WAS,,/,
     1       1H0,I4,I4,I3,I6,10A4,3F9.2)
      CALL EXIT
      END
```

   TURES SUPPORTED
  CS

  REQUIREMENTS FOR
   MON   0   VARIABLES   198   PROGRAM   1308

    OF COMPILATION

      C   01
      S(1130,TIME)

INDEX

Absorption of fixed costs, 312
Achievement plan, budgeting, 322
Acid test ratio, 335
Additives, processed foods, 126
Albers, Carl, 298
Analysis of sales, 330
Anthony, Robert N., 2, 39, 40
ARA Services Inc., 7, 170, 171, 172, 173, 174
    FOCUS system, 168–175
Automation, beverages, 305
Average cover, 331
Average sale per chair, 331
Average sale per guest, 330–331
Average weight charts, 137

Back office computer system, *see* Remote computer
Balance sheet, illustration, 334
Banquet forecasting, 161
Bar chart schedule, 230–231
    illustration, 232
Bar-issues systems, 299
Basic crew, scheduling, 241–242
Basic Four Food Groups, illustration, 25
Beverage cost control, 389–407
Beverage cost formula, 299
Beverages:
    beverage cost formula, 299
    monitoring costs, 298
    production control, 297
    purchasing, 290
    receiving and storage, 292
    security, 293
    stock turn, 292
    temperature, 293
    total dollar use, 299
Bin card, beverages, 294
Blind check receiving, 135–136
Board plan, forecasting, 166

Board plan pricing, 28
Brand, Horst, 226
Breakeven analysis, 339–342
Budget, definition of, 309–310
Budgeting, food service, 309–325
    basis for, 314–318
    budgeting process, 310
    budget planning participation, 318
    budget revisions, 310
    cost behavior, 311
    direct operating costs, 318
    estimating volume, 310
    grouping costs, 311
    historical performance, 314
    industry studies, 314
    large organizations, 323
    objective standard, 309
    participation, 318
    performance responsibility, 319–324
    planning, 309
    time periods, 322
    variable, 311
Budget planning participation, 318
Budget revisions, 310
Buffet, portion control, 207
Buyer, 78

Cafeteria menus, 34
Call brands, 291
Canned foods, *see* Processed foods
Can sizes, 216, 351
Capacity constraints, forecasting, 159
Capital costs, 318
Carnes, R.B., 226
Cash budget, 318
Cash flow:
    estimate, 318

    illustration, 320
    total cash flow in, 318
Cashier's report, 63
Cash report, 61
Categorized food costs, 272
    illustrations 268, 273, 274, 275, 276
Cathode ray tube, 55
    illustration, 56
Chain of control, 247–248
    illustration, 248
Chair turn, 23, 159, 332
    illustration, 160
Check average, 331
Check control, 284
Check-issue sheet, illustration, 284
Check printer, 55
    illustration, 56
Clip-on menu, 22–23
    illustration, 22
Coin dispenser, 57
    illustration, 57
College food service, 165
Collins-Thompson, D.L., 191
Competition, analysis of, 16
Competitive bid buying, 85
    illustration, 86
Computer:
    data base, 44
    downloading, 49
    hardware, 44
    procedures, 44
    software, 44
Computer input summary form, 275
Computerized food cost, 272
    extending and footing, 272
    input summary form, 275
    program, Appendix 2, 355
    reports, 273, 274
Computerized forecasting, 168, 181
Computerized precosting, 222

illustration, 223
Contract buying, 90
Control:
  beverage cost, 289–307
  food cost, 247–262
  illusion of, 6
  management, 39–41
  operational, 39
  storage, 146
  strategic planning, 39
Controllable costs, 2
Control systems, 265
Convenience foods, *see*
    Processed foods
Conversion charts, 215, 345
Corrective measures, 6
Cost, definition of, 2
Cost analysis sheet, 248, 250
  illustration, 249
Cost centers, 322
Cost-per-drink chart, 296
Cost-plus contracts, 91
Costs, principal, 2
Costs varying directly with
    sales, 313
Cost-volume-profit relation-
    ship, 311
Counts, food, 216, 352–353
Credit memorandum, 138
  illustration, 141
Current ratio, 333
Customer, 15, 78
  market planning, 15
Cutability grading, 111
CRT, 55
Cycle menu: 19–20
  average guest stay, 19
  illustration, 21
  menu rotation, 19

Daily food cost, 253
  illustration, 256
Daily purchase journal,
    illustration, 268
Daily report, 60
  illustration, 155
Davis, Gordon B., 43
Dearden, John, 39, 40
Debt to equity ratio, 335
Debt to total assets ratio, 335
Decision making, 327–343
Density, canned food, 128
Dining room register report,
    251, 253

Direct issues, 248, 253, 260
Direct operating expenses, 2
Disk storage, 54
  illustration, 55
Dispensers, portion control,
    200
  illustration, 203–204
Distributed intelligence, 48
Distribution of sales, 330
Dollar sales per employee
    hour, 226
Downloading, 49
Drained weight, canned food,
    80, 128
Drake, Galen G., 164, 292, 298
Dried foods, *see* Processed
    foods
Drucker, Peter, 15

Earnings per share of common
    stock, 336
Economic climate, forecasting,
    156
ECR, 44
Electronic cash registers, 44, 45
  illustration, 46
  presets, 45
Employee time clock report, 70
EPSC, 336
Equity to total assets ratio, 335
Eschbach, Charles E., 148
Established indicators,
    forecasting, 157
Evaluation of operations, 327
Extendible foods, 26
Extending inventory, 271
  computerized, 272

Fair Labor Standards Act, 225
Family restaurant menus, 34
Fast food:
  market, 7
  menus, 33
  portion control, 208
  storage, 150
  under or overuse percent, 208
Fat usage, precosting, 221
Fay, Clifford T., 322, 323
Financial health of a firm, 333
Finished waste report, 66
Fish, *see* Seafood
Fixed costs, 3
  committed, 311–313
  minimum number of
      workers, 227

payroll, 227
  programmed, 311–313
Fixed price contract, 90
FOCUS system, 168–175
Food cost, 213–222, 265
  adjusted for inventory, 266
  daily, 247–262, 260
  formula, 266
  frequency of computation,
      267, 269
  key factor monitoring, 265
  measures, 265
  mechanics, 266
  monthly, 247–262
  per person per day, 267
  remedial action, 285
  specialized controls, 278–285
  standard, 272
  traditional system, 247–262
  variance, 275
Food cost control, 247–262
  accuracy, 260
  cost of control, 260
  "ideal" system, 247
  kitchen to service controls,
      250–252
  mysterious disappear-
      ance, 247
  unbroken chain of control,
      247–248, 253, 257, 260
  uses of traditional system,
      261
  vendor-storeroom-
      kitchen, 248
Food cost control cycle, 3
  illustration, 4
Food cost credits, 256–257
Food cost percent, 267
  formula, 6
Food cost reports, 62, 273
Food issues slip, 248
Food operations computer-
    ized unit systems,
    168–175
Food production control,
    185–210
  chef kitchen, 185
  ingredient control, 191
  leftover control, 189
  marked menu, 191
  methods, 186
  portion control, 193–209
  procedures, 188
  ready foods, 190

Food production control
(*Continued*)
recipe kitchen, 185
recipes, 185–210
Food production staffing, 241–242
Food requisition, 248
illustration, 250
Food service systems
menus, 34
illustration, 36
Footing inventory, 271
computerized, 272
Forecasting, 153–183
acceptability factor, 169, 174, 175
banquets, 161
board plans, 166
capacity constraints, 159
college and university food service, 165
computerized, 168
daily variation in, 164
definition of, 153
economic climate, effect of, 156
established indicators, effect of, 157
fast food, 175–180
hourly forecasts, 175
labor cost, 177
long range planning, 181–182
production planning, 177
FOCUS system, 168–175
freestanding restaurant, 161
health care food service, 165
historical records, 161
hotels, 158
institutional food service, 165
item sales, 163
local events, effect of, 157
popularity index, 164
predicting factors, 153–157
reservations, effect of, 157
special conditions, 156
time, 154
variables, 153
weather, 154
Fortran program, 358
Forward buying, 88
buying and warehousing, 90
contract buying, 90
Free-pouring beverages, 298
Freezer burn, 120

Freshwater, John, 230
Frozen food, production control, 209
Frozen foods, *see* Processed foods
Frozen food storage, 149
Function, market planning, 16

Glaze, seafood, 120
Grade, Poultry, 118
processed foods, 127
produce, 124
seafoods, 120
Grading, 107
Green, Eric F., 164, 292, 298
Group purchasing, 92
Growth ratio, 332
Guest check, 250
illustration, 283
numbered, 283
Guest check control, 282–283
Guest records, 58
illustration, 59
Guests per employee hour, 226
Guide hours analysis, 235
five steps, 237

Hardware, computer, 44
Harris Kerr Forster & Co., 314
Health care food service:
forecasting, 165
illustration, 166, 167, 168
menus, 30
portion control, 194
Heck, William, 321
Hidden costs, precosting, 219
Historical records, forecasting, 161
Horwath, Ernest B., 251, 257, 284, 294
Hourly readings, forecasting, 175
Hourly sales and productivity report, illustration, 176
Hotel menus, 31
illustration, 32
Hotels, forecasting, 158
Huber, Theresa, 17, 193

Ice cream yields, 350
Illusion of control, 6
IMPS, 104, 116
Income and expense statement illustration, 330

Ingredient control, 191
Inspection, 107, 108
meat, 109
poultry, 118
processed foods, 126
produce, 124
seafoods, 120
Institutional cuts, beef, 112
Institutional food service, 165
Institutional Meat Purchasing Specifications, 104, 116
Institutional menus, 32
Inter-register communications, 49
Inventory:
beginning, 266
calculating value, 269, 271
illustration, 271
costs, 101
counting, 269
daily physical, 278
ending, 266, 267
extending, 271
footing, 271
levels, 101
perpetual, 281
physical, 268
summary sheet, illustration, 270
working, 269
Inventory cost analysis reports, 358
Inventory period, 267–269
Inventory summary sheet, 270
Inventory variance report, 62, 285
illustration, 64
Investment, budgeting, 319
Invoice, supplier's bill, 135
Invoice memorandum, 135
Invoice receiving, 135–136
Invoice stamp, 138
illustration, 141
Issuing, special, 280
Item sales, forecasting, 163

Katsigris, Gus, 289, 297
Key factor monitoring, 265
Keys and locks, food cost control, 281
Key variables, 327
Kitchen register report, 251, 253
Kitchen testing, precosting, 218

INDEX

Kotschevar, Lendal, 32, 124, 164
Label, processed foods, 126
Labor cost, 331
   forecasting, 177
   overview, 7
   projecting, 317
Labor cost summary report, 71
Labor intensive menu items, 24
Ladles:
   illustration, 202
   sizes, 200
   yields, 215, 350
Large organizations, budgeting, 323
Latent temperature storage, 191
Laventhol & Horwath, 314, 317
Leftover control, 189
Lesure, John D., 251, 257, 284, 294
Leverage ratios, 335
Levine, Jack B., 46
Levinson, Charles, 298
Limited access storage, 281
Limited menus, 23
   restaurants, 7
Liquidity, 333
Local events, forecasting, 157
Location analysis, 15
Logistic function, fast foods, 143
Logistics, purchasing, 102
Long range planning, 322
   forecasting, 181–182
Longrée, Karla, 134
Lukowski, Robert F., 148

MacLennan, H.A., 191
Magnetic Stripe Reader, 55
Make or buy, 338
Management control, 39, 58, 327
Management information systems, 42–44
Management reports, 58
Managerial control, 39, 58, 327
Marbling, fat in meat, 109
Marked menu, 191
   illustration, 192
Market forms, seafood, 81
   canned food, 128
   seafood, 121
Market planning, 15
Master-slave, 44, 48

Measure conversions, 214–215, 345
"Meat Buyer's Guide," 116
Meat quality, 109–117
   age, 109
   grades, 110
Meat yields, 216, 354
Memorandum invoice, 135
Menu:
   breakfast, 29
   cafeteria, 34
   clip-on, 22–23
   cycle, 19–20
   dinner, 29
   family restaurant, 34
   fast food, 33
   food service systems, 34
   hard back, 28
   health care, 30
   hotel, 31
   hot sheet, 28
   institutional, 32
   limited, 7
   lunch, 29
   printed, 28
   productivity, 241–242
   school food service, 30
   tip-on, 28
Menu analysis, illustration, 174
Menu balance, 23–30
   nutrition, 24
   presentation, 23
   pricing, 27
   production, 24
Menu comparisons, 16
   illustration, price comparison, 16
Menu planning, 14–37
Menu planning concepts, 17
Menu plans, types, 19
Menu popularity surveys, 17
Method cards, 186
Metric conversions, 345
Microprocessor, 48
Minimum wage, 226
MIS, 42
Mixed costs, 3, 313
Modem, 54
Monitoring mode, 6
Month-to-date food cost, 253
   illustration, 258
Morris Graphics Limited, Hosp. Div., 20, 21, 22, 32, 36, 167, 168

Multiplying factor, 217
National Restaurant Association, Estimated Food & Drink Sales, 1980, 8
Negative profit, 2
Net contents, processed foods, 126
Net investment, 337
Non-profit organization, 1
Nonresettable total, 61
Nutrition in menu balance, 24

Objective standard, budgeting, 309
One-stop shopping, 87
Open market buying, 84
   combination system, 87
     illustration, 89
   competitive bid buying, 85
     illustration, 86
   one stop shopping, 87
   selected suppliers, 85
Operating mode, 5
Operating plan, budgeting, 322
Operating ratios, 330
Operating savings, 337
Operational control, 39, 58, 327
Operations needs chart, 230–231
   illustration, 231
Ordering, 77, 98, 102
Organizing for productivity:
   coordinating shifts, 241
   overlapping shifts, 241
Ounce control system, 298, 301
Output statistics, 230
Outstanding check report, 68
Over-and-under scale, 196
   illustration, 197
Overtime, 239
Overtime authorization, 239
   illustration, 240

Packer brands, 111
Par stock, 99
   beverages, 294
Part-time employees, 238–239
   absenteeism, 238–239
   training cost, 238–239
   turnover, 238
Part-time scheduling, 232–235
Patterson, John, 52, 57, 59

Payback period, 337
Payroll control, 225–245
Payroll cost percentage, 229
Payroll costs, 226–228
    categories, 226
    cost percentage, 229
    fixed costs, 226
    mixed costs, 227
    scheduling, 228, 230
    variable costs, 227
Payroll target, 237
Per unit ratio, 329
Percentage, ratio, 329
Percentages, computation, 328–329
Performance reponsibility, budgeting, 319–324
Periodic productivity report, 72
Period-to-date report, 66
Perpetual inventory, 281, 295
    illustration, 282
Physical analysis of use, 285
Physical inventory, 269
Physical volume, estimate, 310
Pilferage, storage, 146
Planning mode, 3
Point of Sales Systems, 6
    back office system, 44
    beverages, 291, 295, 301
    budgeting, 317
    control functions, 58–71
    data base, 44
    dollar costs, 244
    electronic cash registers, 44, 45
    food service, 44
    forecasting, 175
    guest check control, 283
    hardware, 44
    hardware options, 52
    inter-register communication, 49
    inventory variance report, 285
    master-slave system, 44
    perpetual inventory, 281
    POS *vs.* ECR, 51
    procedures, 44
    productivity controls, 243
    selective sales itemizer, 244
    shift reports, 243
    software, 44
    stand-alone registers, 44, 45
        illustration, 46
    summary hours worked, 243
    systems control, 41
    systems presets, 45
    time clock, 243
    waiter tracking, 244
Pollable computer, 48
Polling, illustration, 50
Popularity index, 164
    illustration, 164, 166
Porter, Mary, 289, 297
Portion control:
    approaches, 194
    bakeware, 205–207
    buffets, 207
    count, 201
    determining portion size, 193
    dispensers, 200
    fast food, 208
    ladles, 199–200
    markers, pie and cake, 205
    portioned foods by the piece, 203
    portioned foods by the pound, 201–202
    pumps, 201
    scales, 196–199
    scoops, 199–200
    tools, 196
Portion cuts, beef, 112
Portioning scale, illustration, 197
Portion sizes, illustration, 195
POS, *see* Point of Sales Systems
Potential-sales-value control system, 298, 301
Poultry:
    age, 118
    class, 118–119
    grades, 118
    quality, 118–119
    yields, 216
        appendix 1, 354
Prechecking, 251, 283
    illustration, 251
Precosting, 213–222, 345
    accuracy, 213–214
    beverages, 295
Prepared foods, 18
Prepared-to-order foods, 18, 189
Presets, 15
    variable, 53
Price, 79
Price/earnings ratio, 336
Pricing:
    beverages, 295
    menu balance, 27
Pricing service, illustration, 94
Primal cuts:
    beef, 112
    lamb, 115
    pork, 114
    veal, 113
Prime cost, 331
Principal costs, 2
Procedures, production control, 188
Processed foods:
    additives, 126
    density, 128
    drained weight, 128
    inspection, 126
    label, 126
    market form, 128
    net contents, 126
    product standards, 126
    quality, 125–129
    size and count, 128
    specific gravity, 128
Produce, quality, 122–125
    count, 124
    grading, 124
    inspection, 124
    maturity, 123
    perishability, 123
    seasonality, 124
    size, 124
    variety, 122
Produce trim loss, 356
Product cost, 331
    food, 213–222
Production in menu balance, 24
    illustration, 26
Production planning, forecasting, 177
Productivity:
    definition of, 225
    dollar sales per employee hour, 226
    gross changes, 228
    guests per employee hour, 226
    levels, 227
    limits, illustration, 228
    marginal changes, 228
    organizing for, 240

output statistics, 230
self-service, 243
standard times, 229
statistics, 229
tools for analyzing, 228
Product quality, 107-131
Product research, 107
Product specifications, 107
Profit:
  negative, 2
  zero, 2
Profitability measure, 332
Profit centers, 321
Profit goals, 1
Profit objectives, 309
Programmed activity, 41
Purchase ratio, 266
Purchases, food cost formula, 266, 267
Purchasing, 76-105
  approaches, 84
  beverages, 290
  definition of, 77
  forward buying, 84
  group, 92
  logistics, 102
  open market buying, 84
  price, 79
  service, 80

Quality:
  poultry, 118-119
  product, 78
  seafood, 120-122

RAM (Random access memory), 47
Rate of return computation, 338
Ratio analysis, 328-333
  common uses, 328-333
Ratios:
  acid test, 335
  activity, 332
  current ratio, 333
  earnings per share of common stock, 336
  growth, 332
  leverage, 335
  operating, 330
  percentage, 329
  per unit, 329
  price earnings, 336
  return on investment, 332
  simple, 329

stability, 335
stock analysis, 335
stock yield, 336
turnover, 329
Read only memory, 47
Ready foods, 190
Receiver, 134
  attributes and responsibilities, 136
Receiving, 133-145
  average weight charts, 137
  beverages, 292
  large operations, 140
  logistic function in fast foods, 143
  records, 137-138
  returning merchandise, 138
  small operations, 142
Receiving area, 133
Receiving methods, 135-136
  blind check, 135-136
  invoice, 135-136
Receiving report, 248, 252
  illustration, 254
Recipe, standardized, 185-186
Recipe explosion, 64
Recipe kitchen, 185
Record keeping, precosting, 222
Refrigerated storage, 146
Register reading, hourly, illustration, 156
Remote computer, 44, 47, 48
  illustration, 47
Remote printers, 52
  illustration, 53
Reorder points, beverage, 295
Reports:
  cash, 61
  cashier report, illustration, 63
  daily, 60
  employee time clock report, 70
  finished waste, 66
  food cost, 62
  inventory variance, 62
    illustration, 64
  labor cost summary, 71
  management, 58
  media, 61
  outstanding check, 68
  period-to-date, 66
  periodic productivity report, 72

recipe report, illustration, 65
sales control reports, 65
selective sales itemizer, 67-68
  illustration, 69
  shift, 58
  waiter tracking, 67
Reservations in forecasting, 157
Restaurant forecasting, 161
Return on investment formula, 332
Revenue centers, 322
Rhoads, 322, 323
ROM, 47
Rosenblatt, 322, 323
Runouts, planned, 26

SAGA, 7
Sales, hourly, forecasting, 177
Sales volume, estimate, 310
Sallerthwait, Charles S., Sr., 168
Sayles, I.C.I., 191
Scales, portion control, 57, 196-199
  baker's dough scale, 198
  electronic digital scales, 199
  over-and-under, 196-197
  portioning scale, 197
Schedules for levels of sales, 317
Scheduling, 230
  basic crew, 242
  coordinating shifts, 240
  evaluating, 235-237
  lead employee, 240
  management, 240
  payroll, 228
  service employees, 242
  utility workers, 243
School food service menus, 30
Scoops, sizes, 200, 350
  illustration, 201
  yields, 215, 350
Seafood, quality, 120-122
  breading, 120
  inspection, 120
  market forms, 121
Seafood yields, 216, 354
Seasonal price changes, precosting, 220
Security:
  beverages, 293
  storeroom, 146, 149

372 INDEX

Selected suppliers, 85
Selective sales itemizer, 67–68, 244
   illustration, 69
Service, 80
Service employees, scheduling, 242
Set menu, 19
   illustration, 20
Shellfish, *see* Seafood
Shift reports, 58
Shifts:
   coordinating, 241
   overlapping, 241
Shrinkage, storage, 150
Side work, 242
Simple ratio, 329
Sinclair, Upton, 108
Slip printer, 57
   illustration, 57
Software, 44
Special issuing, 280
Special-issue systems, 265
Specialized controls, food cost, 278–285
Specifications, 81–83
   fruit, fresh, illustration, 83
   meat, 109–117
     illustration, 84
   poultry, 118–119
   processed foods, 125–129
   produce, 122–125
   receiving, 137
   seafoods, 120–122
   vegetables, illustration, 83
Specific gravity, canned food, 128
Split shifts, scheduling, 233, 234
Spoilage, storage, 145
Stability ratio, 335
Staffing strategy, 7
Stand alone registers, 44, 45
   illustration, 46
Standard costs, budgeting, 315
Standard food costs, 272
Standard glassware, beverages, 298
Standard of identity, 83
Standardized recipe, 185, 196, 276
   beverages, 297

Standards, processed foods, 126
Standard times, productivity, 229
Standing orders, 101
Statement of income and expense, 318, 330
Step variable costs, 313–314
Stock analysis ratios, 335–336
Stock turn, 292, 333
Stock yield, 336
Storage, 145–150
   beverages, 293
   control, 146
     beverages, 294
   extending shelf life, 149
   fast food, 150
   frozen food, 149
   layout, 146
   limited access, 281
   location, 146
   pilferage, 146
   proper facilities, 146
   refrigerated, 146
   security, 146
   shrinkage, 145
   spoilage, 145
   storeroom, equipment, 146
     internal arrangement, 146
Storeroom, 147
Strategic planning, 39
Supervisory participation in budgeting, 318
Supplier, 78
Sweeney, F. Jerome, 164, 292, 298
Systems contracts, 91

Temperature, beverages, 293
Thirteen month calendar, 161
   illustration, 162
Time, effect of in forecasting, 154
Time clock, 243
Time periods, budgeting, 322
Total cash flow in, 318
Total dollar use, 299
Toth, Louis, 251, 257, 284, 294
Training mode, 59
Trim loss, produce, 217, 356
Turnover, payroll control, 238

Turnover ratio, 329

Uniform product code, 54, 570
Uniform system of account for restaurant, 2
UPC, 54, 570
Utility workers, scheduling, 243

Van Wijk, Alforms, 46
Variable budgets, 311
Variable costs, 3, 311
   payroll, 227
   relevant range, 313
   step variable, 227
   varying directly with sales, 313
Variable precepts, 53
Variance, food costs, 275
Vender, 78
Volume/weight conversions, 346–349

Waiter tracking, 244
Waiter tracking report, 67
Wand reader, 52
   illustration, 54
Warehousing, 90
Waste factor, precosting, 221
Weather, effect of in forecasting, 154
Weekly schedule, 235
   illustration, 236
Weight conversions, 214–215, 345
Weight and measure conversions, 345
Well brands, 290
   illustration, 291
Working inventory, 269
Wrisley, Albert L., Jr., 148

Yield grading, 111
Yielding, 265, 278–280
   illustrations, 279, 280
Yields:
   ice cream, 350
   ladles, 350
   meat, 216, 354
   poultry, 216, 355
   scoops, 350
   seafood, 216, 355
Yield testing, 79

Zero profit, 2